T0341541

THE UNIVERSITY OF MICHIGAN
CENTER FOR CHINESE STUDIES

MICHIGAN PAPERS IN CHINESE STUDIES
NO. 20

HSIN-LUN (NEW TREATISE)
and
Other Writings by Huan T'an
(43 B.C. - 28 A.D.)

An Annotated Translation with Index
by
Timoteus Pokora

Ann Arbor

Center for Chinese Studies
The University of Michigan

1975

Open access edition funded by the National Endowment for the Humanities/
Andrew W. Mellon Foundation Humanities Open Book Program.

Printed and bound by CPI Group (UK) Ltd, Croydon, CR0 4YY

ISBN 978-0-89264-020-1 (hardcover)
ISBN 978-0-472-03803-9 (paper)
ISBN 978-0-472-12744-3 (ebook)
ISBN 978-0-472-90139-5 (open access)

ACKNOWLEDGMENTS

I owe much to those who have worked on my manuscript since 1970. My sincere appreciation must be extended to Professors Chun-shu Chang, Donald J. Munro, and Rhoads Murphey for their contributions of time and expert advice through all stages of the manuscript preparation. I would also like to thank Christina Whitman and Leslie Swartz Shalen who edited the text for content and grammatical continuity. Finally, my thanks to Judy Dudley, the typist, and Lilly Chai, the calligrapher, for their excellent work.

CONTENTS

viii

INTRODUCTION

Better known in his own times than later, Huan
T'an was a scholar-official, independent in his thought
and unafraid to criticize orthodox currents of his time.
He and his more famous contemporaries Liu Hsin, Yang
Hsiung, and Wang Ch'ung were scholars of the Old Text
exegesis of the Classics.

Huan T'an (ca. 43 B.C.-28 A.D.) lived in the
disturbed period around the time of the Han interregnum
and witnessed political crises, uprisings, and civil
war. He observed the reigns of the Emperors Yüan (48-
33 B.C.), Ch'eng (33-7 B.C.), Ai (7-1 B.C.), and P'ing
(1 B.C.-6 A.D.). He was close to Wang Mang during his
quest for power and the establishment of his Hsin dynasty. Even at the court of the victorious Kuang-wu
(25-56 A.D.), the first emperor of the restored Han
dynasty, Huan T'an remained an honorary official and a
well-known scholar. But he never belonged to the small
group of decision-makers or highest advisors and this
may account for his ability to retain a position in the
court throughout these political changes.

Much of the information we have on Huan T'an
comes from Fan Yeh, the author of the Hou Han shu. In
addition, many important facts about Huan T'an and his
times are found in the fragments[1] of his principal work,
Hsin-lun.

The Hsin-lun differs from other books on political criticism in that it does not deal primarily with
history but takes many examples from contemporary social
and political life. Unfortunately, since the greater
part of his writings is lost, a full evaluation of his
ideas is rather difficult.

While belonging to the Old Text group of court
officials and scholars, Huan T'an differed radically
from them in his stress on direct knowledge, in his
range of practical experience, and in his outspoken
criticism of popular opinions. He was not a systematic
philosopher, but his ideas were influential in the
return to a more worldly conception of Confucianism.

---

*The author feels that his original considerably longer
introduction provides a more adequate setting as well
as additional helpful information. He will be glad to
supply copies of this longer version on request, and may
be addressed Care of Center for Chinese Studies, University of Michigan.

His Life

Huan T'an probably came from Anhwei province. His father was a Prefect of Imperial Musicians, and like him, Huan T'an spent many years as an official of music. But his unorthodox concept of music and his musical talents on the ch'in (zither) often involved him in conflicts with the emperor under whom he was serving. As a result, his career was frequently inter-rupted. It may have been Huan T'an's unsuccessful ca-reer that motivated his interest in the rise of Wang Mang. However, even if a modest new opportunity did open up for him around the time of Wang Mang's accession, he did not achieve any important post and certainly had no direct influence on Wang Mang.

By the end of Wang Mang's reign Huan T'an was sixty-five years old. He remained at the court but soon became embroiled in a conflict with the Emperor Kuang-wu. An experienced and courageous scholar-offi-cial, Huan T'an continued his criticism under the new Emperor. He finished his Hsin-lun and sent it to the Emperor, as it was written as a handbook on political science for a new ruler. From extant memorials and their replies we know that Kuang-wu found Huan T'an's political views incompatible with his own. In particular, Emperor Kuang-wu was infuriated over Huan T'an's criticism of the prognostication texts because the Emperor believed that it was by virtue of the guidance of these texts that he had ascended the throne. While Huan T'an "said again with insistence that the prognostications were contradictory to the canonical books,"[2] Emperor Kuang-wu claimed that their "reliability" was based on the Clas-sics and on Confucius himself. Huan T'an was condemned to be beheaded immediately, but was pardoned later after lengthy kowtowing. He did not, however, go unpunished. He was exiled to Liu-an in Anhwei where he was to be an Assistant Administrator. The aged scholar was unable to endure the long trip and died on the way.

The case of Huan T'an established a precedent. For the first time the Emperor was directly informed that deceitful people may falsely praise the prognosti-cation texts in order to mislead the ruler. Secondly, the furious reaction of the Emperor who had declared the prognostications authentic served as a warning to other scholars to be more cautious in their utterings on the subject. Some influential Old Texters did not

heed these admonitions and later succeeded in imposing
their ideas on the Emperor Chang (76-88 A.D.). In 85
A.D., while on an imperial inspection tour of the East,
Emperor Chang sent a messenger to make a sacrifice at
Huan T'an's tomb. Thus the scholar's critical attitude
towards the prognostication texts and his contribution
to Han thought was officially, if posthumously, recognized and sanctioned.

His Thought

Huan T'an's ideas played a large role in the
development of Han thought. It was Huan T'an who, together with his follower Wang Ch'ung, started the critical trend of thought by attacking the New Text school
and by viewing with skepticism the idealized past.
Along with Yang Hsiung, all three philosophers were
Confucian but had some penchant for Taoism. Huan T'an's
attitude towards Confucius was reserved, even critical.
He rarely referred to Confucius as a sage. This anti-
traditional tendency is illustrated in quotations from
the Hsin-lun. Huan T'an said to Yang Hsiung: "If a
sage should appear to future generations, people will
merely realize that his talents are greater than theirs,
but many will not be able to tell whether he is really
a sage or not."[3] Huan T'an said further: "A sage appears once in a thousand years."[4] He questioned how
people will know who is the proper sage.

In fact modern scholarship has shown that Confucius's reputation is out of proportion with the facts
of his career. An early proponent of this view, Huan
T'an stated: "Confucius was an ordinary man, but he
became eminent and his hand became famous."[5] Huan T'an
had almost nothing positive to say about Confucius's
merit, his ideas, or his contributions to scholarship
and the Classics. He challenged the traditional praise
bestowed upon the Ch'un-ch'iu, which was considered to
be a work by Confucius. "I have written the Hsin-lun
in order to examine and discuss the past and the present, but I also wish to promote successful government.
How does this differ from the praise and blame of the
Ch'un-ch'iu!"[6] Excessive adoration of the past, the
Classics and sages, was an object of his criticism:
"When the literati read the account of success and
failure in political affairs which is found in the
Ch'un-ch'iu, they believe that the Ch'un-ch'iu will

again be written when a new sage appears. I said this
would not be so. Why? Later sages need not necessarily
continue the ideas of earlier sages."[7] When Huan T'an
clashed with Emperor Kwang-wu by pointing out that it
was a mistake to attribute the prognostication texts to
Confucius, he was the first philosopher to oppose the
texts publicly. The Emperor's reaction was to say:
"'Huan T'an opposes the teachings of the sage'...",[8]
which was not accurate.

Huan T'an was something of a self-styled Confucian but, as Pan Ku tells in the Han shu, he had an
interest in Taoism. Pan Ku informs us that Huan T'an
wished to acquaint himself with the texts of Lao-tzu
and Chuang-tzu. Although these texts did not have a
deep influence on him, he was very well informed and
impressed with what H. G. Creel calls "Hsien Taoism"
or Religious Taoism. This is evidenced in the "Wang
hsien fu" (Rhyme-prose on Looking for the Immortals),
which frequently refers to retaining breath, seeking
immortality, and other magico-religious practices.

On Literature

Huan T'an's attitude toward literature differed
radically from that of most Han Confucians. While he
criticized one of the Classics he also defended some
books generally held in contempt. He praised the "unusual treatises" but criticized that which was "unreal"
in Chuang-tzu. Thus, Huan T'an came close to supplying
a theoretical basis for an independent, non-orthodox
development in literature.

In contrast to his Confucian compatriots, Huan
T'an noted some value in the hsiao-shuo genre (fiction).
Comparing the hsiao-shuo with the tuan-shu (short books,
often considered contrary to and inferior to the Classics), he characterized both as short and fragmentary
writings but also acknowledged their value for moral
education. "Now, the authors of the hsiao-shuo represent [those who make] only small and fragmentary utterings. The authors make these short books by clothing
their messages in comparisons with things close at
hand. But they contain words worth heeding on the subjects of self-control and the regulation of one's
family."[9] While other scholars of his day were far
more cautious on the use of these genres, Huan T'an made

an important contribution by proposing the inclusion
of the "heretical" genres in the closed and nearly
sacred realm of literature.

Huan T'an composed at least two _fu_. He must
have been fond of this genre, even a theoretician of
it, because he devoted a chapter of the Hsin-lun,
"Speaking on Rhyme-prose," to the _fu_. Unfortunately,
we have only four fragments of this chapter. Huan
T'an's interest in the _fu_ genre did not excite substantial response among the literati of his time or among
later scholars. If the few extant samples of his
rhyme-prose are representative of the whole work, we
might conclude that Huan T'an was not concerned with
the aesthetic problems of this kind of poetry. Rather,
he stressed that the composition of a _fu_ required extreme concentration and may be detrimental to one's
health. However, Huan T'an stressed his intention to
study the ars poetica by imitating the best specimens
of poetry. "In my youth I studied and liked the Li-sao.
Since I have read extensively in other books, I wish
to repeat my studies ..."10

Of Huan T'an's rhyme-prose, Liu Hsieh said:
"It is definitely shallow and lacking in talent." But
he added: "Therefore, we know that he excelled in his
satirical treatise [i.e., the Hsin-lun] but could not
come up to [the necessary level of] polite literature."11

Liu Hsieh's evaluation of the Hsin-lun as a
satirical or indirectly critical treatise (feng-lun)
is very fitting. Huan T'an mocked Ch'in Kung, a specialist on the Book of Documents, because he needed
more than a hundred thousand words to explain the two
characters in the title Yao-tien.12   In a fictional-
ized caricature of the well-known dialectician Kung-sun
Lung, Huan T'an discussed the thesis "a white horse is
not a horse." He said: "People could not agree with
this. Later, when riding a white horse, he wished to
cross the frontier pass without a warrant or a passport. But the frontier official would not accept his
explanations, for it is hard for empty words to defeat
reality."13

Huan T'an was also critical and satirical of
the bureaucracy. He told how the Great Administrator
P'ang Chen examined the use of the meat remaining after

sacrifices. It was found that there were twenty catties
of raw beef left over. Because P'ang Chen suspected
that the meat was used illegally, he impeached the
Prefect. The investigation proved that the meat was
not stolen, but in the course of the investigation the
officials consumed so much meat, rice, and wine that
in the end the expenditure was far greater than the
price of the original twenty catties of beef.[14]

The variety of literary devices at Huan T'an's
command is impressive. He used parables, proverbs, and
puns as tools of criticism and satire. He was fully
cognizant of the emotional effect of both literature
and music and mentioned it often. Many of the fragments
have several levels of meaning. For example: "When
the people hear the music of Ch'ang-an, they come out
of the gates, look towards the west, and laugh. The
smell of meat is pleasant, so they stand in front of a
butcher's shop, chewing vigorously."[15] On one level,
Huan T'an is saying that many people are unable to
recognize real values. On another, music can move the
hearts and minds of people. Finally, both music and
meat are inaccessible to common people.

The extant fragments may not properly reflect
Huan T'an's ideas on literature. This is because the
compilers of encyclopedias selected factual statements
or curiosities from the Hsin-lun to preserve while ig-
noring his general philosophy and observations on literature. However, we can say that Huan T'an encouraged
independence of mind. He preferred reality, thorough-
ness, and simplicity. He stressed the utility and
profit to be gained from literature. He summed up his
liberal attitude toward literature: "Although there
are unfounded and outrageous passages in Chung Chou and
those other books, we must use what is best in them.
How dare we talk of rejecting them completely?"[16]

On Music

The concept of "new music" as found in Huan
T'an's work and in the work of a few other writers is
very vague, and we cannot say for sure what it means.
The cloud of Confucian phrases is barely penetrable
despite J. P. Diény's serious study of the new music.[17]
Huan T'an spent all his life in musical circles. As

stated in his biography, he secured such a position as
a Prefect of the Bureau of Music because he was "fond
of the [musical] notes and the musical tubes and ...
good at playing the ch'in.... By nature he was fond of
singers and musicians."18 Immediately after the death
of Emperor Ch'eng, Huan T'an's career as the Prefect of
the Bureau of Music was interrupted because the new
Emperor Ai (or his high dignitaries) were opposed to
the new music. During the reign of Wang Mang, Huan T'an
became a Grandee of Music,19 but this position was
inferior to the one he had held previously. Huan T'an
was also a theoretician of music under Wang Mang. For
the most part he was concerned with musical measure-
ments, but in addition to this musicological work he
authored the Ch'in-tao in which he expounded on his
concept of the music performed on the ch'in. The second
interruption in Huan T'an's career as a dignitary of
music occurred when he quarrelled with Wang Mang's Di-
rector of Music, Marquis Hsieh. As a result of the
argument, both officials were dismissed.20

Just as Huan T'an assumed an anti-traditional
posture with regard to literature and the Classics, he
advocated unorthodox music in direct contradiction to
Confucian preferences. Among the three things hated
by Confucius, the Analects say: "I hate the tunes of
Cheng corrupting the court music."21 The "tunes of
Cheng" referred to unorthodox and improper music. In
opposition to Confucius's theory of "three dislikes"
Huan T'an proposed his own "four not equal" (pu ju),
of which the fourth was: "The k'ung and chieh [instru-
ments] are not the equals of the flowing music of
Cheng."22 The stress was on "flowing" in contrast to
"static," "stagnant," and by implication, orthodox
music. Both the k'ung and the chieh, used at the beginning and the end of a performance, belonged to a
group of instruments which produced the kinds of music
which were said to have resembled all things,23 exhorted
people to practice virtue,24 and represented all
things.25 Thus, Huan T'an compared two musical instruments symbolizing virtuous and orthodox court music
unfavorably with the unorthodox, flowing, vivid new
music.

Huan T'an suffered as a result of his critiques
of Confucius's theory of music. He endured public
criticism and was accused of depravity. That turpitude
was associated with the new music appears to have been

the rub, because it was the "lewd" and pleasurable aspects of the new music that made it incompatible with the traditional, proper, orthodox music. The new music was not invented by Huan T'an but we know that the Bureau of Music introduced it and that Huan T'an was its Prefect until it was abolished. Huan T'an's involvement with the new music is further testimony to his courageous anti-traditional activities and attitudes. However, the new music is not even mentioned in either the Lun-heng or the Hou Han shu.

On Natural and Strange Occurrences

At a time when supernatural speculation was popular, Huan T'an stood out as a scholar who insisted on rational approaches to the natural world. Huan T'an based his responses to the questions of his day concerning alchemy, immortality, health, life, and death on his keen observation of nature. The Hsin-lun is rich with reports of the Han weakness for magic. "[Wang Ken] ... accepted the services of Hsi-men Chün-nui, a gentleman versed in the arts of magic, to teach him the art of driving old age away. Chün-hui said: 'The tortoise is said to live for three thousand years and the crane for one thousand years. Considering the qualities of man, why is he not the equal of insects and birds?'"26 But Huan T'an did not accept such musings, even from Hsi-men Chün-hui, an influential specialist in prophesies, and retorted with sarcasm: "Who could live long enough to learn how old a tortoise or a crane is?"27

Knowing the ideas of Wang Ch'ung, we are not surprised that Huan T'an was critical of the supposed will of Heaven and of omens. "In the Empire there are cranes which are eaten in all the commandaries and kingdoms. Only in the Three Capital District does no one dare to catch them because of the custom that an outbreak of thunder will occur if a crane is caught. Could it be that Heaven originally favored only this bird? [No], the killing of the bird merely coincided with thunder."28 In a similar vein, Huan T'an corrected the theory from the Tso chuan which stated that the protruding eyes of two dead men closed only after their corpses received some desired information. Huan T'an explained simply that the eyes might have been open at death but closed as the corpse stiffened. He concluded

that there is no relation between the closing of the
eyes and the received information.[29]

In Huan T'an's view, it is necessary to respect
the interests and needs of the living while paying proper attention to people who have died. He saw death as
inevitable and therefore minimized efforts to evade it.
Huan T'an's ideas on the problems of the body and mind,
life and death, the candle and flame are impressively
described in the longest and most important extant
fragment.[30] In addition to this he drew an analogy to
demonstrate his point: "Liu Tzu-chün believed the vain
speeches of the magicians who said that one may become
a divine immortal through study. I saw that down in
his courtyard grew a great elm, very old, worn, and
broken. Pointing to it, I said, 'That tree has no
feelings, but nevertheless it will decay and become
worm-eaten. Although you may want to care for it and
nurture its life, how can you possibly prevent its
decline?'"[31] Thus, according to Huan T'an, there is no
reason to look for a way to immortality, as Liu Hsin
and others during the Han dynasty did.

Huan T'an demonstrated an interest in and knowledge of medicine. He mentioned the dissection and
inspection of the five viscera by Wang Mang.[32] He discussed the magician Wang Chung-tu who could endure almost any heat and cold; cold and heat (han shu) was a
name for a disease to which Wang was apparently immune.[33]
In the fragment on breathing exercises, Huan T'an is
concerned with keeping oneself in good physical and
mental health. He seems at home with medical terminology and used it to draw analogies between physicians
and rulers, and between medical and political practices.
"Needles, moxa, prescriptions, and medicines are tools
to help the sick, but without a skilled physician, they
cannot cure. Talent, ability, virtue and fine conduct
are tools for ruling a country but without an enlightened ruler they are of no effect. If the physician
does not own the needles and medicines, he may buy them
in order to practice his trade. If the ruler has neither
talent nor virtue, he may appoint wise counsellors and
need not personally possess these qualities. Thus we
can see that talent, ability, virtue, and fine conduct
are the needles and medicines of a country. They are
effective if used as aids to the ruler."[34] Thus, Huan
T'an found medical wisdom similar to political wisdom.

Lest we categorize Huan T'an too neatly, he also related some strange occurrences. For example, there are several different versions of a story about the magician Tung Chung-chün, who "was once tried at law for a serious crime and put into prison. He feigned illness and death. Several days later he rotted and insects grew in him, but he revived."[35] Another fragment tells of an old woman who allegedly died but suddenly rose before being buried and drank wine. Elsewhere a female slave who died, was buried, and several times came to caress her orphaned child. The texts present only the "facts," while the usual critical remarks by Huan T'an are curiously absent. Perhaps all we can say is that in addition to his interest in natural occurrences, Huan T'an also liked to narrate strange stories. This is, I believe, what he had in mind when he spoke of "wonderful treatises and unusual texts."

On Politics, Law and the People

The Hsin-lun was written as a manual on political science for a ruler, probably for the first ruler of the Later Han dynasty. From Huan T'an's observations on politics, it is clear that he perceived a need for such a manual. One of the principal terms in Huan T'an's political deliberations was "Great Substance" (ta t'i). "Without great talent and deep wisdom, the Great Substance cannot be seen. The Great Substance includes all the affairs of the present and those that are to be."[36] In evaluating the shortcomings of such rulers as Emperor Kao and Wang Mang, Huan T'an pointed to their ignorance of the Great Substance.

A crucial question in Confucian political thinking was that of the relation of the House of Han toward other pretenders to the throne. Huan T'an was both realistic and daring enough to state that the abuse of power is bad, whether the ruler is legitimate or illegitimate. "The Way of the King is pure; his virtue is like that. The Way of the Hegemon is dappled and mixed (tsa); his achievement is like this. They both possess the Empire and rule over myriads of people. Their rule passes down to their sons and grandsons. They are the same in substance."[37] To identify the methods of Kings and Hegemons as the same represents a kind of heresy from an orthodox Confucian standpoint.

Huan T'an was not opposed to the study of antiquity, but he did mock those who paid too much attention to it or who accepted it as the only possible model for their times. For example, he said that Wang Mang wished "to imitate antiquity in everything he did.... He ignored things near and modern and chased after the remote past."[38] It is possible that Huan T'an became critical of the use of ancient models because of the way Wang Mang claimed to imitate the Chou dynasty and fancied himself another Duke of Chou.

Some of Huan T'an's political criticisms sound remarkably modern. "Also, to let the enlightened and the wise plan affairs and then bring them down to the masses will certainly be inadequate."[39] One of the reasons he cited for the fall of Wang Mang was that "...in all his acts and endeavors he only wanted to trust and rely on himself while he refused to share responsibility and authority with informed and experienced men."[40] Although Huan T'an did not mention Legalism or any Legalist philosopher and although there is no evidence that he was among those who proposed the blending of Confucianism with Legalism, many of his views on law may strike us as similar to a legalist standpoint. Law, he said, should be entrusted to high dignitaries who will guarantee its impartiality. "A wise government servant or an upright official should conduct affairs and uphold the law in a manner as clear as the red and green used [in painting].... If a crime is properly [defined] it should be possible to punish it.... If the High One happens to neglect the case, if he does not delay it and give it a hearing, then [the accused] is bound to suffer a violent death."[41] There is a suggestion here of equality before the law. In the same fragment Huan T'an admonished officials that abuse of the law will invite dire consequences.

But in the end, Huan T'an had a mind of his own and juxtaposed these Legalist ideas with criticism of matters associated with Legalism. For example, he also warned against excessive severity and punishments disproportionate with the crime. Also, he described Ch'in Shih Huang-ti as follows: "He looked on the masses of people as milling flocks of sheep and as herds of pigs which must be driven with a rod. Therefore he was later overthrown."[42] Huan T'an gave priority to the interests of the people. "...with respect to establishing laws and prohibitions, one cannot completely stop up the evil in the world, but it is enough if the laws and prohibitions meet the wishes of the multitude."[43]

Huan T'an's political discussions included many comments on the circumstances of the common people. In a dry, sarcastic statement he observed: "Since the consolidation of the Han dynasty, the taxes exacted from the people during one year represent more than four billion. Half is spent for the salaries of civil servants."[44] His advice to rulers was succinct: "When the stupid man makes plans, the only ones that are of benefit to government policy are these that are in harmony with the mind of the people and have a grasp of the real state of affairs."[45]

The Translation

The two partial editions of the fragments of Huan T'an, dating from the nineteenth century, were used as basic references for the present translation. Both editions are entitled Huan-tzu Hsin-lun, one by Sun P'ing-i and one by Yen K'o-chün. Quotations from the Hsin-lun are also found in sixty-four sources, primarily encyclopedias and commentaries. Most are short references, mainly illustrating the meanings of words or providing bits of information totally unrelated to the body of Huan T'an's philosophy. Taken out of context, the short fragments are not easy to understand. To deal with this problem I have provided notes which comment on the text, refer to other texts and sources, and explain the people and facts in the fragment. A further complication was that in checking every quotation in the original sources I found many discrepancies, so there are several versions of many of the fragments included herein.

The reconstructed text has not been subject to commentary and its reliability has not been analyzed. Since this reconstructed text cannot pretend to correspond to the arrangement of the original, there is some unavoidable loss of inner coherence. I tried to meet this problem by providing a large index.

References to the previous editions and to the original sources are given in the caption of every fragment. Information on the editions of the Hsin-lun is given in Bibliography I. Bibliography II lists the studies of Huan T'an's ideas and life. Bibliography III has the other sources of the fragments.

The present translation was begun in 1956 at Peking University. Without the use of that library the systematic checking of each fragment would not have been possible. In my studies on Huan T'an published in the early 1960's in <u>Archiv Orientální</u> in Prague, I had already translated some of the fragments; this is noted at the end of the respective fragment. The translation was completed during my stay at The University of Michigan, Ann Arbor.

With no reliable edition of Huan T'an's writings with commentary available, the present translation must be of a preliminary nature. New studies and translations of works by Liu Hsiang, Liu Hsin, Yang Hsiung, and others of Huan T'an's contemporaries will undoubtedly contribute to the understanding of the scattered fragments of Huan T'an. In many cases only the historical context will explain the meaning of a fragment. Still, I hope that my first steps will not be misleading to those who will follow them.

Timoteus Pokora

Prague

February, 1974

NOTES: INTRODUCTION

1.   For an explanation of the fragments, see the section of the "Introduction" entitled "The Translation," page xxii.

2.   Fragment 210.

3.   Fragment 31.

4.   Fragment 18.

5.   Fragment 77.

6.   Fragment 2B.

7.   Fragment 95.

8.   Fragment 210.

9.   Fragment 189.

10.   Fragment 139.

11.   Wen-hsin tiao-lung 10, 47, p. 110, 2; cf. Shih, Literary Mind, p. 253 for a different translation. See also note 60 in the following chapter, Huan T'an's Work and Its Transmission.

12.   Fragment 88.

13.   Fragment 135B.

14.   Fragment 66.

15.   Fragment 79A.

16.   Fragment 2B.

17.   "Musique théorique et musique d'agrément," in the second chapter of J. P. Dieny, Aux origines de la poesie classique en Chine, Leiden, 1968.

18.   Fan Yeh's biography of Huan T'an in Hou Han shu.

19.   Fragment 82.

20.   Fragment 43.

21.   Analects XVII, 18.

22.   Fragment 75.

23.   Wan wu; Hsün-tzu XX, 11 p. 255, a treatise on
music.

24.   Li-chi XVII, 14, a treatise on music.

25.   Po-hu t'ung VI, 51 d, a treatise on music.

26.   Fragment 146A.

27.   Fragment 146A.

28.   Fragment 133; cf. the 47th chapter of the Lun-
heng, "A Last Word on the Dragons."

29.   Fragments 203 and 204.

30.   Fragment 84A.

31.   Fragment 156.

32.   Fragment 38B; cf. fragment 116, note 40.

33.   Fragment 151 and notes.

34.   Fragment 13.

35.   Fragment 152B.

36.   Fragment 32A.

37.   Fragment 3B.

38.   Fragment 32D.

39.   Fragment 28.

40.   Fragment 32C.

41.   Fragment 65.

42.   Fragment 11B.

43.   Fragment 209.

xxvi

Huan T'an's Work and Its Transmission

Huan T'an, like his contemporary Wang Ch'ung, was a prolific writer. In his biography of Huan T'an in Hou Han Shu 28A, the historian Fan Yeh describes Huan's work in some detail:

> In the past[1] [Huan] T'an wrote a book of twenty-nine fascicules, in which he discussed the action which should be taken in his time. He called this the Hsin-lun (New Treatise).[2] When he submitted this work to the Emperor, the Epochal Founder[3] approved it. As the chapter "Ch'in-tao" (The Way of the Zither) was not yet finished, Su-tsung[4] commanded Pan Ku to expand and complete it.[5] In all, Huan T'an has written twenty-six fascicules of rhyme-prose, eulogies, letters and memorials.[6]

Although Fan Yeh suggests that the Hsin-lun is concerned only with "actions which should be taken" in Huan T'an's time, the work in fact covers both contemporary and historical matters. Its great value rests in its adaptation of historical anecdotes as tools for the solution of modern problems.

To this end Huan T'an presented his work for the edification of the Emperor. His purpose is clearly stated in the introduction:[7] "In compiling the New Treatise I have examined and discussed the past, as well as the present age, but I also wish to promote fruitful rule."[8] Huan T'an places his work in the tradition of Lu Chia's Hsin-yü (New Words),[9] which has been called a "Fürstenspiegel,"[10] or treatise on statecraft. Huan T'an's classification was accepted by the early T'ang writer Wei Cheng (581-643 A.D.), who presented a handbook of political science, Ch'ün-shu chih-yao (Essentials of Government From All Books), to the throne in 631 A.D.

It is likely that Huan T'an presented his work to Emperor Kuang-wu. It is unlikely that the Emperor would "approve" the Hsin-lun after his argument with Huan T'an in 28 A.D. over the meaning of the prognostications texts. Sung Hung first recommended Huan T'an to Kuang-wu in 26 A.D. as an eminent scholar (see note 60 below). Subsequently, he received two rather insignificant offices[11] and apparently pleased Kuang-wu with

his zither performances at state banquets. These very
performances may have caused a falling out, however,
for they aroused criticism so severe as to force the
Emperor to recant publicly his "improper behavior."
Huan T'an's status at this time was not helped by his
critical memorials to the throne (see fragments 209
and 210). Thus, it is most likely that the Hsin-lun
was presented in 26 or 27 A.D., towards the end of Huan
T'an's life. Of course, work on the book must have
begun much earlier.

Fan Yeh credits Pan Ku with having completed,
or edited, the "Ch'in tao" chapter of the Hsin-lun.
Since that chapter has been frequently attributed to
Huan T'an,12 it is unlikely that Pan Ku added much of
substance to the text. In any case, "Ch'in tao" existed
in some form before the Hsin-lun was sent to Kuang-wu.
Perhaps it formed a separate book, since Liu Hsin quotes
from it in Part 17 of his Ch'i-lüeh, which discusses the
principles of court music.

Pan Ku, in his chapter on drains and ditches
(Han shu 29), relied heavily on Huan T'an's account
(see fragment 208). Apparently, there may have been a
sort of personal connection between the two court scholars, although they never met. Pan Ku's father, Pan
Piao, taught the young Wang Ch'ung, who greatly admired
Huan T'an. The fact that Pan Ku includes the story of
Huan T'an's vain attempt to borrow Taoist writings from
the Pan family library13 in the last chapter of the Han
shu, which is devoted to the Pan family, may indicate
that Pan Ku associates Huan T'an with the history of
his own family. It should also be noted that they were
both adherents of the ancient text school.

Fan Yeh also notes that Huan T'an left over
twenty-six fascicules of rhyme-prose, eulogies, letters
and memorials. This approaches the number found in his
Hsin-lun, which is composed of twenty-nine fascicules.
In his commentary, the T'ang prince Li Hsien (posthumous
name, Chang-huai) reports that the Hsin-lun contained
sixteen chapters. Three of these (Chapters 1, 15, 16)
were short, while the remaining thirteen were divided
into two parts each,14 in accordance with the wishes of
Kuang-wu. Twenty-nine parts or fascicules were created
from the sixteen chapters originally compiled by Huan
T'an.

Li Hsien's commentary gives the titles of these sixteen chapters. By following Yen K'o-chün's organization of the fragments and comparing the titles given by Li Hsien with similar chapters in the works of other philosophers, we can ascertain the contents of each chapter with some certainty. For instance, the fifteenth chapter, "Mourning a Friend," appears to be devoted to Yang Hsiung, although some eulogies may also have been included in it. The ninth chapter, "Correcting the Classics," discusses the various versions of these ancient texts, and the twelfth chapter, "Speaking on Rhyme-prose," deals, of course, with the _fu_ form. The reconstructed first chapter, which is quite short, gives some background on prominent literary personalities.

Chapters 2 and 3, "Kings and Hegemons" and "Searching for Counsellors," are both concerned with politics and the perennial problem of Chinese administration, how to select eminent advisors. The bulk of Huan T'an's book is devoted to criticism, as is suggested by the titles of five chapters (Chapters 6, 7, 8, 10, 13), "Reprimanding Wrong," "Awakening Insight," "Dispersing Obscurantism," "Recognizing Intelligence," and "Discerning Error."

Efficient criticism presupposes a distinction between right and wrong. Therefore, Huan T'an, like Wang Ch'ung was fascinated by the theory of knowledge. His interest can be seen in the fourth, fifth, and fourteenth chapters, "On Substance," "Observing Evidence" and "Explaining Plans." The eleventh chapter, "Encountering Affairs," is rather informative, dealing with affairs which do not necessarily have any political importance but are of special interest to Huan T'an. This chapter includes, according to Yen's reconstruction, thirty-four fragments, or approximately one-fifth of the entire book.

Several titles in the _Hsin-lun_ are quite similar to those in the _Lun-heng_: "Reprimanding Wrong" (_Ch'ien-fei_, _Hsin-lun_ 6) and "Reprimands" (_Ch'ien-kao_, _Lun-heng_ 42); "Correcting the Classics" (_Cheng-ching_, _Hsin-lun_ 9) and "Statements Corrected" (_Cheng shuo_, _Lun-heng_ 81); and "Recognizing Intelligence" (_Shih-t'ung_, _Hsin-lun_ 10) and "On Intelligence" (_Pieh-t'ung_, _Lun-heng_ 38). Wang Ch'ung's adaptation of some of Huan T'an's titles is not solely due to chance. Similarly, Huan T'an

adopted Lu Chia's Hsin-yü as one of the models for his
own work. In fact, the titles of these two works also
demonstrate some similarities: "Mastering Affairs"
(Shu shih, Hsin-yü 2) and "Encountering Affairs" (Li
shih, Hsin-lun 11); and "Counselling the Government"
(Fu-cheng, Hsin-yü 3), and "Searching for Counsellors" (Ch'iu fu, Hsin-lun 3).[15] One title, "Discerning
Error" (Pien-huo, Hsin-yü 5 and Hsin-lun 13) is common
to both works. The words, pien huo are derived from
the Analects of Confucius. In drawing from the Classics,
both Han philosophers stress "...How virtue was to be
exalted and errors discerned,"[16] an emphasis which many
later scholars share with these sober, rationalistic
Han Confucians.[17] It should also be noted that the 11th
chapter of Hsün-tzu bears the same title as Hsin-lun 2,
"Kings and Hegemons."

Although most of Huan T'an's life was spent
under the rule of the Former Han dynasty and Wang Mang,
the Hsin-lun was not included in the bibliographical
chapter, Han shu 30, because he died in the Later Han.
(However, his musicological work, "Ch'in-tao" was included in the Ch'i-lüeh catalogue.)

The bibliographical chapters of the Chiu and
Hsin T'ang-shu[18] tell us that the Hsin-lun was first
mentioned some six hundred years later in the bibliographical chapter, Sui-shu ching-chi chih (p. 71),[19]
as being a work of seventeen chüan. This number, seventeen, corresponds neither with the sixteen nor the
twenty-nine given elsewhere. It is unlikely that the
seventeenth chüan was the introduction. Sun's suggestion (Introduction 1a) that the seventeenth chüan was
a table of contents is unconvincing. The Hsin-lun subsequently disappears from the bibliographical records
of dynastic histories, which indicates that it was no
longer part of the Emperor's library. In fact, a Ko-
rean source tells us that the Emperor Che-tsung sought
to obtain this work from the Koreans in 1091 or 1092
A.D.[20]

The fact that the work was not in the Emperor's
library does not necessarily mean that it had been ir-
retrievably lost. Rather, the library's copy of the
Hsin-lun, along with many other books, may have been
destroyed during the turmoil after the fall of the T'ang
dynasty. Although a printed edition of Wang Ch'ung's
Lun-heng was issued in 1045, almost fifty years before

the Chinese asked the Koreans for the Hsin-lun, Huan
T'an's book had not been printed. At the end of the
T'ang, the Japanese possessed a copy of the work; it
was cited in the catalogue, Nihonkoku genzaisho mokuroku,[21] written by Fujiwara no Sukeyo (died 898 A.D.),
some time before 891.[22] However, neither a collection
of lost Chinese texts, which was published in Japan in
1797 A.D. under the title I-ts'un ts'ung-shu 佚 存 ,
nor a similar collection found in Japan around 1880
A.D.[23] included the Hsin-lun. This suggests that the
Hsin-lun in Japan, as in China, was never printed and
was probably lost some time after the T'ang.

However, there are quotations from the Hsin-lun
in works by authors from the Sung and subsequent dynasties who could not have had access to a printed edition
or to the manuscript, which is said to have been lost
in either the tenth century (according to Yen) or the
Southern Sung (according to Sun). Three Sung writers
include quotations: fragment 108 by Wu Shu (947-1002
A.D.), fragment 83 by Yüeh Shih (930-1007 A.D.), and
fragment 198 by K'ung P'ing-chung (ca. 1045-1105 A.D.).
This last fragment is not included by either Sun nor
by Yen. Much of the K'ung P'ing-chung quotation appears to be derived from fragment 104, as is the small
fragment 86B quoted by Fang I-chih (1611-1671 A.D.).

New fragments found in later sources are usually
included in the second part of the present translation:
fragments 188 and 202 from Shuo-fu (end of the Yüan period), fragments 176-187 from Tung Yüeh's (1620-1686 A.D.)
Ch'i-kuo k'ao, and fragment 199 from P'ei-wen yün-fu
(compiled in 1711 A.D.).

The newly found fragments probably have several
origins. Some may have come directly from the Hsin-lun
or were quoted in some other source, while others were
simply invented. The authenticity of each of the later
fragments should be examined individually. Even one of
Yen's fragments (78) is unreliable, but only because
Yen misread "Ku T'an" for "Huan T'an."[24] The authenticity of these fragments is important for some of them
represent critical historical information. Tung Yüeh,
for instance, relies on Huan T'an for his information
about Li K'uei's Canon of Laws, a possible source of
ancient Chinese law.[25] It is also essential to determine whether Huan T'an's work was available to later
philosophers if we are to evaluate his impact on them.[26]

The existence of quotations from the Hsin-lun in other compilations of the lei-shu type has led some to say that the work must have been extant in the Ming period.[27] These compilations include: Wu Shu's "Shih-lei fu" (fragment 108 has been discussed above); Shih-wen lei-chü, compiled by various Sung and Yüan authors; Hsieh Wei-hsin's [Ku-chin] ho-pi shih-lei [pei-yao] (1257 A.D.); Ch'en Yao-wen's T'ien chung-chi (1610 A.D.); Tung Yüeh's Ch'i-kuo k'ao (see fragments 176-187).[28] Since these bulky compilations contain no quotations not found elsewhere, I perused only the Ch'i-kuo k'ao.

The theory that the Hsin-lun was in existence during the Ming was also suggested by Ch'üan Tsu-wang[29] (1705-1755 A.D.), who cites Ch'ien Ch'ien-i (1582-1664 A.D.) as his authority. Unfortunately, the catalogue of Ch'ien's library, Chiang-yün-lou shu-mu (ed. TSCC), contains no mention of the Hsin-lun. Moriya Mitsuo (Bibliography IIA 14) points out that Ch'ien's ability to refer to the Hsin-lun precisely may have been due to his good friend Chao Ch'ing-ch'ang (1563-1624 A.D.). According to Sun Ts'ung-t'ien (fl. 1759 A.D.) and Ch'en Chun, whose catalogue Shang-shan-t'ang Sung Yüan pan ching-ch'ao chiu-ch'ao shu-mu is found in the Ch'iu-liao-chai ts'ung-shu,[30] Chao collated a Sung text of Huan-tzu Hsin-lun in seventeen fascicules. Although the contemporary bibliographer Wang Chung-min, also quoted by Moriya, does not believe the information in this catalogue to be reliable, this particular problem, as well as the compilation of catalogues in the Ming period, should be studied more closely. There may have been much unfounded speculation on the riches of Ch'ien Ch'ien-i's library. It is also said, for instance, that an extremely rare Sung edition of Ou-yang Hsün's encyclopedia, I-wen lei-chü (submitted to the Emperor in 624 A.D.) could be found there, but this too is not listed in the Chiang-yün-lou shu-mu catalogue.[31] If we were to accept the information given by Sun Ts'ung-t'ien and Ch'en Chun at its face value, we would have to believe that there was a Sung print (pen 本 ?), collated in the 16th and 17th centuries and known to Sun and Ch'en in the 18th century, which was never seen again. This is hardly possible. (For more detailed discussion, see the studies listed in Bibliography IIA 14 and B 19.)

It should be clear that the existence of a quotation from Hsin-lun in a post-T'ang or a post-Sung work does not mean that the text still existed as a complete book at that time. I have, for instance, translated

fragment 52 from the 18th century dictionary P'ei-wen
yün-fu, but we know that the fragment comes from the
T'ai-p'ing yü-lan, rather than from a full text of Hsin-
lun. The T'ai-p'ing yü-lan is not a primary source.
Its editors merely copied, sometimes in a most disor-
derly fashion, old quotations from earlier encyclopedias. The fact that it was not compiled under the best
of circumstances has been indicated by J. W. Haeger in
his study, The Significance of Confusion: The Origins
of the T'ai-p'ing yü-lan.[32] Moreover, the sources of
the editions of the T'ai-p'ing yü-lan were earlier lei-
shu such as the Hsiu-wen yü-lan (360 chapters) or the
Wen-ssu po-yao (1200 chapters), which are now unknown
but may have been used by some of those who later quoted
from the Hsin-lun. As we have seen, errors are often
made in transfers from one edition to another, and the
quotations often vary among compilations made throughout the centuries.[33]

     Therefore, the occurrence of any fragment in
texts of this sort between and after the T'ang or Sung
periods did not necessarily mean that they came from a
full text of the Hsin-lun. However, the fact that after
the wide use of printing during the Sung there was a
sharp decrease of quotations from the Hsin-lun indicates
that something of importance happened to the full text
at that time. If it did not disappear completely, it
became very rare.

     Since some late quotations might have actually,
if indirectly, come from the original text of the Hsin-
lun, we cannot suspect them in general. At the same
time, we cannot ignore the widespread tendency of amend-
ing texts which have been lost. Remember, for example,
the fate of the text of the Chu-shu chi-nien which disappeared for several centuries before it was rediscovered in 279 A.D., only to disappear again sometime
during the Sung to be later supplanted by a Ming fake.
Fakery is not uncommon in Chinese literature[34] and historical writings.

     As for the authenticity of Huan T'an's frag-
ments, the most suspect case is fragment 188, quoted
from the introduction to the Fei-yen wai-chuan, where
literary motifs were undoubtedly at work. Fragment
202, an anecdote on Kuang-wu, is also highly suspect.
In both cases, personalities from the Han history were
used--or misused--by two unknown authors who referred

to Huan T'an to lend support to their stories. Only
in the second case, that of Chu Yu, did the personality
really exist. The second category of fakes, where the
history is being elaborated on merely to give it more
fullness and detail, is represented by many of the quotations by Tung Yüeh (see especially fragment 176, his
large quotation on the Canon on Laws). The fragments
on the Ming-t'ang (175) probably fall into the same
category. There do not seem to be any such problems
with the other recently discovered fragments.

        There is also the possibility, however faint,
that Huan T'an's Hsin-lun may, in some cases, have been
mistaken for some other Hsin-lun, since works by that
name were numerous. As mentioned in the note 26 to
fragment 84A, T'ai-p'ing yü-lan 375.2b quotes some Hsin-
lun, but it is not clear which one is meant. Huan
T'an's Hsin-lun was the first. A survey of the other
works may be relevant for some future study of the
transmission of ideas and attitudes.

        The commentary to Wen hsüan 17.13b and 27.12b
refers to a Hsin-lun by Chia K'uei (30-101 A.D.), who,
like Huan T'an, was an astronomer and adherent of the
ancient texts school.35 T'ai-p'ing yü-lan 265.10b and
739.12a quotes another Hsin-lun, by Ying Chü (190-252
A.D.). During the Chin dynasty, there were four authors
of such texts--Chou Hsi,36 Hsia-hou Chan (ca. 247-295
A.D.),37 Mei-tzu,38 and Hua T'an (died ca. 320 A.D.).
The books by these last three authors, of which we now
have only a few fragments, were reconstructed by Ma·
Kuo-han. A later Hsin-lun is attributed to Liu Hsieh
(ca. 465-522 A.D.), the author of the Wen-hsin tiao-
lung. The same book is also attributed to Liu Chou
(ca. 516-567 A.D.). Wang Shu-min convincingly demonstrated that the author was Liu Chou. The title Hsin-
lun was given to the book quite late, during the Sung;
the original title was simply Liu-tzu.39

        The difference of one character between the
names of Huan T'an and Hua T'an has given rise to another important question--who was the author of fragment 84A? This fragment Hsing-shen, included into the
Hung-ming chi, was attributed to "Huan T'an of the Chin
period." This is clearly impossible; either the "Chin"
or the "Huan" must be wrong (see Bibliography IIA 7 and
9). To complicate the matter, these two authors of
very similar names both produced a Hsin-lun. Hua T'an

also compiled, among other works, a Han shu,[40] which
indicates his interest in the Han period.

Kung P'ing-chung (ca. 1045-1105 A.D.) was among
the Sung authors who quoted Huan T'an. Although K'ung
entitled his book Heng-huang Hsin-lun, its contents
have nothing to do with Huan T'an's thought. During
the Ming period, the philosopher Chan Jo-shui (1466-
1560 A.D.),[41] who used the style name of Kan-ch'üan
("Sweet Springs"), wrote, among other things, two works
entitled Kan-ch'üan Hsin-lun ("Joyful Treatise of the
Sweet Springs") and Yang-tzu che-chung ("Discriminating
Sincerity of the Yang-tzu"). There are several references in those titles: Kan-ch'üan clearly refers to
the Sweet Springs Palace of the Han; another hsin in
Hsin-lun indicates "New Treatise of Huan T'an," and
finally Yang-tzu refers to Master Yang or Yang Hsiung.

The abundance of books entitled Hsin-lun (or
using "Hsin" as part of their title), as well as the
similarities in the names of their authors created confusion even among the medieval bibliographers. Emperor
Yüan of Liang (reigned 552-554 A.D.) said in his Chin-
lou tzu: "There is a Hsin-lun by Huan T'an and another
by Hua T'an. There is a T'ai-hsüan ching by Yang Hsiung
and another by Yang Ch'üan. When one deliberates upon
it, one sees many mistakes in the form of the characters
and in their pronunciation. Someone said, 'If there is
a Hsin-lun by Huan T'an, why should there be another by
Hua T'an? If there is a T'ai-hsüan ching by Yang-tzu,
why should there be another T'ai-hsüan ching?' All
[questions like that] originate in improper study."[42]

Wang Yin-lin (1223-1296 A.D.), in his Yü-hai
62.4a-b, an encyclopedia written for examination candid-
ates, added the following note to a short biography of
Huan T'an: "Among Confucian [texts] there is also a
Hsin-lun by Hsia-hou Chan in ten chüan, a Hsin-lun by
Hua T'an in ten chüan; a Hsin-yen by Ku T'an of Wu in
ten fascicules,[43] and eight fascicules entitled Hsin-i
by Hsüeh Ying;[44] as well as Chia I's Hsin-shu, Lu Chia's
Hsin-yü, Liu Hsiang's Hsin-hsü and P'ei Yüan's Hsin-
yen."[45]

The Ch'in-ts'ao and the Ch'in-tao

As mentioned above, our information on the
Ch'in-ts'ao is somewhat contradictory. According to

the Tung-kuan Han chi, it originally consisted of one
introductory section. This and Fan Yeh tell us that
Pan Ku must have been the one to complete it. In the
present translation, which is based upon Yen's reconstruction, the Ch'in-ts'ao is found in fragments 169-
174. The first of these, based primarily on Li Shan's
commentaries to the Wen hsüan, is probably the introductory part mentioned by the Tung-kuan Han shi, since
it focuses on the remote past. It is rather improbable
that Pan Ku composed all the remaining parts of this
"booklet on ch'in ideology," to use the term created
by R. H. van Gulik.[46] It is clear, however, that he
was conversant with at least the official court music
since Chapter 22 of the Han shu includes a "Treatise
on the Rules for Ceremonious Behavior and Music."

Ch'in-tao is not mentioned specifically in the
bibliographical chapters of the dynastic histories, perhaps because it was not considered to be a separate
book but merely a chapter of the Hsin-lun. Both of the
T'ang-shu attribute another work of a similar title,
Ch'in-ts'ao,[47] of two fascicules to Huan T'an. The
bibliographies in both of the T'ang histories also
refer to another of Huan T'an's musicological books--
Yüeh yüan ch'i,[48] which is also in two fascicules.[49]

Although the titles of the Ch'in-tao and the
Ch'in-ts'ao are similar, the content of these books
certainly differed. While Ch'in-tao may be translated
as "The Way of the Zither" or "The Doctrine of the
Zither,"[50] Ch'in-ts'ao most probably means "Music Performed on the Zither." The Ch'in-ts'ao is generally
attributed to Ts'ai Yung (133-192 A.D.), the well-known
Late Han scholar. However, his biography in the Hou
Han shu does not mention any Ch'in-ts'ao, but refers
instead to another music treatise--Hsü yüeh 敍樂
("Explaining Music").[51] Ch'in-ts'ao by Ts'ai Yung is
not cited in any dynastic bibliography nor in the commentaries to the Hou Han shu.

There have been several explanations of these
discrepancies. Hou K'ang[52] quotes Ma Jui-ch'en (1782-
1853 A.D.), who suggests that Ch'in-ts'ao might have
been a chapter in Ts'ai Yung's Hsü yüeh, just as Ch'in-
tao was a chapter of the Hsin-lun. In his view both
those works on the ch'in were not cited in dynastic
histories because they were merely chapters of larger
works. Ma Jui-ch'en also points to some contradictions

between both Ch'in-ts'ao and Ch'in-tao which establish
that they were not composed by the same author.53 Finally, Ma Jui-ch'en points out that a commentary to Wen
hsüan quotes from Hsin-lun the same lines that Pei-t'ang
shu-ch'ao quotes from Ch'in-ts'ao54 and suggests that
such identical quotations might represent a contamina-
tion of the works. Hou K'ang feels that Ma's explanation is ingenious but believes that it does not establish Huan T'an's authorship. We might add (see note 48
above) that the Chiu T'ang-shu does not attribute the
Ch'in-tao to anyone. The author of the Hsin T'ang-shu,
who must always differ with the Chiu T'ang-shu, may have
included the information on its authorship merely out
of contrariness.

The problem of the authorship of Ch'in-ts'ao,
however, is even more complicated. The bibliographies
in Sui shu, the two T'ang-shu, Sung-shih and some Sung
catalogues attribute the Ch'in-ts'ao (in one or three
fascicules) to the Chin author K'ung Yen (268-320
A.D.).55 This attribution is supported by forty quotations from the Ch'in-ts'ao in the commentaries to the
Wen hsüan. K'ung Yen's work disappeared, as did Huan
T'an's Hsin-lun, after the Sung dynasty.

Huang Shih collected the fragments of Ch'in-ts'ao
in his great work, Han-hsüeh-t'ang ts'ung-shu, the part
I-shu k'ao (Lost Books) 49.1-43a. A reconstruction of
Ch'in-ts'ao which followed Sun Hsing-yen's (1753-1808
A.D.) edition in the P'ing-chin-kuan ts'ung-shu was republished in the collection Ts'ung-shu chi-ch'eng, along
with a detailed introduction (dated 1805 A.D.) by Ma
Jui-ch'en. Ma, who believed that Huan T'an was not the
author of the work, also says that K'ung Yen was not
the author but only a continuer of the work of Ts'ai
Yung. Ma finds that the Ch'in-ts'ao contains ideas
identical to those in Ts'ai Yung's "Rhyme-prose on the
Ch'in" as quoted in the Pei-t'ang shu-ch'ao; this coin-
cidence, he feels, is proof of Ts'ai Yung's authorship.
It should be pointed out, however, that the range of
ideas and information in literature on the ch'in was
rather limited by the orthodoxy inherent in the subject.
There are many coincidences, but only some of them are
meaningful in proof of shared authorship.

Ma Jui-ch'en's arguments are ingenious, but the
fact remains that no bibliographical chapter in the

dynastic histories attributes the Ch'in-ts'ao to Ts'ai
Yung. On the contrary, two other authors--Huan T'an
and K'ung Yen--are cited.

Whoever wrote the Ch'in-ts'ao--it may not have
been any one single person--it is clear that the Ch'in-
tao and the Ch'in-ts'ao were two distinct books despite
some confusion that created by their similar titles.
The aim of the Ch'in-tao has been discussed above.[56]
According to R. H. van Gulik, the existing Ch'in-ts'ao
is a collection of approximately fifty ancient melodies;
the work contains no musical notation.[57] It is possible
that Huan T'an was associated with the Ch'in-ts'ao. For
instance, on page 26a, the Ch'in-ts'ao mentions a "Song
on Dragon and Snake" by Chieh Tzu-sui, whom Huan T'an
mentions in fragment 132 (see also note 77 ibid.). A
relatively old source, the Ch'in-shih (History of the
Lute) by Chu Ch'ang-wen (1041-1100 A.D.), says: "Both
Huan T'an and K'ung Yen collected zither melodies, while
Ma Yung and Ts'ai Yung, following in the footsteps of
the great Confucians, in their time loved the art [of
playing the zither] greatly."[58] Chu Ch'ang-wen clearly
differentiates between the two pairs of ch'in devotees.
He links Huan T'an with K'ung Yen--three centuries a-
part--and Ma Yung (79-166 A.D.) with Ts'ai Yung--near
contemporaries. Because of Huan T'an's unorthodox activities in the Bureau of Music, disbanded in 7 B.C.,
which, among other things, collected tunes, Chu Ch'ang-
wen's description of Huan T'an's activities (chi ch'in-
ts'ao 集 琴 操) is not surprising.

Although there is no definitive proof that Huan
T'an wrote the Ch'in ts'ao, it is probably not too far-
fetched to suggest that he had some share in this book,
considering the slow process by which such folklore
collections come into being.

Other Works by Huan T'an

According to Huan T'an's biography, in addition
to his Hsin-lun he "wrote twenty-six fascicules of rhyme-
prose, eulogies, letters and memorials."[59]

One of Huan T'an's fu, "Rhyme-prose on Looking
for the Immortals," translated in fragment 205, reveals
an unorthodox and Taoist spirit, but it does not contribute much to our understanding of Huan T'an and Chinese poetry.[60] The other fu is mentioned only in Pei-

t'ang shu-ch'ao 102.3b: "Huan T'an of Later Han, whose
style name was Chün-shan, criticized and scorned all
Confucianists. At seventy years of age, he was appointed to fill a vacancy as Assistant Administrator
of the [distant] Commandery of Liu-an. Affected [by
his exile], he wrote a short fu contemplating the Great
Tao. Later he fell ill..."[61] The Ch'ing scholar Ku
Huai-san reported, that as of his time, "one may now
examine" two of Huan T'an's fu.[62] Evidently, he meant
that the Ch'ing scholars had information on the "Ta-tao
fu," not that it was still in existence at that time.

All the other works referred to in the biography
may have been part of his "Literary Works" (T'an-chi),
mentioned by Li Shan[63] at the beginning of the T'ang.
It is, therefore, surprising that the bibliographical
chapter of the Sui shu[64] tells us that the five chüan
of Huan T'an's chi 桓 譚 集 are lost (wang 亡).
The same bibliography[65] does mention a Huan-tzu in one
chüan, but it probably has no connection with Huan T'an,
since "Huan-tzu" is used only to refer to the man Huan
T'an and never to his work. The Ch'i-lu by Juan Hsiao-
hsü (479-536 A.D.)[66] also credits the "Literary Works
of Huan T'an" with five chüan,[67] but both of the T'ang
shu mention only two.[68] This may indicate that part of
Huan T'an's writings had been lost by the time of the
T'ang shu.

It is still unclear whether some fragments related in Huan T'an's biography (see fragments 206-210)
belong to his Hsin-lun or to his "Literary Writings"
or are quoted by the historian Fan Yeh from some other
source. The fragments 211 and 212 (pien-i 便 宜),
like fragments 209 and 210, appear to be actual proposals made to Kuang-wu. The last fragment, 215 (Shang-
shih 上 事), may also be such a proposal, but the
word shih ("affair") indicates that it had an informa-
tional, rather than an admonishing purpose. The fragments 211-213 and 215 might have come from Huan's memorials (tsou 奏), mentioned by Fan Yeh. Of the letters (shu 書), only two short fragments still exist--
one from Huan T'an's answer to a letter from Yang Hsiung
(fragment 214) and another from a letter to Tung Hsien.[69]

Finally, it should be made clear that another
work, Ch'i-shuo 七 說 , was not written by Huan
T'an. The commentary to Wen hsüan 4.29a quotes a very
short fragment (five characters) of "Huan T'an's Ch'i-
shuo." Another fragment from the Ch'i-shuo is mentioned

in the commentary to <u>Wen hsüan</u> 60.35a, but in this case
the work is attributed to Huan Lin 桓鱗 . There is
a short biography of Huan Lin (ca. 130-170 A.D.)
(apparently the same man with a slight graphical
variation in his name) in <u>Hou Han shu</u> 27 (p. 1338) which
includes some <u>shuo</u> in a list of his works. Li Hsien's
commentary quotes a more precise source, which calls
them <u>Ch'i-shuo</u> ("Seven Explanations" or "Seven Persua-
sions"). This is corroborated by the <u>Wen-hsin tiao-lung</u>
3:14 (<u>Shih</u>, p. 75), in which Huan Lin's work is compared
with other writings in groups of seven.[70] Thus, the
<u>Wen hsüan</u> 4.29a reference is clearly a mistake and should
be read Huan Lin instead of Huan T'an.

Summary of Works

<u>Hsin-lun</u> 新 論 (New Treatise), 16 chapters divided
    into 29 parts. Lost after the T'ang or Sung
    dynasties.

"Ch'in-tao" 琴 道 (The Way of the Zither), last
    chapter of the <u>Hsin-lun</u>, completed and edited
    by Pan Ku.

"Ch'in-ts'ao" 琴 操 (Music Performed on the
    Zither), in two <u>chüan</u>, referred to only by the
    <u>Hsin T'ang-shu</u>. Also attributed to Ts'ai Yung
    and K'ung Yen.

<u>Yüeh-yüan-ch'i</u> 樂 元 起 , in two <u>chüan</u>, lost.

<u>T'an chi</u> 譚 集 (Literary Works), five, and later
    two <u>chüan</u>.

"Wang-hsien fu" 望 仙 賦 (Rhyme-prose on Looking
    for Immortals), in existence; "Ta-tao fu" 大 道
    賦 (Rhyme-prose on the Great Way), known only
    by title.

Reports quoted in Huan T'an's biography.

"Shang pien-i" 上 便 宜 , "Ch'en pien-i" 陳 便 宜 ,
    "Ch'i-shih" 啟 事 , "Shang-shih" 上 事 .

Two letters.

Erroneous attributions: <u>Huan T'an pieh-chuan</u> 桓譚別傳 ,
    post-Sung fragments; <u>Ch'i-shuo</u> 七 說 .

Special case: "Hsing-shen" 形 神 .

NOTES: HUAN T'AN'S WORK AND ITS TRANSMISSION

1.   Before Huan T'an's clash with Kuang-wu in 28
A. D.

2.   Lun 論 is a literary term which, in the
Han dynasty, acquired a special, emphatic meaning stres-
ing the actuality of the text and the importance of its
words. The original meaning of the character, as in
the title of the Lun-yü of Confucius, was "to discuss,
to reason, to argue." The term lun might have had a
pointedly Confucian connotation, as Ho Liang-chün pointed
out in his Ssu-yu-chai ts'ung-shuo (first published in
1567 A.D.): "From the Eastern Han there came Huan T'an's
Hsin-lun, Wang Chieh-hsin's (or Wang Fu) Ch'ien-fu lun,
Ts'ui Shih's Cheng-lun, Chung-ch'ang T'ung's Ch'ang-yen,
and Wang Ch'ung's Lun-heng. From the Wei there came
Hsü Kan's Chung-lun. Even if everyone of (those authors) had his own point of view, not one resembles the
various Taoist philosophers. Their works were called
lun and (were thus) distinguished from other philosophers." (Shanghai: 1959, p. 185) This work was republished in the series Yüan Ming shih-liao pi-chi ts'ung-
k'an. By mentioning Chung-ch'ang Tung's Ch'ang-yen, Ho
Liang-chün includes books like the Fa-yen (Model Words)
by Yang Hsiung, a "hard-line" Confucian. The word hsin
in the title Hsin-lun has its own meaning. See the explanation of the chapter titles below.

3.   I.e., Kuang-wu.

4.   I.e., Emperor Chang.

5.   Tung-kuan Han chi 69b: "Only "The Way of the
Zither" was not yet complete; there was only one introductory section of it." Emperor Chang probably ordered
Pan Ku to complete the Ch'in-tao in the year 85 A.D.,
since it was in that year that he decided to reorganize
the ritual and music. See his edict on the subject in
Hou Han shu 35, p. 1269. Emperor Chang must have been
very pleased by this chapter for in that same year he
gave Huan T'an posthumous honors during his imperial
tour in the East by ordering sacrifices at Huan T'an's
tomb (cf. Huan T'an's biography, p. 1018). This show
of respect, almost sixty years after Huan T'an's death,
was probably not bestowed on the man so much as it was
an indication by the Emperor's interest in re-establish-
ing Huan's conception of music which had been in

disrepute for almost 100 years. (The Bureau of Music, of which Huan T'an was the Prefect, had been abolished in July 7 B.C.)

6.   Hou Han shu 28A, p. 1018; T. Pokora, "The Life," pp. 33-34.

7.   The poet Yü Hsin (513-581 A.D.) mentions that Huan T'an wrote a postface (hsü). Perhaps fragment 2B may be interpreted in this sense. See fragment 204, comm. and note 80.

8.   Fragment 2B.

9.   Ibid. Note the significance of the word hsin ("new").

10.   A. Gabain, "Ein Fürstenspiegel: Das Sin-yü des Lu Kia," MSOS 33 (1930), pp. 1-82.

11.   Pokora, "The Life," I, p. 21 and note 39.

12.   See the section below on the "Ch'in-tao" and the "Ch'in-ts'ao."

13.   See fragment 81, note 15. It should be speci-fied that the 100th chapter of the Han shu mentions not Huan T'an, but Huan Sheng 桓 生 (100A, p. 5819). Yen Shih-ku was the first to identify Huan Sheng with Huan T'an. However, in the time of Huan T'an, there did exist one Huan Sheng who is mentioned in Han shu 88, pp. 5170, as a specialist in ritual; he is also referred to in Liu Hsin's biography in Han shu 36, p. 3423, as Huan Kung 桓 公 from Lu. Clearly, he was a typical Con-fucian scholar. Nevertheless, Yen Shih-ku's opinion was generally accepted; see, for example, Ch'ien Mu, "Liu Hsiang Hsin fu-tzu nien-p'u," Ku-shih pien 5 (1935), p. 133. In view of the personal relations discussed above, I believe Yen's suggestion to be correct. Per-haps Pan Ku did not give the name correctly because he did not want to ridicule Huan T'an as Pan Ssu had done.

14.   Tung-kuan Han chi, as quoted by Li Hsien, says: "When Kuang-wu read it, he decreed that the scrolls were too long and should all be divided into two parts..."

15.   Translation of A. Gabain: Die Methode, Die Regierung stützen.

16. See _Analects_ XII:x:1; Legge, p. 256.

17. My paper, "The Necessity..." in _ArOr_ 30 (1962), pp. 247-250, points out at least two philosophers who entitled their works _Pien-huo_. These were Hsieh Ying-fang (ca. 1300-1397 A.D.) and Ku Liang (15th-16th century A.D.). Other philosophers of the Sung and Ming periods are also discussed in this connection.

18. _T'ang shu ching-chi i-wen ho chih_ (Shanghai: 1956), p. 170.

19. The separate edition of the chapter (Shanghai: 1956).

20. The list of the 118 books which he sought is given in _Koryø-sa_ 10 (P'yongyang: 1957), p. 151. For background information on the Chinese mission, see M. C. Rogers, "Sung-Koryø Relations: Some Inhibiting Factors," in _Oriens_, No. 11 (1-2) (1958), pp. 194-202, especially p. 200.

21. Ohase Keikichi (1865-1944 A.D.), ed., _Nihonkoku genzaisho mokoroku kaisetsukō_ (Tokyō: 1956), p. 11, mentions a _Hsin-lun_ in 17 fascicules.

22. For information on this catalogue, see P. Pelliot, _BEFEO_, No. 2 (1902), p. 333; _BEFEO_, No. 9 (1909), p. 401; _TP_, No. 13 (1912), p. 495; and especially, P. van der Loon, _TP_, No. 41 (1952), p. 369, note 3.

23. P. Pelliot, _BEFEO_, No. 2 (1902), p. 315.

24. A similar mistake of Ku T'an for Huan T'an is made by the Harvard-Yenching indices to the _TPYL_ (p. 234) and to the bibliographical chapters (_I-wen chih erh-shih chung tsung-ho yin-te_, p. 212), as well as by Yao Chen-tsung in his _Hou Han shu i-wen chih_ (who refers to Chang Tsung-yüan, _Sui-shu ching-chi chih k'ao-cheng_; see _Erh-shih-wu shih pu-pien_, II, p. 2371). These three works refer to a _Huan T'an pieh-chuan_. Chang Tsung-yüan wonders why this work is not mentioned in the bibliographical chapters of the _Sui_ and _T'ang shu_. Moreover, the _Huan T'an pieh-chuan_, as quoted in _TPYL_ 775.3b-4a, says that Huan T'an went to Chiao-chih, as well as to the state of Wu; no such trip is mentioned in his biography in _Hou Han shu_ 28A. In fact, the earliest reference to Chiao-chih appears in _Hou Han shu_ 1B, p. 63, which concerns the year 40 A.D. The explanation is

simple: the character "Ku" has been mistaken for "Huan."
For Ku T'an, see the fragment 78.

25.   See Bibliography, IIIB 7 and IIA 15. In my
article, "The Canon of Laws by Li K'uei--A Double Falsification," pp. 113-16, I discuss the date of the dis-
appearance of the Hsin-lun.

26.   See my article, "The Necessity," ArOr, No. 30
(1962), pp. 246-50.

27.   For example, according to Huang Hui, Lun-heng
chiao-shih (p. 1025), the [Ku-chin] Shih-wen lei-chü
21 quotes Huan-tzu Hsin-lun, as follows, "There is a
proverb of Kuan-tung: 'When the people hear the music
of Ch'ang-an, they come out of the gates, look towards
the west and laugh.'" These lines are actually a small
part of fragment 79A, which is frequently quoted in
pre-Sung sources.

28.   See Chung-kuo che-hsüeh-shih tzu-liao hsüan-chi:
Liang Han chih pu (Peking: 1960), p. 207.

29.   Chi-ch'i t'ing wai pien, 40. 15a-16a (ed. SPTK).

30.   See the 1929 edition, p. 260. Another, shortened title of the work is used: Shang-shan-t'ang shu-mu.

31.   This edition was republished in Peking in 1959.
See D. Holzman, RBS 5, No. 586. For Wang Chung-min's
short study of the catalogue, see his "Chiang-yün-lou
shu-mu pa" ("Postface to the Catalogue of Chiang Yun
Lou, the Library of Ch'ien Ch'ien-yi"), Kuo-li Pei-
p'ing t'u-shu-kuan yüeh-k'an (Bulletin of the National
Library of Peking), No. 3 (5) (1929), pp. 577-79.

32.   JAOS, No. 88 (3) (1968), pp. 401-10. The hap-
hazard editing of the TPYL resulted in the inclusion
of several different versions of a single Hsin-lun
fragment.

33.   Wang I-t'ung described this phenomenon, using
the example of the Tzu-hai dictionary in his article,
"Tz'u-hai k'an-wu" in Tsing Hua Journal of Chinese
Studies, No. 2 (1960), pp. 131-42.

34.   The influence of falsely attributed works and
imitations was studied by Liang Jung-jo in "Chung-kuo

wen-hsüeh-shih shang ti wei-tso i-tso yü ch'i ying-hsiang," Tung-hai hsüeh-pao, VI (1) (1964), pp. 41-53.

35.   Chia K'uei's Hsin-lun is not mentioned in the Hou Han shu, but Chia K'uei's biography discusses him with Huan T'an and Cheng Hsing (Hou Han shu 36, p. 1316).

36.   See Wen T'ing-shih (1856-1904 A.D.), Pu Chin-shu I-wen chih, p. 3754 (in Er-shih-wu shih pu-pien III), quoting from PTSC 63 (9b). TPYL 241.9b gives the name as Chou Shao.

37.   Hsia-hou Chan was a friend of the poet P'an Yu. For P'an Yu, see note 23 to fragment 84A. For Hsia-hou Chan, see note 26 to fragment 84A.
38.   As early as the time of the bibliographical chapter of the Sui shu, p. 72 (see note 19 above), nothing was known of Mei-tzu.

39.   Wang Shu-min, "Liu-tzu chi-cheng," introduction to the Monographs of the Institute of History and Language, XLIV (T'aipei: 1961), particularly p. 6a-b.

40.   Wen T'ing-shih (see note 36 above), p. 3717, quotes this work from PTSC 62 (9b), but he feels that Hua T'an may have been confused with Hua Ch'iao (died 293 A.D.), who compiled a Hou Han shu.

41.   Ming-shih 288.3b-4b.

42.   Chapter "Tsa chi," 13B, p. 16b, in the Chih-pu-tsou-chai ts'ung shu edition. See also the introduction to Sun's edition, 4a.

43.   Ku T'an lived in the 3rd century A.D. The reconstruction of his work is entitled Ku-tzu hsin yü: see fragment 78.

44.   Hsüeh Ying died in 282 A.D. See San kuo chih, Wu chih 8.

45.   P'ei Yüan is known as P'ei Hsüan 裴 玄 . He was a contemporary of Hsüeh Ying.

46.   See R. H. van Gulik, The Lore of the Chinese Lute: An Essay in Ch'in Ideology, Monumenta Nipponica Monographs (Tokyo: 1941).

47.   P. 31 (see note 18 above). <u>Chiu T'ang-shu</u> does not mention the author of the <u>Ch'in-ts'ao</u>. It is surprising that none of the works attributed to Huan T'an is mentioned in the bibliographical chapter of the <u>Sui shu</u>.

48.   <u>Ibid</u>.

49.   Tseng P'u (1871-1935 A.D.), in his <u>Pu Hou Han shu i-wen chih p'ing k'ao</u> (<u>Er-shih-wu shih pu-pien</u> II, p. 2581), proposes that the title should read <u>Yüeh-yuan yü</u> and refers to a book written by King Hsien of Ho-chien (155-130 B.C.). Tjan Tjoe-som, <u>Po-hu t'ung</u> I (p. 105), however, says that <u>Yüeh-yüan yü</u> is a <u>wei</u> appendix to the <u>Book of Music</u>.

50.   R. H. van Gulik, "The Lore," p. 34 (see note 46 above), explains that <u>Ch'in-tao</u> means, "...the inner significance of the Lute, and how to apply this in order to find in the Lute a means for reaching enlightenment."

51.   <u>Hou Han shu</u> 90B, p. 2169.

52.   <u>Pu Hou-Han shu i-wen chih</u> (<u>Erh-shih-wu shih pu-pien</u> II, p. 2110).

53.   <u>Ibid</u>.

54.   <u>Wen hsüan</u> 31.4b and <u>PTSC</u> 132.6b--fragment 171; quoted only partially in some sources.

55.   For a detailed account, see Juan Yüan (1764-1849 A.D.), <u>Ssu-k'u wei-shou shu-mu t'i-yao</u> (Shanghai: 1955), p. 12.

56.   See note 50.

57.   P. 167 (see note 46 above).

58.   <u>Ch'in-shih</u> 6, according to the Chinese text reprinted by van Gulik (pp. 55-56); my translation differs in some points from his.

59.   See note 6 above.

60.   Liu Hsieh was critical of Huan T'an's "Wang-hsien fu." <u>Wen-hsin tiao-lung</u> 10:47, p. 110.2, states: "[The owner of] Huan T'an's works is said to be as rich

as I Tun, and Sung Hung has praised and recommended him.
But, in comparison with [the rhyme-prose of Ssu-ma]
Hsiang-ju and other rhyme-prose written in the Palace
of the Assembled Spirits, Huan's is definitely shallow
and lacking in talent. Therefore, we know that he excelled in his satirical treatise [i.e., the Hsin lun]
but could not come up to [the necessary level of] polite
literature." This cryptic statement by Liu Hsieh was
misunderstood by V. Y. C. Shih, The Literary Mind,
p. 253: "Huan T'an's works have been acclaimed as being
as rich as I Tun, and Sung Hung has compared him to [Ssu-
ma] Hsiang-ju in his recommendation. However, judged on
the basis of his own 'fu on the Palace of Chi-ling' and
other works, he is definitely shallow and lacking in
talent...." In note 27, Shih refers to Sung Hung's
biography where Huan T'an is compared to Yang Hsiung,
Liu Hsiang and to Liu Hsin, but not to Ssu-ma Hsiang-ju.

In fact, Liu Hsieh's text paraphrases Wang
Ch'ung's Lun-heng (20:61, p. 862; Forke, II, p. 274),
which compares Ssu-ma Hsiang-ju's invitation from Emperor Wu with Yang Hsiung's participation in the imperial hunts of Emperor Ch'eng. The point of similarity
is the fact that Ssu-ma Hsiang-ju, Yang Hsiung and Huan
T'an served their rulers both as officials and as poets.
Forke misunderstood the text in translating the name
"I Tun." For I Tun, see Watson, Records II, p. 483;
for a correction of Forke, see P. Pelliot, in JA, XX
(1912), p. 165; for Sung Hung, see Hou Han shu 26, p.
956. In any case, Huan T'an wrote no "Fu on the Palace
of Chi-ling." Sung Hung is evidently Sung Chung-weng
of the fragment 45.

61.   PTSC 102.3b is probably based upon Hsieh Ch'eng's
Hou Han shu, quoted by Yao Chih-yin in Hou-Han-shu pu-i
4a; see also Hui Tung's commentary in Hou-Han shu chi-
chieh 28A, p. 1018, and Huan T'an's Fu (bibliography IIB
48), p. 355, notes 10-11.

62.   Pu Hou-Han shu i-wen chih, Er-shih-wu shih pu-
pien II, p. 2270.

63.   See the beginning of the commentary to fragment
190.

64.   P. 112 (cf. note 19 above).

65.   P. 78. "Huan-tzu" is also listed in the third
part of the Sui-shu bibliography, which is devoted to

the philosophers, as "Huan T'an's _Hsin-lun_;" although
the _Hsin-lun_ belongs to the category of Confucian
writings, "_Huan-tzu_" is listed among the miscellany.
Ch'en Te-yün, _Ku chin jen-wu pieh-ming so-yin_ (1937),
pp. 82-83 (reprint, T'aipei: 1965), lists four men
from the Ch'un-ch'iu period, one from the Warring States
period and one from the Chin dynasty who used Huan-tzu
as a second name.

66.   The reference to _Ch'i-lu_ is from Tseng P'u, _Pu
Hou Han shu i-wen chih p'ing k'ao_, _Erh-shih-wu shih pu-
pien_ II, p. 2542, which does not give the name of Juan
Hsiao-hsü, who lived during that dynasty.

67.   Ku Huai-san (note 62 above), p. 2270, states
that during the Liang dynasty there were also five chüan.
He does not give his source for this statement but he
evidently means Juan Hsiao-hsü who lived during that
dynasty. See preceding note 66.

68.   P. 291 (see note 18 above).

69.   For two letters from Yang Hsiung to Huan T'an,
see note 12 to fragment 80C and note 123 to fragment
214. For another letter to Tung Hsien, see fragment
207.

70.   See also Hervouet, _Sseu-ma Hsiang-jou_, p. 157,
note 2.

List of Abbreviations

AM   Asia Major.

Ar Or   Archiv Orientální.

BEFEO   Bulletin de l'Ecole Française d'Extrême-Orient.

BMFEA   Bulletin of the Museum of Far Eastern Antiquities.

BSOAS   Bulletin of the School of Oriental and African Studies.

DKJ   Morohashi Tetsuji, Dai Kan Wa Jiten, Vol. 1-13, Tokyo, 1960.

ECCP   A. H. Hummel, Eminent Chinese of the Ch'ing Period. Vol. 1-2, Washington, 1943-44.

HFHD   H. H. Dubs, The History of the Former Han Dynasty by Pan Ku. Vol. 1-3, Baltimore, 1938, 1944, 1954.

HJAS   Harvard Journal of Asiatic Studies.

IWLC   I-wen lei-chü. See Bibliography IIIA 23.

JA   Journal Asiatique.

JAOS   Journal of the American Oriental Society.

JAS   Journal of Asian Studies.

Liang Han pu-fen Chung-kuo che-hsüeh-shih tzu-liao hsüan-chi. Liang Han pu-fen. Peking, 1960. See Bibliography I 7.

MH   E. Chavannes, Les Mémoires Historiques de Se-ma Ts'ien. Vol. I-V. Paris, 1895-1905; reprinted with VIth additional volume, Paris, 1968-69.

MSOS   Mitteilungen des Seminars für Orientalische Sprachen.

PTSC	Pei-t'ang shu-ch'ao, see Bibliography IIIA 37.
Pu-pien	Erh-shih-wu shih pu-pien. See Bibliography IV 3, 32, 54, 75, 90.
PWYF	P'ei-wen yün-fu. See Bibliography IIIA 38.
RBS	Révue bibliographique de sinologie.
SPPY	Ssu-pu pei-yao.
SPTK	Ssu-pu ts'ung-k'an.
Sun	Sun P'ing-i, Huan-tzu Hsin-lun. See Bibliography I 1.
TP	T'oung Pao.
TSCC	Ts'ung-shu chi-ch'eng.
WYWK	Wan-yu wen-k'u.
Yen	Yen K'o-chün, Huan-tzu Hsin-lun. See Bibliography I 2.
ZDMG	Zeitschrift der deutschen Morgenländischen Gesellschaft.

I. HSIN-LUN (New Treatise)

As Reconstructed by Yen K'o-chün

Chapter 1. Creation

1

Commentary to the Wen hsüan 40.17b.   Yen 13.2a. Sun 14a.

The Ch'in chancellor[1] Lü Pu-wei encouraged his
noble and excellent scholars to compose the Spring and
Autumn of Mr. Lü. The King of Huai-nan [Liu An] of the
Han dynasty enticed his brilliant and penetrating scholars to write sections and chapters [of the book Huai-
nan-tzu]. When they were finished,[2] both books were put
on display at the market place in the capital, and a
reward of one thousand catties of gold was publicly
offered to attract scholars to criticize the books.
Nevertheless, no one was able to propose any change.
Their contents were concise and captivating, their substance full and language subtle.

2

A TYPL 976.5b   Yen 13.2a. Sun 26a.

Tung Chung-shu concentrated all his spirit on
handing down the past. Before he reached the age of
sixty he did not glance at the greens in the garden.[3]

B TPYL 602.3b   Yen 13.2a. Sun 23a.

I have written the New Treatise in order to
examine and discuss the past and the present, but I
also wish to promote successful government. How does
this differ from the praise and blame given in the
Ch'un ch'iu! There are now people who doubt everything.
They say that the oyster is not a bivalve, that two
times five is not ten.

I, Huan T'an, wrote my New Treatise, after having
consulted Liu Hsiang's New Arrangement, and Lu Chia's
New Words.[4] In his parables[5] Chuang Chou mentions that
Yao questioned Confucius; Huai-nan-tzu says that the

boundaries of earth were smashed when Kung-kung was
fighting to become Emperor.[6] Everyone believes that
these are ridiculous statements, and therefore many
people now say that these are deficient books which
cannot be used. But nobody understands the space under
Heaven better than a sage. Although there are unfounded
and outrageous passages in Chuang Chou and those other
books, we must use what is best in them. How dare we
talk of rejecting them completely?[7]

NOTES: CHAPTER 1

1.   The edition by Yen K'o-chün (hereafter Yen) does not give the title hsiang 相 ("chancellor").

2.   Yen's text has shu 書 ("book").

3.   The story of Tung Chung-shu may be found in his biography in the Shih chi (121, p. 26; O. Franke, Studien zur Geschichte, p. 91): "For three years Tung Chung-shu did not look at his cottage and garden. Such was his spiritual force!" Wang Ch'ung also relates this story in his Lun-heng (26 p. 370; A. Forke, I, p. 504) but, in his usual skeptical way, he adds that three years is an exaggeration. Later, this anecdote, which praises Tung Chung-shu's zealous study of the Ch'un ch'iu while revealing a rather ironical attitude towards his bookishness, was adopted by Han Yü, who, in turn, was criticized for it by Chu Hsi. Cf. T. Pokora, "The Need for a More Thorough Study of the Philosopher Wang Ch'ung and of his Predecessors," pp. 238-239.

4.   An autobiographical fragment by Lu Hsi, which is quoted in his biography (Chin shu 54.11b), says, "Liu Hsiang examined [Lu Chia's] New Words and wrote his New Arrangement. Huan T'an studied the New Arrangement and wrote his New Treatise.

5.   Yü-yen ("parables") is the title of Chuang-tzu Chapter 27, translated by J. Legge as "Metaphorical Language" and by J. R. Ware as "Symbols." But the discussion between Yao and Confucius is mentioned neither there nor in the other chapters of the existing text of Chuang-tzu. Huan T'an apparently was speaking, not of the title of Chapter 27 nor of metaphors in general, but of fiction (hsü 虛) as opposed to fact (shih 實).
      Huan T'an's use of the term yü-yen can best be understood in the context of the analyses by Ju. L. Kroll, who offered much helpful advice on this manuscript, especially on those sections derived from Huan T'an's biography (fragments 206-10). Kroll writes in his letter of June 5, 1965:
      When studying the Shih chi I came upon an interesting device, a Han term denoting fictive speech put into the mouth of a fictive personality. This term, yü-yen 寓言 , has usually been translated as "allegory." At the beginning of Chuang Tzu's Chapter 27,

entitled Yü-yen, the term is explained as
words put into the mouth of an outsider
(according to the commentary, "a fictive
personality") in the hope that those words
will be more readily believed because the
outsider is not interested in the matter.
　　Ssu-ma Ch'ien uses the expression (Shih
chi 63, p. 10) as a ready-made term for a
certain literary device. (He believes that
everything written by Chuang Tzu is just
yü-yen.) Liu Hsiang, in his Pieh lu (ibid.,
quoted in the So-yin commentary), also explains the term: "Again, [Chuang Tzu]
created the surnames and personal names of
people, having them talk with one another.
This means he put words in [the mouths] of
these people. In Chuang-tzu there is,
therefore, a chapter entitled "Words put
[into the mouths of others]." Liu Hsiang
felt that such an approach had also been
used in Lieh-tzu. Finally, Pan Ku applied
the term of the rhyme-prose by Ssu-ma
Hsiang-ju (Han shu 100 B, p. 5866).
　　Thus we have before us the tradition of
"fiction," including invented dialogue,
which reaches from the philosophers of the
Warring Kingdoms period to the Han rhyme-
prose. There is an opposed tradition,
centered upon "real facts" (shih-shih 實事)
and represented by Ssu-ma Ch'ien. As a
matter of fact, Ssu-ma Ch'ien systematically
evaluated the works of Chuang-tzu and Ssu-ma
Hsiang-ju with the terms shih 實 and hsü
虛 , and states that they contain much
"fiction"(hsü, k'ung-yü 空語) and
exaggeration.
Also see Kroll's book on Ssu-ma Ch'ien, Syma Czjan-
istorik, pp. 43-45.

6.　　This legend is explained in detail in Chapter
31 ("T'an t'ien") of Wang Ch'ung's Lun-heng.

7.　　It is difficult to explain why Yen combined
these two quite different fragments. However, this
is typical of his approach in editing Huan T'an.

Chapter 2. Kings and Hegemons

3

A The Cheng-i commentary to Shih chi 5, p. 54;[1]

TPYL 77.5a.   Yen 13.2a-b Sun 11a.

In the distant past Three Sovereigns and Five
Supreme Rulers were established. Later, there were
Three Kings and Five Hegemons. These were the highest
rulers in the world. Therefore, it is said that the
Three Sovereigns regulated[2] by using the Way, while
the Five Supreme Rulers achieved moral transformation
through virtue. The Three Kings followed benevolence
and righteousness, while the Five Hegemons used authority and knowledge.

It has been said: When there were no laws,
regulations, chastisements or punishments, the ruler
was called "Sovereign." When there were laws and
regulations but no chastisements or punishments, the
ruler was called "Supreme Ruler." When the good were
rewarded, the bad punished, and the feudal rulers came
to court to perform their duties, the ruler was called
"King." When armies were raised, alliances pledged,
and sincerity and righteousness used to reform the
age, the ruler was called "Hegemon."

B I lin 3.7a.   Yen 13.2b. Sun 4b-5a.

The Three Sovereigns ruled by using the Way.
The Five Supreme Rulers achieved moral transformation
through virtue. The Three Kings followed benevolence
and righteousness. The Five Hegemons used authority
and knowledge. When there were no regulations, chastisements or punishments, [the ruler] was called Supreme
Ruler. When the good were rewarded, the bad punished,
and the feudal rulers came to court, [the ruler] was
called King. When huge armies were raised and alliances and vows pledged,[3] [the ruler] was called Hegemon.[4]

King [wang 王] means "to go towards" [wang
往]. This means that, because his kindness and
favor are great, the Empire comes to the King. The Way
of the King is pure; his virtue is like that. The Way
of the Hegemon is dappled and mixed; his achievement
is like this. They both possess the Empire and rule

over myriads of people. Their rule passes down to their sons and grandsons. They are the same in substance.

This fragment can also be found in Chao Jui's (8th century A.D.) Ch'ang-tuan ching 3.27a (in the "Shih pien" 適 變 chapter); in edition Tu-shu chai ts'ung-shu. It is a short mixture of 3A and 3B. A very short version of 3B can be found in T'ai-p'ing yü-lan 403.3b.

Cf. Liang-Han chih pu II, p. 351.

4

Commentary to the Wen hsüan 48.25b.   Yen 13.2b.   Sun 14b.

For a long time T'ang and Wu dwelt as chiefs of the region among the feudal lords. Their virtue and kindness reached the hundred families.

5

Ch'u-hsüeh chi 9.17b.   Yen 13.2b.   Sun 18a.

The virtue of a ruler who follows the Way of Kings supports and encompasses, and thus unites with Heaven.

6

A   TPYL 77.5a.   Yen 13.2b-3a.   Sun 20a.

One of the literati might say, "If one unsuc- cessfully aspires to become a true king, he may yet become a hegemon."[5] This statement is incorrect. Tradition says, "Among Confucians even boys five cubits tall[6] do not discuss the affairs of the Five Hegemons because they oppose the hegemons' disregard of benev- olence and righteousness and for might and deception."[7]

B   I lin 3.7a.   Yen 13.2b.   Sun 5a.

If one unsuccessfully aspires to become a true king, he may yet become a hegemon.[8]

NOTES: CHAPTER 2

1.   The text of the Shih chi to which the Cheng-i
commentary is attached refers to the year 343 B.C. (the
nineteenth year of the Duke Hsiao of Ch'in) and says,
according to Chavannes' translation: "Le dix-neuvième
année, les Fils du Ciel conféra [au duc Hsiao] le titre
d'hégémon," (in the nineteenth year, the Son of Heaven
gave the title of Hegemon to Duke Hsiao); MH II, p. 66
(and I, p. 304).

2.   "Regulate" is li 理 . Yen's text has chih
治 ("to rule"), taken from 3B.

3.   Again, Yen adds two characters from 3B.

4.   The 3A text has po 伯 for "hegemon," while
3B has pa 霸 . Huan T'an's terminology is also used
by Wang Ch'ung. Cf. Lun-heng 1, p. 3; Forke, Lun-heng
II, p. 32 and note 4.

5.   Hsü Yüeh makes a similar statement at the end
of his memorial to Emperor Wu. Cf. Shih chi 112, p. 20;
Watson, The Records II, p. 231. Hsü Yüeh says that he
has heard this statement, but neither he nor the commentary refers to a specific source. Later, the very text
used here is quoted by Wang Ch'ung as a proverb. Cf.
Lun-heng 4, p. 29; Forke, I, p. 315. Wang Ch'ung adds,
"Hegemons are frustrated pretenders to the King's
throne."

6.   This term is used in Mencius III:I:IV:17;
Legge, p. 256. A similar term, "of six cubits" is used
in the Analects VIII:6; Legge, p. 210, translated this
as referring to a child of about fifteen years. See
also Lü-shih ch'un-ch'iu 10:5, p. 103; Wilhelm, p. 129.

7.   The traditional statement is a paraphrase of
Tung Chung-shu. See Tung's biography in Han shu 56,
p. 4020. Franke, Studien zur Geschichte, p. 96 and
note 2.

8.   The meaning of version B differs somewhat from
A, but this is evidently due to its having been shortened.

Chapter 3. Searching for Counsellors

7

I lin 3.7a.   Yen 13.3a. Sun 5a

Ruling a country is at the root of being a
counsellor. Those who are so employed all possess
great talent. Those of great talent are the legs and
arms, the feathers and pinions of the ruler.

8

TPYL 187.8a.   Yen 13.3a. Sun 20b.

The kings, dukes and high officials are happy
to receive excellent teachers and brilliant counsellors.
The common people and the masses are pleased to cultivate
benevolent worthy men, as well as wise gentlemen. All
of these are the pillars and beams of the country, the
feathers and wings of all men.1

9

Jen-tzu,2 quoted in I lin 5.7b, suggests Huan T'an.

Yen 13.3a.

It is easy to support a king, but it is difficult to help a hegemon.

10

TPYL 404.8a.   Yen 13.3a. Sun 21a.

In former times, although I Yin of the Yin
dynasty, T'ai-kung of the Chou, and Po-18 Hsi of the
Ch'in all had Heavenly3 talents, they rose to become
teachers of kings and hegemons only after the age of
seventy.

A <u>Ch'ün-shu chih-yao</u> 44, p. 763   Yen 13.3a-b.   Sun 20a.

    The king of Ch'in saw the ruling house of Chou lose its power and might to the feudal lords. ... He, therefore, relied only upon himself and did not enfeoff others or allow them to become feudal lords. Later, Ch'en Sheng, and the rulers of Ch'u[4] and Han, all rose from the common people and were never enfeoffed as rulers with land. Together they annihilated Ch'in.

    When Emperor Kao conquered the Empire, he remembered that King Hsiang Yü had come through the Han-ku pass, while he himself had come from the Wu pass.[5] He ignored the passes and erected and strengthened the defenses. He filled the inner area with his three armies and organized frontier garrisons on the outside. He established a penalty of relentless punishment[6] for the formation of bands, and posted heavy rewards for information on subversives.

    But, later, when Wang Weng [i.e., Wang Mang[7]] usurped the throne he did not break through the passes, bridges and strategic defenses, but won everything sitting down. Wang Mang saw how he himself won the Empire by taking the government into his own hands, so he suppressed the great ministers and took to himself all the powers of his subordinates. Once he obtained the power, he personally handled all matters[8] whether they were great or small, deep or shallow. But later when he lost his throne, it did not come about through the great ministers.

    The Keng-shih Emperor saw that Wang Mang's Empire perished because he lost the affection of the people. Therefore, when he came to the western capital,[9] he trusted in the people's joy and happiness and allowed himself to enjoy peace and contentment. But he would not listen to the criticism and proposals of the ministers and counsellors. The Red Eyebrows surrounded him without, while the ministers rebelled within. Then the city fell.

    From this we can see that calamities and perils are strange and uncanny things, never of the same kind. How can one successfully overcome them, by building defenses or by planning preventive measures? The best defense and prevention is to assess the wise, intelligent and greatly talented, to foresee and forestall, and then perhaps be saved.

B <u>TPYL</u> 86.7a.   Yen 13.3a. Sun 20a.

     The First Sovereign Emperor of the Ch'in saw
how the house of Chou had lost its power. He believed
that it was necessary to keep the Nine Provinces in his
own hands. He looked on the masses of people as milling
flocks of sheep and as herds of pigs which must be
driven with a rod. Therefore, he was later overthrown.

12

<u>I lin</u> 3.7b.   Yen 13.3b. Sun 5a.

     The clear mirrors are the tortoise and straws
of divination. The regulations and rules are the bushel
and peck. The scales and measures are the yard and the
foot.

13

<u>Ch'ün-shu chih-yao</u> 44, pp. 763-764.   Yen 13.3b-4a.

     Needles, moxa, prescriptions, and medicines are
tools to help the sick, but without a skilled physician
they cannot cure. Talent, ability, virtue and fine
conduct are tools for ruling a country, but without an
enlightened ruler they are of no effect. If the physician does not own the needles and medicines, he may buy
them in order to practice his trade. If the ruler has
neither talent nor virtue, he may appoint wise counsellors and need not personally possess these qualities.

     Thus we can see that talent, ability, virtue
and fine conduct are the needles and medicines of a
country. They are effective if used as aids to the
ruler.

     Tradition says, "Better have one Po-lo than ten
fine horses. Better have one Ou Yeh than ten sharp
swords."[10] Better have a few who know good things than
have many good things. When he who knows good things
brings out the excellent and the precious [in them],
precious things multiply and are not limited to a mere
ten.

14

PTSC[12] 11b.   Yen 13.4a.
[13]
      To face the descendants of the Nine Provinces.

15

TPYL 212.6a.   Yen 13.4a. Sun 9a.

      Yao once tested Shun at the foot of a great
mountain. The people of the mountain directed him to
record the affairs of the empire,[14] as the officials
of the Office of the Masters of Writing do today. Only
when one finds great worthies, as well as men of knowledge, is it possible to make a decision and still be
fair.

The same, somewhat shortened, text is found in IWLC
48.17a and PTSC 59.2a.   The last sentence is missing
in the text quoted in the commentary to Hou Han shu 34,
p. 4137.

16

Commentary to Wen hsüan 56.17a.   Yen 13.4a. Sun 15a.

      The Duke of Chou clarified and respected the
Way of Chou, and brought benefits to all within the
four utmost limits.

17

PTSC 44.2a.   Yen 13.4a. Sun 15a.

      Run the prison like water.

18

Commentary to Wen hsüan 60.27b.   Yen 13.4a. Sun 14a.

      A sage appears once in a thousand years. Worthy
and superior men think of him but cannot see him.

See also the commentary to <u>Wen hsüan</u> 37.35b. The first
sentence of the fragment is repeated in the commentaries
to <u>Wen hsüan</u> 57.35 and 52.24a.

19

Commentary to <u>Wen hsüan</u> 36.27b.   Yen 13.4a.   Sun 14a.

He who is perfectly straight, loyal and upright
dares to criticize and protest as did Chi An.[15]

20

<u>I lin</u> 3.7b.   Yen 13.4a.   Sun 5a.

The eminent men of past generations secured
their merit and left their names to posterity. Their
pictures are in the imperial palaces and inner apart-
ments. They are the great invaluable treasures of the
nation. One could gather the jade of Pien Ho,[16] pile
up the jade ornaments of the Hsia, hoard the pearls
of the Marquis of Sui,[17] store pearls which shine in
the night--but even that would not sufficiently compare.[18] What age lacks ministers like I Yin or Lü
Shang, Chang Liang or Ch'en P'ing? But the rulers of
men do not recognize them, and the lower ministers are
not employed.

21

<u>Ch'ang-tuan ching</u> 3.16b.   Yen 13.4b.

When a person is capturing wild animals, he
does not allow a beauty to raise her hands.[19] When a
person is fishing for a giant fish, he does not allow
a boy to make careless preparations. It is not that
he dislikes them, but that their strength is inadequate
for the task. Now, what about a ruler of [a country
with] ten thousand chariots who does not select the
best men?

22

<u>TPYL</u> 684.5b-6a.   Yen 13.4b.   Sun 24a.

Tradition says that Prince Mou of Wei met the
King of Chao in the north. The King had just commanded

his hat-maker to put the official hats in order and
bring them forward.

He asked Mou how to govern his country. Mou
replied, "Great King, if you could sincerely treat the
country as seriously as you treat that two-foot strip
of silk,[20] then the country would be well-governed and
at peace." The King said, "I received this country
from my ancestors. The ancestral temple and the gods
of soil and grain are very serious matters. How can
you compare them to a two-foot strip of silk?"

Mou said, "When you, Great King, order your
hats to be made you do not call on your relatives or
those close to you to do the job. Instead, you invariably seek out skilled craftsmen. Don't you do this because you fear that the silk would be ruined and the
hats not be made? Now, if those who govern the country
are not skilled, then the gods of soil and grain will
not be at peace and the spirits of the ancestral temple
will not accept blood offerings. Great King, you do not
seek out skilled men, but you consult your personal
favorites instead. Doesn't this practice take the
country less seriously than a two-foot piece of silk?"

The king said nothing in reply.

PTSC 127.2b has a short version of this fragment. Huan
T'an's anecdote appears to be based on Chan-kuo ts'e,
"Chao ts'e" 3, 15.

23

Commentary to Wen hsüan 45.28b and 46.37b.

Yen 13.4b. Sun 14b.

Human nature is difficult to fathom, difficult
to know. Therefore, those of an extraordinary and
strange nature are often ignored by the vulgar.

24

A TPYL 897.2b and IWLC 93.10b. Yen 13.4b-5a. Sun 17b.

The old man of Hsieh,[21] who lived at Ch'ang-an,
was an expert in judging horses. In the frontier

outposts he found a noble horse. The old man rode into market on the horse, but no one noticed him coming or going. Later, someone complimented him on the horse and asked to see it.

The old gentleman said, "All these officials have no eyes. They are not worthy to see it."

B   The commentary to Wen hsüan 4.30a (Sun 12b) gives a short quote which Yen has interpolated into the one above: A horse expert said, "The Duke of Hsieh bought a horse which looked ugly but had a proper gait. He called it Chi-tzu."[22]

25

A   IWLC 93.3b.   Yen 13.5a. Sun 17b.

Domestic animals are quite common, but all of them which were especially fine have been recorded in the texts. Thus there are horses named Hua-liu[23] and Chi-lu,[24] and the oxen Kuo-chiao and Ting-liang[25] are praised.

B   The subcommentary to Li chi 35.7b (edition Shih-san ching chu-su, Shanghai, 1926) has a version given by neither Yen nor Sun: Domestic animals are quite common, but all of them which were especially fine have been recorded in the texts. The best are called Han-lu[26] and Sung-ts'u.[27]

26

I lin 3.7b.   Yen 13.5a. Sun 5a-b.

Is there any period which has no men like I Yin or Lü Shang, Chang Liang or Ch'en P'ing? The ruler of men does not recognize them, so many worthy men are not employed.[28]

Worthy men are of five classes.[29]

Some are careful and diligent in their family affairs, and honor their elders when in social groups. These are the gentlemen of the villages.

Some do their work with energy. They understand profit, writing, and the [Work of] Shih [Chou]³⁰ These are the gentlemen of the districts and the courts of justice.

Some are trustworthy and sincere, respectful in their demeanor, incorrupt and honest, and fair and reasonable. When in a lowly position, they devote their attention to those above. These are the gentlemen of the prefectures and the commandaries.

Some have mastered classical scholarship. Their name is eminent and their behavior skilled. They penetrate so deeply as to participate in governing. They are broadminded, as well as persistent. These are the gentlemen among the dukes and counsellors.

Some of high and excellent talents rise above the multitude as does a mountain. They have many ideas and great plans, make plans for the age, and thus establish their great merit. These are the gentlemen of the Empire.

27

Commentary to Wen hsüan 50.10a.   Yen 13.5a.   Sun 14b.

The man who follows principle when living at home, who is peaceful and obedient in his village, who is respectful and reverent in his comings and goings, whose words are serious and modest--that man is a perfect gentleman.

28

Ch'ün-shu chih-yao 44, p. 764.   Yen 13.5a-6a.

Once counsellors and assistarts have been found, there remain three great difficulties and two bars to excellence.

Among those now in charge of affairs, many are mediocre men, and only a few have great talent. Those few cannot overcome the many; one mouth cannot argue against an entire nation. To hold a solitary and individual opinion against the consensus,³¹ to argue from a viewpoint which disdains what is petty against minds which prize what is petty will never create cooperation. This is the first difficulty.

The creation of something strange and remark-
able, the making of something extraordinary, cannot be
understood by vulgar men. Also, to let the enlightened
and the wise plan affairs and then bring them down to
the masses will certainly be inadequate. This is the
second difficulty.

If at the moment when the plan which has been
heard and accepted is about to be put into action but
is not yet completed, carping men take an instant dislike to it, then the half-complete plan will meet suspicion and the voice which proposed it becomes the butt
of accusations. This is the third difficulty.

Wise men exhaust all their minds and voices in
the service of the nation, but the masses watch them
with malice, and they become the objects of suspicion.
If one is not accepted as a conformist, he is slandered.[32] His virtue may be ten times perfect, but a
single fault will do him in. This is the first bar to
excellence.

Gentlemen of talent and ability are the envy of
the world. When they meet a wise ruler they rise at
once, rejoicing. But once the ruler has been lucky
enough to find men of talent, he insists that they
follow the masses and not the men of wisdom. Though
they be Yu Jo or Chung-ni, they are still dismissed.
This is the second bar to excellence.

Therefore, unless the relations between a ruler
and his ministers are most intimate and stable, unless
they have such great trust that they would tear out
their hearts for each other, unless their actions are
above suspicion and doubt--as when I Yin and Lü Shang
were employed when Fu Yüeh was discovered in a dream,[33]
or when Kuan Chung and Pao Shu-ya were appointed with
trust--it is difficult to carry out an act and bring
an idea to fruition.

Again, the arguments of ministers have too many
angles. When they wish to see someone employed, they
pressure the ruler with quotes from the ancient sage
counsellors; when they wish to remove someone from the
ruler's favor, they call him a usurper who endangers
the country.

Now, father and son are the closest of kin, but
in the ruling families there was the matter[34] of Kao-
tsung and Hsiao-i[35] and, later on, during the reigns of

the Emperors Ching and Wu, the affairs of the crown-princes Li[36] and Wei.[37] There are loyal ministers with lofty ideals, but over the years there have been the unhappy affairs of Kuan Lung-feng, Pi Kan, Wu Yüan, and Ch'ao Ts'o.[38] There are so many similar cases they cannot be fully listed. So, how can matters be accomplished? How can they be simply learned? However, by analyzing what has happened in the past we may get a good look at the problem and be forewarned.

Noble and excellent men of great talent prize the opportune moment.[39] They all want to reach the heights of the sages and shine their light down through the ages. Why would they ruin their names, turn from righteousness and indulge in wild and vile behavior? Lu Chung-lien refused gold and the kingdom of Ch'i.[40] The kingdom of Chao gave gold and titles to Yü Ch'ing, but he laid aside his fief of ten thousand families and his position as chancellor of the country.[41] Then they rejoiced that they had made a name for themselves and were also free to do what they pleased. Did they beg again? Did they curry favor or hasten after wealth?

The depraved, disobedient, and rebellious ministers, when closely observed, are all greedy men, arguing over trifles. None of them had great talent. Thus we can come to fully understand, during our lifetimes, the behavior, the feelings, and the sense of responsibility of eminent gentlemen of extraordinary talent and ability. If we don't[42] regard this as being of the greatest importance, then we begin to suspect them. If we find it impossible to acknowledge, accept, and effectuate their plans, then these plans, although born of broad knowledge and past success, will be useless.

29

<u>I lin</u> 3.7b.   Yen 13.6a.   Sun 5b.

Had Chia I not been degraded and disappointed, his literary elegance would not have been produced.[43] Had Liu An, the Prince of Huai-nan not been noble, successful, and wealthy, he could not have employed a host of eminent scholars to compose a book.[44] Had the Grand Historian [Ssu-ma Ch'ien] not been responsible for keeping records, he would not have been able to put them into order and come to know both the past and the present.[45] Had Yang Hsiung not been poor, he could never have written his Mysterious Words.[46]

Previous translation of the last part: T. Pokora, "The Life" II, p. 546.

30

I lin 3.8a.   Yen 13.6a. Sun 5b.

The three virtuous men of the Yin dynasty[47] were all obscure in their own time but shown forth brilliantly in later times. What good is that to [our] time?[48] What is their help for the ruler?

31

Wang Ch'ung, Lun-heng, 16, 50, p. 720.   Yen 13.6a.

Huan Chün-shan said to Yang Tzu-yün,[49] "If a sage should appear to future generations, people will merely realize that his talents are greater than theirs, but many will not be able to tell whether he is really a sage or not."

Tzu-yün replied, "This is true indeed."

Previous translation by A. Forke, Lun-heng, p. 361.

NOTES: CHAPTER 3

1.   In his commentary, Sun 20b mentions a very
short text by Huan Chieh, as quoted in PTSC 29.3a:
"A great minister [is like] a beam." Yen 13.3a is
skeptical about attributing this statement to Huan Chieh
(whose biography can be found in San-kuo chih, Wei chih
22). Another quasi-biography of Huan Chieh, the Huan
Chieh pieh-chuan, is quoted six times in the TPYL, but
there is no mention of a book by him. The commentary
to the PTSC 29.3a says that Ch'en Yü's edition of the
same work attributes this statement to Huan Chieh, while
Ma Kuo-han in his Yü-han shan-fang chi-i shu says this
fragment is from Huan Fan's Shih-yao lun. Ma puts Huan
Fan in the category of Legalists (fa chia 法 家). Although Yen had some doubts, he included the quotation
under Huan T'an. Nevertheless, the Huan Chieh pieh-
chuan, as quoted in TPYL 431.7a, just says that Huan
Chieh is a "great minister [is like] a beam" (liang-
tung ta ch'en 樑棟大臣). Thus the four characters apparently have nothing to do with Huan T'an's
Hsin-lun.

2.   Jen-tzu is a book in ten ch'üan by Jen I, according to the commentary to the I lin. However, the
bibliographical chapter of the Sui history, the "Sui
shu ching-chi chih" 3 (p. 74) mentions a Jen-tzu tao-lun,
also in ten ch'üan, which is attributed to Jen Ku 嘏
of Wei. Chung-kuo jen-ming ta tz'u tien (p. 224, 3),
says that Jen I, who lived during the Later Han, wrote
a Jen-tzu, but the authority for this assertion is unknown. Jen I may be Jen Shuang 爽 , who is mentioned in the San-kuo chih, wu chih 12. Jen-tzu tao
lun, as reconstructed by Ma Kuo-han, can be found in
Yü-han shan-fang chi-i shu, vol. 78.

3.   Yen proposes ta 大 ("great") instead of t'ien
天 ("heavenly").

4.   The leaders of Ch'u, like Hsiang Yü, who fought
against Liu Pang after the death of Ch'en Sheng, were
mostly heirs of noble families.

5.   See, for example, HFHD I, pp. 6 and 54.

6.   For this meaning of ch'iung-chih 窮治
see Chavannes, MH III, p. 558 and note 4 ("punir
jusqu'au bout").

7.   Here, and in other fragments by Huan T'an, quoted in the Ch'ün-shu chih-yao, the text has Wang Weng (or Wang weng 王翁). The commentary to the I lin 2.8a correctly states: "'Venerable old Wang' [Wang weng] refers to Wang Mang. Since Huan T'an had served under Wang Mang, he could not abuse him, nor could he call him ruler." For further arguments on this point, see T. Pokora, "Life" I, pp. 62-64 and notes 38, 45, 46. Henceforth, the term Wang weng will be translated as Wang Mang.

8.   The same is said of the First Emperor of Ch'in in the Shih chi 6, p. 56; Chavannes II, p. 178. Both statements appear to be historically correct, but they undoubtedly reflect the attitude of officials who did not like to be pushed from their own spheres of authority, even by the Emperor, and were also afraid that the ruler's authority would be undermined by his involvement in trivial affairs.

9.   The capital referred to is Ch'ang-an.

10.   Lü-shih ch'un-ch'iu 24:2, p. 309; Wilhelm, p. 420. Ou Yeh, a famous smith, and Po Lo, a legendary judge of horses, are referred to in Han Fei Tzu 50 (translated by B. Watson as "Eminence in Learning").

11.   For another perspective on the value of knowledge, see fragment 138.

12.   The quotation in PTSC is attributed to Hua T'an's Hsin-lun and does not belong to Huan T'an. Nevertheless, the term "Nine Provinces" (chiu chou 九州) is also found in fragment 11B.

13.   Instead of hou 後 ("descendant"), Yen has chün 俊 ("eminent").

14.   This information reflects Han ideas on the origin of Chinese historiography.

15.   Chi An was a morally upright official who dared to criticize even Emperor Ching.

16.   For an explanation of this famous treasure see Shih chi 87, p. 8; Bodde, China's First Unifier, p. 18 and note 3.

17.   Cf. note 16 above.

18.   This is the end of the text of the Sung edition of the I lin, as reprinted in the collection Ssu-pu pei-yao. Nevertheless, both Yen and Sun add the two following sentences which, according to the Sung edition, belong to the beginning of fragment 26.

19.   "Raise her hands," i.e., take part in the hunt.

20.   Instead of ts'ung 縱 , I read shih 綕 .

21.   This probably refers to the famous T'ien Wen, Lord of Meng-ch'ang. T'ien Wen, according to Shih chi 75, p. 12, returned to Hsieh in his old age. He is also known as Wen of Hsieh. In the account appended to Shih chi 96, p. 22, T'ien Wen is described almost as Huan T'an pictures the old man in the fragment above.

22.   Chi was a legendary horse who could run one thousand li in a day. Confucius mentioned the horse in Analects XIV: 35; cf. the explanation by Legge, p. 288, sub 35.

23.   Hua-liu is mentioned in Yang Hsiung's Fan Li-sao, quoted in Han shu, 87A, p. 5060. According to Yen Shih-ku's commentary, Hua-liu was of a sorrel color

24.   For Chi, see note 22 to fragment 24A. Lu was one of the horses of King Mu of Chou, as was Hua-liu. Sometimes the names of Chi and Lu are combined.

25.   Both oxen are only mentioned in this fragment. For Kuo-chiao, see PWYF 771.2 and DKJ 39474.146; for Ting-liang, PWYF 4040.1 and DKJ 2.214.

26.   Han-lu, a very great dog, is mentioned in Shih chi 79 (p. 16) and defined in the So-yin commentary, which refers to the Chan-kuo Ts'e. The name may be literally translated as "the hound of Han."

27.   Evidently Sung-ts'u is "a dog of Sung." This term can also be found in PWYF 3896, 3. Both "Han-lu" and "Sung-ts'u" were first used by Huan T'an. They cannot be found together in early texts, but are only used in later lexicons. Even the origin of the terms is not clear, for in K'ung-ts'ung-tzu, 17, 20 b, ed. SPTK, it is pointed out that all other animal names reflect either the shape or the color of the animal.

28.   For the first two sentences, see note 18 to fragment 20.

29.   Wu p'in 五 品 ("five classes"). See the Book of History, II:i:19; Legge, p. 44.

30.   Wang Hsien-ch'ien, in Tung-fang Shuo's biography in Han shu 65 (p. 4380), explains wen-shih 文史 ("writings") as referring to the different ways of writing. For the Work of Shih Chou (or "Historian Chou"), see D. Bodde, China's First Unifier, p. 147.

31.   The term lei-t'ung 雷同 is used in a memorial to Huan T'an which is quoted in his biography in the Hou Han shu 28A, p. 1016; Pokora, "The Life," I, p. 31, note 108.

32.   In accordance with an anonymous commentator of the Ch'ün-shu chih-yao, I prefer su 愬 ("to slander") for hsiang 想 ("to consider").

33.   Shih chi 3, p. 22; Chavannes, MH I, p. 195.

34.   The text, which I have followed, has she 設 . The commentary to the Ch'ün-shu chih'yao proposes ch'an 讒 ("to slander"), while Yen gives shih 失 ("to lose," "to miss," "to err").

35.   Hsiao-i is said to have been a crown prince, son of Kao-tsung (or Wu-ting, ca. 1324-1265 B.C.). Although Hsiao-i was a paragon of filial piety, his father mistreated him after the death of his mother. Hsün-tzu (17:23, p. 295; Köster, p. 310) briefly mentions Hsiao-i with Confucius' disciples Tseng Shen and Min Tzu-ch'ien.

36.   Shih chi 11, p. 8; Chavannes, MH II, p. 511; Watson, Records I (p. 370) says that Li was deposed in 150 B.C. His name was Liu Jung according to Han shu 5; HFHD I, p. 316.

37.   The crown prince Liu Chü, with his mother, the Empress Wei Tzu-fu, mobilized an army on September 1, 91 B.C., for an attack on the Lieutenant-Chancellor. After their defeat, both mother and son committed suicide. Cf. HFHD, II, p. 114. The revolt was brought about by the disgrace of Wei Tzu-fu. Huan T'an also mentions Wei Tzu-fu at the beginning of his own biography in the HHS; cf. Pokora, "The Life," I, pp. 18-19.

38.   "Unhappy affair" (pien 變) is a euphemism for the execution of ministers. In Chuang-tzu (10, p. 55; Legge I, p. 283), three of these virtuous counsellors are mentioned: "Formerly Lung-feng was

beheaded; Pi Kan's heart was torn out; Ch'ang-hung was ripped open; and Tzu-hsü was reduced to pulp." Kuan Lung-feng was a minister to Chieh of Hsia; Pi Kan, to King Chou of Shang; Wu Yüan (or Wu Tzu-hsü), to Fu-ch'ai of Wu; Ch'ao Ts'o, to Emperor Ching of Han. Ch'ao Ts'o, who is also mentioned in a memorial by Huan T'an (cf. "The Life," I, p. 25 and fragment 209, note 58) proposed the abolition of fiefs in 154 B.C. This proposal led directly to the Rebellion of the Seven Kingdoms. The Emperor Ching tried to save the situation by sacrificing Ch'ao Ts'o.

39.   The commentary prefers ho 合 ("agreement," "the opportune moment," i.e., "the right time for action"). Chiu 咎 ("calamity") is found in other versions.

40.   Shih chi 83, pp. 14-18; Kierman, Four Late Warring States Biographies, pp. 44-47, especially p. 44. The Lord of P'ing-yüan wished to give a fief and gold to Lu Chung-lien, who adamantly refused them.

41.   The biography of Yü Ch'ing, a wandering politician of the third century B.C., can be found in the second part of the Shih chi, Chapter 76 (pp. 11-22), but the source of Huan T'an's statement is Shih chi 79, p. 32. Yü Ch'ing is the reputed author of the Yü-shih ch'un-ch'iu. He rose very quickly as an advisor to King Hsiao-ch'eng of Chao (265-245 B.C.), but too much in demand by other rulers, he did not wish to amass honors and wealth and so gave up his position.

42.   Instead of the pu 卜 of the text, Yen has hsia 下 .

43.   Evidently refers to Chia I's Hsin-shu.

44.   Huai-nan-tzu.

45.   Shih chi.

46.   T'ai-hsüan ching.

47.   The three virtuous men of Yen were Wei-tzu, Chi-tzu and Pi Kan, according to the Analects XVIII:1.

48.   The Ssu-pu pei-yao edition of the I lin, which has chün 君 ("ruler") instead of shih 世 ("times"), is evidently mistaken.

49.   Huan T'an and Yang Hsiung.

Chapter 4. <u>On Substance</u>

32

A <u>Ch'ün-shu chih-yao</u> 44, pp. 765-66.   Yen 13.6b-7a.

Everything which the ears hear and the eyes
see, which the heart and mind know and recognize, which
the feelings and dispositions like and dislike, which
is welcomed or thrown away because of its use or harm--
all men are equal in the attention which they pay to
these things.

Talent and ability, great or small; wisdom and
plans, deep or shallow; hearing and vision, dark or
bright; disposition and behavior, thick or thin--people
possess these qualities in different degrees. Without
great talent and deep wisdom the Great Substance[1] cannot
be seen. The Great Substance includes all the affairs
of the present and those that are to be.[2]

The man whose speech is correct and whose plans
are appropriate, who meets a crisis with power, who
abides by the constant and holds to the proper, who is
not perplexed when he meets a problem, who carries a
measured judgment within which he cannot be upset or
shifted or deceived by the cunning and strange--such a
man understands the Great Substance.

But, although he may be as powerful as Wang
Mang, as discriminating and quick as Kung-sun Lung, as
clever and glib[3] as Tung-fang Shuo, and as adept at
explaining disasters and abnormalities as Ching Chün-
ming; although he may have seen much and heard much,
have written as many as ten thousand chapters, and
taught Confucianism to hundreds and thousands of stu-
dents--if he has no great talent he just increases his
ignorance of the Great Substance.

Wang Mang surpassed the people of his time in
three ways: he had enough intelligence to disguise the
wrong and diminish the right; he could stump the so-
phists with his arguments; his power terrified his subordinates and several times he secretly cut down those
he disliked. Therefore, none of his ministers could
refute or respond to his arguments. No one dared to
contradict, correct, or remonstrate with him.

Finally he came to defeat and death. This is the disaster of the Great Substance.

B   Emperor Kao understood the Great Substance. He said, "Chang Liang, Hsiao Ho, Han Hsin--these three gentlemen are all outstanding among men! It was because I was able to use them that I won the empire."[5] This is the fruit of knowing the Great Substance.

C   When Wang Mang first took over the government, he thought that he understood fully the worthies and the sages, and that none among his ministers could surpass his talent and intelligence. Therefore, in all his acts and endeavors he only wanted to trust and rely on himself, while he refused to share responsibility and authority with informed and experienced men. He put forth his ideas as soon as he thought of them, and once an idea came he would use it. Therefore, he seldom achieved success and finally met ruin and death. This was a man who did not know Great Substance.

Emperor Kao was very shrewd and could evaluate himself. While his ministers regulated affairs and fixed laws, he would say, "I am not high, but low. Let's evaluate our ability to carry these out and make that our guide and measure." Within his realm, he relaxed the government of the land to meet the needs of the times. Therefore, both his people and his ministers were happy and joyful, and future generations remembered him. This was a man who knew the Great Substance.

D   Wang Mang praised and admired[6] the government of earlier sages, but he despised and was contemptuous of the law and ordinances of the House of Han. Therefore, he changed and altered many things, wishing to imitate antiquity in everything he did. He praised the regulations of earlier sages but did not realize that he could not carry them out himself. He ignored things near and modern and chased after the remote past. What he esteemed was not that to which he should have devoted himself. Therefore, he fell from lofty principle into ruin and confusion. This was a man who did not know the Great Substance.

When the Eminent Founder (Emperor Kao) wished to attack Wei, he sent men to spy on its Chancellor, its generals and its leaders, as well as on other men of authority. When he learned the ruler's name, he said, "None of them equal Hsiao Ho, Ts'ao Shen,7 Han Hsin, Fan K'uai and my other men. It will be easy to deal with Wei."8 Then he attacked and destroyed it. This was a man who knew the Great Substance.

E   Once Wang Mang planned to attack the Hsiung-nu in the North. Later he attacked the followers of the Red Eyebrows in Ch'ing, in Hsü, and in many other commanderies.9 He would never choose excellent generals, but instead employed members of the great families, and trustworthy and cautious civil officials. Or he would put in command the sons and grandsons of those close to him, or those whom he had loved for a long time. None of this was shrewd or intelligent. Wretched deputies led the army and managed the multitude when they went out to meet a mighty enemy. Therefore, when the armies joined in battle, his army met with defeat, and his officers and men scattered and fled.

His fault lay in not selecting excellent generals. His generals, as well as the ruler himself, did not know the Great Substance.

This text, quoted by Yen, is divided into five parts (A-E) in the <u>Ch'ün-shu chih-yao</u>.

33

<u>PTSC</u> 116.1a-b.   Yen 13.7a. Sun 15b.

To move like striking thunder, to be still like a standing mountain, to attack like hurtling lightning, to seize like a swift storm, to be light in the beginning and heavy later on, full inside and empty outside...

34

<u>PTSC</u> 115.5a.   Yen 13.7a. Sun 15b.

Chou Ya-fu, because of Li's severity, ferocity and billowing, deserves to be called "the greatest general of the country."10

35

A The <u>Chi-chieh</u> commentary to the <u>Shih chi</u> 91, p. 15.[11]

   <u>Ch'ang-tuan ching</u> 6.17a.   Yen 13.7b.   Sun 10b.

There is a game called "strategic chess" [<u>wei-ch'i</u> or "go"] which is said to belong to the art of war.

When one starts, the best strategy is to spread the pieces far apart and stretch them out, to encircle and attack, and thus win by having many roads open. The next best strategy concentrates on cutting off the enemy to seek advantage. Therefore, victory and defeat are uncertain, and plans and calculations are needed to decide the outcome. The lowest strategy is to defend the borders and corners, hastily building "eyes" so as to protect oneself in a small area.[12]

But, nevertheless, it is best to analyze the words of Lord Hsieh. His best plan was: seize Wu and Ch'u, add Ch'i and Lu, then Yen and Chao. This is what is meant by "extending the roads and territories." His next best plan was: seize Wu and Ch'u, add Han and Wei, block Ch'eng-kao, and occupy Ao-ts'ang. This is what is meant by "hastening to cut off the enemy and to seek advantage." The lowest plan was: seize Wu and Hsia-ts'ai, and occupy Ch'ang-sha to overlook Yüeh. This is what is meant by "defending borders and corners, hastily the building 'eyes'."

A shorter, corrupt version of this fragment can be found in <u>TPYL</u> 753.4b, where it is attributed to <u>Hsin-yü</u>.[13]

B <u>I lin</u> 8a. Commentary to <u>Wen hsüan</u> 52.23a.

   <u>TPYL</u> 753.4b.   Yen 13.7b.   Sun 5b and 10b.

There is a game called "strategic chess," which is said to belong to the art of war.

The best strategy is to spread out and stretch far, and thus to win victory by many outlets. The next best strategy concentrates on cutting off the enemy's advantage and profit. The lowest strategy is to defend the borders and corners, hastily building "eyes" to protect oneself in a small area.[14] But, nevertheless,

it is best to analyze words like those of the Lord
Hsieh, who said that Ch'ing Pu was going to revolt.
Hsieh's best plan was: seize Wu and Ch'u, extend the
roads and territories. His next best plan was: block
Ch'eng-kao, hasten after strategic roads and seek some
advantage. His lowest plan was: rely on Ch'ang-sha to
overlook Yüeh, defend the borders and corners, hastily
building "eyes."

The generals and Chancellor of the Keng-shih
Emperor could not put up a defense and thus allowed the
dead pieces of chess within the encirclement to come
alive again.

36

Ch'u-hsüeh chi 24.14b.   Yen 13.7b.   Sun 18a-b.

When the Keng-shih Emperor arrived at Ch'ang-an,
his great ministers were assigned to work in the Eastern
Palace,[15] so the people below laughed at them. Moreover, half of the city was used as barracks to house the
small guard.[16] Therefore, we know that they did not
belong to the company of Hsiao [Ho] and Ts'ao [Shen].[17]

Previous translation: T. Pokora, "The Life," II,
p. 522.

37

Ch'ün-shu chih-yao 44, p. 766.   Yen 13.7b.

[The importance of] words and actions lies in
their beauty and goodness, not in their quantity. When
a man utters one beautiful word and performs one beautiful act, the Empire follows him. When one man conceives
one wicked idea or one shameful deed, the ten thousand
people oppose him. Must not one, then, be cautious?

Thus the I Ching says, "Words and actions are
the hinge and the spring of the superior man. The
movement of that hinge and spring determines glory or
disgrace. It is this which moves Heaven and earth."[18]

30

A <u>Ch'ün-shu chih-yao</u> 44, p. 766.   Yen 13.8a.

     Wang Mang punished and killed people; then he
would use poison to deface their corpses. When men were
burned alive he filled the muscles of their corpses with
vinegar and five kinds of poison. As they were buried
they were covered and laid upon prickles and thorns.[19]
Already dead, these people were just like wood or earth.
Though he multiplied their wounds and added poisons,
what good or harm could it do to corpses?

     The Accomplished T'ang restricted hunting.[20]
This in no way helped the scholars and commoners, but
the people turned to him because they admired his virtue
and kindness.

     Duke Hsüan of Ch'i saved the life of an ox.[21]
This was of no use to the sages, but those sages who
praised him admired his benevolence.

     King Wen buried the dried bones.[22] This was of
no use to the multitude of commoners, but those who rejoiced at it were moved by his mercy[23] and righteousness.

     Wang Mang defaced the dead. This did not hurt
the living, but those living men who hated him did so
because he had revealed his cruelty and oppressiveness
to them.

     In all these four instances what is imperceptible
and minute is also outstanding and important. The tiny
is also the great. Therefore, the two sages prospered,
and the King won praise, while Wang Mang perished. Thus,
there is a great difference between the man who knows
the Great Substance and the man who does not know the
Great Substance.

Cf. <u>Liang Han pu-fen</u> II, pp. 351-52; Pokora, "The Life,"
I, pp. 67-68.

B <u>I lin</u> 3.8a.   Yen 13.8a.

     King Wen buried the dried bones. This was of
no use to the multitude of commoners, but they rejoiced
at it, moved by his mercy and righteousness. Wang
Mang's inspection of the five viscera[24] did not hurt the
living, but living men hated his cruelty and oppressiveness.

39

Ch'ün-shu chih-yao 44, p. 767.   Yen 13.8a.

When the sage kings ruled the country, they
revered propriety and yielding, and manifested benevolence and righteousness. They made respect for worthy
men and love for the people their affair. Therefore,
divinations by tortoise-shell and straws were seldom
performed, sacrifices to the gods and the dead were
rare.

40

Ch'ün-shu chih-yao 44, p. 767.   Yen 13.8b.[25]

Wang Mang, who liked to divine with tortoise-
shell and straws, observed the [lucky and unlucky] hours
and days, and fervently served the demons and the gods.
He incurred great expenses in building temples and
sacrificial sites,[26] and by washing, fasting, and offering sacrificial victims, meals and savory food to
the gods and the dead. The hardships of the officials
and servants responsible for arranging these rituals
were unspeakable.

Since he governed poorly, he was confronted with
rebellion in the Empire. When difficulties arose and
war broke out, he had neither the wit nor the foresight
to save and extricate himself. Instead, he rushed to
the Southern Altar to pray at the suburban sacrifice.
He struck his chest and cried out about injustice, pas-
sionately calling out and shedding tears, bowing and
praying for commands, imploring Heaven to take pity and
help him. On the day when the troops entered the Palace
and arrows flew all about, a great fire broke out. Wang
Mang escaped under the Tower Bathed by Water, but he
still carried in his arms the book of Heavenly mandates
and portents, and the majestic tou-measures which he had
made.[27] This may be called an extreme case of error and
delusion.

Cf. Pokora, "The Life," I, pp. 66-67; Liang Han pu-fen
II, pp. 342-43. The last words of this fragment suggest
that it was originally part of the thirteenth chapter
of the Hsin-lun, "Discerning Error" (Pien-hou). Nevertheless, Yen included it in the Chapter Four, "On Substance."

41

TPYL 526.6a.   Yen 13.8a-b.   Sun 22b.

King Ling of Ch'u was arrogant and contemptuous
of the people below him.   He treated men of worth rudely
and devoted himself to demons.   He believed in the religion of the shamans and in their incantations, and
fasted and abstained to make himself pure and fresh
when sacrificing to the Lord on High.   When performing
rites for the many Spirits,[28] he would clutch a feather
sash in his hand and start to dance before the altar.
When the men of Wu came to attack his country, people
rushed to tell him, but King Ling kept on dancing as if
nothing had happened.[29]   Turning to the messengers, he
replied, "I am sacrificing to the Lord on High and en-
tertaining the Bright Spirits.   I shall be receiving
their blessings and do not dare go to the rescue."

Then the soldiers of Wu arrived and captured
his Crown Prince and his Queen.[30]   It was tragic indeed.

This fragment is reproduced in Tung Yüeh, Ch'i-kuo k'ao,
pp. 233 and 275.   Cf. introduction to fragments 176 ff.

NOTES: CHAPTER 4

1.   Ta t'i 大體 ("Great Substance"). This term
was first used by Mencius, who answered a question from
his disciple Kung-tu with: "Those who follow that part
of themselves which is great are great men; those who
follow that part of themselves which is little are little
men." Mencius VI: I: XV:1; Legge, translation, p. 417.
The term is common in ancient texts.

2.   Huan T'an gives "the Great Substance," a much
broader meaning than does Mencius (see note 1 above).

3.   For min-chieh 敏給 ("glib"), see, e.g.,
Shih-Chi 2, p. 4; Chavannes, MH I, p. 99. Chavannes
refers to the Ta Tai Li-chi.

4.   Ching Fang, the I Ching specialist.

5.   A shortened account from the Shih chi 8, p. 66;
Chavannes, MH II, p. 384. See also HFHD I, p. 107.

6.   Instead of mu 慕 ("to admire," "to think of
affectionately"), perhaps another mu 摹 ("to follow,"
"to copy") should be inserted.

7.   Ts'ao Shen is Ts'ao Ts'an. See Hulsewe, Remnants I, p. 373, note 147.

8.   This short evaluation was actually made by Fan
Tseng; see Shih chi 7, p. 54; Chavannes, MH II, p. 303.
The successful attack against Wei was undertaken in
204 B.C.

9.   The rebels are mentioned in Han shu 99 C (under
January 23 A.D.), as quoted and translated by Dubs in
HFHD III, p. 456.

10.   Nothing similar is found in Chou Ya-fu's biography in Shih chi 57, pp. 14-24, or in Han shu 40,
pp. 3515-22. Chou Ya-fu, like Ch'ao Ts'o, quarreled
with Emperor Ching (see fragment 28 and fragment 209,
note 58); cf. HFHD I, pp. 297-99. Pan Ku also, like
Huan T'an, criticized Emperor Ching and applauded both
men; see Hulsewe, "Notes on the Historiography of the
Han Period," p. 40.

11.   Huan T'an's text, found in the commentary to
the biography of Ch'ing Pu (or Ying Pu), reflects the

ideas of Lord Hsieh, former Prime Minister of Ch'u. See Watson, Records I, pp. 204-205. The chess analogy was introduced by Huan T'an. Wei-ch'i was probably first mentioned by Yang Hsiung in Fa Yen 4, p. 12, although traditionally its first mention has been attributed to Shun (DKJ 4806.9).

12.   "Eye" (mu 目) is a technical term for a type of formation of the pieces in wei-ch'i. If·a group of pieces have an "eye" in the center, they cannot be "killed" by encirclement.

13.   TPYL 753.4b does not include the last paragraph on Keng-shih.

14.   Instead of the kuai 罫 of fragment 35A, I lin has kua 罣 . Both Yen and Sun give kuai-mu 罫目 .

15.   The Eastern Palace was the Empress' residence. See Watson, Records II, p. 122, note 6. The passage suggests that it was an indignity for great ministers to be assigned to work in the women's quarters.

16.   The term hsiao wei lou 小衞樓 is not quite clear. PWYF 1371.2 attributes it only to the Hsin-lun.

17.   Ts'ao Shen was a minister of Liu Pang. Huan T'an is corroborated by other sources. Keng-shih's colonel Wang Hsien, who called himself General-in-Chief of the Han, lived in the Eastern Palace, used Wang Mang's robes and carriages, and took the women of his harem. Cf. HFHD III, p. 466, and H. Bielenstein I, p. 132.

18.   The Great Appendix I:8:42; Legge, pp. 361-62. Huan T'an's fragment paraphrases this section of the I Ching.

19.   Huan T'an's account evidently inspired the authors of Wang Mang's biography in Han shu 99C; HFHD III, p. 451: "[Wang Mang] had Tung Chung's clan and relatives arrested. He buried them together in one pit with strong vinegar; poisonous drugs; foot-long, naked, two-edged blades; and a thicket of thorns." This text has also been translated by Hulsewé, Remnants I, p. 120, sub 16; and by Bielenstein, The Restoration I, p. 125. For the thorns of the ching and the chi plants, see Yü Ching-jang, "Shih ching chi."

20.   Lü-shih ch'un-ch'iu 10:5:102; Wilhelm, p. 128.

21.　　Mencius I:VII:4; Legge, p. 139.

22.　　Lü-shih ch'un-ch'iu (10:5, p. 103; Wilhelm, pp. 128-29) says that King Wen saw that corpses which were found in digging a pond were properly dressed and buried.

23.　　In accordance with I lin 3.8a, I read en 恩 ("mercy") for ssu 思 ("thought").

24.　　This seems to be one of Huan T'an's favorite terms. Cf. fragments 80 and 116.

25.　　Fragments 39 and 40 are combined in Ch'ün-shu chih-yao. Yen separated them, inserting fragment 41 between them.

26.　　This is the reading of chao 兆 given by Couvreur in his Dictionnaire classique, p. 67. This character may also be read as t'iao 祧 ("ancestral hall").

27.　　A similar account is given in Wang Mang's biography in the Han shu; cf. HFHD III, p. 464.

28.　　Yen, unlike Sun, erroneously gives ch'en 臣 ("ministers") for shen 神 ("spirits").

29.　　The first part of the fragment, up to this point, is given in a shorter form in TPYL 735.4b.

30.　　The text has two meaningless characters, i hsia 以下 , omitted by Yen and Sun.

Chapter 5. Observing Evidence

42

A I lin 3.8a-b.   Yen 13.8b.   Sun 6a.

Because Tung-fang Shuo was a man of few and
simple words, he was believed to be honest and trustworthy. Everyone says that Shuo was a man of great
wisdom and that no sage after him has been Li's equal.

But Huan T'an says, "There are people[1] who take
a fox for a wild-cat, a zither for a harp.[2] This means
not only that they do not know what a zither or a fox
is, but that they also do not know what a wild-cat or
a harp is. These words not only show ignorance about
Shuo, they also show ignorance about the sages after
him."[3]

B IWLC 44.13b.   Sun 17a.

Rustics call a fox a wild-cat and mistake a
zither for a harp. This shows not only that they do
not know what a fox or a zither is, but also that they
do not know a wild-cat or harp.

43

TPYL 496.9a.   Shuo fu 59.3b-4a.   Yen 13.8b.   Sun 22a.

When I was a Grandee in the Directorship of
Music it once happened that birds started to cry in the
trees in the courtyard, frightening all the people who
worked in the Bureau. Later I quarreled with the Dir-
ector of Music, Marquis Hsieh. Both of us were tried,
dismissed and sent away.

The shorter version in TPYL 927.6a omits the words,
"dismissed and sent away."
Previous translation and explanation in Pokora, "The
Life," I, pp. 59-60. Cf. also fragment 82.

44

TPYL 816.9b.   Shuo fu 59.3a.   Yen 13.8b-9a.   Sun 17a.

On the way back to P'ei I fell ill.[4] I covered myself with a quilt and a loose robe[5] of red wool. Riding a bay-horse, I rode towards the Eastern Commune[6] of the Hsia-i prefecture for night lodgings. The Chief of the Commune, fearing that we were bandits, sent his servants into the night to apprehend us. I ordered my men not to fight, and after asking some questions, they went away.[7] Thus [I achieved] peace and self-preservation.

The first part of the fragment is also found in TPYL 693.7b, IWLC 75.8b, and PTSC 129.20a. PTSC explains that Huan T'an was returning from Ch'ang-an.

45

I lin 3.8b.   Yen 13.9a.   Sun 6a.

If people use words to praise me, they must also use words to condemn me. Wang Mang sent the Chief Commandant Meng Sun to T'ai-shan to make sacrifices. On the way he went through Hsü province, where Sung Chung-weng, the Governor of Hsü, told him that my talents and knowledge could be compared to those of Ch'en P'ing or the Marquis of Liu [Chang Liang]. Meng Sun returned joyfully and said to me, "Chung-weng has praised your virtue abundantly. You are indeed as he said."

I replied, "We have kept company for four or five years, and you have never praised me. Now you hear one word from Chung-weng, and you marvel at it. If somebody were to slander me, you would believe him too. I am afraid of you."

Previous translation: Pokora, "The Life," II, pp. 536-37.

46

Commentary to Wen hsüan 26.41b.   Yen 13.9a.   Sun 14a.

The I Ching of the Chou dynasty says, "Retiring in a noble way will be advantageous in every respect."[8]

47

<u>TPYL</u> 684.6a.   Yen 13.9a. Sun 24a.

King K'ang of Sung[9] made caps for bodies without heads and showed them to the brave.[10]

48

A <u>Ch'ün-shu chih-yao</u> 44, p. 767.   Yen 13.9a-b.

Shun-yü K'un came to a neighboring house where he saw that the stove-outlet went straight up and that firewood had been piled beside it. He said, "This will cause a fire!" He told [the household] to change it, to bend the outlet and move the firewood away. The family who owned the stove-outlet would not listen to him. Later, flames reached the piled-up wood and ignited the house. The neighbors all gathered to help fight the fire until it was put out.

[The family] boiled a sheep and set out wine to reward and thank those who fought the fire. They bent the stove-outlet and moved the firewood away, but stubbornly refused to invite Shun-yü K'un to drink and eat.

A wise man ridiculed them, saying, "He told the members [of the household] to bend the stove-outlet and move the firewood, but they stubbornly refused to show any grace or favor to him. On the contrary, those with burnt heads and broken foreheads[11] become the most honored guests." Thus he lamented the slighting of the root and the honoring of the end.[12]

Is the removal of danger restricted to the stove-outlet and the firewood? Indeed, the problem is the same in the case of illness in man and disorder in the state. Therefore, a good physician cures what has not yet appeared, and an enlightened ruler breaks off plots at the root. We of later generations ignore the method of stopping up what has not yet sprouted, and busy ourselves attacking what has already become established fact. Ministers who draw up plans receive little reward, while fighting men are glorified.

This situation resembles the case of that household. It misses the relative importance and unimportance of things. By analyzing the warnings of Shun-yü K'un, it is possible to understand everything. This belongs to the category of observing evidence.[13]

40

B IWLC 80.9b.   Sun 17a-b.

      Shun-yü K'un came to a neighboring house where
he saw that the stove-outlet went straight up and that
the firewood had been piled up beside it. He said,
"This will cause a fire. You should bend the stove-
outlet and move the firewood." The family would not
listen to him. Later, their house indeed caught fire.
The neighboring families helped fight the fire and put
it out.

      [The family] boiled a sheep and set out wine to
thank those who fought the fire, but they refused to invite K'un. A wise gentleman ridiculed them, saying,
"Shun-yü K'un told them to bend the stove-outlet and
move the firewood, but they will not show any grace or
favor to him. Instead, those with burnt heads and
broken foreheads become the most honored guests." Thus
he lamented the slighting of the root and the honoring
of the end.

C Ch'u-hsüeh chi 25.30a.   Sun 17b (commentary).

      Tradition and the records say that Shun-yü K'un
came to a neighboring house where he saw that the stove-
outlet went straight up and that the firewood had been
piled up beside it. He told them, "This will cause a
fire. Change it--bend the stove-outlet and move the
wood."

Previous translation (from Huai-nan-tzu, see note 12
below): E. Haenisch, Lehrgang der klassischen chinesischen Schriftsprache IV, pp. 132-33.

49

TPYL 400.7b.   Yen 13.9b. Sun 20b.

      A disciple of the Erudite Master Han,[14] who
lived in the east, had bad dreams for three consecutive
nights. When he asked some people about it, they told
him to get up at daybreak and pray in a privy. After
three mornings, the people reported him to the authori-
ties for uttering curses. He was seized and tried and
died some days later.

In addition to the version mentioned in note 14 below,
there is a similar version in Shuo fu 59.3b.

50

TPYL 695.2b-3a.   Yen 13.9b.   Sun 24a.

        Expectant Appointee Ching Tzu-ch'un had long
been familiar with soothsaying. Once he was involved
in a lawsuit and was imprisoned. His father-in-law,
Chu,[15] came to the prison gate and sent a message saying
that he was leaving a jacket and trousers for him.

        Tzu-ch'un became frightened and exclaimed,
"Mister Chu came with a message. [The name] Chu can be
taken for [the word] chu or 'execution,' and trousers
and jacket are separated in the middle. Then I am to
be cut in two at the waist." Later he was executed in
this manner.[16]

51

TPYL 15.11b.   Yen 13.9b.   Sun 25a.

        The personal home of Yang-ch'eng Tzu-chang was
Heng.[17] He was a man from the Shu commandery. [During
the reign of] Wang Mang he and I were both Libationers
Expounding the [Classic of] Music.[18] When he was in bed
ill, I bought inner and outer coffins [for him]. I
lined them with silk, put on a cover and dug a grave
for him.

Previous translations: H. H. Dubs, HFHD III, p. 192,
note 19.1 (without the last sentence); Pokora, "The
Life," I, p. 62. For a correction of the latter translation, which is based on Yen, see note 17 below.

42

NOTES: CHAPTER 5

1.   See the different beginning in fragment 42B.

2.   K. Reinhard, Chinesische Musik, p. 31, suggests that the harp (k'ung-hou) did not appear in China until after the fall of the Han dynasty, i.e., during the 3rd-4th centuries A.D. This reference to it by Huan T'an places it in the early first century A.D. at least. Nevertheless, I would agree with L. E. R. Picken's statement that "there is no evidence that [the Han] k'ung-hou was a harp, or that it was linked with the k'ung-hou of later times other than by name." In support of this thesis, Picken presents some instances in which the k'ung-hou is associated with the zither (se), as it is in the present text. Thus, we may agree with Picken that "it would be reasonable to suppose that this particular k'ung-hou was a [type of] zither" (L. E. R. Picken, "T'ang Music and Musical Instruments," pp. 115-16). There is also a special article by Kishibe Shigeo, "Kugō no engen." See also his "The Origin of the K'ung hou."

3.   Wang Ch'ung was greatly preoccupied with the problem of giving proper recognition to worthy men during the Han dynasty. The 80th chapter of his Lun-heng is entitled "Ting hsien," ("A Definition of Man of Worth").

4.   The text of the Shuo-fu has two misprinted characters at this place.

5.   The text has ch'an 襜   , while TPYL 693.7b has ch'an-yü 襜褕 ·

6.   "Commune" (t'ing 亭) may also be translated "Police Post." The Police Posts were also used as official resthouses, and their Chiefs had to ensure the safety of the principal roads. See Hulsewé, Remnants I, p. 16.

7.   The three last sentences are given somewhat differently in IWLC 75.8b; the last, summarizing sentence is omitted. Yen 13.9a includes the character kung 攻 ("attack") in the line which ends "to apprehend us," indicating that the servants were sent to attack Huan T'an and his cortege.

8.   I Ching, hexagram XXXIII; Legge, p. 128. The first phrase is also understood to mean "a fat pig."

9.   K'ang, also known as Yüan or Yen, was the last ruler of the Sung. K'ang is reportedly his posthumous name; cf. Shih chi 38, p. 42, the So-yin commentary; Chavannes, MH IV, p. 247, note 1. His traditional dates are 328-286 B.C., but Ch'ien Mu, Hsien Ch'in chu-tzu hsi-nien, pp. 402-404, argues that he came to the throne in 318 B.C. The name "K'ang" is used repeatedly in Lü-shih ch'un-ch'iu (II:4, VII:4, XV:5, XXIII:4, XXIV:3).

10.   Traditionally, King K'ang has been considered a most despotic ruler. This story can also be found at the end of the fourth chapter of Hsin hsü, where kuan 棺 ("inner coffin") is substituted for kuan 冠 ("cap").

11.   A common phrase. See Matthews, Chinese-English Dictionary No. 721.13, and S. Couvreur, Dictionnaire classique, p. 552.

12.   Huai-nan-tzu 16, p. 274 briefly mentions the advice of Shun-yü K'un, but only the appended commentary by Kao Yu gives the story in detail, without attribution. Han shu 68, p. 4492, quotes the memorial of Hsü Fu, which gives the entire story but does not refer to Shun-yü K'un.

13.   With Yen, I prefer cheng 徵 ("evidence") to wei 微 ("minute"), as "Observing Evidence" is the title of the fifth chapter of the Hsin-lun.

14.   Han sheng. The version of this fragment in TPYL 186.7a, which contains several misprints, adds here: "He lived in the Eastern court [tung ssu 東寺]."

15.   The text has Chu chün, while Sun gives Chu Jo; the latter has been adopted, with reservations, by Yen.

16.   Yao chan 腰斬 ("to be cut in two at the waist") was a punishment for impious (pu-tao) and intractable (ni) crimes. See Hulsewé, Remnants I, pp. 111-12.

17.   Both Yen and Sun add the character hsing 姓 after Yang-ch'eng Tzu. The translation would then be: "The surname of Yang-ch'eng Tzu was Chang, and his personal name was Heng." That would give that eminent

44

specialist of music the name of Chang Heng, which is
apparently incorrect. Yang-ch'eng is a double surname.

18.   Sun, and Yen following Sun's text, gives hsüeh
      學 ("studies"), instead of yüeh 樂 ("music").
Hsüeh is erroneous here. The position "chiang-hsüeh
chi-chiu 講學祭酒 [Libationer Expounding the Stud-
ies] did exist during Wang Mang's reign, but the only
holder of that office was Kung Sheng in 9 A.D. (Han shu
72, p. 4616). Hou Han shu does not mention the title
"chiang-hsüeh chi-chiu."

Chapter 6. Reprimanding Wrong

52

Ch'ün-shu chih-yao 44, pp. 767-68.   Yen 14.1a-b.

When kings begin their ascendancy, they all first
build their base. They set up broad fences and screens
in order to establish their own adherents and strengthen
the country's foundations. Therefore, when King Wu of
Chou defeated the Yin dynasty, even before descending
from his war chariot, he enfeoffed the descendants of
the Yellow Emperor and those of Yao, Shun, Hsia and Yin,
as well as those among his relatives whose conduct was
virtuous, and ministers of merit. Thus he made them
his pinions, supports, and assistants, and his Mighty
Undertaking could continue forever through his descendants.

In the past, the mighty Ch'in Shih huang-ti did
away with feudal rulers and depended on, and was responsible to, himself alone. None of his sons and
brothers were enfeoffed. He was solitary, weak, and
had no one with whom he could consult on work. Therefore, he had been Emperor [only] for fourteen years
when he died.

When the Eminent Founder of the Han dynasty first
settled the Empire, he turned his back on the short-
sighted plans of the fallen Ch'in. He followed the far-
sighted ways of Yin and Chou. He praised and honored
merit and virtue, and generously enfeoffed his sons
and brothers. Although many of them later met defeat
or ruin because of their arrogance and laziness, the
foundation of the Han had been fixed and established
so other families and powerful ministers could not sub-
vert it again. When it came to the time [of the Em-
perors] Ching and Wu, the feudal kings made several
rebellions, and, as a result, were suppressed and
stripped of their power and position. After that, the
kings only enjoyed an empty rank and passively sub-
sisted on the incomes derived from their rents and
taxes.

Consequently, the Han dynasty became weak, solitary and alone. Thus, Wang Mang, without waging war
or commanding territory, could take the Empire away.
Greedy for merit and desiring to rule autocratically,

he refused to enfeoff his sons and grandsons, his relatives with the same surname, or his relatives by mar-
riage, who could have been his fences and supports. As
a result, when war broke out there was no one to aid
him.

Tradition says, "He who suffers from the same
disease[1] as a dead man cannot be a physician. He who
pursues the same policies as a defeated country cannot
be consulted in preparing plans." The actions of Wang
Mang were very similar to those of the violent Ch'in.
Therefore, he too perished after fifteen years of rule.

The hunter and marksman who is after birds and
beasts desires to hit them but first fears that the
wound will not be great enough. But once he has captured his prey, he is annoyed that there is so much
injured meat. Once a rustic man found a fish sauce[2]
which he liked very much. When meal time came, he disliked the idea of having to share it, so he spat a little
into it. This angered those who shared the meal with
him, so they blew their noses into his sauce and left.
Consequently, no one[3] could eat.[4]

The defeated Ch'in and Wang Mang were both, at
the time when they intended to seize the Empire, pleased
to share it with others. But once they attained it,
they loved it dearly and refused to share it. This is
like loving the meat and spitting into the sauce.

P'ei-wen yün-fu, p. 3248.2, sub "t'ing chiang" 脡 醬
("strips of dry meat and sauce"), quotes the fish sauce
anecdote from this text. The last part of the anecdote
is somewhat different: "....but the people who were
sharing the meal with him blew their noses into his
sauce. Thus it was thrown out, and no one got [what he
wanted]. The fallen Wang Lang[5] of the Hsin dynasty was,
at the time when he intended to seize the Empire, pleased
to share it with others. But once he attained it, he
loved it dearly and refused to share it. This is like
loving the sauce and spitting into it." The PWYF version seems to be based on TPYL 492.5a (see note 4 below).

53

Ch'ün-shu chih-yao 44, pp. 768-69.   Yen 14.1b-2a.

Once Duke Huan of Ch'i went out to see the ruins
of an ancient land. When he inquired about it, he was

told, "There are the ruins of Mr. Kuo."

Once more [the Duke] asked how Mr. Kuo had come to this. The answer was, "He favored good and hated evil."

Duke Huan said, "If he favored good and hated evil, then his land should have been preserved but, on the contrary, it has been ruined. How has this happened?"

The answer was, "He favored the good, but he could not use it. He hated evil, but he could not abolish it. The good people knew that he honored them but could not use them. Therefore, they murmured against him. The bad people saw that he despised and detested them. Therefore, they hated him. The good people murmured against him and the bad people were his enemies. How could he hope to avoid defeat?"6

Wang Mang approved of the worthy, wise, talented and able gentlemen of the Empire. He sent inquiries to them and assembled them all together, but he did not use them. Consequently, these men criticized and murmured against him. Emperor Keng-shih hated the many kings with assumed titles who were devoid of righteousness, but he could not get rid of them. Consequently, each of them hated him in his heart and looked on him as an enemy. Therefore, Wang Mang was attacked and killed, while his palaces were consumed by flames. Emperor Keng-shih was driven out by the many kings with assumed titles, and his city and its suburbs were destroyed.

Both rulers favored good and hated evil and therefore could not escape calamity and disaster. Finally, the great capital Ch'ang-an was destroyed and fell into ruins because of them. Their acts were Great Faults indeed!

The ancestors of the Northern Man barbarians co-existed with China for countless years. They could not [be induced] to come to China by virtue, nor could they be annexed to China by force. Theirs was a violent and ferocious nature; they gathered like beasts and scattered like birds. It was difficult to bend their might or to make peace with them. Therefore, the sage kings held them in check but did not rule them.

In the past, when the Chou dynasty was in decline, the I and Ti barbarians attacked it constantly.

However, China did not perish, but survived with a
thread of life. Thus, when King Hsüan brought about the
restoration he was able to recover those territories
which had been invaded.[7]

The First Ch'in Emperor, although he commanded
four hundred thousand armored men, did not dare to peep
into the region west of the Yellow River. He built the
Great Wall to separate China from the barbarians. After
the establishment of the Han, the Eminent Founder was
surrounded at P'ing-ch'eng.[8] During the reign of Empress Lü the shan-yü Mao-tun made irregular suggestions,[9] and during Emperor Wen's reign the Hsiung-nu
launched great invasions. Signal fires[10] and mounted
scouts[11] came as far as the Palace of Sweet Springs in
Yung. During the reigns of the Emperors Ching and Wu
armies were sent out several times and met with disaster.
In the end [the Hsiung-nu] could neither be captured nor
controlled. Then China entered into an alliance with
them, making peace and forming royal marriages. From
then on the frontier people[12] won peace and China found
repose.

Later, internal dissension broke out among the
Hsiung-nu, and they split into five groups, each following a shan-yü. Kan Yen-shou was able to meet their evil
with his profound virtue. Thus the shan-yü Hu-han-yeh
agreed to offer tribute and called himself [Kan's] subject.[13] He came to court and saw there the House of
Han. The House of Han could spread forth its virtue and
extend its eminence, so its authority was revealed to
all men within the four seas. There was no one who
would not submit to them, and for generations there were
no invasions. Now, [in the time of Wang Mang], it was
still uncertain whether there will be peace or peril.
The Hsiung-nu were suddenly attacked. Their seals and
ribbons of office were seized; the titles and ranks of
their great ministers were degraded and diminished;
their customs and regulations were altered; and the territories of the shan-yü were divided into fifteen
states.[14] As a result hatred and fury arose, and the
events ended in discord and struggle. Wang Mang refused
to blame himself or show remorse.

When rebellion broke out[15] Wang Mang maintained
an unyielding and unreasonable attitude. Many generals
and commanders were appointed; soldiers and horses were
drafted and sent out; and provisions and materials were
transported until the entire Empire was exhausted.[16]
Throughout the Empire there was grief, hatred, anger and

suffering, which gave rise to great disturbances. In the end not a single barbarian suffered any setback or injury. The result was merely self-exhaustion and self-depletion.

The **Book of Documents** says, "Calamities sent by Heaven may be avoided, but there is no escape from calamities brought on by oneself."[17] This is what is meant by that statement.

When Emperor Kao was surrounded he did not eat for ten days.[18] When he managed to escape, he showed no anger, for he knew it was not wise to attack nor profitable to be angry. Now, the Hsiung-nu wronged Wang Mang, and he invaded forthwith, hampered, and harassed them.

Thus the present mess came about. Indeed, isn't this what is meant by "the meat of itself produces worms and man of himself produces misfortune?" When affairs that were not urgent become so critical it is an extreme case of self-created trouble.

54

Liu Chao's commentary to Hou Han shu 38, p. 4220 (Po-kuan 5).   Yen 14.2b.   Sun 9b.

In the reign of Wang Mang the Western Seas Commandery was established. All officials [were paid] one hundred **shih** for attending to their duties. Another source says the pay was 400 **shih**. After two years of service they were transferred to another job.

55

TPYL 627.8a.   Yen 14.2b-3a.   Sun 23b.

Since the consolidation of the Han dynasty, the taxes[19] exacted from the people during one year represent more than four billion. Half is spent for the salaries of civil servants. The remaining two billion is deposited in the Imperial Treasury as "forbidden money."[20] Eight billion and three hundred million[21] from the cultivation[22] of orchards and grounds[23] managed by the Privy Treasurer are given to the Palace for upkeep and defraying the cost of gifts and rewards.

The first part of the fragment is quoted in the commentary to Wen hsüan 36.15a (Sun 14a). The present fragment, shortened at the beginning, is also reproduced in Wang Ying-lin's K'un-hsüeh chi-wen 12.7b.

56

TPYL 531.8a.   Yen 14.3a. Sun 22b.

Wang Mang erected nine ancestral temples,[24] which had bronze pillars and rafters supporting the tiles, as well as[25] gold and silver engravings on the ceilings.

57

TPYL 871.5b.   Yen 14.3a. Sun 25b.

A raised fire rises in the night, ignites charcoal, and dries the walls.

58

Ch'ün-shu chih-yao 44, pp. 769-70.   Yen 14.3a.

Calamities[26] and abnormalities have always been present in the Empire; there was no age without them. If the calamities and abnormalities conjoin with an enlightened ruler and a wise minister, or with a prudent gentleman and a benevolent man, these men will regulate their virtue, improve their administration, examine their offices, and act with care, responding in this way to the calamities and abnormalities. The ill luck and misfortune will be erased, and misfortune turn into fortune.

In the past Ta-mou[27] found the abnormality of a mulberry and a paper-mulberry growing together in his court,[28] but he won the title of Central Ancestor. Wu-ting[29] saw the abnormality of a crying pheasant alighting on a tripod,[30] but he enjoyed a long life-span of one hundred years.[31] King Ch'eng of Chou was beset by a calamity--wind and thunder which broke trees--but as a reward he received a contrary wind and a fruitful year.[32] Duke Ching of Sung was upset because the planet Mars stood in the constellation of the Heart, but [during the same night] it passed through three solar mansions.[33]

From this point of view, no one was more [predetermined] than these men when they responded by stopping calamities and abnormalities with their virtue, righteousness and sincerity. Therefore, the Book of the Chou says, "When the Son of Heaven sees an abnormality, he improves his virtue. When the feudal rulers see an abnormality, they improve their administration. When the great ministers see an abnormality, they improve the performance of their offices. When gentlemen and commoners see an abnormality, they improve their persons."[34] The spirits cannot injure the Way, and evil omens cannot injure Virtue. In a time of decadence and evil customs, among the ruler and his ministers great immorality and arrogance, as well as bad administration, can be found. Among gentlemen and commoners, there are many crooked hearts and evil actions. Therefore, many calamities and abnormalities appear. Moreover, these people cannot look inside and concentrate on themselves, nor can they fear Heaven's authority. Instead, they look outside and concentrate on slander and criticism, asking questions and digging out causes. They are deluded by the glib-tongued and the stupid, deceiving themselves as a result and incurring disasters and calamities. They all disobey Heaven and go contrary to the Way!

Cf. Liang Han pu-fen II, p. 343.

59

The So-yin commentary to Shih chi 28, p. 77.

Yen 14.3b. Sun 11a.

When Emperor Wu left [the capital he carried] the Imperial Signet, the official seal and an [ink] stone. Wealth manifested itself in omens. But Tzu-hou had no seal. The Emperor dreaded and loathed him, so he killed him.[35]

60

A **I lin** 3.8b.   Yen 14.3b.   Sun 6b.

In the past, when I was Wang Mang's Grandee in Charge of the Doctrine, there was a man who killed his mother. An imperial edict commanded that he be executed and his corpse be burned. I said that it was not proper to announce such a thing to the public.[36]

I sent [the Emperor] a sealed memorial which said: "Once during the reign of Emperor Hsüan, the dukes, ministers and grandees of the court were assembled. When his turn came the chancellor said, 'The owl gives birth to young which devour their mother when they grow up, and thereupon they become able to fly.'

"A wise man responded, 'I have only heard that the young of the owl [grow up] to feed their mother.'

"The chancellor was greatly ashamed and regretted his improper words. All those present disapproved of the Chancellor and approved of the wise man. The words of the worthy man benefitted Virtue and Moral Transformation. Therefore, the gentleman covers up evil and spreads good abroad. If it is improper to mention the matter when talking of birds and beasts, how much more when talking of people. It is not fitting for the matter to be broadcast."

B **TPYL** 491.7a.   Yen 14.3b.   Sun 21b-22a.

Once during the reign of Emperor Hsüan the dukes, ministers and grandees of the court were assembled in the palace. When his turn came, the Chancellor said, "I have heard that the owl gives birth to young which devour their mother when they grow up, and thereupon they become able to fly. Is that really true?"

A virtuous man responded, "I have only heard that the young of birds [grow up and] feed their mother in their turn."

The Chancellor and the Grand Commandant were much ashamed and regretted their improper words. The many gentlemen there all disapproved of the Chancellor and approved of the virtuous man's words because they benefitted Virtue and Moral Transformation.

Therefore, the superior man hides evil while spreading good abroad. [If such things] are shunned with respect to birds and beasts, how much more should they be shunned with respect to people!

C The version in TPYL 927.6a is essentially the same as version B, but it has an introduction somewhat similar to that in version A. Yen, as usual, combined all three versions: "During the reign of Wang Mang a young man, Pi K'ang, killed his mother. An imperial edict commanded that his corpse be burned and his crime exposed to the Empire. I sent [the Emperor] a sealed memorial....

61

Shu-i chi 1A,8b-9a.[37]   Yen 14.3b.   Sun 9b.

Take off one's clothes and expose one's body[38] at the Stream of the Naked.[39]   On the sea there is a Minister of the Naked.[40]

62

Commentary to Wen hsüan 1.3a and 57.28a.   Yen 14.3b.

Li Hsien's Commentary to Hou Han shu 70A, p. 1429.

Sun 12b.

Tung Hsien's younger sister became a Brilliant Companion.[41] The residence where she lived was called Pepper Wind.[42]

63

TPYL 776.3a.   Yen 14.3b.   Sun 16a.

In the Ch'u capital, Ying,[43] the wheel hubs on the carriages bumped into each other,[44] people rubbed shoulders in the market,[45] and roads paralleled and crossed one another. This is described as "A dress which is new in the morning and shabby in the evening."

The version in PTSC 129.3b is identical, with the exception of the variations noted in the notes 44 and 45.

54

The <u>Shuo fu</u> 59.3a version is identical to that in <u>TPYL</u>
776.3a.

64

Commentary to <u>Wen hsüan</u> 4.30b.　　Yen 14.4a.　　Sun 13a.

　　　The roads were filled with weeds. They were a
wide, empty and confused [wasteland].

65

<u>Ch'ün-shu chih-yao</u> 44, pp. 770-71.　　　　　　　Yen 14.4a.

　　　Someone said, "In the past, the dukes, lords,
important ministers and all the multitude[46] would speculate on who would be assigned to a vacant post, saying,
'A or B should hold that post.' Later, it would turn
out as they had predicted. How did they manage to know
this, and how could they share the mind of the Emperor?
Confucius said of Tzu-kung: 'When he makes a guess it
is invariably correct.'[47] Now,[48] could the multitude
be as good as Tzu-kung?"

　　　I responded, "Men who hold office all come from
the same class and do not differ greatly. Those whose
good qualities are somewhat better are already apparent
to those above and below. Those whose intelligence is
different see things differently, while those whose
intelligence is equal see things in the same way. What
the multitude below privately say to themselves often
agrees with what the Emperor [thinks].

　　　For instance, in the past T'ang and Wu employed
I Yin and Lü Shang; Kao-tsung chose Fu Yüeh; and Duke
Huan of Ch'i and Duke Mu of Ch'in received[49] Kuan Chung,
Ning Ch'i, Yu-yü and Po-li Hsi.[50] How could the multitude know such men? Although the multitude below may
have liked to speculate on their suitability for em-
ployment, how could they have selected these men as fit
for the posts[51] of the great ministers and assistants?

　　　The state establishes the hierarchy of officials
and the system of punishments in order to set apart the
evil and the crooked. Within, the Palace Assistant to
the Imperial Clerk[52] is appointed[53] to bring order into
the Imperial Capital. Therefore, wise and experienced
men[54] are usually employed.

In the beginning the hope was to revere the true law, but in the end contempt for the true law gradually crept in. Severity became the rule, and cruelty exceeded its bounds. Officials exerted all their energies to win merit and reward.[55] Or, one who wanted to make his abilities known feared the criticism of base and weak men. Therefore, these [base men] were restrained by flogging,[56] and crimes were created by the manipulation of the written word. So now, when the matter has become accomplished fact, and sentence has been passed, even if one wished Kao Yao[57] to hear the case, he could not hear it. It is truly tragic.

For a few trivial words, a man and his entire clan are executed. [This state of affairs] has come about gradually. Often, when someone in the court is angry, he does not check out the source of the slander which he hears. This creates contradiction and confusion in the Empire. The people of the Empire mock the cruelty of the officers of the law by saying, "The lower officers enforce severity so that they can let the High One dispense mercy and grace."[58]

This statement is completely inaccurate. A wise government servant or an upright official should conduct affairs and uphold the law in a manner as clear as the red and green used [in painting].[59] Therefore, if a word is proper, it should be possible to carry it out. If a crime is properly [defined], it should be possible to punish it. Why should anyone harbor the strange desire to accuse whomever he wishes? If the High One happens to neglect the case, if he does not delay it and give it a hearing, then [the accused] is bound to suffer a violent death.[60]

Under Emperor Ai, Wu K'e, an expectant appointee, was summoned to a royal audience several times because he knew the stars and enjoyed feats of magic. Later, he was tried in court because of the Emperor's[61] affair and imprisoned. At the end of his prison term, it was discovered in interrogation that he had once said to some people, "The Han dynasty will produce a courageous, and reckless young man, a man like Emperor Wu." The cruel and violent [administrator of the law] thought these words improper and highly disrespectful for they called a late emperor "a reckless young man."[62]

Now, if words are occasionally excessive or amiss, the speaker should not be punished and executed; when words are slanderous and deceptive they can, without exception, be considered criminal.

The Book of Changes says, "The great man produces his changes like the tiger,...the superior man
produces his changes like the leopard."[63] Now, if one
uses this when speaking of the ruler of men, he might
say, "Why am I compared with birds and beasts?" If
one compares the wisdom of the ruler to Yao and Shun,
he might be angered and say, "Why am I compared to the
dead?" The assistants and officers of unenlightened
rulers follow and obey them,[64] complying with and exe-
cuting their words. Are they not doubling the dark
ignorance of their rulers?

66

TPYL 863.5b.   Yen 14.4b. Sun 25a.

P'ang Chen,[65] Great Administrator of Chiu-
chiang, made an inspection to see that the Prefects
were continuing the custom inherited from the remote
ancestors[66] of sacrificing the remaining meat[67] to the
spirits of the earth. He found twenty catties of raw
beef.[68] P'ang Chen charged the Prefect, asking the
Master in Charge of Robbers[69] to chase and arrest him.
The imperial edict[70] stated that remaining meat should
not be stolen.[71] In all the yamens and prefectures the
officials set right[72] the winter sacrifices, the worship
of ancestors and the sacrifices to the God of Kitchen.
They presented not only hot food, but also much meat,
rice, wine, and dried meat. Numerous delicacies also
increased the abundant [feast]. Every commandery and
yamen even slaughtered several cows.

NOTES: CHAPTER 6

1.   This is a slight modification of Huai-nan-tzu
17, p. 293.

2.   The K'ang-hsi tzu-tien gives the pronunciation
of the character 鮏 as shen or t'ing. Its exact
meaning is unknown, but it appears to be a kind of fish
or fish sauce (cf. DKJ 46176). PWYP 3248,2, quoting
this fragment, has t'ing 脡 ("strips of dried
meat").

3.   In accord with the commentary to Ch'ün-shu
chih-yao, I read chü 俱 instead of tan 但 . PWYF
also has tan, while both TPYL quotations (see the following note), have chü.

4.   TPYL 492.5a (Sun 22a) quotes the anecdote, as
well as the concluding paragraph of this fragment,
while TPYL 865.8a (Sun 22a, commentary) only relates
the anecdote of the fish sauce. Both versions are very
similar to that found in the Ch'ün-shu chih-yao.

5.   "Wang Lang" 王朗 appears to be a misprint
for Wang Mang 王莽 .

6.   The same anecdote can be found in the fourth
chapter of Liu Hsiang's Hsin hsü (11b-12a). Liu
Hsiang's point is somewhat different: Kuan Chung re-
proves Duke Huan for not having asked the name of his
informant, who was invited in and rewarded.

7.   The Chou ruler Li was in exile from 841 to 828
B.C. King Hsüan became his successor (827-783 B.C.).
Cf. Chavannes, MH I, pp. 275-76.

8.   Kao-tsu was surrounded by the Hsiung-nu at P'ing-
ch'eng. Cf., e.g., Shih chi 110, pp. 26-27; Watson
II, pp. 165-66. Huan T'an suggested a method which Kao-
tsu may have used in his escape seven days after he was
encircled; see fragment 159, as quoted in the Chi-chieh
commentary to Shih chi 56, p. 14 (cf. Watson I, pp.
160-61).

9.   This is alluded to several times in the Shih
chi (e.g., in chapter 100, p. 4), but only Han shu 94A,
p. 5314, reproduces Mao-tun's letter to Empress Lü.
The shan-yü suggested that, since they were both old
and alone, they might marry.

10.   In 158 B.C.   Cf. <u>Shih chi</u> 110, p. 42; Watson II, p. 176.

11.   In 162 B.C.   Cf. <u>Shih chi</u> 110, p. 37; Watson II, p. 173.

12.   In accordance with the commentary to the <u>Ch'ün-shu chih-yao</u>, I read <u>min</u> 民 ("people") for the <u>yung</u> 甬 of the text.

13.   In the year B.C. 58, the <u>shan-yü</u> sent his younger brother to pay court; <u>HFHD</u> II, p. 246. See also Kan Yen-shou's disproportionately short biography in <u>Han shu</u> 70, which mentions only that Kan Yen-shou killed the <u>shan-yü</u> Chih-chih in 36 B.C. Three years later Chih-chih's rival, the <u>shan-yü</u> Hu-han-yeh, came to court and was among other things, given a Chinese court lady for his wife. Cf. <u>HFHD</u> II, pp. 331, 335, and 281-85.

14.   The last measure was announced by Wang Mang in a message in late 10 A.D.; cf. <u>HFHD</u> III, p. 305. The same source says: "The title of the Hsiung-nu <u>shan-yü</u> was changed, and he was called the 'Submitted Captive [Fu-yü] of the Surrendered Slaves [<u>Hsiang-nu</u>]'"; <u>ibid.</u>, p. 304.

15.   In accordance with the commentary to the <u>Ch'ün-shu chih-yao</u>, I read <u>fan</u> 反 for <u>chi</u> 及 .

16.   In accordance with the commentary to the <u>Ch'ün-shu chih-yao</u>, I read <u>tan</u> 彈 for <u>t'an</u> 彈 .

17.   <u>Shang shu</u> IV:V:ii:3; Legge I, p. 207. Also see <u>Mencius</u> II:I:IV:6; Legge, p. 199.

18.   Instead of "ten days" the text should read "seven," according to <u>Shih chi</u> 56, p. 14; Watson I, p. 161. Moreover, the So-yin commentary to the <u>Shih chi</u> quotes a fragment of the <u>Hsin-lun</u> which also reads "seven;" see fragment 159.

19.   Instead of <u>fu-chien</u> 賦斂 ("to exact taxes"), the commentary to <u>Wen hsüan</u> 36.15a has <u>fu ch'ien</u> 賦錢 ("exacted money," i.e., tax money).

20.   <u>Han shu</u> 64B, p. 4374 mentions that, under Emperor Wu, the cost of a military expedition of less than one thousand <u>li</u> was four hundred million. Any

deficit was covered by the "forbidden money" of the
Privy Treasurer. Yen Shih-ku comments that the re-
sources of the Privy Treasurer were used for the Emper-
or and therefore called "forbidden money."

21.　　This fragment contains important information
on the economic history of China. As Yü Ying-shih says,
"The annual revenue of the Later Han period is not reported in the Hou Han shu. Fortunately, the well-in-
formed scholar, Huan T'an...has provided us with a clue,
which may lead to breaking the otherwise hopeless dead-
lock. According to him, from Emperor Hsüan's time on
[73-49 B.C.], the totality of annual fu-ch'ien [see
note 19 above--T.P.], or tax money, collected by the
Han government amounted to more than 4,000,000,000 cash,
of which, he further states, half was used to pay the
salaries of all the officials of the Empire. On the
other hand, as for the total annual revenue of the Shao-
fu, or the Emperor's purse, Huan gives the amount of
8,300,000,000, which was used for the upkeep of the
imperial palace and for various kinds of imperial gifts."
[Trade and Expansion in Han China, p. 62 and note 76].

　　This fragment was also studied by Lao Kan in his
Ch'in-Han shih, p. 136. He believes that the character
pa 八 ("eight") was a mistake for fan 凡 ("all, "in
general"). Lao Kan thinks that the income of the Privy
Treasurer could not be two times that of the Ministry
for State Expenditure (ta ssu-nung; for the relation of
the two institutions, see RBS 5, No. 99). If Lao Kan's
interpretation is correct, the income of the Privy
Treasurer would total only one billion and three hundred
million cash. The problems with this short fragment
reveal how uncertain the study of Han economic history
still is.

22.　　For an explanation of tso-wu 作務 , see Chou
Shou-ch'ang's commentary to Han shu 90, p. 5230.

23.　　Instead of yüan ti 園地 ("orchards and
grounds"), the text should probably read yüan-ch'ih 園
池 ("orchards and ponds"), in accordance with Shih
chi 30, p. 4 and Chavannes III, p. 542 ("...les parcs
et les marais").

24.　　See HFHD III, pp. 395-400, especially pp. 398-99.

25.　　The text has tai 帶 , instead of the ta 大
of Yen and Sun. Tai also occurs in another context in
Wang Mang's biography (HFHD III, p. 399, note 9.11).

26.   Instead of fu-i 夫異, I read tsai-i 災異 ("calamities"). Tsai-i is used again near the end of the
fragment.

27.   Ta-mou, or T'ai-mou, is Chung-tsung, the ninth
ruler of the Yin dynasty.

28.   This legend is treated in more detail by Wang
Ch'ung; cf. Lun-heng 5, 19, pp. 203-204; Forke, II,
p. 161. For different traditions concerning the two
trees, see Huang Hui's commentary to the Lun-heng 2:7,
p. 59.

29.   Wu-ting, or Kao-tsung, is the 22nd ruler of the
Yin. He may have lived ca. 1230 B.C. Cf. Shih chi 3,
p. 23; Chavannes, MH I, p. 196.

30.   Preface to the Shu-ching 29; Legge, p. 7.

31.   The various texts confuse T'ai-mou and Wu-ting;
cf. note 4 in A. Forke, Lun-heng II, pp. 161. In both
cases, however, the two rulers were exhorted by a Tsu-
chi to reform their way of ruling, with the success
described by Huan T'an.

32.   Shu-ching V:vi:16-19; Legge, pp. 359-60. When
King Ch'eng harbored ill-founded suspicion against the
Duke of Chou, Heaven sent down a calamity; later, when
the King repented, acknowledging the Duke's innocence
and loyalty, all the damage which had been done was made
whole.

33.   This story is related in Lun-heng in the beginning of the 17th chapter, pp. 191-92; Forke, II, pp.
152-53. Duke Ching averted the calamity with three
virtuous maxims.

34.   The source of this quotation is not clear. A
similar idea is put forward in Li chi XX:3; Legge II,
p. 203.

35.   Apparently Tzu-hou is Ho Tzu-hou, i.e., Ho Shan,
the son of the famous general Ho Ch'ü-p'ing who is mentioned twice in the 28th chapter of the Shih chi (Chavannes III, pp. 501, 504). Shih chi mentions that Ho
Shan died suddenly in 110 B.C. and cites Huan T'an's
fragment as an explanation of his mysterious death.
Nevertheless, Shen Ch'in-han objects to this explanation, referring to the Wen-hsin tiao-lung 13 (Shih, The
Literary Mind, p. 69): "The Emperor expressed his grief

in a poem..." Shen Ch'in-han believes that this establishes that Emperor Wu could not have killed Ho Shan. Chavannes' opinion (III, p. 504, note 1) is different: "Il est probable que l'empereur Ou fit empoisonner Tseheu pour être sûr qu'il ne divoulguerait pas ce qui s'était passé lors du sacrifice fong dont il avait été le seul témoin." In any case, we may only conclude that there may be no one reliable explanation of Ho Shan's death. Also see Chavannes, Le T'ai-chan, p. 19. For another fragment involving T'ai-shan, see fragment 117.

36.   There has been a general tendency to conceal information like this. See Hulsewé, Remnants I, pp. 111-12.

37.   The text of the Shu-i chi begins: "In southeastern Kuei-lin, along the sea, there is Lo-ch'uan. Huan T'an's Hsin-lun says...."

38.   For ch'eng 呈 ("to present") I read another ch'eng 裎 ("to take off the clothes and expose the body").

39.   Both Yen and Sun end the fragment here.

40.   DKJ 34371.19 gives also the full two sentences. The term "Lo-ch'uan" is mentioned neither in the P'ei-wen yün-fu, nor in the Chung-kuo ku-chin ti-ming ta tzu-tien. Huai-nan-tzu refers to the Country of the Naked (Lo kuo 裸 國), which lies southwest of China, but this has nothing to do with Huan T'an's Lo-ch'uan.

41.   "Brilliant companion" (chao-i 昭儀) is a very high rank, next to that of Empress. Emperor Ai bestowed it on Tung Hsien's sister; see HFHD III, p. 8, and Han shu 93, p. 5291.

42.   "Pepper Wind" (chiao-feng 椒風) is mentioned in Tung Hsien's biography in Han shu 93, p. 5291. Han kuan i B.la-b (Plate XVI of Chen Tsu-lung, Index du Han-kuoan ts'i-tchong) says that the walls of the Empress' residence were covered with plaster which contained pepper because it gave warmth. On the other hand, the term may have come from the pepper-tree, Zanthoxylum, which is a symbol of fecundity because it bears a great deal of fruit. Also, pepper has a fine smell which gives comfort to the aged (Shih ching IV:I:iii:v; Legge, p. 603).

43.   Sun has Ngo 鄂 instead of Ying 邟 .

44.　　　Instead of chü kua ku 車掛轂, I follow
the PTSC 129.3b version, chü ku chi 車轂繫.

45.　　　Instead of chiao 交 , PTSC 129.3a has p'ai-t'u
排突 ("push against each other").

46.　　　'The multitude below' refers to the courtiers.

47.　　　Analects XI:18; Legge, p. 243.

48.　　　I prefer chin 今 ("now") for ling 令 .

49.　　　I prefer shou 受 ("receive") for shou 授
("to give to, confer on").

50.　　　Kuan Chung and Ning Ch'i were chancellors of
Duke Huan, while Yu-yü and Po-li Hsi were chancellors
of Duke Mu. Po-li Hsi and Ning Ch'i are both referred
to in Shih chi 83, p. 24. Yu-yü was originally an envoy
of the Jung barbarians. See Shih chi 5, pp. 32-35;
Chavannes, MH II, pp. 41-44, where both Po-li Hsi and
Yu-yü are mentioned. All these men are said to have
lived in the 7th century B.C.

51.　　　The character 真 is unknown. It may be a mistake for either tse 責 ("duty, responsibility") or chen
真 ("true"). The commentary to Ch'ün-shu chih yao
prefers chen while I believe it should be tse.

52.　　　For chung-ch'eng yü-shih 中丞御史 ("Palace assistant to the Imperial Clerk"), see Chavannes,
MH I, Appendix I, p. 514, sub III.

53.　　　In accordance with the commentary to the Ch'ün-
shu chih-yao, I prefer chih 置 ("to establish, appoint") to liang 量 ("to measure, deliberate").

54.　　　Ming hsi 明習 ("wide and experienced men");
cf. Hulsewé, Remnants I, pp. 340, 394, note 224.

55.　　　The character wei 未 is superfluous.

56.　　　For a detailed explanation of ch'u 楚 ("flop-
ping sticks"), see Bodde and Morris, Law in Imperial
China, p. 80. Bodde, however, believes that ch'u were
first used in the Liang dynasty, long after this was
written.

57.　　　Kao Yao was a minister to the legendary ruler
Shun. He is traditionally believed to have introduced
penal law. Cf. Hulsewé, Remnants I, p. 27.

58.   "The High One" apparently refers to the Emperor.

59.   Tan ch'ing 丹青 ("cinnabar and azurite," or "red and green"). For a detailed explanation, see HFHD III, p. 441, note 21.2.

60.   For a discussion of the Emperor's personal roles in the affairs of the Empire, see fragment 11A, note 8, and the relevant text.

61.   The commentary says that ti 帝 ("emperor's") is superfluous.

62.   Ta pu-ching 大不敬 ("highly disrespectful"); see Hulsewé, Remnants I, pp. 156ff. Wu K'e committed some heinous crime, evidently "uttering imprecations against the Emperor;" see Hulsewé, p. 158. See also fragment 49, in which another man was arrested for a similar crime.

63.   I ching 49 (hexagram ko); Legge, p. 168.

64.   The term chih shih shun ch'eng 執事順成 is also used in Tso chuan, Hsüan 12; Legge, pp. 312, 317.

65.   P'ang Chen has no Han shu biography, nor is he mentioned in the Hou Han shu. But, since he was a high official, chapter 19B of Han shu has some information on him: In 14 B.C., as Great Administrator of Ho-nan, he came to Tso-p'ing-i commandery, where he served for three years (p. 1304). In 8 B.C. he was a Privy Treasurer. He became Commandant of Justice and, two years later, Privy Treasurer of the Ch'ang-hsin Palace.

66.   Both Yen and Sun give kao 高 ("high") alone, which does not by itself have any reasonable meaning. The text has kao ts'eng 高曾, which refers to a great grandson of a kao-tsu, which is an ancestor in the fifth generation. I believe that the meaning of the term is more general, perhaps "remote ancestors." Pan Ku, at the end of his Hsi-tu fu ("Fu on the Western Capital," Wen hsüan 1.7b) mentions that the Shang followed the model (kuei-chü) of their kao ts'eng.

67.   "Remaining meat" is the meaning of li 䐑 , according to the Yü-p'ien, as quoted in DKJ 40146 sub 9. For other explanations, see the commentaries to Shih chi 84, p. 35.

68.   The beef which should have been sacrificed had been hidden for the private use of the Prefect.

69.   Chu shou tao 主守盗 ("Master in Charge of Robbers"). Chu shou ("Master in Charge of...") was, according to DKJ 100.119, a general title for officials who managed stores, prisons, etc. In this case the official was specifically assigned to handle robbers. This title is not listed in the dynastic histories or other official sources for the Han period.

70.   Instead of shang ch'ing 上請 , I read ch'ing-shang 請上 . For an explanation of the term ch'ing, see my review of the reissue of D. Bodde, China's First Unifier, p. 132. The Emperor's assistance may have been requested because a misuse of a sacrifice could be an "impious" crime (pu-tao 不道). For a similar case, see Hulsewé, Remnants, p. 168, example 14.

71.   Pu-tsang 不贓 ("not stolen"). Sun says that in his text these two characters are illegible; Yen has pu-shun 不賑 , which might mean that the Emperor should not offer the meat as a sacrifice.

72.   Instead of yüan-shih 緣是 , I read yüan-shih 掾諟 ("the officials set right").

Chapter 7. Awakening Insight

67

I lin 3.8b.   Yen 14.5a. Sun 6b.

If the dragon does not have even one foot of water, there is no way for him to ascend to Heaven. If the sage does not have even one foot of soil, there is no way for him to rule the Empire.

68

I lin 3.9a.   Yen 14.5a. Sun 6b.

Prognostications[1] are derived from the Chart of the Yellow River and the Book of [the River] Lo.[2] They were only omens, but they could not be ascertained. Later, foolish people constantly added to and enlarged [the original texts], using them as bases for various theories. They claimed that K'ung Ch'iu was the author of the texts. Their error is great indeed![3]

Previous translation: Pokora, "The Life," I, p. 30, note 97.

69

I lin 3.9a.   Yen 14.5a. Sun 6b-7a.

Chang Tzu-hou[4] said, "Yang Tzu-yün[5] is a Confucius of the Western Parts,[6] but he is so poor."

I replied, "Tzu-yün is also a Confucius of the Eastern Parts. Was Chung-ni[7] only Confucius of Lu? He was also a sage of Ch'i and Ch'u."

70

I lin 3.9a. TPYL 68.4b.   Yen 14.5a. Sun 7a.

Drawings on water and engravings on ice dissolve and melt with time.

71

<u>I lin</u> 3.9a.   Yen 14.5a.   Sun 7a.

Confucius taught four skills[8] to gentlemen, each according to his taste. Like a market where many different goods are displayed, those who wish to buy[9] arrive together.

72

Commentary to <u>Wen hsüan</u> 20.20a.   Yen 14.5a.   Sun 13b.

The sage greatly surpasses [other] men with his heavenly manner.

This fragment is quoted by Hui Tung in an explanation of a memorial by Ti-wu Lun; <u>Hou Han Shu</u> 41, p. 1484.

73

Commentary to <u>Wen hsüan</u> 41.32a.   Yen 14.5a.   Sun 14b.

Yen Yüan was [a man of] eminent and excellent talent, second only to the sages. Upon hearing one point, he knew ten.[10]

74

Commentary to <u>Wen hsüan</u> 53.20a and 59.1a.

Yen 14.5b.   Sun 15a.

Tzu-kung said to Duke Ching of Ch'i,[11] "In serving Confucius I am like a thirsty man who carries a cup and goes to drink from a river or a sea. When [his stomach] is full[12] he goes away. How is he to know the depth of the river or the sea?"[13]

75

<u>TPYL</u> 569.8a.   <u>Ch'u-hsüeh chi</u> 15.9b.

Yen 14.5b.   Sun 18a.

A house without trimming is not the equal of O-pang Palace. An uncarved beam is not the equal of a polished rafter. Dark-colored liquors[14] are not the equals of Ts'ang-wu wine.[15] The k'ung and chieh [instruments][16] are not the equals of the flowing music of Cheng.[17]

Previous translation: J.-P. Diény, Aux origines de la poesie classique en Chine, p.37.

76

TPYL 404.8a.   Yen 14.5b. Sun 21a.

A proverb says, "Three years of study [alone] does not equal three years with a selected teacher."

Previous translation: A. Forke, Geschichte der mittel-älterlichen chinesischen Philosophie, p. 103 and note 3.

77

TPYL 860.9b.   Yen 14.5a. Sun 25a.

Confucius was an ordinary man,[18] but he became eminent and his hand became famous. When they come to his tomb, those of high-rank sacrifice beef, mutton, chicken and pork, while the lower people offer wine, dried meat and a cold repast.[19] After paying their respects they leave.

78

TPYL 932.3a.   Yen 14.5b.

Fragment 78 was not written by Huan T'an, but by Ku T'an. The biography of Ku T'an, who wrote a Hsin-yü, can be found in San-kuo chih, Wu chih 7.10b-12a. Ku T'an was from a good family; his grandfather Ku Yung (168-243 A.D.) was a chancellor of Wu for nineteen years. In the second half of the third century A.D., Ku T'an was imprisoned and banished to Chiao-chih, where he died two years later at the age of forty-one. The confusion of Huan T'an and Ku T'an may be due to the simple fact that their names are quite similar (Huan 桓 resembles Ku 顧), as are the titles of

their books (<u>Hsin-lun</u> and <u>Hsin-yü</u>). The fragments of
<u>Ku-tzu hsin-yü</u> (two double-pages) were collected in Ma
Kuo-han, <u>Yü-han shan-fang chi i shu</u>, vol. 75. After
the restoration of the Han, the name Chiao-chih appears
only late in the first century A.D.; for a detailed explanation, see Ch'en Ching-ho, <u>Chiao-chih ming-ch'eng
k'ao</u>.

NOTES: CHAPTER 7

1.   The first character, given by Yen as ch'an 讖
("prognostications"), was illegible to the editor of
I lin.

2.   Legge, I Ching, Appendix III, p. 374.

3.   For a detailed account, see, for example, Tai
Chün-jen, Ho-t'u Lo-shu ti pen-chih chi-ch'i yüan-lai
ti kung-yung. A short and brilliant explanation of Ho-
t'u 河圖 , ("the River Chart"), can be found in
W. A. Rickett, Kuan-tzu: A Repository of Early Chinese
Thought, pp. 183-88. Ch'en P'an, who systematically
studied the ch'an and wei texts explains the two middle
sentences of Huan T'an's difficult text: "This means
that the Chart of the Yellow River and the Book of the
River Lo which, according to the tradition, were extremely old, originally had no inscriptions, but merely
some streaks resembling characters or sketches. Some
of them were recognizable, while others were not.
Later, people modified and embellished them, saying that
the Chart and the Book, the ch'an and the wei, etc.,
were proving this or that. Therefore, their number was
always increasing." Ch'en P'an, Ch'an-wei ming-ming
chi ch'i hsiang-kuan chih-chu wen-t'i, p. 26.

4.   This is apparently the only reference to this
man, who is otherwise unknown.

5.   Yang Tzu-yün is Yang Hsiung.

6.   Yang Hsiung was born in Szechwan, which is in
western China.

7.   Chung-ni was the tzu 字 ("style name") of
Confucius.

8.   For ssu k'o 四科 ("four disciplines"), see
Analects XI:II.2. They are virtue, able speech, administrative ability, and literary attainment.

9.   Sun is incorrect in thinking that the character
chih 置 is erroneous; one of its meanings is "to buy."

10.   Analects V:VIII:2; Legge, p. 176.

11.   Sun does not include "of Ch'i."

12.   "Stomach" has been added by Yen.

13.   This story is not found in the <u>Analects</u>. An account of Tzu-kung's conversation with Duke Ching can be found near the end of Chapter 11 of the <u>Shuo-yüan</u>, but it does not contain this statement. However, the preceding story in that chapter of the <u>Shuo-yüan</u> tells of Tzu-kung's conversation with Chao Chien-tzu, in which he compares Confucius to a river or a sea. This apparently inspired Huan T'an's simile. For another anecdote which Huan T'an derived from Chapter 11, see fragment 171.

14.   Li chi VII:I:10; Legge, I, p. 370 and note 2.

15.   Ts'ang-wu was a large commandery, covering most of Kwangtung and Kwangsi. It dates from the time of Emperor Wu.

16.   S. Couvreur, Li Ki II, p. 91, remarks, "Deux instruments qui servent à donner le signal, l'un au commencement, l'autre à la fin des morceaux de musique."

17.   The Confucian literati considered the tunes of Cheng to be notoriously frivolous, although no one has ever clearly defined what was improper about them.

18.   <u>Cheng fu</u> 正夫 . Both Yen and Sun give <u>p'i fu</u> 匹夫 .

19.   <u>DKJ</u> 7239.96 identifies the <u>han-chü</u> 寒具 ("cold repast") with the modern <u>san-tzu</u> 饊子 , which is fried, puffy shredded dough. <u>Han shih</u> 寒食 ("day of cold food") is a day in spring when people travel to visit graves; see, e.g., F. W. Mote, <u>The Poet Kao Ch'i</u>, p. 136.

Chapter 8. Dispersing Obscurantism

79

A I lin 3.9a.   Yen 14.5b-6a.   Sun 7a.

Since Yen Yüan's allotted span was short,[1] he thought affectionately of Confucius, wishing to return[2] to him in his later years. He heard the words of the eastern village:[3] "When the people hear the music of Ch'ang-an, they come out of the gates, look towards the west and laugh. The smell of meat is pleasant, so they stand in front of a butcher's shop, chewing vigorously."[4]

Similarly, people of today, although they cannot discern the sage, still admire him with delight. A common horse and an excellent, fine horse chase each other's bit and tail, but then, in the evening, the excellent horse neighs and eats as usual, while the common horse hangs down his head and will not eat.

How does this differ from Yen Yüan and Confucius's being fit or unfit?

B TPYL 897.2b.   Yen 14.5b-6a.   Sun 25b-26a.

Since Yen Yüan's allotted span was short, he thought affectionately of Confucius, [wishing to] return to him in his later years. Similarly, a common horse and an excellent horse chase each other, but then, in the evening, when they are placed together in the halting place, the excellent horse neighs and eats as usual, while the common horse hangs down his head and will not eat again.

How does this differ from Yen Yüan and K'ung Ch'iu's fitness and unfitness?

C Yen 14.5b-6a.   Sun 7a.

The following sources give similar versions of the anecdote of Ch'ang-an music and the smell of meat:[5] TPYL 391.7a, 496.4b, 828.2b, and 863.5b; PTSC 145.4a; IWLC 72.6a; Ch'u-hsüeh chi 26.14a; Commentary to Wen hsüan 41.22a; and Po K'ung liu t'ieh 16.6b.

72

80

A <u>I lin</u> 3.9a-b.   Yen 14.6a.   Sun 7a-b.

In my youth I saw the beautiful writings of Yang
Tzu-yün and wished to follow them. Once I wrote a small
<u>fu</u>, and, having strained my mind too much, I immediately
fell ill. Tzu-yün has said that when Emperor Ch'eng
ordered him to write the "<u>Fu</u> on the Kan-ch'üan [Palace],"
he, too, violently strained himself. He became tired
and lay down. He dreamed that his viscera fell out on
to the floor. He gathered them up with his hand and put
them back again. Later he awake, with an ailment of
the breath which lasted for a year. Therefore, one may
say that exhausting the mind injures one's vitality and
one's spirit.

B <u>PTSC</u> 102.2a.   Yen 14.6a.

During the reign of Emperor Ch'eng, when the
Brilliant Companion Chao Fei-yen was in great favor,
Yang Tzu-yün was charged by Imperial edict to write <u>fu</u>.
Every time an Imperial progress was made to the Kan-
ch'üan [Palace] Yang violently strained his mind and
vitality, and, after he completed the <u>fu</u> at great pains,
he was tired and took a nap. He dreamed that his viscera fell out and that he put them back again with his
hands. Later he awoke with his breath greatly diminished. One year later he died.

C <u>IWLC</u> 56.18a and 75.8b. <u>TPYL</u> 75.8b, 587.7a and

739.2a.   Yen 14.6a.   Sun 13a.

In my youth I saw the beautiful writings and
noble essays of Yang Tzu-yün. I did not appreciate my
youth or the fact that I was a novice,[6] but wished to
overtake him at once. Inspired by an event,[7] I wrote
a small <u>fu</u>. Having strained my energy and my mind too
violently, I immediately found that I had become ill.[8]

Tzu-yün has said that Emperor Ch'eng, while
travelling to the Kan-ch'üan Palace, charged him by
Imperial edict to write <u>fu</u>. Because he had exerted
himself violently, he was tired and had a little nap.
He dreamed that his viscera fell out on to the floor.
He put them back in with his hands. When he awoke, his
breath was greatly diminished. He was ill for a year.[9]

In my youth I liked his writings.[10] Tzu-yün
labored on his _fu_ and odes.[11] I wished to learn from
him. Tzu-yün said, "If you can read a thousand _fu_, then
you will be skilled at writing them!"[12]

D Commentary to Wen hsüan 17.4a.   Yen 14.6a. Sun 13a.

(the first paragraph only)

Huan T'an wished to learn the art of writing _fu_
from Yang Tzu-yün. Tzu-yün said, "If you can read a
thousand _fu_, then you will be skilled at writing them!"
T'an admired Tzu-yün's writings. Having exerted his
mind on a small _fu_, he instantly suffered an attack of
illness. He recovered only after a whole day.

Tzu-yün said that Emperor Ch'eng, when sacrificing at the Kan-ch'üan Palace, ordered Yang Hsiung to
write _fu_. He violently exerted his mind and vitality,
became tired, and took a little nap. He dreamed that
his viscera fell out and he put them back in with his
hands. Later he awoke and felt ill. He was breathless
and palpitating, and his breath was greatly diminished.

Fragment 80D seems to be a summary of Huan T'an's information written by someone else.

E The following sources tell, more or less, the same
story of Yang Hsiung's sufferings as was told in the
other fragments: TPYL 393.7b and 399.6a; PTSC 102;
3b-4a; commentary to Wen hsüan 7.1a; Po K'ung liu t'ieh
86.4a; and Shuo fu 59.3b.[13]

Previous translation of Yen's full text: Pokora, "The
Life," II, p. 543.

81

I lin 3.9b.   Yen 14.6a. Sun 7b.

Chuang Chou [Chuang Tzu] was seriously ill, and
his disciples were weeping around him. He replied to
them, "I am dying now, so who [dies] first? [Compared
to someone] born a hundred years from now, who dies
last?[14] No one can escape death, so why should one
covet these moments?"[15]

82

A   <u>TPYL</u> 740.5a-b.   Yen 14.6a-b.   Sun 11b.
                                             (commentary)

      When I was a Grandee in the Directorate of
Music, I received the memoirs of the musicians. They
said that Emperor Wen of Han obtained the musician Sir
Tou, who was 180 years old and had lived since the
period of Marquis Wen of Wei. He was blind in both
eyes. The Emperor asked what food he ate in order to
reach such an age. Sir Tou replied, "I lost my sight
when I was thirteen years old. My father and mother
taught me music and how to play the <u>ch'in</u> [zither].
I did not use Taoist calisthenics and do not know how
I reached this great age."

      I felt that this explanation was plausible be-
cause Sir Tou, having been blind from youth, concentrated on the One and looked inward.

B   <u>TPYL</u> 383.10b.   Yen 14.6a-b.   Sun 11b.
                                             (commentary)

      In the past, when I was Wang Mang's Grandee in
the Directorate of Music, I read the memoirs of the
musicians.[16] [They said] that Emperor Wen [of Han]
obtained the musician Sir Tou, who was 180 years old
and had lived since the period of Marquis Wen of Wei.
He was blind in both eyes. Emperor Wen, wondering at
this, asked what he ate in order to reach such an age.
Sir Tou replied, "I lost my sight when I was thirteen
years old. My father and mother pitied me and taught
me how to play the <u>ch'in</u> [zither]. Every day I studied
and practiced until it became my regular occupation.
I cannot perform [Taoist] calisthenics, nor do I follow
a [special] diet.

      Huan T'an thought that Sir Tou's [strong] con-
stitution and [long] life span were attributable to
the benefits of his having always lived in retirement
and carefree contentment, since he was blind from
youth.

C Ts'ao Chih, "Pien tao lun," Kuang Hung ming chi

5.3a-b.   Yen 14.6a-b.

In the past I was Wang Mang's Grandee in the Directorate of Music and read in the memoirs of the musicians[17] that Emperor Wen of Han obtained the musician Sir Tou, who was 180 years old and had lived since the period of Marquis Wen of Wei. He was blind in both eyes. The Emperor, wondering at this, asked him how he had reached such an age. Sir Tou replied, "I, your servant, lost my sight when I was thirteen years old. My father and mother pitied my inability to learn any craft and taught me how to play the ch'in [zither]. Your servant was also[18] able to practice Taoist calisthenics and does not know by what power he has reached his great age."

Huan Chün-shan discussed this and said, "Mister Tou put the fact that he was blind from youth to great use and, concentrating on the One, he looked inward. His sensibility was not aided by outward perception." [Ts'ao Chih continues], "In the past Chün-shan rebuked Liu Tzu-chün,[19] saying that inner vision was useless. In the discussion of Sir Tou he used the argument of non-perception. I do not see any consistency in his theories."[20]

D Yen Shih-ku's commentary to Han shu 30, p. 3108.

                        Yen 14.6a. Sun 11b.

Sir Tou was 180 years old and blind in both eyes. Emperor Wen, wondering at this, asked him how he had reached such an age. Sir Tou replied, "I, your servant, lost my sight when I was thirteen years old. My father and mother pitied my inability to acquire different skills and taught me how to play the ch'in [zither]. I have practiced Taoist calisthenics, but have swallowed no pills."[21]

A shortened version of 82D is found in Tung Yüeh's Ch'i-kuo k'ao, pp. 72-73. See commentary to fragment 176.

Previous translation: Pokora, "The Life," I, p. 59.

83

A <u>T'ai-p'ing huan-yü chi</u> 12.15a-b.

Yen 14.6b. Sun 26a.

During his travels Duke Huan of Ch'i met a man from Mo-ch'iu[22] and asked him his age. The man replied, "Eighty-three years." The Duke said, "Would you bless me with your long life?" The man answered, "If you are to live a long life, you must hold gold and jade lightly and consider men to be your treasures."[23]

B <u>Ch'u-hsüeh chi</u> 8.8b.   Yen 14.6b. Sun 26a.
                                        (commentary)

During his travels Duke Huan of Ch'i met a man from Mo-ch'iu.

84

A <u>Hung-ming chi</u> 5.4b-5b: "Chin, Huan T'an: <u>Hsin-lun</u>,

<u>Hsing shen</u>."   Yen 14.6b-8a.

I once paid a visit to Tu Fang,[24] a former prefect of Ch'en, from my commandery. I found him reading the book of <u>Lao-tzu</u>. He said, "Through quietude, equanimity,[25] and the nourishing of his own nature, Lao Tzu lived several hundred years. Now, if we follow his way, can we not increase our years and avoid old age?"

I answered, "Although [people may have the same] body and name, their dispositions and innate natures, their talents and abilities differ in degree. Their constitutions are strong or weak, robust or fragile. By taking care of and nourishing [one's own body] when it is used, only a slight degree of improvement may be achieved. In contrast, if clothing, shoes, and utensils are cared for they remain intact for a long time."

By his side I saw a hemp candle from which about one foot of ash hung down. Using it as an example, I said, "The spirit lives in the body like the flame blazing in the candle. If [the candle] is properly tended and turned so that it follows the flame,

[the flame] need not be extinguished until the candle
is all used up. Of course, if the candle has no flame,
it cannot become active in the void, nor can its ashes
be lighted later. The ashes are like man's old age:
The teeth fall out, the hair turns white, the muscles
and flesh wither and dry up, and the spirit cannot
moisten and lubricate the body.[26] When such a state
prevails inside and outside the body, the breath expires and the man dies, just as the flame and the
candle are both used up.

"If a man unfortunately encounters some evil,
injury, or illness and receives neither care, nourish-
ment, nor an excellent doctor, he may die an untimely
death. In such a death the muscles, flesh, sinews and
bones are usually like flame which dies in a gust of
wind, neither rescued nor protected. Such circumstances
lead to death, although there is ample flesh and the
stem of the candle is still long."

Once at night, while sitting and drinking inside, I lit a hemp candle. Half of the candle pressed
down as if about to go out. Now, I said to myself,
"Let's watch it carefully." I saw that its surface was
cracked and gnarled. Then I tended it and turned it so
that the flame passed over and revived. Now, man's
body may also suffer loss and cracking, but if it is
cared for immediately and supported well, it too may
pass through [intact].

Moreover, since no one knows the time of his
own birth, one should grow old and die without any
knowledge of one's self. In the distant past, when the
world was equitable and harmonious, people[27] were born
with beauty and wealth. All were robust and strong and
lived to a great age, some reaching as long as 100
years before their death. Death came to them imper-
ceptibly, as if it were a sleep. It was like fruit and
corn which fall by themselves after a long period of
ripeness. Later generations encountered weak, poor and
evil fluids. They married at improper times, and toiled
and labored to excess. Therefore, they and their children were all injured. Their sinews, bones, blood, and
energy were neither stout nor strong, so their lives
were full of misfortune. Their lives were cut short,
and they died prematurely in their prime. When they
fell ill, they would suffer and grieve, and then their
lives would end. Thus, everyone mourns and abhors
death.[28]

Once Duke Ching of Ch'i, glorifying his country and praising his own pleasure, said, "Suppose that there was no death in the past, what would happen to [the pleasure of the people of this time]?" Yen-tzu said, "The Lord on High considers man's death to be good. For the benevolent it is a rest, for the non-benevolent it is a going away. Now, you do not think of striving to increase your learning every day in order to reach understanding and thus establish yourself and make your name famous. Instead, you are only greedy for profit and longevity, craving to extend your life and increase your years. You are a man whose errors have not been dispelled."[29]

Somebody objected, saying, "I am afraid that your comparison of the candle and the flame with the body and the spirit appears [to be right, but is actually] wrong. Sometimes muscles and skin crack and are injured, but they recover by themselves because the energy of the blood circulates. If the hemp of the candle is broken or injured it cannot recover and be made whole again, even if a flame resides within it. Therefore, the spiritual fluid makes birth and growth possible, but the lighted candle cannot repair itself and become whole because it is of a different character in this respect. How can you wish to identify them?"

I responded, "The flame arises from one end, whereas the spiritual fluid of man is in the whole body and emanates gradually from the inside to unite with the outside or goes from the outside flesh to the inside. Thus it does not necessarily go from [only] one end. Let's compare it to a charcoal flame which burns red. If some water is poured over it, it too expires to a certain degree but it revives. It is the same as man's blood fluid, which gives birth and growth to the muscles and flesh. If we look at their outcome, they either burn or become ash. Why should they not be compared?"

Later, I sat one night in conversation with Liu Po-shih, and we lit a flame in some fat. The fat in the lamp was almost used up, and the wick was scorched, bald and about to die. Using it to make my idea clear to Liu Po-shih, I said, "Man's decline and old age is like a bald lamp." Then I repeated the previous discussion on lighting the hemp candle.

Po-shih said, "If a lamp or candle is about to go out, one should add fat or replace the candle.

Likewise, when a man is old and infirm, he either per-
ishes or perpetuates himself."

My answer was, "The existence of man, who
possesses form and body, is like a lamp or a candle.
When the wick is totally used up and reaches its end,
how can it resupply or replace itself? Its resupply
and replacement clearly depends on man. Perhaps[30] the
extinction of man also depends on Heaven, or Heaven may
arrange for him [to continue his life].

"If his muscles, bones and blood energy are
rich and strong, then his body and spirit may be supported and live for a long time. If all this is bad,
then [the body and the spirit] are broken and injured[31]
just as the flame dies out slowly or quickly according
to the quantity of fat and the length of the candle.
One cannot wish that the lamp and candle would resupply or replace themselves, but if the fat on the side
is quickly pressed so it soaks the tip of the wick and
if the stem [i.e., the hemp], as well as the trunk
[i.e., the candle], are turned or inclined accordingly,
the flame becomes quiet and the light will usually be
restored. But once the root is exhausted, the lamp
and the candle cannot be rescued.

"Now, man, in cultivating his nature, may, like
the pressing of the fat and the turning of the candle,
grow his fallen teeth back again, turn his white hair
black again, or make his muscles and flesh radiant and
moist. But when the end of his life is reached he, too,
can only die.

"The intelligent man knows how difficult it is
to strive for [the prolongation of life] and therefore
he does not exert himself for it. The foolish man de-
ceives himself with hopes that 'the candle will change
when the fat is used up.' Therefore he takes many pains
and gives himself no rest.

"Grass, trees and the five kinds of grain come
into being on earth through the energy of yin and yang.
When they grow big and bear fruit, the fruit returns
to the earth where it may grow again. In the same way,
man, as well as the birds, beasts and insects, all
reproduce by intercourse between female and male.
Birth is followed by growth, growth by old age, and old
age by death--like the alternations of the four seasons.
To wish to change one's nature, to strive after strange
ways, is a delusion which I cannot understand."

B TPYL 870.3a gives a short version of Huan T'an's

discussion with Liu Po-shih. [Yen 14.7b]. Sun 25b.

One night when I was sitting with Liu Po-shih, the fat in the lamp [was almost used up], the wick was bald, and [the flame] was about to die out. I said to Po-shih, "Man's informity and old age is like a bald candle wick."

Po-shih said, "If man is weak and old, he has to continue himself [i.e., prolong his life]."

I said, "By enriching one's own constitution white hair may grow black again, but when the end of one's life is reached, one must die."

Previous translations: A Forke, Geschichte der mittel-älterlichen chinesischen Philosophie, pp. 106-108 (partially); Liang Han chih pu, pp. 211-14. See also Liang Han pu-fen, pp. 347-50.

85

TPYL 897.2b.   Yen 14.8a.   Sun 26a.

In the burial ground of Empress Wei[32] there were ten horses which were used as mounts or to draw carriages at funerals. The officials and servants tended and fed them well and saw that they were well watered. They could not be ridden. And all the horses lived to the age of sixty.[33]

86

A TPYL 990.5a.   Yen 14.8a.   Sun 26a.

I told Liu Tzu-chün that cultivating one's nature does not help [postpone old age]. His elder brother's son, Liu Po-yü,[34] said, "If Heaven produces drugs which kill man, it must certainly produce drugs which give man life." I said, "The plant ourouparia rhynchophylla[35] does not agree with man, so eating it causes death. But it is not produced for the purpose of killing man. Similarly Szechwan beans[36] poison fish, arsenic kills rats,[37] cassia injures otters, and apricot stones kill dogs.[38] But these are not made by Heaven for this purpose.

B Fang I-chih, <u>Wu-li hsiao-chih</u> 11, p. 273 (ed. <u>Wan-yu</u> <u>wen-k'u</u>).

The cassia injures otters. Apricot stones kill pigs. The loach [<u>fen-ch'iu</u>] fears pepper, and the centipede, oil.[39]

Previous translation: Pokora, "The Life," II, p. 538. Cf. <u>Liang Han pu-fen</u> II, p. 345.

NOTES: CHAPTER 8

1.　　Analects VI:2; Legge, p. 185.

2.　　Instead of shang 殤 ("die young"), I follow TPYL 897.2b, which has fu 復 ("return").

3.　　Wen tung li yü ("words of the eastern village") may be wrong. TPYL 496.4b, among others, replaces it with Kuan-tung yen-yü ("a proverb of Kuan-tung"), i.e., "east of the Han-ku pass." This region was thought of as rustic.

4.　　Both the music and the meat are unattainable, and the people can only listen or look from a distance. But, while they despise the music of the capital, they are greedy for the meat. The latter part of the proverb is still common today.

5.　　The anecdote is also mentioned in a letter by Emperor Wen of Wei, Ts'ao P'i, in Wen hsüan 42, third item. See also TPYL 828.2b.

6.　　Hsin-chin 新進 ("novice"). Only found in TPYL 739.2a.

7.　　Only found in TPYL 739.2a.

8.　　Commentary to Wen hsüan 17.4a gives three additional characters which mean: "I recovered only after a whole day." See fragment 80D.

9.　　TPYL 739.2a adds, as in fragment 80B, that Yang Hsiung died the next year. A similar text is TPYL 75.8b. The next paragraph beginning "In my mouth..." is found only in IWLC 56.18a and TPYL 587.7a.

10.　　TPYL 587.7a. IWLC 56.18a has: "I once liked his writings."

11.　　Sung 頌 . Only in TPYL 587.7a.

12.　　This last paragraph is a short version of fragment 140 (Yen 15.5a); see also fragment 80D. The saying about a thousand fu is quoted in Hsi ching tsa chi 2.4a, but Huan T'an is not mentioned ("Somebody asked..."). In fact, this is a quotation from Yang Hsiung's reply to a letter from Huan T'an which evaluated Ssu-ma

Hsiang-ju's rhyme-prose: "Ssu-ma Ch'ang-ch'ing's fu do
not originate from [the hands of] men, but their divinity approaches magic and should be studied carefully.
There is a proverb which says, 'Even all the ingenious
gods of Fu Hsi will not pass the door of those who
practice.'" Cf. Yen, Ch'üan Han wen 52.10a. For another letter by Yang Hsiung to Huan T'an, see fragment
214, note 123. Another comment by Yang Hsiung on Ssu-
ma Hsiang-ju's rhyme-prose is in Ssu-ma Ch'ien's Shih
chi 117, p. 105, but it cannot be found in his Fa yen.

The comment quoted by Ssu-ma Ch'ien appears to
be a late and very awkward interpolation. The reliability of Yang Hsiung's letter to Huan T'an, which also
concerns Ssu-ma Hsiang-ju's rhyme-prose, might also be
called into question. For his source Yen merely refers
to "Yang Shen ch'ih-tu ch'ing-ts'ai" 楊慎赤牘清裁 .
If ch'ih 尺 is substituted for ch'ih 赤 , it appears
that this source is a book by Yang Shen (1488-1559 A.D.)
entitled "Correct Selection of Collected Correspondence,"
which I have not been able to examine. Yang Shen's book
was probably rather popular, as it was later amended by
another well-known Ming writer, Wang Shih-chen (1526-
1590 A.D.) and reissued under the title [Tseng chi]
Ch'ih-tu ch'ing-ts'ai 增集尺牘清裁 . Yen is
departing from his usual habit when he quotes a source
as late as the 16th century for the first century Yang
Hsiung. See my article, "Huan T'an and Yang Hsiung on
Ssu-ma Hsiang-ju."

13.   In Chapter 6.26 (Shen-ssu) of his Wen-hsin tiao-
lung, Liu Hsieh discusses Yang Hsiung and Huan T'an, as
well as Wang Ch'ung, in the same context as the present
fragment. Shih translates (The Literary Mind, p. 156)
as follows: "...Yang Hsiung had nightmares because of
his inability to continue writing, Huan T'an fell ill
because of onerous thinking, Wang Ch'ung exhausted his
vitality in his intellectual labors...."

14.   In other words, "I am the first to die, compared to you who weep. But compared to one born a
hundred years from now, you will be first to die. If
I am first to die and you are also first to die, then
what's the point of weeping because I die first?"

15.   In light of Chuang Tzu's well-known relativism,
"these moments" apparently symbolize one's whole
life. This quotation corresponds exactly with the
famous discussion between Confucius and Lao Tzu recorded in Chuang-tzu XXII:II:XV; Legge I, p. 64.

Huan T'an's quotation is particularly interesting in two respects. First, Huan T'an's own point of view is revealed in his stress on the inevitability of death. Second, Huan T'an's quotation may present some evidence that Chuang Tzu's text was known and used during the Han period and thus was written before the Ch'in dynasty.

Wen I-to's Ku tien hsin i, p. 279, says, in a chapter devoted to Chuang Tzu, that he became influential only during the Wei and Chin periods. Wen I-to even declares that "Huan T'an did not even see the Chuang-tzu." He says that no Lao-Chuang ideas were discussed during the Later Han, and that only the Huang-lao doctrine was known. He also asserts that no commentary to the Chuang-tzu was written during the Han periods.

We possess quite specific information on Huan T'an's interest in and knowledge of Chuang Tzu and Lao Tzu from Pan Ku. The last chapter of the Han shu (100, A, pp. 5819-20) tells us that Pan Ku's uncle, Pao Ssu, refused Huan T'an's request to read these books, both of which were apparently owned by the rich Pan family. Although there is still no evidence that Huan T'an was ever allowed to read the Taoist literature in the Pan family's library, it is clear that he had at least potential access to the Chuang-tzu text. However, the text must have been quite rare; otherwise a Confucianist like Huan T'an would not have risked the mockery of the Taoist Pan Ssu.

Wen I-to's negative attitude is questioned by Chiang Shih-jung in "Yu kuan Chuang-tzu ti i-hsieh li-shih tzu-liao." Chiang quotes this fragment, as well as others from Huai-nan-tzu, Shih chi, and Han shu, to prove that Huan T'an did indeed read the Chuang-tzu. He also refers to Ma I-ch'u, who believes that this fragment represents a lost text by Chuang Tzu.

16.   Fragment 82B has shu-chi 書 記 , instead of the chi 記 of 82A.

17.   Yüeh chi 樂 記 ·

18.   The text has yu 又 ("also"), instead of the pu 不 ("not") of the two previous versions, changing the meaning radically. It is possible that this is a misprint. See note 21 below.

19.   Liu Hsin.

20.   Although we know of several discussions between
Liu Hsin and Huan T'an (see, for instance, fragments 86A
and 156), it is not clear which discussion Ts'ao Chih
has in mind. See also the chapter on Huan T'an's relation with Liu Hsin, in Pokora, "The Life," II, pp. 537-
42.

21.   This fragment is quoted in Yen Shih-ku's commentary to the music section of the bibliographical
chapter of the Han shu. Confucius' theory of music is
explained and its decline attributed, as usual, to the
pernicious influence of the tunes from Cheng and Wei.
Surprisingly, the well-known hero, Marquis Wen of Wei,
is credited with the patronage of musical literature:
"Among the rulers of the Six Kingdoms, Marquis Wen of
Wei was most fond of the past. Emperor Wen obtained
his musician, Sir Tou." Perhaps Pan Ku adopted this
curious theory from Huan T'an.

        The historian Ch'i Shao-nan (1706-1768 A.D.),
quoted by Wang Hsien-ch'ien, has carefully calculated
Mister Tou's age to prove that Huan T'an was mistaken
in giving it as 180 years, rather than ca. 230 years.
Ch'i Shao-nan's chronology is undoubtedly correct, but
the problem is not one of chronology.

22.   Mo-ch'iu was a town in Ch'i, now Shantung, according to Chung-kuo ku-chin ti-ming ta-tz'u-tien,
p. 873.4. Chavannes, MH V, p. 106, note 5 could not
identify the place.

23.   Huan T'an's source is, again, Hsin-hsü (4.9b-
10b).

24.   Tu Fang belonged to the family of Huan T'an's
friend, Tu Lin (Hou Han shu 36, p. 1297). For Tu Shih,
Governor of Nan-yang, see fragment 128, note 68. Huan
T'an's connection with the Tu family appears to have
been very close. At least two men belonging to this
group must have been rather unconventional, for they
were included in the collective biography of the yu-chi
("wandering knights"): Ch'en Tsun and Chang Sung (Hou
Han shu 27, p. 986). Chang was criticized by Huan T'an
for his "error," which Han thought unworthy of a "perceptive man" (see fragment 103). In his youth Chang
Sung studied with Tu Lin's father, Tu Yeh (Han shu 85,
p. 5019). For other instances of Huan T'an's acquaint-
ance with the yu-chi, see fragment 188, which is of

doubtful authenticity. The connection between Huan T'an and Tu Lin has been mentioned by both Lo Hsiang-lin (p. 141) and G. E. Sargent (p. 166) in Symposium on Historical, Archeological and Linguistic Studies on Southern China, South-East Asia and the Hong Kong Region. K'ang Yu-wei, who believed that Huan T'an was a disciple of Chang Sung, agrees; Hsin Hsüeh wei ching k'ao, p. 14.

25.   These terms are found in Tao-te ching 31 and in later Taoist literature, such as Huai-nan-tzu 2.

26.   Jun-tse   潤 澤   , which originally meant "softening and moistening," is also used by Mencius (III:1:20; Legge, p. 245).

TPYL 375.2b quotes another statement on hair which might also have come from Huan T'an's Hsin-lun: "The hair on the head is born on the skin. If the hair is removed, the skin does not know about it." TPYL introduces this with "Hsin-lun yü-yüeh" 新 論 語 曰 which may mean either "the New Analects say" or, more plausibly, "a quotation from the Hsin-lun says." These sentences may be associated with the reference to hair in this fragment, or with Ts'ao Chih's comment on skin (see fragment 152F, note 28). This is only conjecture; it must be stressed that TPYL lists these sentences after quotations on the subject of the skin from Pao-p'u tzu and Hsi ching tsa chi, which suggests that the quotation belongs to one of the many treatises entitled Hsin-lun which followed Huan T'an's.

As a matter of fact, I lin quotes a fuller version of these sentences, attributing it to a Hsin-lun which contains ten chüan. Since I lin says that Huan T'an's Hsin-lun contains seventeen chüan, the quotation from TPYL 375.2b should probably be attributed to Hsia-hou Chan (243-291 A.D.), who also wrote a Hsin-lun. Or, it could have come from another Hsin-lun in ten chüan also quoted in I lin, which the editor attributes to Hua T'an (d. ca. 230 A.D.). See I lin 6.5a and 6a.

27.   The text has jen min 人 民 , while Yen has jen wu 人 物 .

28.   Chi-t'ung 疾 痛 and ts'e-ta 惻 怛 ("mourns and abhors") are two binomes also found in the beginning of Li chi XXXII; Legge II, p. 375.

29.   <u>Yen-tzu ch'un-ch'iu</u> 7:4, p. 180, says that Duke Ching was criticized by Yen-tzu for asking what men of the remote past had delighted in when there was no death: "Duke Ching, drinking wine, was enjoying himself tremendously. He said, 'In the remote past they had no death, but what was their pleasure?' Yen-tzu answered, 'If there was no death in the remote past, just that was their delight. Duke, how might you gain such pleasure?'" The relevant text of <u>Yen-tzu ch'un-ch'iu</u> is quoted in more detail in P'an Yu's "Ch'iu hsing fu," <u>Wen hsüan</u>, 13.26.

30.   For <u>tang</u> 黨 ("association") I read <u>t'ang</u> 儻 ("perhaps"). The latter character is given by Yen.

31.   For a similar comparison, see fragment 156.

32.   I believe that Huan T'an is referring to the chorus girl Wei Tzu-fu, who became the Empress of Emperor Wu in 128 B.C. She is mentioned in Huan T'an's conversation with Fu Yen, Marquis of K'ung-hsiang, which is related in the beginning of Huan T'an's biography. Wei Tzu-fu was quite popular with later Han writers.

33.   The age of sixty is clearly a deliberate exaggeration, since the average life of a horse is between fifteen and twenty years, although some have been known to live for forty years.

34.   Sun gives "Liu Po-sheng." Fragment 84 indicates that Huan T'an had similar discussions with Liu Po-shih. In a series of personal names only the second characters usually differ (e.g., Po-yü, Po-sheng, Po-shih, etc.). Therefore, Liu Po-yü and Liu Po-shih may have been brothers, since their names belong to the same series. Liu Po-yü was probably the son of Liu Chi; see also fragment 98. W. Bauer explains the customs concerning personal names in "Das <u>P'ai-hang</u>-System in der chinesischen Namengebung." Bauer explains, in his book on the same subject, that the <u>p'ai-hang</u> system for the names of brothers was already in existence in the Former Han period, while the complete <u>p'ai-hang</u> system for generations only appeared at the end of the Han; see W. Bauer, <u>Der chinesische Persone name</u>, pp. 165-66, note 2.

35. <u>Kou-teng</u> 鈎藤 ("<u>ourouparia rhynchophylla</u>") given in Sun and translated in O. Z. Tsang, <u>A Supplement to a Complete Chinese-English Dictionary</u>, p. 362,

according to DKJ 40319.81, is a creeping plant. The text, however, has kou-wen 鈎吻 , which is also classified with the creeping plants by DKJ 40319.90.

36.   Pa-tou 巴豆 ("Szechwan beans") is mentioned twice in the "Yen-tu" chapter of the Lun-heng (66, p. 947 and 952 of Huang Hui's edition); Forke I translates pa-tou as "croton oil beans" (p. 298) and "croton seed" (p. 300). Croton oil is a radical purgative, which Wang Ch'ung says can cause death when eaten in large quantities.

37.   Huai-nan-tzu 17 (p. 295) is similar: "People die from eating arsenic, but it satisfies the hunger of the silkworms. Fish die from eating Szechwan beans, but rats grow fat on it." Instead of pa-tou, Huai-nan tzu has pa-shu 巴菽 , which is an oil-producing tree from Szechwan.

38.   The text has kou 狗 ("dog"), while Sun, Yen and fragment 86B give chu 猪 ("pig").

39.   The second part of this fragment is quoted only by the Ch'ing scholar Fang I-chih (1611-1671 A.D.), but this does not necessarily mean that the whole Hsin-lun was at his disposal. Fang may have found it in one of the numerous lei-shu ("encyclopedias"). For information on Fang I-chih, see the article on him by Hou Wai-lu.

Chapter 9. Correcting the Classics

87

Commentary to Wen hsüan 20.34a.   Yen 14.8b. Sun 13b.

Students are already very ignorant and in darkness. Moreover, teaching methods are faulty. This is how stupidity is cultivated.

88

Yen Shih-ku's commentary to Han shu 30, p. 3129.[1]

Yen 14.8b. Sun 11b.

Ch'in Chin-chün[2] could explain the title of the "Yao-tien"[3] chapter. His explanation of these two characters was over a hundred thousand words, but his explanation of "examining into antiquity"[4] reached thirty thousand words.

Previous translation: Pokora, "The Life," II, p. 564.
Explanation: Pokora, "An Important Crossroad," p. 75.

89

I lin 3.9b.   Yen 14.8b. Sun 7b.

Tzu-kung asked Chü Po-yü,[5] "Sir, how do you govern a country?"

[Chü Po-yü] answered, "I govern by not governing."[6]

Previous translations: F. Hirth, "Bausteine zu einer Geschichte der chinesischen Literatur," pp. 435-36; Pokora, "The Life," II, p. 565.

A   TPYL 608.5a.   Yen 14.8b-9a. Sun 23a-b.

        The first Book of Changes is called "Manifesta-
tions of Change in the Mountains;" the second, "Flow
and Return to Womb and Tomb;" the third, the "Book of
Changes of the Chou Dynasty." "Manifestations of
Change in the Mountains" consists of 80,000 words;
"Flow and Return to Womb and Tomb," of 4,300 words.

        The Old Text version of The Book of Documents
previously consisted of 45 scrolls and 58 p'ien.[7] The
compiled Old Text version of the Li chi consists of 56
scrolls. The Old Text Analects consists of 21 scrolls.
The Old Text Classic of Filial Piety consists of one
scroll, 20 sections, and 1,872 characters;[8] it differs
from the New Text version in more than 400 characters.

        These are a forest and a marsh of excellent
treatises, a deep sea of texts and ideas!

B   Yen Shih-ku's commentary to Han shu 30, p. 3122.

                                    Yen 14.8b-9a. Sun 7b.

        The Old Text Classic of Filial Piety consists
of one scroll, 20 sections, and 1,871 characters; it
differs from the New Text version in more than 400
characters.

C   PTSC 101.2a.   Yen 14.8b. Sun 15b.

        "Manifestations of Change in the Mountains"
[Li-shan][9] is deposited in the Fragrant Terrace; the
"Flow and Return to Womb and Tomb" is deposited in
/the office of the/ Grand Augur.

This quotation is attributed to Huan Mao's Hsin-yü,
but it is clearly from the Hsin-lun by Huan T'an.

D   Wang Ying-lin, K'un-hsüeh chi-wen 1.7a.

                                    Sun 4b (preface):

        "Manifestations of Change in the Mountains"
consists of 80,000 words; "Flow and Return to Womb and

Tomb" of 4,300 words.[10] The Book of Changes of the
Hsia dynasty is detailed, while the Book of Changes of
the Yin dynasty is simple. The basis for this statement has yet to be examined.[11]

E Commentary to Lu Te-ming, Ching-tien shih-wen 1.2b.

Yen 14.8b. Sun 12b.

The text differs in more than 400 characters.[12]

Previous partial translation: Pokora, "The Life," II,
pp. 562-63.

91

TPYL 329.5a.   Yen 14.9a. Sun 20b-21a.

In the fourth month Crown Prince Fa[13] offered
a sacrifice on the heights of Pi. Down below he travelled as far as the north of the Meng ford. By this
time he had become King Wu. Having completed his three
years of mourning,[14] he wished to complete his father's
mission. He climbed into a boat and caught a fish.[15]
This was the response of the Earth. After he performed the sacrifice of the burnt offering,[16] a bird
descended. This was the response of Heaven.[17]

Two years later [King Wu] heard that Chou [Hsin]
had killed Pi Kan and imprisoned Chi-tzu.[18] The Grand
Tutor and Junior Tutor[19] had fled to Chou,[20] carrying
their musical instruments in their arms. On the chia-
tzu day, the moon [shone] like strung jade, and the Five
Planets [glistened] like strung pearls[21] at early dawn.
King Wu had by morning travelled as far as the Southern[22]
Suburb and the Wilderness of Mu.[23] Following [the will
of] Heaven, he punished Chou [Hsin]. Thus a soldier
stained his sword with blood. The Empire was pacified,
but not settled.

92

Wu-hsing ta-i 4, p. 85.   Yen 14.9a.

Man possesses the form of Heaven and Earth,
holds within him the pure vital spirit, and, among

living things, is the most intelligent. Therefore, in his demeanor he moves as wood. In his speech he is as trustworthy as metal. In his sight he is as clear as fire. In his hearing he is as receptive as water. In his thought he is as wise as the Earth. His use of the five forces consists of movement, quietness and returning, so that they unite with the spirits.

If his demeanor is respectful, he is full of gravity, of gravity like seasonable rain. If his speech accords [with reason], he is full of serenity, serenity like seasonable sunshine. If his sight is clear, he is full of wisdom, wisdom like seasonable heat. If his hearing is receptive, he is full of deliberation, deliberation like seasonable cold. If his heart is grave, he is full of saintliness, saintliness like seasonable wind.[24]

Metal, wood, water and fire are all contained in the Earth. Rain, sunshine, heat and cold all come from the wind. Demeanor, speech, sight and hearing are all born in the heart.

Previous translation: A. Forke, Geschichte der mittel-älterlichen chinesischen Philosophie, pp. 108-109 and note 2.

93

A TPYL 533.8b. Ch'u-hsüeh chi 13.18b.

Yen 14.9a. Sun 18a.

The kings built the Hall of Light[25] and the Jade Dam[26] to receive and transmit Heaven and propagate moral transformation.[27]

B TPYL 534.2a. IWLC 38.27a. Yen 14.9b. Sun 17a.

The kings built a circular pond in the shape of a round piece of jade [pi], filled it with water and encircled it with a dam [yung].[28] Thus it was called pi-yung. It symbolized the reception from above of [the mandate of] Heaven and Earth to spread teachings and ordinances, to propagate the Way of Kings, to rotate a full circle[29] and then to start all over again.

C IWLC 38.24b.   Yen 14.9b. Sun 9a
                                        [commentary]

        The kings built the Hall of Light. Above it
was circular, below square, thus symbolizing the sky
and the earth. Thus was created a hall with four sides,
each with its own color, in the pattern of the four
directions.30 Because Heaven is [full of] light, [this
hall] was named the "Hall of Light."

D Liu Chao's commentary to the 8th treatise (the second

   treatise on the sacrifices) in the Hou Han shu,

   p. 3587.   Yen 14.9a-b. Sun 9a.

        Because Heaven is [full of] light, [the hall]
was named the "Hall of Light." Above it was circular
imitating the sky, and below it was square imitating
the earth. Eight windows imitated the winds from the
eight directions. Its four extremities imitated the
four seasons. Nine chambers imitated the nine provinces.
Twelve seats imitated the twelve months. Thirty-six
doors imitated the thirty-six rains. Seventy-two lat-
ticed windows imitated the seventy-two winds.31

Huan T'an may have written this description of the Hall
of Light and its associated buildings in connection with
the plans for constructing them. In 4 A.D., Wang Mang
proposed the erection of the Hall of Light, the Pi-yung
and the Spiritual Tower [Ling t'ai]; cf. HFHD III, p.
191. Dubs, however, translated this to say that Wang
Mang "memoralized and built...these monuments." Ac-
coring to Huan T'an's biography (Hou Han shu 28A, p.
1017), Emperor Kuang-wu called a meeting to determine
the site of the Spiritual Tower, and on this occasion
he clashed with Huan T'an because of their radically
divergent interpretations of the omens (The Life I,
p. 32). Finally, we know from Hou Han shu, the second
treatise on the sacrifices (p. 3587), and from Yüan
Hung's Hou Han chi (8, p. 51; cf. The Dates of Huan
T'an, p. 672), that all three buildings were built in
56 A.D. Ssu-ma Kuang erroneously concluded that Huan
T'an's dispute with Kuang-wu took place in that year.
In my article, "The Dates of Huan T'an," I demonstrate
that this dispute arose in 28 A.D. My opinion is shared
by M. Maspero; see his article cited in note 25 below.
Since only the Spiritual Tower was under discussion in

28 A.D., and since Huan T'an died under circumstances indirectly connected with the dispute later in that year, Huan's descriptions of the Hall of Light were probably associated with Wang Mang's proposals in 4 A.D.

The second chapter of the large treatise, Ming-t'ang ta-tao lu by Hui Tang (1697-1758 A.D.), includes three quotations from Huan T'an's Hsin-lun which are not quoted by either Yen or Sun. Therefore, these quotations are translated below, with their recently discovered quotations (see fragment 175).

A TPYL 610.7b.   Yen 14.9b.   Sun 12b.

[The Tradition of Tso...].[32] More than a hundred years later Ku-liang Ch'i, a man from Lu, wrote a Ch'un-ch'iu. It was damaged and much of it lost. There was also Kung-yang Kao, a man from Ch'i, who, following the text of the Classic,[33] wrote [his own] Tradition which covered and obscured the original facts. The Tradition of Tso bears the same relation to the Classic[34] as the outside of a garment does to a lining--both exist only by mutual dependence. Even a sage who pondered for ten years behind locked doors could not understand the Classic without the Tradition.

B Lu Te-ming, Ching-tien shih-wen, introductory chap-

ter 20a.   Yen 14.9a.   Sun 12b.

The Tradition of Tso declined during the Warring Kingdoms because it was hidden. More than a hundred years later, Ku-liang Ch'i, a man from Lu, wrote[35] a Ch'un-ch'iu. It was damaged, and much of the text of the Classic was lost. There was also Kung-yang Kao, a man from Ch'i, who, following the text of the Classic, wrote [his own] Tradition which greatly departed from the original facts.

C I lin 3.9b. Liu Chih-chi, Shih t'ung 14.14b.

                                 Yen 14.9b. Sun 7b,12b.

[The Tradition of] Tso. The Classic and the Tradition bear the same relation as the outside of a garment does to a lining[36]--both exist only by mutual dependence.

Previous partial translations: A. Forke, Geschichte der mittelälterlichen chinesischen Philosophie, p. 109, note 3; Previous full translation: Pokora, "The Life," II, pp. 565-66.

95

PTSC 95.6b.   Yen 14.9b-10a.   Sun 15a.

When the literati read the account of success and failure in political affairs, which is found in the Spring and Autumn Annals, they believe that a Spring and Autumn Annals will again be written when a new sage appears. I said this would not be so. Why? Later sages need not necessarily continue the ideas of earlier sages.[37] All that the sages and worthies have transmitted contain, in the same degree, the Way, virtue, benevolence and righteousness, creating wonderful treatises and unusual texts which are all good and well worth studying.[38]

Previous translation: Pokora, "The Life," II, p. 564.

96

Ku-wen yüan 11B, p. 272.   Yen 14.10a.

Usurpation, regicide and annihilation in Wu-- the source of this trouble was Chi Cha.[39] Chi Cha would not consider the idea[40] of imitating the regency of the Duke of Chou of antiquity and, as far as more recent times were concerned, he admired the modest yielding of Ts'ao Mo.[41] His reputation is already very small. How can one say that the significance found in the Spring and Autumn Annals lies therein?

96

I lin 3.9b.   Yen 14.10a.   Sun 7b.

    [It is said that] Yao could approach [the
greatness of] Heaven because his ability to appoint
the two sages Shun and Yü as his ministers is admired.

NOTES: CHAPTER 9

1. Criticizing the immense commentaries to the Classics, the author (probably Liu Hsin) of the bibliographical chapter of the Han shu complained, "The explanation of a text of five characters could be as long as twenty or thirty thousand characters." Yen Shih-ku used Huan T'an's fragment to demonstrate the truth of this statement.

2. Ch'in Chin-chün 秦近君 appears to be the scholar Ch'in Yen-chün 延君 , also known as Ch'in Kung 恭 , from Hsin-tu, the home of Wang Mang. Ch'in Kung's teacher was the erudite Chang Shan-fu, an expert on the Book of Documents (see Table II in Tjan Tjoe Som, Po Hu T'ang I, p. 86ff). The author of Chapter 88 (p. 5158) of the Han shu also remarks with some sarcasm that Ch'in Kung followed the path of his teacher in writing explanations as long as one million words. It is expected that Huan T'an and Pan Ku, both followers of the Old Text school, would ridicule Ch'in Kung who belonged to the New Text school of Classical criticism. Ch'in Yen-chün, erroneously called Ch'in Chün-yen, is also mentioned in Wen-hsin tiao-lung 18.51a. See Shih, The Literary Mind, p. 104 for an explanation of the title, "Yao-tien."

3. The first chapter of the Book of Documents.

4. The first words of the Book of Documents. For details, see Legge, The Shoo King, p. 16.

5. Chü Po-yü was a disciple of Confucius who is said to have become a Taoist. According to Analects XV:6, Confucius esteemed him very highly. The recorder, Yu, also praised by Confucius, tried in vain to persuade Duke Ling of Wei to employ Chü Po-yü. Two commentaries by Kao Yu provide more information on Chü Po-yü. The first of these (Huai-nan-tzu 9, p. 129) merely says that his name was Chü Yüan and that he was a tai-fu ("great official") in Wei. The second commentary (Lü-shih ch'un-ch'iu 20:8, p. 264) states, among other things, that his name was Chü Chuang-tzu, his posthumous name, Ch'eng-tzu, and that he was the son of Chü Wu-chiu. According to Lü-shih ch'un-ch'iu 20:8 (p.264; Wilhelm, p. 357), Chü Po-yü was a chancellor in Wei. At that time Confucius, Tzu-kung and Shih-yü (i.e., Tzu-yü or Yü-tzu) were in Wei. For information on Chü Po-yü's alleged conversion to Taoism, see Chuang-tzu XXV:III:iii:8; Legge, p. 124.

6.   This text is, with insignificant exceptions, the same as that given in Huai-nan-tzu (9, p. 129). Huai-nan-tzu points out that Chü Po-yü was a chancellor. Tzu-kung's discussion with Chü Po-yü is mentioned in Lun-heng 18:54, p. 778; Forke, I, p. 95.

7.   Yen has 18 (十八) p'ien instead of 58 (五十八) p'ien, but he remarks that something appears to be missing. The missing element is the character for 5 (五) which should precede 十八.

8.   Compare with fragment 90B. For a detailed account of the Classic of Filial Piety, see Chou Shou-ch'ang, Han shu chu chiao-pu 28, pp. 471-72.

9.   Li-shan appears to be a misprint for lien-shan.

10.   This sentence is quoted by Wang Ying-lin in his Han shu i-wen chih k'ao-cheng, p. 4 (p. 1390 in the anthology Erh-shih-ssu-shih pu-pien II). Wang Ying-lin remarks that neither book is listed in the bibliographies.

11.   The last sentence appears to be Wang Ying-lin's addition. I include it because it is part of Sun's text.

12.   The introductory chapter of Ching-tien shih-wen says that the arrangement of the Old Text version of the Analects differs from that of the Ch'i and Lu versions. The commentary to this statement appends this quote from the Hsin-lun. However, both Yen and Sun give another version of the fragment: "The text of the Old Text version of the Analects differs in more than 640 characters from that of the Ch'i and Lu versions."

13.   Fa was the personal name of King Wu of Chou. See Shih chi 4, pp. 15 and 19; Chavannes, MH I, pp. 221 and 224, note 4. See also J. Legge, The Shoo King V:I:I:6; p. 285.

14.   As was customary during the mourning period, King Wu continued to act as if his father, King Wen, were still alive and retained his previous title of Crown Prince. His speeches and actions are described in "Great Declaration," Chapters 27 and 28 of the Book of Documents and, according to that account, in Shih chi 4, pp. 18-23; Chavannes, MH I, pp. 222-28.

15.   Catching a fish is an auspicious omen.

16.   For the sacrifice of the burnt offering see
Po-hu t'ung 18; Tjan Tjoe Som I, p. 240 and especially
p. 332, note 319. The source is, once more, the Book
of Documents (V:III:3; Legge, p. 309) from the chapter
entitled "The Successful Completion of the War."

17.   Wang Ch'ung (Lun-heng 3:12, p. 116; Forke I,
p. 130) more specifically states that a white fish and
a red crow appeared to King Wu. This is undoubtedly a
later elaboration of the information given in the Book
of Documents and the Shih chi.

18.   Chi-tzu may be a name or refer to Viscount of
Chi.

19.   This probably refers to Chi-tzu (or the Viscount
of Chi) and Pi Kan, but cf. Chavannes, MH I, p. 206,
note 2. Both dignitaries are mentioned in the Book of
Documents IV:XI:1; Legge, p. 273.

20.   Shih chi 3, p. 32; Chavannes, MH I, p. 206.

21.   This description may reflect Chuang-tzu XXXII:
III:X:14; Legge, p. 212. It may, however, refer to the
legend in the introduction to the first chapter on
astronomy in the Hou Han shu (treatise 10, p. 3624),
which says that the heavens were so arrayed in the Gold-
en Age as a sign of total harmony. See also fragment
112B.

22.   Instead of nan 南 ("southern"), Yen has Shang
商 ("suburb").

23.   The Book of Documents (V:III:9; Legge, p. 315)
and Shih chi (3, p. 33; Chavannes I, p. 207 and note 1)
mention only the Wilderness of Mu, but Cheng Hsüan,
quoted ibid., in the Chi-chieh commentary, says that
the Wilderness of Mu is a name for Chou Hsin's "Southern Suburb" (Nan-chiao).

24.   For this terminology, see the Book of Documents,
"The Great Plan" (V:IV:6; Legge, pp. 326-27). For the
correlation of phenomena, see ibid., V:IV:34; Legge,
p. 340. Huan T'an's fragment is almost a direct quote
from the Book of Documents. It should not be taken to
represent his ideas, since the context in which he discussed it is unknown.

25.   Among the many studies of the Ming t'ang 明堂 ("Hall of Light"), the more important are: 1) Wang Kuo-wei, "Ming-t'ang miao t'ung-k'ao," translated by J. Heffer in "Ming-t'ang miao ch'in-t'ung-k'ao: Auschluss über die Halle der lichten Kraft, ming-t'ang, über den Ahnentempel miao, sowie über die Wohnpaläste (Wohngebäude) ch'in." 2) A. C. Soper, "The 'Dome of Heaven' in Asia." 3) W. E. Scothill, The Hall of Light. 4) H. Maspero, "Le Ming-t'ang et la crise religieuse avant les Han." 5) R. Goepper gives a very concise account in W. D. von Barloewen, Abriss der Geschichte aussereuropäischer Kulturen II, p. 175.

26.   Pi-yung 璧雍 ("Jade Dam"). For an explanation of this curious term, see fragment 93B.

27.   Hsing 行 is not included in TPYL 533.8b.

28.   There are various ways of writing the characters for pi-yung, as well as various etymologies of the word. Therefore, O. Franke (Geschichte des chinesischen Reiches III, p. 161) believed that the term was not of Chinese origin. M. Quistorp, "Männergesellschaft und Alterklassen im alten China," pp. 21-22, suggested that pi-yung was a home for men (Männerhaus).

29.   IWLC 38.27a has chou 周 ("to rotate a full circle"), while TPYL 534.2a gives chung 終 ("to end").

30.   Instead of chiao 郊 ("sacrifices"), in accordance with Yen and Sun, I prefer fang 倣 ("to imitate, follow the pattern of").

31.   In Han China it was believed that in times of Great Equality, there was one wind every five days and one rain every ten days. Therefore, there were seventy-two winds and thirty-six rains every year. S. Camman believes that this description of the ming-t'ang demonstrates that the whole structure "was apparently a vast space-and-time diagram, reflecting contemporary beliefs" ("Types of Symbols in Chinese Art," in A. F. Wright, ed. Studies in Chinese Thought, pp. 201 and 229, note 9).

32.   For the missing words, see fragment 94B.

33.   I.e., the Ch'un-ch'iu.

34.   The characters in the text appear to be misplaced: "The Classic of Tso bears the same relation to

the Tradition..." I follow fragment 94C, Liu Chih-chi's
version; see note 36 below. Note Huan T'an's unrestricted praise of the Tso chuan and his sharp criticism of
the Kung-yang chuan.

35.   Tso 作 , while 94A has wei 為 .

36.   The Shih t'ung text ends here. It begins, "The
Tradition of Tso and the Classic..." Liu Chih-chi then
adds his own opinion, "Tung-kuan Han chi quotes Ch'en
Yüan's memorial; 'When Kuang-wu came to power, [the
Tradition of] Tso was established. But Huan T'an and
Wei Hung slandered it, and therefore [this text] devoted to the middle way was abolished.'" For an explanation of "the middle way" (chung tao 中道),
see Pokora, "The Life," II, p. 566, note 193. The short
quote mentioned by Liu Chih-chi is found in the very
brief biography of Ch'en Yüan in Tung-kuan Han chi 16,
p. 68a. It differs radically from Huan T'an's opinion
of the Tso chuan, as revealed in the present fragment.

37.   Sun's text ends at this point. For Huan T'an's
comparison of his Hsin-lun with the Ch'un ch'iu, see
fragment 2B.

38.   Yen says that his text is based on both PTSC
95 and TPYL 68. However, TPYL 68 only includes one
quotation from Hsin-lun and that is fragment 70 on ice
(ping 冰). TPYL 68 also discusses ch'ao 潮
("tide") and ch'uan 川 ("streams"). None of these
three words is mentioned in the present fragment, so I
cannot explain Yen's mistake.

        In any case, for the sake of completeness, here
is Yen's version: "When the literati read the account
of success and failure in political affairs which is
found in the Spring and Autumn Annals, which sets forth
righteous principles, they believe that a Spring and
Autumn Annals will again be written when a new sage
appears. This is also the opinion of most learned
scholars like the Grand Historian. I think it will not
be so. Why? Later sages need not necessarily continue
the ideas of earlier sages. All that the sages and
worthies have transmitted contain, in the same degree,
the Way, virtue, benevolence and righteousness, creating
wonderful treatises and unusual texts which are all good
and well worth studying. In the same way, all people
include in their diet fish, meat, vegetables and egg-
plants, for raw and cooked meals are of different fla-
vors but they are still delicious."

102

For a similar, "liberal" espousal of the idea
of a free choice of spiritual "foods," see fragment 71.

39.   Chi Cha, who lived in the sixth century, was a
man of excellent character. He refused to reign over
Wu, although he was a twentieth-generation descendant
of its founder and his brother had become its ruler.
Instead, Chi Cha chose to leave his country and live
in the principality of Yen-ling. He is mentioned often
in the Tso chuan and in Shih chi 31 (Chavannes, MH IV,
pp. 6, 7, 11, 13, 15; V, pp. 23, 200, etc.). Huan T'an
may have been interested in Chi Cha because of his love
of music; Tso chuan, 29th year of Hsiang (Legge, pp.
545-46 and 549-51) has a long section on Chi Cha's
evaluation of various types of music. See also fragment 104, note 29.

40.   The Ku-wen yüan text originates from a text by
Li Yen, which records a discussion, probably fictional,
between Li and a guest. Yen's version of this text
has shu 書 ("book"), while the full text by Li Yen,
as reprinted by Yen, Ch'üan Hou Han wen 82.1b, has ssu
思 ("idea"), in accordance with the text of Ku-wen
yüan in the Wan-yu wen-k'u edition.

41.   The text has "Ts'ao Tsang" 曹臧   , evidently a corruption of Ts'ao Kuei 劌, who is mentioned
in Tso chuan Chuang 10. Ts'ao Kuei is Ts'ao Mo, a
courageous general of seventh century Lu. In 618 B.C.
Ts'ao Mo forced Duke Huan of Ch'i to return to Lu its
territories which had been seized in three battles;
cf. Chavannes, MH IV, p. 50 and note 2. Ts'ao Mo has
a short biography in Shih chi 86, the first of the
biographies of the "assassins;" cf. D. Bodde, Statesman, Patriot, and General in Ancient China, p. 29,
note 42.

Chapter 10.   Recognizing Intelligence

98

A   I lin 3.9b.   Yen 14.10a.   Sun 7b.

Liu Tzu-cheng, Liu Tzu-chün and Liu Po-yü, the
son of Liu Tzu-chün's elder brother,[1] were all intelligent men. They especially admired [the Tradition of]
Tso. They taught it to their sons and grandsons, and
even down to the women, all of whom read and recited
it. This, too, is error.

B   PTSC 98.7b.   TPYL 610.8a and 616.7a.   Shuo fu 59.3b.

Yen 14.10a.   Sun 15b.

The three men, Liu Tzu-cheng, Liu Tzu-chün and
Liu Po-yü, especially valued [the Tradition of] Tso.
They taught it to their sons and grandsons,[2] and even
down to the women, all of whom read and recited it.[3]

Previous translation: Forke, Geschichte der mittel-
alterlichen chinesischen Philosophie, p. 109, note 3.

99

Commentary to Wen hsüan 23.28b.   Yen 14.10a.   Sun 13b.

The Eminent Founder of the Han established a
mighty foundation; his merit equaled[4] that of T'ang and
Wu. When he fell ill he had a good physician but would
not use him. He entrusted himself exclusively to his
wife and submitted to the will of Heaven. In this he
was also mistaken. This must be called the error of
an intelligent man.

Cf. Liang Han pu-fen, p. 345.

100

TPYL 88.3b [see also notes 14 and 16 below].

Yen 14.10a-b. Sun 20a-b.

The Eminent Exemplar, the Han Emperor Wen, possessed the virtues of benevolence, knowledge and per-
spicacity. He took over [the Han Empire] when it was
newly consolidated. Personally, he was frugal and
thrifty[5] so that he might benefit and give rest to the
people, and save and aid those in difficulty and want.
He abolished corporal punishment and liberalized the
statutes and laws,[6] [he promoted] economy in funerals[7]
and burials, and reduced [the number of] royal carriages
and the expenses for official robes. This is called "to
reach the essence of nourishing the living and burying
the dead."[8]

When he was first asked [to leave] Tai,[9] he
deliberated, being full of doubt,[10] and was able to
follow the advice of Sung Ch'ang.[11] He answered the
call and came quickly. After ascending the throne, he
quieted the movements of war and practiced peace.[12] He
dispensed and spread forth great mercy. Wishing to stop
war, he established peace through marriages[13] with the
Hsiung-nu. He presided over the system,[14] and, therefore, he was later praised and exalted with the title
of "Eminent Exemplar."

But he gave himself over to private counsels[15]
and drove away his talented ministers. Nor would he
rise above his private preferences, as when he disturbed the proper order of ranking by permitting his
favorite concubine, Lady Shen, to sit with the Empress.[16]
This is an example of one who is perspicacious but still
errs.

101

PTSC 15.4a.   Yen 14.10b. Sun 19b.

A strong, great and rich.

This fragment belongs to fragment 136 which is, in
turn, related to fragment 100.

TPYL 88.10b.　IWLC 12.17b-18a.　　　　Yen 14.10b-11a.

Sun 16b-17a.

   The talent and disposition of the Han Emperor
Wu were high and excellent.　He practiced the guiding
principles of the veneration of his ancestors and the
extension of his rule.　Therefore, after ascending the
throne, he carried out his great aspirations.　He studied and combined antiquity and the present,[17] and mod-
eled himself[18] on the sages of the past.　This led him
to establish New Year's Day,[19] create regulations and
laws, and invite and select excellent and outstanding
men.[20]

   He spread forth his fierce authority, imposed
a martial spirit in all four directions, so all against
whom he marched submitted to him.[21]　He initiated the
Six Arts and encouraged Confucian studies.　The House
of Han has reached the greatest glory of all dynasties
since creation.　Therefore, he shines as the Epochal
Founder.　He was indeed a ruler of unsurpassed excellence.

   Nevertheless, the Emperor had many faults and
committed many errors.　He wished to extend the fron-
tiers and enlarge his territory, coveted profit, and
fought over useless things.　Hearing that Ta-yüan,[22]
the country of the Western barbarians, had famous
horses, he sent a great army which campaigned for
several years.　Many of its officers and men died, but
he got [only] a few dozen [horses].

   Again, when the chorus girl Wei Tzu-fu became
greatly favored and loved by the Emperor, he secretly
tried to find some misbehavior on the part of Empress
Ch'en and for this dismissed her.[23]　When Wei Tzu-fu
was established [as Empress], her son was appointed
Crown Prince.　Later, [the Emperor] gave ear to the
slanders of evil ministers, and the Empress died of
grief,[24] while the Crown Prince [Liu Chü] left [the
court] to perish in some unknown place.[25]

   [The Emperor] believed in witchcraft and black
magic.[26]　He invited and consorted with many evil men
and sought out frivolous magicians.　His construction
of palaces exhausted the storehouse and treasuries

within, and exhausted the Empire without. It is impossible to count the number of people who died and perished. This may be called an example of the errors of a perceptive man.

Cf. Liang Han pu-fen II, pp. 345-46.

103

Han shu 92, p. 5272.   Yen 14.11a.

The Han shu's collective biography of the "wandering knights" [yu-hsia 游 俠] says that one of its heroes, Chang Sung was killed by bandit soldiers after the fall of Wang Mang in 23 A.D. (p. 5272). In his commentary Yen Shih-ku points out that Li Ch'i (fl. ca. 200 A.D.) said, "[Chang] Sung knew that bandits were coming and that he ought to leave. But it happened that it was a taboo day,[27] so he did not leave. Because of this he was killed by the bandits. Huan T'an says, 'This was the error of a perceptive man.'"[28]

104

TPYL 556.1b.   Yen 14.11a.   Sun 22b.

Yang Tzu-yün, who was a Gentleman, lived in Ch'ang-an. He was always poor. When he lost his two sons recently, he mourned deeply and carried both of them back to Shu for burial there. As a result, he became impoverished and in want. Yang Tzu-yün attained the Way of the sages and understood death and life. He should, therefore, not be ranked lower than Chi Cha.[29] Nevertheless, he mourned[30] his sons and resented their death. I[31] could not restrain his [excessive] love by appealing to propriety.[32] He brought great expenses upon himself and so became impoverished.

Previous translation: Pokora, "The Life," II, p. 547. See also Archiv Orientální No. 29 (1961), p. 494, and fragment 197.

NOTES: CHAPTER 10

1.   Liu Hsiang, Liu Hsin and, probably, a son of
Liu Chi. For the latter, see fragment 86, note 34.

2.   The last eight words are found only in TPYL
616.7a and Shuo fu 59.3b. The Shuo fu quotation ends
here.

3.   TPYL 610.8a has: "...recited and treated it."

4.   Instead of hsü 徐 ("grave, dignified"), I
read mou 侔 ("to equal"), in accordance with both
Yen and Sun.

5.   For this point, see also fragment 136.

6.   Pan Ku's eulogy at the end of the "Annals of
Emperor Wen," (HFHD I, pp. 274-75), although quite en-
thusiastic about the Emperor, does not credit him with
this radical a change in the penal law: "Verdicts [of
capital punishment] were pronounced in [only] several
hundred cases, [so that he] almost succeeded in setting
aside [such] punishments."

7.   "Simplicity of Funerals" is the title of the
67th chapter of the Lun-heng.

8.   The text has sung chung 送 終 ("burying the
dead"), while Sun has sung ssu 送 死 , but these two
terms are essentially the same.

9.   Emperor Wen, at that time called Liu Heng, was
the oldest son of Emperor Kao. He was King of Tai from
196 to 180 B.C. After being selected by the most influential men, he was invited to reign over the Empires
but he refused with the usual proper reluctance before
he was finally installed. Cf. HFHD I, pp. 215-16, the
introduction to the "Annals of Emperor Wen," as translated by H. H. Dubs.

10.   Hu-i 狐 疑 ("full of doubt"), is translated
by Chavannes MH II, p. 458, as "défiant comme le renard,"
and explained in detail in note 2, ibid.

11.   The Palace Military Commander of Tai, Sung
Ch'ang, disagreed with the Chief of the Gentlemen-at-
the Palace, Chang Wu, and felt that Liu Heng should

accept the invitation to go to the court. Liu Heng
followed this advice only after a divination and other
precautionary measures. Cf. Chavannes, MH II, pp. 444-
48; HFHD I, pp. 222-26.

12.   King Wu also receives credit for this in the
Book of Documents V:III:2; Legge, pp. 308 (translation)
and 309 (explanation). Instead of the hsing 行 of
the text, Yen has hsiu 修 which corresponds to the
Book of Documents.

13.   This refers to the well-known policy of political marriages of Han princesses to Hsiung-nu chieftains.

14.   This phrase is found only in PTSC 15.1b.

15.   The text has su 俗 ("vulgar, common"), while
Yen and Sun give ssu 私 ("private, secret"). Emperor
Wen was very superstitious.

16.   The commentary to Wen hsüan 49.27b quotes Huan-
tzu, Hsin-lun: "Emperor Wen's Lady Shen disturbed the
proper order of ranking by sitting with the Empress."
Sun 14b. See Watson, Records I, pp. 521-22. It is
surprising that Huan T'an's opinion of Emperor Wen coin-
cides with that of H. H. Dubs (HFHD I, pp. 214-19).

17.   This phrase is quoted in PTSC 12.1b-2a.

18.   Instead of mo-fan 模範 ("to model oneself
on"), TPYL 88.10a has huo 獲 ("to obtain"). In that
case the translation would be: "He obtained precedents
from the sages of the past."

19.   This probably refers to the introduction of
the new T'ai-ch'u calendar, by Ssu-ma Ch'ien, among
others. It did not follow the earlier practice of
rotating the beginning of the year, so the year regu-
larly began in the first month. Cf. B. Watson, Ssu-ma
Ch'ien, pp. 209-10, note 60.

20.   Huan T'an appears to refer to the Emperor's
adoption of Tung Chung-shu's proposals for the recruit-
ment of talented young men.

21.   Part of this sentence is quoted in PTSC 13.5a.

22.   Ferghana.

23.   This sentence is found only in TPYL 88.10b.

24.   Han shu says the Empress committed suicide on
September 9, 91 B.C.; HFHD II, p. 114.

25.   This refers to the famous and tragic affair in
August 91 B.C. and at the end of 93 B.C., when Wei Tzu-
fu's son, Crown Prince Liu Chü, was charged with witchcraft and black magic. He had attempted a rebellion
which was quickly suppressed, but during which several
tens of thousands of people were killed.

26.   Cf. J. J. M. de Groot, The Religious System of
China V, pp. 826-44; H. Y. Feng and J. K. Shryock, "The
Black Magic in China Known as Ku." This form of black
magic, ku 蠱 , involved the use of a love potion to
punish a faithless lover. It is ironic that the dis-
missal of Empress Ch'en in 130 B.C. to make way for Wei
Tzu-fu was very similar. The only differences were
that it was the Empress's daughter Ch'u-fu who perished
on that occasion and that the heads of all the persons
involved were impaled in the market place; cf. HFHD II,
p. 41. The original meaning of the character ku was
"hallucination;" cf. R. F. Bridgman, "La médecine dans
la Chine antique," pp. 172-73. See also Hulsewé, Remnants I, p. 33, sub k. For the importance of black
magic in Chinese law generally, and ku sorcery in particular, see the detailed account by T'ung-tsu Ch'ü,
Law and Society, pp. 222-25.

27.   The day fan-chih 反支 . A similar story
told in Wang Fu's Ch'ien-fu lun, chapter "Ai-jih" 愛日 ,
as quoted in his biography in Hou Han shu 40, p. 1766.
This has a long commentary by Li Hsien, who refers to
the books on yin and yang. This was a taboo of the common people, not an official taboo.

28.   Li Ch'i's information is reliable, since both
Chang Sung and Huan T'an belonged to a certain group
of men associated with the Old Text school. Cf. Pokora,
"The Life," II, p. 522, note 6 and p. 570; see also
fragments 84A, note 24 and 94C, note 36. Ts'ao P'i
(see fragment 79, note 5) thought highly of Chang Sung
and criticized Ch'en Tsun. A fragment of his Tien-lun,
quoted in I lin 5.4b, says, "I-wu [i.e., Kuang Chung]
was extravagant, while Pao shu-[Ya] was modest--their
will was not the same. Chang Sung was pure, while
Ch'en Tsun was filthy--their behavior was not alike."
This statement is not included in Ts'ao P'i's "Tien-
lun lun-wen" in Wen hsüan 52.

29.　　　For Chi Cha, see also fragment 96, note 39. In the present fragment Huan T'an refers to the extravagant care given to the burial of Chi Cha's eldest son in 515 B.C. Huan T'an was extremely critical of Chi Cha's belief that the bones of his son should be in the earth while his spirit moved around freely. Cf. Li chi II:II: III:13; Legge I, pp. 192-93, especially note 2 on p. 192.

30.　　　TPYL has lien 戀 ; both Yen and Sun have mu 慕 .

31.　　　The text has yü 予 ("I"), while both Yen and Sun give tzu 子 ("you"), which would totally change the meaning of the sentence.

32.　　　The last four characters i i ko en 以義割恩 ("restrain his [excessive] love by appealing to propriety") are also used in Hou Han shu 29, p. 1065; for Pan Ku's use of Huan T'an's terminology, see Pokora, "The Life," II, p. 547, note 77.

Chapter 11.   Encountering Affairs

105

I lin 3.9b-10a.   Yen 15.1a.   Sun 5a.

      If a net is raised by drawing the rope, all
its eyes spread open; if a fur coat is shaken out and
held at the collar, then its ten-thousand hairs arrange
themselves. The government of a great country should
be like this.1

106

A   TPYL 402.8b.   Yen 15.1a.   Sun 8a, 21a.

      To replace a worthy man with a worthy man is
called obedience [to the right]. To replace a worthless
man with a worthless man is called disorder.

B   I lin 3.10a reproduces this fragment, but it has
graphical variations in two characters: instead of
tai 代 ("to replace") it has fa 伐 ("to chastise"),
and instead of shun 順 ("obedience"), it has fan 煩
("trouble"). With these changes the translation would
read: "To chastise a worthy man with a worthy man is
called trouble..."

107

Yen Shih-ku's commentary to Han shu 29, p. 3083.

                                   Yen 15.1a.   Sun 11b.

      The style name of Kuan Ping2 was Tzu-yang.3   He
was talented, wise, perceptive and penetrating.

Previous translation: Pokora, "The Life," I, p. 48,
note 2.

108

A <u>TPYL</u> 61.3a-b. Wu Shu, <u>Shih-lei fu</u> 6.11a.

Yen 15.1a-b. Sun 20a.

The Commander-in-Chief Chang Chung[4] discussed [the problem] and said, "The waters of the Yellow River are muddy, and one picul (<u>shih</u>) of water contains six <u>tou</u> of mud, but people fight to open[5] the banks of the River to irrigate their fields, causing[6] the obstruction of its course. Then, in the third month, when the peach trees begin to flower[7] the waters come and burst their banks since the flow is blocked. People[8] should be prohibited from diverting the River."[9]

B Yen Shih-ku's commentary to <u>Han shu</u> 29, p. 308,

quoting <u>Tsa-lun</u>.[10]   Yen 15.1a. Sun 12a.

[Chang Jung's] style name was Chung-kung.[11] He studied the problems of irrigation.[12]

Previous translation: Pokora, "The Life," I, p. 49, notes 8 and 11.

109

Yen Shih-ku's commentary to <u>Han shu</u> 29, p. 3084.

Yen 15.1b. Sun 11b.

[Han Mu's] style name was Tzu-t'ai. He understood the problems of water control.

Previous translation: Pokora, "The Life," I, p. 50, note 12.

110

<u>I lin</u> 3.10a.   Yen 15.1b. Sun 8a.

Wang P'ing-chung[13] said, "The <u>Chou Genealogy</u>[14] says, 'In the fifth year of King Ting[15] the Yellow River

shifted from its former course.'[16] The present [bed]
in which it flows swiftly[17] is not [the bed] which Yü
excavated."[18]

Previous translation: Pokora, "The Life," I, p. 50 and
note 17.

111

A Shui-ching chu 1, 1, p. 2.   Yen 15.1b-2a.   Sun 11b.

Of the sources of the Four Rivers,[19] [the source]
of the Yellow River is the highest, and [that river] is
longest. It flows down from on high. The flow tumbles
down steep [mountains] and, therefore, is swift.

B IWLC 9.2a.   Yen 15.1b-2a.   Sun 11b.
                                              (commentary)

Of the sources of the Four Rivers, [the source
of the Yellow River] is the highest, and [that river]
is the longest. It flows down from on high. The flow
is turbulent and, therefore, brings calamities and suffering to the lowlands.[20]

Previous translation: Pokora, "The Life," I, p. 52,
note 23.

112

A Ch'u-hsüeh chi 4.22a.   Han 0, Sui hua chi-lu 4.5a.

                           Yen 15.2a.   Sun 18a.

Specialists in the calendar and mathematics use
the following method of calculation: They investigate
and test the beginning from Heaven's beginning[21] in the
remote past up to the eleventh month, the chia-tzu day
at midnight on the first day of the new moon at winter
solstice.

B <u>Ch'u-hsüeh chi</u> 4.22a.   Yen 15.2a.   Sun 15b.

     The sun: from Heaven's beginning up to the
eleventh month, the first day of the new moon at early
dawn in winter solstice, when the sun and the moon are
like strung jade.22

                         113

A <u>Ch'u-hsüeh chi</u> 25.2b.23   Yen 15.2a.   Sun 16a.

     When I was a Gentleman I was in charge of the
water clock.24 Dryness and humidity, cold and warmth
are [reflected] by changing different degrees. [I had
to adjust them] at dusk and dawn, by day and by night,
comparing them to the shadow of the sun.25

B <u>TPYL</u> 2.12b.   Yen 15.2a.   Sun 16a.
                                                     (commentary)

     [In using] the water clock, dryness and humidi-
ty, cold and warmth are [reflected] by different degrees. I had to compare them by day with the shadow
of the sun and by night with the mansions of the stars.
Then I could adjust them.

Previous translation (of the fragment as given by Yen):
J. Needham, <u>Science and Civilization in China</u>, Vol. III,
pp. 321-22.

                         114

A <u>TPYL</u> 2.11a-b.   Yen 15.2a.   Sun 19b.

     Yang Tzu-yün26 loved astronomy. He questioned
an old artisan who had helped make an armillary sphere
at the Yellow Gate.27 He28 said, "When I was young I
could do such work [just] by following the specifications in feet and inches, but I could not really understand their meaning. Gradually I came to understand
more and more. Now I am seventy, and I feel that I am
just now beginning to know it. But I am old and will
die soon. Now, I have a son who also likes to learn
how to make [these instruments]. He, too, must repeat
my years of [experience]; only then will he understand

and know the instruments. But he will also have to repeat [my experience] of death!" How sad and how funny were his words!

B PTSC 130.12a.   Sun 19b. (commentary)

Yang Tzu-yün loved astronomy. He questioned an old artisan who attended an armillary sphere at the Yellow Gate about it. Hung[29] said, "When I was young I made such things but I could not really understand their meaning. Now I am seventy, and I feel that I am just beginning to know it. But, I am old and will die soon."

Previous translations: J. Needham, Wang Ling, and D. J. Price, Heavenly Clockwork: The Great Astronomical Clocks of Medieval China - A Missing Link in Horological History, p. 129; J. Needham, Science and Civilization in China, Vol. III, p. 358; partial translation by T. Pokora, in a review of Heavenly Clockwork; "The Life," II, pp. 548-50.

115

A Chin shu 11.4a.[30]   Yen 15.2a-b.

[Huan Chün-shan said,] "At the spring equinox the sun rises from the point where the Prime Vertical begins and sets at the point where the Prime Vertical ends. This is the Prime Vertical of the human observer, not that of Heaven. The Prime Vertical of Heaven always passes through the Pole Star, which is in the center of the heavens. When we look at it, the Pole Star appears in the north above the observer.[31] Moreover, at the spring and autumn equinoxes the sun rises and sets south of the Pole Star. If Heaven turns like a millstone towards the right, then, since the northern path is farther and the southern path nearer,[32] the number of quarter-hours for the day and for the night on the water clock would not be equal."

Later, at the time of making reports to the throne, he sat in the western gallery [with Yang Hsiung][33] waiting for information. Feeling cold, he turned his back to the sun, but after a time the sunlight left the gallery, and he could no longer sun his back. [Huan] Chün-shan then said to an adherent of the k'ai-t'ien theory,[34] "If Heaven turns like a millstone towards the right, the sun's light should shine under this gallery when it moves towards the west. Instead of leaving the gallery, it should shift slightly towards the east. As it does in fact leave the gallery, [its movement] accords with the hun-t'ien theory."[35]

Previous translation: Ho Peng Yoke, The Astronomical Chapters of the Chin shu, pp. 56-57.

B TPYL 2.6b-7a. Shih-lei fu 6.1b.

Yen 15.2a-b. Sun 18b-19a.

The brilliant Yang Tzu-yün followed the literati's theory of Heaven, believing that Heaven, like an umbrella, rotated constantly towards the left, while the sun, moon, stars and planets accordingly moved from east to west.[36] So he drew diagrams of these bodies and of the degrees of movement relating them to the four seasons and the calendar, to darkness and light, and to day and night. He wished to set up principles for people and to bequeath the law to later generations.

I argued with him, saying, "At the spring and autumn [equinoxes] day and night must be equal. At dawn the sun rises from the point where the Prime Vertical begins, just in the east, and in the evening it sets at the point where the Prime Vertical ends, just in the west. Now, if the people of the Empire observe and watch it, then this is the Prime Vertical of the human observer, not that of Heaven. The north star must be the Prime Vertical of Heaven; this star is the pivot of Heaven.[37] This pivot is Heaven's axle, just as the umbrella has an axle.[38] The cover of the umbrella may revolve but the axle does not move. Likewise, Heaven also revolves, while the Pole Star is permanently fixed, as we know, in the center of Heaven. When we look up at it, the Pole Star appears in the north and not immediately above man. At the spring and autumn equinoxes the sun rises and sets south of the Pole Star. If the cover revolves, then the northern path is near and the southern path is far. How could the recorded number of days and nights be equal?" Yang Tzu-yün could offer no explanation.

Later, at the time of making reports to the
throne, I was sitting with Yang Tzu-yün in the gallery
of the White Tiger Hall. Feeling cold, I turned my
back to the sun,[39] but after a time the sunlight left,
and I could no longer sun my back. I used this to
demonstrate [my point] to Yang Tzu-yün: "If Heaven
revolves like a cover and the sun moves towards the
west, the sun's light should shine under this gallery
and shift slightly towards the east. Does not the contrary occur, in accordance with the hun-t'ien theory?"

Yang Tzu-yün immediately destroyed his work,
and so the literati's belief that Heaven revolves towards the left is erroneous.

116

Introduction to Seng-yu's "Shih chieh chi" [世 界 記],

"Shih chieh chi mu-lu hsü" 5, in Ch'u san-tsang

chi chi 12, p. 73.

Yen 15.2b. See also

Yen, Chüan Liang wen

72.11a.

In his responses to questions Huan T'an used
the metaphor of the five viscera.[40]

117

TPYL 536.11a. Ch'u-hsüeh chi 13.17a.

Yen 15.2b. Sun 18a.

It is said[41] that on[42] T'ai-shan there are al-
together over 1800 places with engraved stones, but
only 72[43] of them are recognizable.

118

Liu Yao, Liang shu 50.9b. Liu Chih-chi, Shih t'ung

3.1a. Yen 15.2b.

In his "Chronological Table of the Three Dynasties,"[44] the Grand Historian[45] [wrote] on horizontal and vertical lines and imitated the Chou Genealogy.[46]

Previous translation: T. Pokora, "The Life," I, p. 50, note 17; see also Pokora, "The First Interpolation in the Shih chi," p. 313.

119

Commentary to Wen hsüan 18.6b and 40.19b.

Yen 15.2b. Sun 13b.

The three rulers of the Han set up musicians and singers[47] at the Yellow Gates in the Inner [Palace].

120

PTSC 55.5b.   Yen 15.3a. Sun 15a.

Under Emperor Hsiao-ch'eng I was Prefect of the Bureau of Music. In all, I supervised[48] and registered over one thousand actors, jugglers, acrobats and musicians.[49]

Previous translations: Pokora, "The Life," I, p. 41 and note 19. J. P. Diény, Aux origines de la poésie classique en Chine, p. 87.

121

Commentary to Wen hsüan 46.17b.   Yen 15.3a. Sun 14b.

The genius of the sages and worthies does not show itself in this age,[50] and their marvelous and excellent skills are not passed on.

122

TPYL 565.5b.   Yen 15.3a. Sun 23a.

Yang Tzu-yün was a man of great talent, but he did not understand musical tones.[51] I grew detached

from the court music[52] and came to prefer modern tunes.[53]
Tzu-yün said, "It is very easy to be pleased[54] by shallow
things, but the profound can be understood[55] only with
difficulty. It is fitting that you do not like the
court odes and delight in the tunes of Cheng."

Previous translation: Pokora, "The Life," II, p. 544.

123

Commentary to Wen hsüan 52.9b.   Yen 15.3a.   Sun 15a.

The human heart understands of itself that a
father cannot sacrifice his son and an elder brother
cannot teach his younger brother.

124

TPYL 701.3b-4a. PTSC 132.10b.   Yen 15.3a.   Sun 4a.

Each of the five sounds follows its own direction: spring corresponds with chüeh, summer with chih,
autumn with shang, and winter with yü; kung stays in
the center, uniting the four seasons of the year. The[56]
five tones are incomplete without kung. This can be
illustrated by a flowery, five-colored screen in a hall-
way. If we look at it from a distance, then each color
--green, red, white, yellow and black[57]--is distinct,
but if we examine it closely, they all have a yellow
base adorned by the four other colors.[58] If you want
the music of the four seasons and the five elements,
then all music should have the kung sound as base with
the four other sounds [chüeh, chih, shang, and yü]
adorning it.

125

TPYL 215.9a.   Yen 15.3a.   Sun 20b.

When I was seventeen years old,[59] I became a
Gentleman of Imperial Carriages,[60] guarding the Palace's
Western Gate at the Small Park.[61]

126

A   Liu Chao's commentary to <u>Hou Han shu</u> 9 (Treatise

29A), pp. 4246-47.   Yen 15.3a-b.   Sun 9b.

          Huan T'an said to Yang Hsiung,[62] "Sir,[63] when
you were a Gentleman at the Yellow Gate, you lived in
the palace and often saw the Emperor's carriage deco-
rated with mortices of precious stone, sunshades with
pictures of flowers and fungi, and three canopies with
pictures of male and female phoenixes.[64] Everything
was painted with the two colors of Heaven and earth,[65]
as well as with the five colors. Its decoration was
of gold and precious stones, kingfisher's feathers,
cords of pearls, and embroidered and ornamented cushions."

B   Commentary to <u>Wen hsüan</u> 16.26b.   Yen 15.3a-b.   Sun 13a.

          I said to Master Yang, "You have often seen
carriages with embroidered and ornamented cushions."

There are six other short versions of this fragment
with minor and unimportant variations: <u>PTSC</u> 141.9a;
Li Hsien's commentary to <u>Hou Han shu</u> 40A ("The Biography of Pan Ku"), p. 1436; and commentaries to <u>Wen
hsüan</u> 1.23a, 1.13b, 22.23b, and 57.33a.

127

<u>PTSC</u> 141.9a.   Yen 15.3b.

          Although I have not seen any ancient carriages
of state,[66] I have frequently heard my teacher say that
they were only simple carriages with rush mats.

128

<u>TPYL</u> 829.10a.[67]   Yen 15.3b.   Sun 25a.

          Fu Hsi invented the mortar and pestle, which
have helped vast numbers of people. Later, others
worked energetically to increase its effectiveness by
using the weight of the body to tread on the tilt-

hammer. The effectiveness of this device was ten times that of the simple mortar and pestle. Still later, mechanisms were installed so that donkeys, mules, oxen, and horses, as well as water power could be used for pounding.[68] Its effectiveness then increased as much as a hundred times.[69]

Previous translations: E-tu Zen Sun and J. deFrancis, Chinese Social History: Translations of Selected Studies, p. 114: Yang Lien-sheng, Study of Great Families of Eastern Han; J. Needham, Science and Civilization in China IV, p. 392.

129

Liu Chao's commentary to Hou Han shu 15 (Treatise 5),

p. 3525.   Yen 15.3b.   Sun 9a.

Liu Hsin's instrument for bringing rain was an earthen dragon which blew a pitch-pipe. All of the many magicians were prepared to arrange it. Huan T'an asked why he made an earthen dragon for the purpose of seeking rain.[70] His answer was, "When the dragon appears, then wind and rain arise to meet and escort him. Therefore, copying the appearance of its kind, I created the earthen dragon."

130

Lun-heng 16:47, p. 693.   Yen 15.3b.

[Huan Chün-shan] also took exception [with Liu Hsin] on the ground that amber and a loadstone could not raise straws or attract needles[71] unless they were genuine. [Liu] Tzu-chün was at his wits' ends and had nothing to say in reply.

Previous translation: Forke, Lun-heng II, p. 356.

131

A Liu Chao's commentary to Hou Han shu 29 (Treatise

19), p. 3833.   Yen 15.3b.   Sun 9a.

122

T'ai lies in the prefecture of Ch'i.[72] There
the people meet on a fixed day to buy and sell at a
night market. If this event does not take place, then
disasters and misfortunes occur.

B TPYL 827.8b.   Yen 15.3b.

In the communes and circuits of Pin is the
prefecture of Ch'i in Fu-feng, it is said that [Pin]
originally was the home base of the Great King.[73]
There the people meet on a certain day to buy and sell
at a night market. If this event does not take place,
they are ashamed.

There are two other shorter versions in TPYL 191.7a
and Ch'u-hsüeh chi 24.27b. They differ only slightly
in their descriptions of the resulting calamities.

132

IWLC 3.25b.[74] TPYL 27.5b.   Yen 15.4a.   Sun 16a.[75]

During the height of winter, the people of
the T'ai-yüan commandery do not eat hot food for five
days.[76] Even in cases of disease and emergency, they
dare not violate this rule because of Chieh Tzu-t'ui.[77]

133

TPYL 13.8a.   Yen 15.4a.   Sun 19b.

In the Empire there are cranes which are eaten
in all the commanderies and kingdoms. Only in the Three
Capital Districts does no one dare catch them because
of the custom that an outbreak of thunder will occur
if a crane is caught. Could it be that Heaven originally favored only this bird? [No], the killing of the
bird merely coincided with thunder.

See Liang Han pu-fen II, p. 345. A very similar fragment is found in TPYL 925.8a, quoting Huan T'an's
Hsin-yü.

134

Tao-shih, Fa-yüan chu-lin 7.16a-b.

Yen 15.4a-b. Sun 18b.

During my youth I heard this story told in the gates of the quarters and villages:[78] "When Confucius was travelling in the East, he saw two small children arguing and asked them why. The first child said, 'I believe that when the sun first rises it is near, while at noon, it is far.' The other child thought that the sun is far when it first rises and near at noon."[79]

The Colonel of the Ch'ang River Encampments, Kuan Tzu-yang,[80] believed that the sun[81] above was far from people, while the four sides of the world were near.

The stars, when they rise at dusk in the east, are very far apart, and they are separated by more than one chang. But if one looks up at them at midnight, they are much more numerous, separated by only one or two ch'ih.[82]

The sun is the yang of Heaven, while fire is the yang of earth. When the yang of earth rises, the yang of Heaven falls. Now, if a fire is made on the earth and its temperature is observed from the side and from above, then from very different distances, the heat differs by half. If the sun is exactly at midday, we are exposed to the attack[83] of Heaven's yang, and therefore it is hot. Also, when the sun first rises, it comes from the Great Yin, and therefore it is still cold.[84] When the sun sets in the west on the tops of mulberry trees and elms,[85] although the amount [of its heat may be] the same, the air [of the evening] is not the same as the air of the clear dawn.

Sui Shu 19.3a[86] (Yen 15.4a-b) is very similar, with slight differences, such as: 1) The first paragraph is omitted; 2) "How can one know if it is true?" is added to the end of the second paragraph; 3) The third paragraph ends with, "If we look at them with a measure, it is even clearer. Therefore, we know that Heaven above is more distant than the sides of the world;" and 4) A final paragraph is added which says, "Huan Chün-shan said, 'How could the words of Kuan Tzu-yang be correct?'"

135

A **TPYL** 464.5a.   Yen 15.4b.   Sun 21b.

   Kung-sun Lung was a dialectician who lived at
the time of the Six Kingdoms. He wrote a treatise on
"Hard and White" and, to illustrate his theory, said
that a white horse is not a horse. To show that a
white horse is not a horse he said that "white" is that
by which one names the color and "horse" that by which
one names the form. The color is not the form, and the
form is not the color.[87]

Previous translation: A. C. Graham, "The Composition
of the **Gongsuen Longtzyy**," p. 175, and"Two Dialogues
in the **Kung-sun Lung-tzu**: "White Horse" and 'Left and
Right'," p. 132. The two translations differ somewhat.

B **Po K'ung liu t'ieh** 9.9a.   Yen 15.4b.   Sun 16b.

   Kung-sun Lung often argued thus: "A white
horse is not a horse." People could not agree with
this. Later, when riding a white horse, he wished to
pass through the frontier pass without a warrant or a
passport.[88] But the frontier official would not accept his explanations, for it is hard for empty words
to defeat reality.[89]

136

A **TPYL** 35.2b.   Yen 15.4b.   Sun 19b.

   Everyone now says that the Han Emperor Wen led
the Empire with his personal example of frugality and
economy[90] and his cultivation of the Way and its Power.
Accordingly, the Empire was morally transformed,[91] becoming strong, great and rich.[92] The grace of the Emperor reached down to the common folk, so that even a
shih of grain came to cost only several dozen cash.[93]
There was abundance and surplus both above and below.

B **PTSC** 156.9b.[94]   Yen 15.4b.   Sun 19b.[95]

   Everyone now says that the Han Emperor Wen was
personally frugal and thrifty. Accordingly, the Empire

was transformed, becoming strong, great and rich. Even
a _shih_ of grain came to cost only several cash.

C _TPYL_ 837.7a.   Yen 15.4b. Sun 19b.

Everyone says that the grace of the Han Emper-
or Wen reached down to the common folk, so that even
a _shih_ of grain came to cost only several cash.[96]

137

A The _So-yin_ commentary to _Shih chi_ 12, p. 15.[97]

Yen 15.4b. Sun 11a.

[Huan T'an's _Hsin-lun_] suggests that the Grand
Historian composed his book and when it was completed,
showed it to [Tung-fang] Shuo. [Tung-fang] Shuo undertook
to revise it; therefore, the inscription of "The Grand
Historian" was added at the end of each chapter by
[Tung-fang] Shuo.

B The _So-yin_ commentary to _Shih chi_ 130, p. 63.

Yen 15.4b. Sun 11a.

Huan T'an says that when Ssu-ma Ch'ien completed the book which he had written, he showed it to
Tung-fang Shuo. Shuo added "The Grand Historian" to
all the chapters.

Previous translation: T. Pokora, "The First Interpolation in the _Shih chi_," pp. 311-12, and note 9.

138

TPYL 805.5b.   Yen 15.5a. Sun 24b.

Chi Yu-pin of Lo-yang had a small jade letter.
The Internuncio of the Guards, Shih Tzu-po,[98] loved
things made of jade. Having seen the jade, he marveled
at it and sent me to tell Chi Yu-pin that he wanted to
buy it for thirty-thousand cash. Chi Yu-pin said, "I
have passed it around among those who like and understand such things, and it has already brought an offer

of one-hundred-thousand cash, not a mere thirty thousand." Amazed, I said, "If I were to see it on the
street, I would not guess that it could be offered on
the market for even one thousand. Therefore, it follows
that there is a very great distance between knowledge
and ignorance!"

NOTES: CHAPTER 11

1.   Part of this text is quoted in TPYL 694.6a,
but not in Sun or Yen.

2.   For Kuan Ping, see also fragment 134.

3.   Instead of "Tzu-yang," Sun gives "Tzu-ch'ang"
子 場 , which is clearly erroneous. Yang may be
written in two ways (揚 or 陽), as in the surname
of Yang Hsiung.

4.   See 108B, note 11 below.

5.   Instead of chüeh 決 ("to burst, open"), Yen
has yin 引 ("to lead").

6.   TPYL 61.3a has chin 今 ("now"), while Shih-lei
fu has ling 令 ("to cause").

7.   Li chi IV:I:II:4 (the section on the second
month of spring in the Yüeh-ling chapter): "Rain begins to fall. The peach tree begins to blossom..."
(Legge I, p. 258). See also Yen Shih-ku's commentary
to Han shu 29, p. 3075.

8.   Shih-lei fu 6.11a adds, "From now on..."

9.   Shui-ching chu 1, p. 3, quoting [Yang Ch'üan's]
Wu-li lun, reproduces fragment 108A with some minor
variations but fails to indicate its source. The quotation from Wu-li lun ends with a short sentence stating
that the name of the Yellow River is derived from the
mud in its waters.

10.   Instead of Tsa-lun 雜 論 , the Chung-hua
shu-chü edition of Han shu (in the collection Ssu shih,
p. 865.3) has Hsin-lun. Tsa-lun is clearly a misprint
for Hsin-lun, since Yen Shih-ku not only fails to identify the author of Tsa-lun, but also frequently refers
to the information from Huan T'an's Hsin-lun which is
found in chapter 29 of Han shu (on drains and ditches).
See fragment 208.

11.   Chang Jung was, according to Han shu 29 (p.
3083) an Officer of the Commander-in-Chief. Fragment
108A says that he was himself the Commander-in-Chief
and gives his name as Chang Chung 張 仲 . Since

fragment 108B gives his style name as Chung-kung 中功 ,
108A's "Chang Chung" may be the same name with the
second character missing. Chou Shou-ch'ang, in his
Han shu chiao-pu 27, p. 456, says that two characters,
shih 士 ("officer") and kung 功 (a part of the style
name), are missing, but he is still not certain that
the two texts refer to the same man.

12.   The text of Han shu, undoubtedly based on the
Hsin-lun, is more detailed and somewhat different:
"An Officer of the Commander-in-Chief, Chang Jung of
Ch'ang-an, said, 'The nature of water is to flow down-
hill. If its motion is quick, it scrapes, empties and
slightly hollows [the river bed]. The waters of the
Yellow River are heavy and muddy; it is said that one
picul (shih) of water contains six tou of mud. Now,
in all the western commanderies up to the capital and
beyond to the east, people always divert the water of
the Yellow River, the Wei River and the mountain streams
to irrigate their fields. During spring and summer
drought there is a period of little water. Therefore,
[the people] slow the flow and store up the river
[water], and silt it to make it rather shallow. If
there is a great rain so the water rushes in, it over-
flows and bursts [the dikes]. But there are several
state dikes blocking [the water]. The dikes are slightly higher than the [adjacent] plain, and, holding up
the water, they resemble erected walls. But if everything would be left to follow its nature so [the water]
is no longer used for irrigation, then all the streams
would flow, and there would be no calamities caused by
the overflowing or breaking of [the dikes].'"

13.   Yen Shih-ku says that P'ing-chung was the style
name of Wang Heng, who was a Division Head of the Grand
Ministry of Works, according to Pan Ku (Han shu 29,
p. 3084).

14.   See fragment 118, note 46.

15.   602 B.C.

16.   With the exception of the introductory words,
"Wang P'ing-chung said," this fragment is quoted in
Han shu 29, p. 3084: "The Chou Genealogy says, 'In
the fifth year of King Ting the Yellow River shifted.'
Therefore, the present [bed] in which it flows is not
[the bed] which Yü excavated." Its source is not
given. The words "course" (ku tao 故道) are not

found in <u>Han shu</u>, but <u>Shui-ching chu</u> 5.1, p. 87, says
that Pan Ku uses the term <u>ku tu</u> 故 瀆 ("former river").

17.　　"Swiftly" is not found in <u>Han shu</u>. Instead,
both Yen and Sun give <u>ch'u</u> 處 ("place"): "...The
present place in which it flows is..." I prefer this
version.

18.　　Yü, the legendary founder of the Hsia dynasty,
is said to have controlled the great floods which were
plaguing the Empire by marvelous feats of engineering,
including the cutting of river gorges through mountains.
Wang Heng's remarks, as quoted in <u>Han shu</u> 29, pp. 3084-
85, are much longer; for a translation, see "The Life"
I, pp. 50-51.

19.　　The Four Rivers are the Yangtze River, the
Yellow River, the Huai River, and the Chi River. They
are mentioned in Pan Ku's eulogy to <u>Han shu</u> 29, p. 3085;
cf. "The Life," I, p. 52.

20.　　Yen, as usual, combines both versions.

21.　　<u>T'ien-yuan</u> 天 元 ("Heaven's beginning"). Chavannes, <u>MH</u> III, p. 322, translates: "...l'origin [qui
vient] du Ciel fondamental..." See also note 5, <u>ibid</u>.
on the reforms of the calendar.

22.　　These two different quotations, given separately
in <u>Ch'u-hsüeh chi</u> (and by Sun), are combined by Yen.
For the poetic metaphor at the end, see fragment 91,
note 21. For calendrical computations in the Han period, see note 9 to fragment 163A.

23.　　The text in <u>PTSC</u> 130.12a is similar but somewhat corrupt.

24.　　For a reform of the water clock in which Huan
T'an may have been involved, see <u>HFHD</u> III, p. 30.

25.　　See fragment 197.

26.　　Yang Hsiung.

27.　　The text (and Yen) has: "Wen chih yü huang-men
tso hun-t'ien lao-kung," but Sun has: "Wen chih yü
Lo-hsia Huang Hung i hun-t'ien chih shuo. Hung yeh..."
Lo-hsia Hung is a famous second century B.C. astronomer.
This text is explained in detail in "The Life," II,
pp. 548-49, note 84. Sun's text should be disregarded.
See also note 29 below.

28.   This may refer to either Yang Hsiung or the old artisan. J. Needham, Wang Ling and D. J. Price, in Heavenly Clockwork, p. 129, believe that it is the artisan who is speaking. In my review of this book, pp. 493-94, I argue that the speaker is Yang Hsiung. The last words of the fragment support my position, for they seem to be Huan T'an's criticism of Yang Hsiung's attitude towards death. See also fragment 104.

29.   "Hung" may be the name of the artisan, or, more probably, it may mean "[the old artisan at the armillary sphere which was made according to the specifications of Lo-hsia] Hung." This may seem to be a great elaboration on the simple word "Hung," but the paragraph in PTSC which quotes Huan T'an is entitled "Lo-hsia Hung's armillary sphere." On the other hand, this heading may explain Sun's emendation (see note 27 above). For Lo-hsia Hung, see also J. Needham, Science and Civilization in China, Volume III, p. 358, note d.

30.   Chin shu appears to quote Ko Hung, who bases his information on Huan T'an.

31.   The explanation in fragment 115B is exactly the opposite.

32.   Again, fragment 115B is exactly the opposite.

33.   For this emendation, see fragment 115B.

34.   Yang Hsiung.

35.   Huan T'an, unlike Yang Hsiung, was an adherent of the hun-t'ien theory. For an explanation, see J. Needham, Science and Civilization in China, Vol. III, pp. 216-19, especially p. 219, which discusses the present fragment. By the end of the Han the hun-t'ien theory was already generally accepted.

36.   The second half of this sentence is found in Ch'u-hsüeh chi 1.2b.

37.   T'ien shu 天 樞 ("the pivot of Heaven"), i.e., the North Star.

38.   Huan T'an's main arguments are reproduced by Wang Ch'ung without acknowledgment in Lun-heng 11, 32, pp. 491-92; Forke I, p. 260.

39.   This sentence, somewhat shortened, is found in the commentary to Wen hsüan 26.7a.

40.   The term tsang 藏 ("viscera") is relatively recent. It appears for the first time in Chou li and is used in the phrase wu tsang 五 藏 ("five viscera"), in Chapter 105 of the Shih chi. For an analysis of the character, see Bridgman, La médecine, pp. 155-56. Huan T'an's interest in anatomy was surely aroused by the first known official dissection, ordered by Wang Mang in 16 A.D. and mentioned by Huan T'an in fragment 38B. Cf. HFHD III, p. 365 and note 30.5. The text of Han shu 99B has also been studied by H. Maspero in "Les procédés de 'nourrir le principe vital' dans la réligion taoïste ancienne," pp. 187-88. The term wu tsang is also used figuratively as a symbol of the mind; cf. Ti-wu Lun's memorial in Hou Han shu 41, p. 1483.

41.   Only given in Ch'u-hsüeh chi 13.17a.

42.   Only given in TPYL 536.11a.

43.   The number 72 clearly refers more to numerology than to reality. Since the second century B.C., the mountain T'ai shan and the number 72 have been connected with the feng sacrifices. At that time it was believed that the feng sacrifice had previously been performed at that site by 72 rulers. See, e.g., Ssu-ma Hsiang-ju's treatise on the feng and shan sacrifices in Shih chi 117, translated by Watson, Records II, pp. 336-39; Yang Hsiung's discussion in Han shu 87A, p. 5089; and the opinions attributed to Kuan Chung, probably those of Kuan-tzu, quoted in Han shu 25A, p. 2083. Huan T'an may have discussed this problem with Yang Hsiung, although we have no definite evidence.

The figure of "over 1800 places with engraved stones" is more puzzling. Chou Shou-ch'ang took up the problem in more detail in his Han shu chu chiao-pu 18, pp. 261-62. He quotes several texts, including Chuang-tzu: "When the surname [of the ruler] is changed [i-hsing 易 姓], [someone else] becomes king. [On this occasion] those who performed the feng sacrifice on T'ai shan and the shan sacrifice on Liang-fu numbered 72. There are indications of this in the existence of over 1800 places with carved reliefs and engraved stones."

Chuang Tzu's text, as it is quoted here, agrees, on the whole, with Huan T'an's. Unfortunately, there is nothing like this in the present text of <u>Chuang-tzu</u>, and the terminology of <u>i-hsing</u> (or <u>i-hsing ko-ming</u> 易 姓革命, "the transfer of the mandate to another dynasty") is clearly derived from Tung Chung-shu. Perhaps Huan T'an did not present any opinion of his own in this fragment, but rather quoted from some prognostication texts (note that he begins with "it is said"). This seems even more probable when we take into account the fact that one of the texts quoted by Chou Shouch'ang attributes the study of <u>i-hsing</u> to Confucius himself.

For the state of Huan T'an's knowledge of Chuang Tzu, see fragment 81, note 15. See also Y. Hervouet, <u>Sseu-ma Siang-jou</u>, pp. 198-99, note 2.

44.   This is Chapter 13 of <u>Shih chi</u>, entitled "San-tai shih piao." The present fragment has <u>San shih piao</u>.

45.   Ssu-ma Ch'ien.

46.   Practically nothing is known about the <u>Chou P'u</u> 周譜 ("Chou Genealogy" or "Chou Genealogies"). Liu Yao of the Liang dynasty, who quotes Huan T'an, suggests only that it must have been written during the Chou dynasty. Liu Yao's text is repeated in <u>Nan shih</u> 49.8a (not quoted by Yen), as well as in the commentary to <u>Shih chi</u> 14, p. 3. In the <u>Shih chi</u>, however, Huan T'an is not acknowledged as his source and the title of the <u>Shih chi</u> chapter is given as "San tai hsi piao." Liu Yao's conclusion has also been reached by Chang Shun-hui in <u>Chung-kuo li-shih yao-chi chieh-shao</u>, pp. 132-33. Liu Fang, quoted in <u>Hsin T'ang shu</u> 199.10a, says that Ssu-ma Ch'ien shortened the <u>Shih pen</u> and, when writing his <u>Shih chi</u>, followed the model of the <u>Chou p'u</u> in order to emphasize that part of his book was devoted to the Hereditary Houses. Of course, the theories of Liu Yao and Liu Fang are not based on any ancient source. The most ingenious explanation is that of the first Chinese historiographer, Liu Chih-chi. Basing his theory on this fragment, he says at the very beginning of his chapter on tables (in his <u>Shih t'ung</u> 3) that the term <u>p'u</u> originated in the Chou period and that the tables (<u>piao</u>) follow the form of the <u>p'u</u>. The bibliographical chapter of the <u>Han shu</u> (Chapter 30) mentions several books of this type but not a <u>Chou p'u</u>. Therefore, I agree with Chao I, quoted by Takigawa

Kametarō in his commentary to <u>Shih chi</u> 13, p. 2, that
Huan T'an refers to the genealogies of the Chou dynasty
in general, rather than to any particular volume. However, fragment 110 contains a very specific quote from
the <u>Chou p'u</u>.

47.　　<u>Kung ch'ang</u> 工倡 ("musicians and singers").
See Gimm, <u>Das Yüeh-fu tsa-lu</u>, pp. 274-75, items 4 and
6.

48.　　Sun does not give the character <u>ling</u> 領 ("to
supervise, to lead"). Apparently Yen added it in re-
constructing the text, since the character in <u>PTSC</u>
55.5b is illegible. I find another <u>ling</u> 伶 ("musician") more appropriate.

49.　　There are insignificant differences between the
texts of Yen and Sun. <u>PTSC</u> 55.5b adds a phrase which
they both lack: "...[ch'ien jen] chih to yeh; chu jen
yeh" 千人之多也者人也("over one thousand registered
men"). One thousand seems to be fairly high, but the
records of later dynasties have even higher figures.
During the T'ang dynasty the average number of court
musicians was fifteen or twenty thousand; cf. Gimm,
<u>Das Yüeh-fu tsa-lu</u>, pp. 576-77.

50.　　For similar ideas see, for example, fragments
31 and 95.

51.　　See fragment 174, note 41.

52.　　<u>Ya-ts'ao</u> 雅操, i.e., <u>ya yüeh</u> 雅樂 ("court
music"), as for example, in <u>Analects</u> XVII:18: "...
the Master said...'I hate the tunes of Cheng corrupting
Court music.'" (Cf. Legge, p. 326).

53.　　<u>Hsin sheng</u> 新聲 or <u>hsin nung</u> 新弄 ("modern
tunes").

54.　　The text has <u>hsi</u> 喜 ("to be pleased"), while
both Yen and Sun have <u>shan</u> 善 , which would make the
sentence, "It is very easy to master shallow things..."

55.　　Instead of <u>shih</u> 識 ("to understand") which
rhymes with <u>hsi</u> 喜 , Sun has <u>shen</u> 深 , evidently
a misprint for <u>t'an</u> 探 ("to try, to essay") which
rhymes with <u>shan</u> 善 . Thus, the sentence would read,
"It is very easy to master shallow things, but the profound can be fathomed only with difficulty."

134

56.　　PTSC 132.10b begins here.

57.　　Only PTSC 132.10b. includes black.

58.　　The text has "wu se wen chih shih" 五色文之
世 , but I prefer Yen's version, "ssu se wen shih
chih" 四色文飾之("adorned by the four other colors").
Sun has "wu se wen shih chih," 五色文飾之 ("adorned
by the five other colors").

59.　　Sun gives Huan's age as seventy, rather than
seventeen.　This is clearly erroneous.

60.　　Feng ch'e lang 奉車郎("Gentleman of Imperial
Carriages").　This text, unlike Yen's, also has the
character chung 中 , which may make the title feng-
ch'e lang-chung ("Gentleman at the Palace in Charge of
Imperial Carriages").　In the preface to his "Rhyme-
prose on Looking for the Immortals," Huan T'an again
mentions that he was a Gentleman, but the various editions of this fu have three different versions of his
title: lang 郎 ("Gentleman"), chung-lang 中郎
("Gentleman of the Palace"), and feng ch'e lang 奉車
郎 ("Gentleman of Imperial Carriages").　See fragment
205, note 3.　On the other hand, perhaps the character
chung 中 is associated with the next character wei 衛
("Palace Guard").　This term, however, did not become
prominent until much later, during the Chin period.
See also "The Life," I, p. 39 and fragment 142.

61.　　Hsiao-yüan hsi-men 小苑西門 ("Western Gate
at the Small Park").　The Han shu (72, p. 4812) says
that Hsiao Wang-chih received the title of "Marquis of
the Eastern Gate of the Small Park."　In his commentary
Wang Hsien-ch'ien suggests that the title should read
"Lower Park" (hsia-yüan 下苑), instead of "Small
Park," but this fragment indicates that he is mistaken.
Huan T'an makes it clear that this refers to a gate of
the Palace, and not to a gate of the city, as Wang suggests.

62.　　This introduction appears to have been added
later, although Liu presents it as a quotation from
Hsin-lun.

63.　　Both the text and Yen have chün 君 ("Sir"),
but Sun gives wu 吾 ("I"), which would change the
meaning radically.　This wu probably belongs to the
beginning of the fragment.　See fragment 126B which

begins, "I said to Master Yang, 'You....'" Pan Ku's postscript (tsan) to Yang Hsiung's biography (Han shu 87B, p. 5134, based on Yang Hsiung's own account) says that when Yang Hsiung first came to court he was over forty years old, and that he first held concurrently the office of "Gentleman" and "Servant Within the Yellow Gates."

64.   Some of these terms are derived from Yang Hsiung's Kan-chüan fu.

65.   The term hsüan huang 玄黃 ("black and yellow" or "the colors of Heaven and earth") is used in Yang Hsiung's essay Chü Ch'in mei hsin. See also Book of Changes I:II:6; Legge, p. 61.

66.   The term lu-ch'e 路車 ("carriage of state") is found only in the Book of Songs, where it occurs frequently.

67.   See also TPYL 762.5a.

68.   Lo Jung-pang, in "China's Paddle-wheel Boats: Mechanized Craft Used in the Opium War and Their Historical Background," (p. 202), says, "...in 31 A.D., the Governor of Nan-yang, Tu Shih, built water-bellows (shui-p'ai), a device whereby the flow of water was used to turn wheels to operate bellows, which forced air into furnaces for forging farm implements. A contemporary of his, Huan T'an, wrote of 'water-pestles' (shui-ch'ung or shui-tui) which were driven by water and which, he said, were a great improvement over manually-operated machines."

69.   Jan Chao-te, in "Kuan-yü Han-tai sheng-ch'an nu-li yü sheng-ch'an-li shui-p'ing wen-t'i," p. 56, bases his opinion that water-mills existed in China during the reign of Wang Mang on this fragment. Other types of mills did exist, as is shown by Huan T'an's fragment 115, which refers to a millstone.

70.   This is the famous question which Wang Ch'ung tried to elucidate in the Lun-heng chapter, "A Last Word on Dragons" (Luan lung; 16, 47). Wang Ch'ung refers to this question by Huan T'an and acknowledges the weight of Huan's arguments against Liu Hsin's device, but indirectly takes issue with Huan T'an. However, even if Wang Ch'ung did accept the efficacy of Liu Hsin's instrument, he opposed Liu Hsin's theory. Wang

Ch'ung's principal idea, which he hoped would be "the last word on dragons," was that things of the same kind attract one another from a distance. Thus, he felt that it was the attraction between a "real" and an earthen dragon which brought rain. Cf. fragment 130. Yang Hsiang-k'uei in, <u>Chung-kuo ku-tai she-hui yü ku-tai ssu-hsiang yen-chiu</u>, p. 469, concluded on the basis of this fragment and fragment 156 that Liu Hsin undoubtedly did favor magicians and believed in the existence of the immortals.

71.　　Huang Hui, <u>Lun-heng chiao-shih</u>, p. 692, suggests that <u>chen</u> 針 ("needle") is a mistake for <u>t'ieh</u> 鐵 ("iron"). He bases this suggestion on a similar text in <u>Lü-shih ch'ün-ch'iu</u> IX:5, p. 92; Wilhelm, p. 114.

72.　　In Shensi.

73.　　The Great King (<u>T'ai-wang</u> 太王) is Tan Fu or Ku-kung Tan Fu ("the Old Duke Tan-fu"). Mencius calls him <u>T'ai-wang</u> and relates him to Pin in <u>Mencius</u> I:II:XV:1; Legge, pp. 175-76. <u>Shih chi</u> 4, pp. 6-8 (Chavannes, <u>MH</u> I, pp. 213-18) refers to him as Ku-kung and says that he was driven out of Pin by barbarians.

74.　　The texts in <u>TPYL</u> 849.5a and <u>PTSC</u> 143.8a are practically the same but omit the reference to Chieh Tzu-t'ui.

75.　　On page 16a, Sun gives two quotations from <u>PTSC</u> 143.8a, the second of which belongs to Sun Ch'u and has nothing to do with Huan T'an.

76.　　<u>TPYL</u> 27.5b has "five months" (<u>wu-yüeh</u> 五月) which should be read as "the fifth month;" see note 77 below.

77.　　Chieh Tzu-t'ui, or Chieh Chih-t'ui (7th century B.C.), was a faithful friend of Duke Wen of Chin until they quarreled. <u>Tso chuan</u>, Hsi 24, tells us that Chieh Chih-t'ui, who had once cut off a portion of his own thigh to relieve his ruler's hunger, chose to leave the court with his mother after this quarrel. Later the Duke realized his mistake and gave Chieh a field on Mien-shang Mountain (Legge, pp. 189 and 191-92).

　　<u>Shih chi</u> 39 (pp. 49-51; Chavannes, <u>MH</u> IV, pp. 294-96) repeats the story of this fragment with some elaborations but makes no reference to the cold meals.

Hsin-hsü (quoted by Li Hsien in his commentary to Hou Han shu 61, p. 2192), however, says that Duke Wen burned down the mountain where Chieh Tzu-t'ui was hiding, but Chieh's burnt corpse could not be found. Thereafter, the use of fire was forbidden during the Ch'ing-ming festival at the beginning of the fourth month (PTSC 143.8a; see note 75 above). Huan T'an's account is corroborated by the biography of Chou Chü (Hou Han shu 61, p. 2192), who became an Inspector of T'ai-yüan under Emperor Shun. This peculiar custom is described by Fan Yeh, and Li Hsien mentions that the affair is described in Huan T'an's Hsin-lun, page 2193. Nevertheless, Shen Ch'in-han, quoted in Wang Hsien-ch'ien's commentary, objects, stating that Huan T'an could not have known Chou Chü and that the true source of this information is Hua T'an's Hsin-lun. Wang is confused, for Li Hsien apparently meant that Huan T'an told the story not of Chou Chü, but of Chieh Tzu-t'ui. H. A. Giles, A Chinese Biographical Dictionary, No. 353, also is mistaken in his statement that "...The origin of the Cold-meat Festival has been erroneously attributed to the tragic fate of Chieh Chih-t'ui." For an explanation of the Ch'ing-ming Festival, see DKJ 7239.217.

The story of Chieh Tzu-t'ui found its way into Chinese fiction; see A. Lévy, "Études sur trois récueils anciens de contes chinois," pp. 112-13. IWLC 4.26a has an interesting quotation from Ch'in ts'ao on Chieh Tzu-sui, who is the same as Chieh Tzu-t'ui. It says that Duke Wen set the woods which covered the mountain on fire in order to smoke out Chieh Tzu-sui, but Chieh clasped his hands around a tree trunk and died in the flames. Thereafter, the Duke instructed his people not to use any fire for five days in the fifth month. Although Huan T'an possibly wrote a Ch'in ts'ao, several works of the same title have been written, and thus, this fragment was not necessarily written by him.

78.   This sentence has been translated and analyzed by A. C. Graham, "The Date and Composition of Liehtzyy," p. 163.

79.   This story is also told in Lieh-tzu 5, p. 58 (ed. Chu-tzu chi-ch'eng), but Huan T'an gives only the first part. In Lieh-tzu the children's conversation continues: "'When the sun first rises it is as big as the cover of the car; by noon it is small as a plate or a bowl. Don't you think it must be nearer when it is big than when it is small?' The other child answered,

'When the sun first rises the air is cool, but soon it
is like dipping your hand in hot water. Don't you think
it must be nearer when it is hot than when it is cool?'
Confucius could not decide the question. The two children laughed, 'Who says you are a learned man?'" Translation by A. C. Graham, The Book of Lieh-tzu, pp. 104-05.

It appears that Huan T'an's fragment is incomplete since the main point--Confucius' embarrassment--
is missing. In a note to her translation of Lieh-tzu,
Ateisty, materialisty, dialektiki dreynego Kitaja. Jan
Czu, Leczy, Czuanczy "(Atheists, Materialists, and Dialecticians of Ancient China: Yang Chu, Lieh Tzu, Chuang
Tzu," p. 345, note 38), L. D. Pozdneeva explains the
children's discussion as a Taoist critique of Confucius; this is probably incorrect.

The main significance of this quotation, as
A. C. Graham pointed out in 1961 (see his article, pp.
142 and 163, cited in note 78 above), is that this quotation, along with others, establishes that the present
text of Lieh-tzu was composed in the 4th century A.D.
by Chang Chan. Therefore, I follow J. Needham (Science
and Civilization in China, Vol. III, p. 226), who says
that such stories "belong to a whole corpus of legend
and folk-tale centering on a quasi-Taoist puer senex,
Hsiang T'o, who, together with other small boys, always
defeats Confucius in a riddle." As a matter of fact,
it was Huan T'an's follower Wang Ch'ung who discussed
Hsiang T'o in his Lun-heng 26:79, pp. 1070-74; Forke,
II, pp. 120-24. See also M. Soymié, "L'entrevue de
Confucius et de Hsiang T'o;" A. C. Graham, "The Date,"
p. 142, note 3 (see note 78 above); A. Walley, Ballads
and Stories from Tun-huang, pp. 89-96. The present
story, quoted from Lieh-tzu, can be found in the chapter on astronomy in Sui shu 19, p. 6a-b, following its
version of fragment 134.

80.   I.e., Kuan Ping, according to fragment 107.

81.   In accordance with Yen, I prefer "sun" (jih
日) to the "heaven" (t'ien 天) of the text.

82.   A ch'ih is one-tenth of a chang.

83.   Instead of heng 衡 ("yoke, horizontal"), I
read ch'ung 衝 ("attack"), in accordance with Sui shu
19.3a.

84. Yen's text has yin 陰 , while Sun's text has yang 陽 . Yin makes sense here, while yang makes no sense.

Chang Chan's note to Lieh-tzu 5, p. 58 (cf. note 79 above), while explaining the meaning of the four characters here translated as "cold" (ts'ang-ts'ang liang-liang 滄滄涼涼), says that Huan T'an narrates this story and writes ts'ang as 愴 ("sad," "sorry"). The same comment is found in Yin Ching-shu's Lieh-tzu shih wen (T'ang), p. 2.5a (quoted by Yen).

Chang Chan's statement is significant because: 1) It indicates that Huan T'an's fragment originally was larger (see note 79 above). The other part of the Lieh-tzu story discussed in note 79 probably also comes from Huan T'an, especially since these four characters are also found there. We need not look for a written source from which Huan T'an derived this story since he clearly states that he heard it from the common people. This corroborates Needham's theory of a folk-tale origin (note 79 above); and 2) If Chang Chan really compiled the Lieh-tzu, as Graham suggests, his reference to Huan T'an shows his artfulness. The same device was used by the author of Chao Fei-yen wai-chuan; see fragment 188.

This discussion on the variation in the size of the sun corresponding to the distance of the observer is not as unsophisticated as it might appear. J. Needham discusses this point, as well as the present fragment, in his Science and Civilization in China, Vol. III, p. 226.

85. These tall trees symbolize the sunset (and also old age) because the last rays of the sun in the evening touch only their tops.

86. This version is quoted in Huang Hui's commentary to Lun-heng 11:32, pp. 495-96, since Huang believes that it was the source of Wang Ch'ung's thought; see Forke, I, p. 263. Wang Ch'ung himself does not refer to his source.

87. This fragment, like the previous one, is significant for what it tells of the authenticity of a well-known text. In this case the text is that attributed to Kung-sun Lung. A. C. Graham, in his penetrating study, "The Composition of the Gongsuen Long-tzyy,"

concludes, among other things, that the text was probably composed in the 6th century A.D. and that only chapters two ("White Horse") and three ("Meanings and Things") are authentic writings by the dialecticians who lived in the Warring States period (p. 181). One of the bases for his belief in the authenticity of the "White Horse" chapter is the present fragment, since Graham feels that, through it, "the gap" between the Han and Sui periods of information on Kung-sun Lung can be satisfactorily bridged in the case of the "White Horse."

However, this fragment has also been used to support a radically different conclusion. T'an Chieh-fu, Kung-sun Lung-tzu hsing-ming fa-wei, pp. 5 and 82, suggests that Huan T'an composed the first part of the first chapter of Kung-sun Lung-tzu. First, instead of entitling the treatise "Hard and White" (Chien-pai lun), as Huan has, T'an Chieh-fu suggests the title "Shou-pai lun," given in the bibliographical chapter of the Sui shu. Huan T'an's reading, however, is corroborated by Lun-heng 29:83, p. 1159; Forke, I, p. 463. Second, T'an Chieh-fu says that Huan T'an was born in the last years of the Western Han, that is, during the first decade A.D. This appears to be incorrect. Third, T'an Chieh-fu believes that Huan T'an's fragment has been shortened. While this is possible, T'an offers no proof in support of his belief. Fourth, T'an Chieh-fu presents two quotations to show that Huan T'an was akin to the spirit of the Kung-sun Lung-tzu. The first, from Huan T'an's biography, says, "On the whole, he followed Liu Hsin and Yang Hsiung in discerning doubtful and strange occurrences." ("The Life," I, p. 18). The second, from Lun-heng (13:38, pp. 608-09; Forke, II, p. 298) says, "Besides, Huan Chün-shan wrote the New Treatise, in which he treats the affairs of his times and discerns and clarifies the positive and the negative. Not one single void or false word, nor any artificial or embellished term stands the test of his proofs and judgments." These two quotations hardly bear out T'an Chieh-fu's conclusion that Huan T'an "without a doubt" compiled a part of the Kung-sun Lung text. Moreover, Wang Ch'ung (Lun-heng 29:83, p. 1159; Forke, I, p. 463. See also T'an Chieh-fu, p. 96) is very critical of Kung-sun Lung, and there is no reason to believe that Wang Ch'ung departed in this one instance from his typically unrestricted enthusiasm for Huan T'an's ideas.

88.   For the regulation of travel through the frontier passes in Han times, see M. Loewe, Records of Han
Administration, pp. 107-17. In 146 B.C., it was proposed that full-grown horses not be allowed outward
passage (p. 108), so horses were registered when crossing the frontier (p. 109).

89.   T'an Chieh-fu quotes this fragment without
comment on p. 96. Ch'en P'an examines it, along with
other information on Kung-sun Lung, in his discussion
of the possibility of the existence of Buddhism in
China in 214 B.C.; see "'Chin pu-te tz'u; ming-hsing
ch'un hsi-fang' chi chu wen-t'i," p. 370. Ch'en P'an
demonstrates that the paradox of the white horse was
in use several centuries before Huan T'an during the
Warring States period. Thus, he corroborates Graham's
opinion on the "White Horse" chapter, discussed in
note 87 above.

90.   See fragment 100 and note 5.

91.   Shih chi (10, p. 40; Chavannes, MH II, p. 487)
says that the Emperor's virtue transformed the people.

92.   See fragment 101. The last part of this short
quotation is found in the Shih chi at the place quoted
above. See also HFHD I, p. 274 (and note 1 on p. 272)
for a possible interpolation.

93.   Fragments 136B and 136C do not give the "dozen"
of the phrase "several dozen cash."

94.   PTSC 15.4a includes the small fragment mentioned
in note 92 above.

95.   Sun incorrectly gives the number of the TPYL
chapter as 56.

96.   Yen says that, according to Feng-su t'ung, "The
Emperor Ch'eng asked Liu Hsiang..." should be added to
this fragment.

97.   Ssu-ma Cheng (8th century A.D.), who wrote this
commentary to the Shih chi with the rather challenging
title of "Tracing Out the Hidden Meaning" (So-yin
索 隱)was not a very reliable historian, as Chavannes
has already pointed out (MH I, p. CCXVI). If he was
not a mere fictional character, it is still highly improbable that Tung-fang Shuo, who was allegedly Ssu-ma

Ch'ien's contemporary, worked on the text of the <u>Shih chi</u>. In fact, more reliable information shows that Huan T'an himself may not have believed this story. <u>Wen-hsin tiao-lung</u> (48, p. 714, of the edition by Fan Wen-lan, <u>Wen-hsin tiao-lung chu</u>) says, "Chün-ch'ing (Lou Hu), a man of great eloquence, overestimated his own ability when he dabbled in literary discussion. He once said, 'The historian Ssu-ma Ch'ien sought advice from Tung-fang Shuo when writing his work.' Huan T'an and his group greeted this with sneering laughter." (Translation by Shih, <u>Literary Mind</u>, p. 260.) <u>Wen-hsin tiao-lung</u> refers not to a "group" of Huan T'an's followers, but to people who shared his point of view.

Furthermore, at the beginning of Ssu-ma Cheng's commentary to Tung-fang Shuo's biography (<u>Shih chi</u> 126, p. 15; Ch'u Shao-sun's text), Chung-ch'ang T'ung is quoted, "Ssu-ma Ch'ien wrote the 'Biography of Ironical Critics' [<u>ku chi</u>], the postface [<u>hsü</u>] of which discusses only the affair of the 'actor' [<u>yu</u>] Chan, but fails to mention Tung-fang Shuo. This is a mistake. Should not the career of Tung-fang Shuo be compared directly to [the careers of the two 'actors'] Chan and Meng? Huan T'an agrees with Ssu-ma Ch'ien's omission, and in this he too is wrong."

It is not surprising that Chung-ch'ang T'ung, the fiery critic of contemporary social conditions, admired the bohemian Tung-fang Shuo. However, Ssu-ma Ch'ien's neglect of this semihistoric and legendary figure is understandable in that he differs from the so-called actors Chan and Meng in two important respects: First, he was not a dwarf, as they may have been. Second, Tung-fang Shuo lived during the Han, while Chan and Meng belonged to the Warring States period. For more information, see my study, "Ironical Critics at Ancient Chinese Courts (<u>Shih chi</u> 126)," (<u>Oriens Extremus</u> 20 (1973)). See also the essay by Han Ch'üeh, "'T'an so wei 'ku chi chia' Tung-fang Shuo" (The So-called 'Ironical Critic' Tung-fang Shuo), <u>Fan kung yüeh k'an</u>, No. 256 (July 1963), pp. 21-24; the title reveals the author's doubts about including Tung-fang Shuo's biography in Ch'u Shao-sun's Chapter 126.

The problems related to this fragment are discussed further in my article, "The First Interpolation in the <u>Shih chi</u>."

98.　　　Instead of the <u>wei yeh-che</u>　衛 謁 者　("Internuncio of the Guards") of the text, both Yen and Sun
give <u>yeh wei-che</u>　謁 衛 者　which I feel is wrong.
Shih Tzu-po is not mentioned in other Han sources. If
the <u>shih</u>　史　could be interpreted as <u>shih</u> 使 ("clerk"
or "messenger"), then it may refer to Han Jung, whose
style name was Tzu-po. He was an Associate Protector-
General and Colonel of the Western Frontier Regions who
was sent on a mission to the Hsiung-nu in 8 B.C. (<u>Han</u>
<u>shu</u> 94B, p. 5370). Although Han Jung was a contemporary
of Huan T'an's, I do not find this tentative identification very believable.

Chapter 12.   On Rhyme-prose (Fu)

139

PTSC 97.5a.   Yen 15.5a.   Sun 15b.

In my youth I studied[1] and liked the Li-sao.
Since I have read extensively in other books, I wish to
repeat my studies...[2]

140

A   I lin 3.10a.[3]   Yen 15.5a.   Sun 8a.

Yang Tzu-yün was expert at fu.   Wang Chün-ta[4]
was skilled with weapons.   I wanted to study with both
these masters.   Tzu-yün said, "If you can read a thousand fu, you will be good at them."[5]

Wang Chün-ta said, "If you can look at a thousand swords, you will understand them."

A proverb says, "He who lies low and practices
to be like one who is marvelously skilled will not pass
by the door of the man whom he imitates."

Previous translation: Pokora, "Huan T'an's Fu," p. 353,
and "Huan T'an and Yang Hsiung on Ssu-ma Hsiang-ju,"
p. 433.

B   IWLC 56.18a.   Yen 15.5a.   Sun 8a.

In the past I liked literature.   Yang Tzu-yün
was expert at fu, so I wished to study with him.   Tzu-
yün said, "If you can read a thousand fu, you will be
good at writing them."[6]

C   PTSC 122.12a-b.   Yen 15.5a. [commentary]
                                         Sun 16a.

Chün-ta was expert at the names of all kinds of
swords.   If he could only see a weapon from a distance
he would know what kind it was.   There was no need for
him to take it into his hand and study it closely.

141

<u>TPYL</u> 496.4b.   Yen 15.5a-b.   Sun 14b.

    A proverb says, "By looking at a section of a
dwarf, we can tell how tall he is."

    Confucius said, "If I explain one corner of a
subject to someone, and he cannot infer the other three
corners from that, I will not continue to teach him."[8]
A look at the two <u>fu</u>[9] which I wrote in my youth[10] is
likewise sufficient to determine whether I have a talent
for writing <u>fu</u>.

Previous translation: Pokora, "Huan T'an's <u>Fu</u>," p. 337.

142

<u>PTSC</u> 102.4a.   Yen 15.5b.   Sun 15b.[11]

    In my youth, when I was a Gentleman of the Im-
perial Carriages, Emperor Hsiao-ch'eng made sacrifices[12]
at Kan-ch'üan [Palace] and Ho-tung [commandery]. The ar-
rangements were first made by the circuit officials in
the Palace of the Assembled Spirits, which was built by
Emperor Wu at Hua-yin. On its gate was the inscription,
"Looking for Immortals," and in its hall was the inscription, "Keeping the Immortals." Wanting to inscribe something on the wall, I composed a <u>fu</u> eulogizing and praising the actions of the two Immortals.[13]

Previous translation: Pokora, "Huan T'an's <u>Fu</u>," p. 362,
note 58.

NOTES: CHAPTER 12

1.   Neither Yen nor Sun gives hsüeh 學 ("study").

2.   It is not clear whether Huan T'an wants to reread only Li-sao or the other books as well.

3.   See also fragments 80C and 80D.

4.   I have not been able to identify Wang Chün-ta. Chün-ta was the style of Hsün Jen, a contemporary of Huan T'an, who lived in retirement; see Hou Han shou 53, p. 1874.

5.   This is alluded to in Wen-hsin tiao-lung 2:8, p. 24.1; Shih, The Literary Mind, p. 49 and note 19.

6.   The version in PTSC 102.3a is almost exactly like this.

7.   Analects VII:8; Legge, p. 197.

8.   These two fu were "Wang hsien fu" 望仙賦 ("Rhyme-prose on Looking for the Immortals") and "Ta-tao fu" 大道賦 ("Rhyme-prose on the Great Tao"). For the former, see fragment 205; for the latter, see Pokora, "Huan T'an's Fu," p. 355, note 11.

9.   Instead of hsiao shih 小時 , I read shao shih 少時 ("youth"), in agreement with other frag- ments, such as fragment 139.

10.   Sun's text is somewhat different, although he attributes it to the same source. For a translation of it, see "Huan T'an's Fu," p. 362, note 58.

11.   In accordance with Yen, I prefer tz'u 祠 ("sacrifices") to tz'u 詞 ("words").

12.   Huan refers to Wang Ch'iao and Ch'ih Sung. This text is a short version of the preface to Huan T'an's "Wang hsien fu" as given in IWLC 78.16b (Yen 12.7b).

Chapter 13.   Discerning Error

143

I lin 3.10a.   Yen 15.5b. Sun 8a.

There are five kinds of good fortune: long
life, wealth, honor, peace and happiness, and to have
many sons and grandsons.

Previous translation: F. Hirth, "Bausteine zu einer
Geschichte der chinesischen Literatur," p. 436.

144

I lin 3.10a.   Yen 15.5b. Sun 8a.

The insect of a hundred feet--they all support
one body. How could it not be saved?

145

Po-wu chih 5.6a.   Yen 15.5b. Sun,
                                                      Preface 3b.

[Huan Chün-shan thought] that there was no such
thing as the Way of the Immortals[1] but that it had been
invented by those who like strange things.[2]

See Liang Han pu-fen II, p. 346.

P'ei Sung-chih's concluding notes to the "Annals
of Emperor Wen of Wei" (San kuo chih, Wei shu 1, Chien-
an year 25) gives another assessment of Huan T'an by
Chang Hua. P'ei quotes Chang Hua's Po-wu chih on people
whom the Emperor admired: "Huan T'an and Ts'ai Yung
were familiar with tones and music."

146

A I lin 3.10a.   Yen 15.5b. Sun 8a-b.

The Marquis of Ch'ü-yang[3] accepted the service
of Hsi-men Chün-hui, a gentleman versed in the arts of

magic,[4] to teach him the art of driving old age away.
Chün-hui said, "The tortoise is said to live for three
thousand years and the crane for one thousand years.
Considering the qualities of man, why is he not the
equal of insects and birds?"[5]

    I replied, "Who could live long enough to learn
how old a tortoise or a crane is?"

B   TPYL 720.5b.   Yen 15.5b. Sun 24b.

    Wang Ken, the Marquis of Ch'ü-yang, accepted
the services of Hsi-men Chün-hui, a gentleman versed in
the arts of magic, to teach him the art of cultivating
long life and driving old age away. Chün-hui said,
"The tortoise and the crane are said to live for three
thousand years. Considering the qualities of man, why
is he not the equal of insects and birds?"

Previous translation: Pokora, "The Life," II, pp. 540-
41. See Liang Han pu-fen II, p. 346.

147

I lin 3.10b. Commentary to Wen hsüan 21.21a.

Yen 15.5b. Sun 8b and 13b.

    Why do the sages not study the way to become
immortals,[6] but instead allow themselves to die?

    The bodies of all the sages are released and
they depart as immortals. When we speak of their "dying," it is merely to show people that they have come
to an end.

148

A Commentary to Wen hsüan 12.27a.

Yen 15.6a. Sun 13a.

    There are five kinds of spiritual men in the
Empire: first, divine immortals; second, hermits and
recluses; third, those who command ghostly beings;[7]

fourth, those who foreknow;[8] fifth, those who cast doubts.[9]

B   Commentary to Wen hsüan 21.21a, 27.6a, 39.32a.

Yen 15.6a.   Sun 13a.

There are five kinds of spiritual men in the Empire: the second is hermits and recluses.

149

TPYL 812.7a.   Yen 15.6a.   Sun 24b.

Sao,[10] the son of the King of Huai-nan, welcomed a magician[11] to create gold and silver. He said that the character for lead [ch'ien 鈆] is composed of "gold" [chin 金] and "sire" [kung 公].[12] Thus, lead is the sire of gold, while silver is the brother of gold.

150

A   Commentary to Wen hsüan 23.25b.

Yen 15.6a.   Sun 13b.

When Lady Li, whom Emperor Wu loved, died, the magician Li Shao-chün claimed that he could bring forth her spirit. Then, in the night, he set up a candle within some curtains and had the Emperor stay within other curtains. From a distance the Emperor saw a beautiful woman who appeared to be Lady Li. The Emperor often returned to the tent to sit within the curtains.[13]

B   PTSC 132.5b.   Yen 15.6a.   Sun 13b
                                        (commentary).[14]

Lady Wang, whom Emperor Wu cared for died. The Emperor loved her greatly. The magician Li Shao-chün claimed that he could bring forth her spirit.[15] Then, in the night, he set up a candle within some curtains. From a distance the Emperor saw a beautiful woman who looked like the Lady.

C TPYL 699.3a.   Yen 15.6a. Sun 13a
                                              (commentary).

    Li Shao-chün arranged for the image of Emperor
Wu's Lady Li to be placed within some curtains and let
the Emperor see it.

D The Chi-chieh commentary to Shih chi 12, p. 813.

                                   Yen 15.6a. Sun 9b.

    Lady Wang, Emperor Wu's beloved and favored
concubine,[16] was modest and retiring,[17] beautiful in
appearance, character and disposition, and sweet and
flattering in speech.

                         151

A Shui-ching chu 3:19, pp. 106-07. (San-fu huang-t'u

   5.8b-9a. TPYL 34.2a. IWLC 5.4b. TPYL 34.7b and

   869.7a-b, PTSC 156.6b).   Yen 15.6a-b. Sun 12a.

    When Emperor Yüan fell ill, an extensive search
was made for magicians.[18] The Han-chung [commandery]
sent a man of the Tao,[19] Wang Chung-tu. When he was
officially interrogated about his abilities, he replied
that he could endure both cold and heat. Then, on a
bitterly cold day in a sharp winter, he was commanded
to take off his clothes and was brought in a four-horse
carriage to Lake K'un-ming in Shang-lin [Park]. He was
driven around the ice by drivers heavily wrapped in
fox skins, who were shivering from the cold. Only
Chung-tu did not appear to be affected. He lay on a
terrace on the lake, smoking[20] with heat and unper-
turbed. In summer, during a great heat, he was ordered
to sit under the burning glow [of the sun] and was surrounded with the fires of ten stoves. But he did not
say he was hot, nor did he sweat.

Previous translation: Pokora, "An Important Crossroad,"
p. 70.

B Ch'u-hsüeh chi 3.9b.   TPYL 22.4b (TPYL 757.7b).[21]

Yen 15.6a-b.   Sun 12a.

On a very hot day when summer was at its peak, the Han-chung [commandery] sent Wang Chung-tu to sit under the burning glow [of the sun]. Moreover, he was surrounded with the fires of ten stoves. But he did not say he was hot, nor did he sweat.

C Po-wu chih 5.5b-6a (just before fragment 145) mentions Wang Chung-tu's hardiness and adds, "Huan Chün-shan believed that Wang Chung-tu could bear cold and heat because of his natural disposition." See Sun's preface 3b.

Ko Hung, in his Shen-hsien chuan 10.5a-b, devotes a paragraph to Wang Chung-tu. In addition to the anecdotes told by Huan T'an, Ko Hung tells us that Wang was two hundred years old, that he used cinnabar, and that he was transformed into an immortal. At the end Ko Hung says, "In his Hsin-lun, Huan Chün-shan mentions this man." Ko Hung also mentions Wang Chung-tu in Pao-p'u tzu Chapters 8, 12 and 15; see J. Ware, Alchemy, pp. 150, 208 and 249. For another reference to Wang, see Han Ao's Sui-hua chi-li 2.7a.

The poet Hsi K'ang varied the story a bit, saying that, according to Huan T'an, Wang Chung-tu could "occasionally" (ou 偶) bear cold and heat. See Hsi K'ang chi 4, as quoted by Holzman, La vie, p. 172, translation on p. 114, and also note 3 on p. 114. Wang Chung-tu's ability to endure cold and heat was especially admired since "cold and heat" (han shu 寒 熱) was one of the most feared diseases in ancient China; cf. Bridgman, La médecine, pp. 159, 172.

A TPYL 643.10a.   Yen 15.6b.   Sun 23b.

Recently, in the reign of Emperor Ai or Emperor P'ing, the magician Tung Chung-chün from the Lin-huai [commandery] was tried at law and put into prison, where he fell ill and died. Some days later his eyes fell in, and insects grew within them. The bailiffs cast him away, but he returned to life and left.

B   TPYL 944.3b.   Yen 15.6b.   Sun 23b
                                       (commentary).

        In the Sui-ling district lived Tung Chung-chün
who liked to inquire into the tricks of magicians. Once
he was tried at law for a serious crime and put into
prison. He feigned illness and death. Several days
later he rotted and insects grew in him, but he revived.

C   TPYL 737.8a.   Yen 15.6b.   Sun 23b
                                       (commentary).

        The magician Tung Chung-chün was guilty of some
wrongdoing.22 Put into prison, he feigned death. His
eyes fell in, and he became rotten and [full of] insects. Thus, we know that in the southern towns of the
Man people there are barbarians with flying heads. This
is not a delusion.

D   Fa-yüan chu-lin 76.22b.   Yen 15.6b. (Sun 23b).

        The magician Tung Chung-chün was guilty of some
wrongdoing.23 Put into prison, he feigned death. His
eyes fell in, and he became rotten and [full] of insects. Thus we know that there is nothing impossible
in delusion, trickery24 or non-existence.

        Moreover, he could blow his nose, sing through
his mouth, show his tongue and his teeth, shake his
eyebrows and move his eyes. In Ching-chou25 dwell the
Man barbarians who can drink with their noses, and in
the Southern Regions there are barbarians with flying
heads. These are not delusions.

E   Po-wu chih 5.3a-b.   Yen 15.6b. (Sun 23b).

        [Huan T'an's Hsin-lun] says that Tung Chung-
chün was a magician who was26 tried at law and put into
prison. He feigned death and was stinking. His eyes
fell in, and [insects] came out of them. Then he revived.

F   Ts'ao Chih, "Pien-tao lun," in Kuang Hung ming chi
       5.3b.27

[Chün-shan also says], Tung Chung-chün was a magician. He was put into prison, where he feigned death. Some days later his eyes fell in, and insects came out of them. He died and revived, but later he finally died.28 What is born must die. A superior man knows this. What is the use of illustrating it?29

Cf. Liang Han pu-fen II, p. 346.

153

TPYL 466.9b.   Yen 15.6a. Sun 21b.

During the reign of Emperor Ai, an old man, Fan Lan, claimed to be three hundred years old. When he first met someone, he was pleased and responded with kindness. But if this happened two or three times, he would curse the man and drive him away.

154

Pao-p'u-tzu, Nei-p'ien 16, p. 72.   Yen 15.6b.

When he was named an official of the Lieutenant Chancellor,[Shih Tzu-hsin]supervised the building of houses. He mobilized civilian officials and soldiers, as well as government slaves to furnish [the labor necessary] to produce gold. When he was unsuccessful, the Lieutenant Chancellor himself believed that the labor supply was inadequate and told Empress Fu about it.30 However, the Empress saw no advantage in making gold until she heard that it could be used as a drug to prolong one's life. Then she became favorably disposed, and Shih Tzu-hsin was given the title of Gentleman and housed in the Northern Palace, where he was attended by messengers.31

Previous translation: J. R. Ware, Alchemy, p. 266.

155

TPYL 382.6a.   Yen 15.6b-7a. Sun 21a.

Once when I was out with the Gentleman Ling Hsi, we saw an old gentleman who was picking his food from excrement. Since his face was dirty and ugly, I could not bear to look at him. [Ling] Hsi said, "How do you know that he is not a divine immortal?"

I said, "If the Way had to be embodied in this fashion, then there would be no Way at all!"[32]

Previous translation: Pokora, "An Important Crossroad," pp. 69-70. See Liang Han pu-fen II, pp. 346-47.

156

A TPYL 956.2a-b. IWLC 88.21a.   Yen 15.7a. Sun 17b.[33]

Liu Tzu-chün believed the vain speeches of the magicians who said that one may become a divine immortal through study. I saw that down in his courtyard grew a great elm, very old, worn and broken. Pointing to it, I said, "That tree has no feelings, but, nevertheless, it will decay and become worm-eaten. Although you may want to care for it and nurture its life, how can you possibly prevent its decline?"

B Ts'ao Chih, "Pien-tao lun," in Kuang Hung ming chi 5.3a.[34]   Yen 15.7a.

This tree has no feelings and wishes which it could repress. It has no ears or eyes which it could close. But, nevertheless, it will rot, wither and become putrid.[35]

Previous (partial) translation: "The Life," II, p. 538. See also "An Important Crossroad," pp. 75-76; and Liang Han pu-fen II, p. 346.

157

A Pao-p'u-tzu, Nei p'ien 16, p. 72.   Yen 15.7a-b.

Ch'eng Wei, a Gentleman of the Yellow Gate, enjoyed the art of yellow and white.[36] He married a girl from a family which possessed and understood prescriptions. Once when he was very upset at having to participate in the Emperor's processions without wearing the clothes appropriate to the season, his wife said, "Let two pieces of taffeta appear." Immediately and from no source the taffeta appeared.

Ch'eng Wei's efforts to make gold by following the Chen-chung and Hung-pao [formulae]had been unsuccessful.37 His wife went to watch him, and just at the moment when Wei was fanning the coals to heat a tube of mercury,38 she said, "I would like to have a try at something." Then she took a drug from her pouch and put a bit of it into [the tube]. After the time span of a meal, they opened the tube to find perfect silver.

Greatly amazed, Wei said, "Why didn't you tell me before that the formula was as near to me as you are?" His wife replied, "One cannot have it unless one is destined. Then Wei tempted her day and night to give him the formula. He sold his land and buildings to give her the best food and clothing, but she still refused to tell him. Then Wei plotted with a friend to make her give in by beating her with bamboo.

When his wife found out, she told him, "The formula may only be passed on to the proper person. If the proper person were found--even if we met on the road-- I would teach it to him. If, however, he were not the proper man--if his words were proper but his heart was not--the formula would not be forthcoming even though I were to be cut into bits and the limbs torn from my body." Wei kept up his pressure, however, until his wife finally went mad. Running away naked, she smeared herself with mud. Later, she died.39

Previous translation: A Waley, "Notes to Johnson's A Study of Chinese Alchemy," pp. 4-5. H. H. Dubs, "The Beginnings of Alchemy," p. 78; see also Dubs, "The Origin of Alchemy," p. 31. J. R. Ware, Alchemy, pp. 264-65.

B TPYL 812.4b.   Yen 15.7a-b. Sun 24b.

[Ch'eng]Wei, a Gentleman Attendant at the Gate,40 was fond of the matters of yellow and white. The wife he married was a strange girl. When [Ch'eng]Wei had no [proper] clothes, his wife made two rolls of silk appear. Later, she saw her husband just at the moment

when he was fanning coals to heat a tube of mercury.
She took a drug from her [pouch][41] and put it into the
tube. Her success was instantaneous. At once [Ch'eng]
Wei tried to find out the formula, but he could not get
it. She went mad and died.

158

A TPYL 905.2b.[42]   Yen 15.7b. Sun 25b
                                        (commentary).

When Lü[43] Chung-tzu's female slave died, she
had a four-year old child. After she was buried, she
returned several times to care for and cuddle it. She
could also wash the child's head. Since this was much
disliked by the people, they told a magician,[44] who
said, "There is a dog. If you kill it,[45] then the female slave will not return."

The old woman of the Yang Chung-wen family[46]
died. When her corpse had been dressed for burial but
not yet buried, she suddenly rose, seated herself before the inner coffin and drank wine. When she had
become drunk, the shape of a dog appeared, and it was
killed.

B TPYL 885.8b.   Yen 15.7b. Sun 25b.

When Lü Chung-tzu's female slave died, she had
a four-year old girl. She returned several times to
wash the child's head and to rinse and wash [her robes].
The magician[47] said, "There is a green dog[48] in the
family which does this. If you kill it, [the affair]
will come to an end.

Yang Chung[49] also said he knew a family where
an old woman, who had died suddenly, rose, drank and
ate. After she had become drunk, she sat down and
sacrificed on the bed. After she had done this three
or four times, the family became disgusted. Thereafter,
whenever she became drunk, her form became ruined.[50]
But [the family] got an old dog and beat it to death.
Later, an investigation revealed that the dog belonged
to a local dealer's family.

Notes: CHAPTER 13

1.   Chang Hua's <u>Po-wu chih</u>, Chapter 5, says, "Yang Hsiung also said, 'There is no such thing as the Way of the Immortals.' Huan T'an was of the same opinion."

2.   See my article, "Huan Tan's <u>Fu</u>," p. 366.

3.   Wang Ken. Cf. fragment 146B.

4.   "A gentleman versed in the arts of magic" is a clumsy translation of the term <u>fang-shih</u> 方士 . Since Hsi-men Chün-hui is identified in <u>Han shu</u> 99C, p. 5798, as a <u>tao-shih</u> 道士 ("gentleman of the Way"), Dubs concludes (<u>HFHD</u> III, p. 446, note 22.10) that <u>tao shih</u> does not refer only to Taoists. For the sake of simplicity, I generally translate both terms, as well as the term <u>tao-jen</u> 道人 ("man of the Way"), as "magician." See also fragment 149, note 11.

5.   The ancient Chinese classified the tortoise in the same species as insects and reptiles (<u>ch'ung</u> 蟲).

6.   Only <u>I lin</u> gives this part of the fragment, while the following section is found in both sources.

7.   <u>Shih kuei wu</u>   使鬼物 ("those who command ghostly beings"). This term is not mentioned in <u>PWYF</u> or <u>DKJ</u>. It is found in <u>Han shu</u> 36, p. 3382, in connection with the books of Liu An (see fragment 157, note 37): "The books tell of the divine immortals' ways of causing ghostly beings to produce gold."

8.   <u>Hsien-chih</u>   先知 ("those who have a priori knowledge or foreknowledge") is clearly of Taoist origin since it can be found in <u>Lao-tzu</u> 38 (as <u>ch'ien-shih</u> 前識); in <u>Lü-shih ch'un-ch'iu</u> (Chapter 20: 1, pp. 256, and 8, p. 272 as <u>hsien-chih</u> 先知); and in <u>Hsi K'ang chi</u> (Chapter 4; see D. Holzman, <u>La vie et la pensée de Hi K'ang</u>, pp. 97 and 164 as <u>ch'ien-shih</u> 前識).

9.   Instead of the <u>i</u> 疑 ("doubts") of the text, Yen gives <u>ning</u> 凝 ("solidify"). The phrase would then read, "those who cast and solidify [metals]," or "alchemists."

10.   Liu An, the King of Huai-nan, did not have a son named Sao; Sun does not give this character.

160

11.　Tao jen 道人 ("magician"); see 146A, note 4.

12.　The text has only tzu chin yü kung 字金與公, but, in accordance with Yen, I read ch'ien tzu chin yü kung 鉛字金與公.

13.　There are several versions of this story. Of Huan T'an's four fragments, two mention Lady Li (as does Han shu), and two mention Lady Wang (as does Shih chi). Other sources call the magician Shao-weng 少翁, instead of Li Shao-chün. See, e.g., Shih chi 12, p. 11 or 28, p. 52 (Chavannes III, p. 470). Shih chi includes this anecdote in its history of the year 121 A.D. and gives much more detail on the shadow-play.

14.　Sun, quoting PTSC 132, has a rather different version which Yen does not include.

15.　Fragment 150A has shen 神 for "spirit," while 150B has shen kuei 神鬼.

16.　I 姬 ("imperial concubine"). For this term, see Dubs's detailed explanation in HFHD I, p. 221, note 1.

17.　This alludes to the beginning of the Book of the Songs; see Legge, p. 1, and the explanation on p. 3 where Yang Hsiung is quoted.

18.　Fang shih 方士 ("magicians").

19.　Tao shih 道士 ("a man of the Tao") probably means the same as fang shih (note 18). See fragment 146A, note 4.

20.　The text has an unknown character, 瞳, while fragment 151B (as well as Yen and Sun) has hsün 曛 interchangeable with hsün 熏 ("smoking"). Huan T'an's biography in Hou Han shu 18, p. 1017, has mo-jan 默然 ("silent").

21.　TPYL 22.4b differs from the text of Ch'u-hsüeh chi 3.9b only in insignificant details. The TPYL 757.7b version has two points of difference: in the beginning it mentions Emperor Yüan, and in the end it does not mention "sweat."

22.　Shih 事 (translated here as "wrongdoing") could mean "matter" or "case" in Han legal terminology;

see, e.g., Hulsewé, Remnants I, pp. 48 and 51. In the present context, however, shih may mean "service," since so-called "Service Statutes" (shih lü 事 律) were enacted during the Han; see Hulsewé, p. 29, and especially p. 65, note 24.

23.   See the preceding note 22.

24.   "Delusion" and "trickery" are, respectively, the Buddhist Māyā and ṛddhi.

25.   The Ching province is the territory of the former kingdom of Ch'u.

26.   I read mu 目 ("eye"), instead of the tzu 自 ("self") of the text.

27.   See fragments 82C and 156B for other paragraphs from this essay by Ts'ao Chih. Ts'ao Chih's essay is quoted in Hou Wai-lu et al., "Wei Chin Nan-pei-ch'ao ssu-hsiang," p. 339.

28.   The two subsequent sentences were probably added by Ts'ao Chih. The text continues as follows: "Even the highest spirit does not surpass Heaven and earth. He cannot allow the hibernating insects to hide in summer, nor can he produce the noise of thunder in the winter. If the time changes, then beings come into movement; if the breath shifts, then things respond to it. If Tung Chung-chün could restrain his breath within himself, change his body into a corpse, rot his skin, and let insects grow, is this anything to be surprised at?"

29.   A very short "biography" of Tung Chung-chün in Ko Hung's Shen-hsien chuan 10.4a gives a short and less sober version of this fragment without attribution, mentioning that Tung Chung-chün's breath exercises kept him looking quite young at the age of one hundred.

30.   This might have taken place in 3 B.C., when Huan T'an was an advisor to Fu Yen, the Marquis of K'ung-hsiang and the father of Empress Fu, who was the wife of Emperor Ai. Evidently the Empress listened to the magicians, since Huan T'an warned her father, "...perhaps she will send frantically for doctors and sorcerers, or summon magicians and wizards from outside the court." (Pokora, "The Life," I, p. 19, translating Huan T'an's biography in Hou Han shu 18A, p. 1012). See also fragment 206.

31.　　Pao-p'u tzu adds, "As though a divine prescrip-
tion of this sort could be effected in a palace with
all sorts of ordinary people in attendance! It is common knowledge that even dyers of silks do not wish to
have all kinds of people watching them for fear their
work will be spoiled. How much truer is this for the
transforming of yellow and white!" (J. R. Ware's translation, pp. 266-67.)

32.　　Apparently the old gentleman was a "Gentleman
of the Way," a tao shih 道 士 or "magician."

33.　　This fragment is associated with fragment 84.

34.　　After a general introduction to his essay, Ts'ao
Chih says, "Huan Chün-shan was one of the authors of
substantial treatises during the restoration. There is
much that is good in his writings and narrations. Liu
Tzu-chün once asked whether a man could really avoid
his decline and exhaustion by repressing his lust and
desires, and by closing his ears and eyes? At that time
an old elm grew in the courtyard. Huan Chün-shan pointed
to it and said..."

35.　　Ts'ao Chih then comments, "Then Liu Tzu-chün
said that he was wrong when he claimed that one could
avoid decline and exhaustion. Huan Chün-shan's comparison with the elm is not quite correct. Why?" Ts'ao
Chih then proceeds with Huan T'an's fragment 82C.

36.　　"The art of yellow and white" is alchemy or,
more specifically, the artificial production of gold
(yellow) and silver (white). The sixteenth chapter of
Pao-p'u-tzu is devoted to this art.

37.　　The Hung-pao and Chen-chung treatises are attributed to Liu An in Pao-p'u-tzu (2, p. 7; Ware, p. 51).
Han Shu (25B, p. 2146) says that Liu Keng-sheng (i.e.,
Liu Hsiang) and others presented Emperor Hsüan with
"Huai-nan's prescriptions Chen-chung ("In the Pillow"),
Hung-pao ("Great Treasure") and Yüan-mi ("Secrets of
the Garden")." Han shu (36, p. 3381) says that these
books were also in Liu An's possession. Yen Shih-ku's
commentary explains that the "Great Treasure" and the
"Secrets of the Garden" are both titles of chapters in
books of Taoist formulae which were hidden in a pillow
(chen chung 枕 中). The works are mentioned neither
by the Shih chi, nor by the bibliographical chapter of
Han shu.

38.   The term for "mercury" translated literally means "water-silver" or "liquid silver."

39.   _Shen-hsien chuan_ 7.2b-3a has a short version of this story entitled "The Wife of Ch'eng Wei." In that version, as is fitting in a treatise on immortals, the wife dies a supernatural death, leaves her body and becomes an immortal.

40.   The title given here ("a Gentleman Attendant at the Gate") is also that used in _Shen-hsien chuan_ 7.2b.

41.   Sun has _ssu_ 笥 ("box").

42.   The text consists of two quotations which are actually two different stories, indicated here by two paragraphs. The text given in Sun's commentary has several variations.

43.   The text has _chan_ 占 , which is not a Chinese surname. I read _Lü_ 呂 in accordance with fragment 158B.

44.   _Fang-shih_ 方士 ("magician"). See note 47 below.

45.   The _hsiao_ 効 of the text makes no sense. Again I follow fragment 158B (as well as Yen and Sun) in reading _sha_ 殺 ("kill").

46.   Generally, it is impossible to identify people associated with magicians in the dynastic histories, but this tale may refer to the Yang family of Hsin-tu in Szechwan (not to be confused with Wang Mang's Hsin-tu in Honan). One of its members, Yang Ch'un-ch'ing, a general who served Kung-sun Shu, was well versed in the _ch'an_ texts. Even his great-grandson, Yang Hou, wrote a book which attempted to enhance the _ch'an_ texts with the authority of Confucius. This was precisely what Huan T'an opposed: "Today all the artful and foxy magicians of small talent and the soothsayers disseminate and multiply diagrams and documents, falsely praising the records of prognostications;" see fragment 210. For the Yang family, see _Hou Han shu_ 30A, pp. 1100-01.

47.   Here the word which I translate as "magician" is _tao-shih_ 道士 , while the fragment 158A has _fang-shih_ 方士 . These different denominations for the same kind of magician corroborate H. H. Dubs's conclusion referred to above (fragment 146, note 4).

164

48.   In the Han period the color green is associated with many animals, but I find no other reference to a green dog.

49.   Both Yen and Sun have Yang Chung-wen; cf. 158A.

50.   Both Yen and Sun have "[ch'i hou tsui] hsing huai yüan" 其後醉行壞垣 which makes no sense. I prefer the TPYL text, which has "[ch'i hou tsui] hsing huai. Tan" 形壞但 ("whenever she became drunk, her form became ruined. But...").

Chapter 14. Explaining Plans

159

A   The Chi-chieh commentary to Shih chi 56, p. 14.

Yen 15.7b-8a. Sun 10a-b.

Someone said, "It is said that Ch'en P'ing's
raising of the siege of Emperor Kao at P'ing-ch'eng was
such a secret affair that no one today knows exactly
what happened. The job was done in a very adroit and
excellent manner, so it remained hidden and was not
spread about. Could you, perhaps, reflect upon and
comprehend this matter?"

I answered, "To the contrary, the plan was mean
and low, clumsy and bad. That is why it was kept secret
and not disclosed.

"When Emperor Kao was besieged for seven days,
Ch'en P'ing went to plead with the consort[1] of the shan-
yü. When she subsequently spoke to the shan-yü, he re-
leased the Han Emperor. From this we know the method
Ch'en P'ing used to persuade her.

"Ch'en P'ing must have told her: 'Han women
are excellent and beautiful. Their appearance is beyond compare in the entire world. Being besieged, [the
Emperor has] sent messengers to rush back and return
with [women] which he intends to offer to the shan-yü.
When the shan-yü sees the women, he will certainly love
them deeply, and if he loves them, you, his consort,will
become increasingly estranged from him. The best thing
to do is to let the Han escape before [the messengers]
arrive [with the women], because once the Han are freed,
they will not bring their women.'

"The consort and [the shan-yü's] women had
jealous natures and they certainly would have despised
[the Han women]; therefore, they spurred[2] the shan-yü
to let the Han go. This explanation is simple and to
the point. Once the ruse proved effective, [Ch'en
P'ing] wished to present it as something mysterious,
and therefore he kept it secret so it would not leak
out."

When Liu Tzu-chün heard my words, he immediately praised them and expressed his agreement.[3]

Previous translation: H. H. Dubs, HFHD I, pp. 116-17, note 2. Pokora, "The Life," II, p. 539.

B TPYL 381.3b.   Yen 15.7b-8a. Sun 10b
                                        (commentary).

Someone said, "Ch'en P'ing's [method of] raising the siege of Emperor Kao at P'ing-ch'eng remained hidden and was not spread about. Can you understand it?"

I said, "Ch'en P'ing won over the consort with the statement that the Han had marvelous women whose beauty was beyond compare in the entire world. He told her that the Emperor had sent messengers who were to rush back with the [women]; that the Emperor intended to offer them to the shan-yü; and that when the shan-yü saw these women, he would certainly love them. Then the consort spoke to the shan-yü and Emperor Kao was spared."

This text was analyzed in P. Pelliot, "Notes sur quelques artistes des Six dynasties et des T'ang," pp. 216-17 and note 3.

C Pai K'ung liu t'ieh 21.8a.   Yen 15.7b-8a. Sun 10a.
                                        (commentary).

Besieged at P'ing-ch'eng, the Eminent Founder won over the [shan-yü's] consort by saying that the Han had beautiful women who were beyond compare in the entire world; that he was hurriedly offering them to the shan-yü; and that the shan-yü would surely love them deeply and his favor towards the consort would decline. This is called "a marvelous escape plan."

D IWLC 18.4a.   Yen 15.7b-8a. Sun 10b.
                                        (commentary).

Ch'en P'ing persuaded the shan-yü's consort by saying that the Han had excellent and beautiful women whose appearance was beyond compare in the entire world; that as soon as they were rushed over, they would be offered to the <u>shan-yü</u>; and that on seeing them, the <u>shan-yü</u> would surely love them deeply and neglect the consort.

NOTES: CHAPTER 14

1.   The Chi-chieh commentary quotes Su Lin as saying
that the yen-chih 閼氏 (here translated as "consort")
is "like the Han empress." Therefore, B. Watson (Records
I, p. 161) translates the term as "consort." But, H. H.
Dubs (HFHD I, p. 116, note 2) translates Yen-chih as a
name. Nevertheless, in his introduction to the translation of Chapter 9 of the Han shu (HFHD II, p. 282),
among other places, Dubs translates yen-chih as "Empress." A detailed explanation of the expression yen-
chih is given by P. Pelliot in Journal Asiatique, Vol.
20(1912), pp. 169-70, where he analyzes a similar term
in the Lun-heng. See also his note in TP, Vol. 24
(1925), p. 279.

2.   The term tzu 刺 ("to spur") is given by the
Ssu shih edition of the Shi chi (Shanghai, 1935, p. 352-
53) and was adopted by both Yen and Sun. Takigawa Kame-
taro's edition, Shih chi hui-chu k'ao-cheng, has shih
事 , which Dubs (see note 1 above) translates as "she
mixed [in the affairs]."

3.   P'ei Yin, the author of the Chi-chieh commentary,
adds that, in essence, Huan T'an's account agrees with
Ying Shao's account in his Han shu yin-i; P'ei is not
sure whether Ying Shao based his account entirely on
Huan T'an or whether he also used other sources. Ying
Shao's text is quoted by Yen Shih-ku in Han shu 1B,
p. 77, and differs in some important details from Huan
T'an's account. Ying Shao says, "Ch'en P'ing arranged
to have some portraits of beautiful women painted and
sent someone to give one to the [shan-yü's] consort.
The man said, 'The Han have beautiful ladies like this.
Now the Emperor, being besieged and in difficulty, intends to offer these [pictures to ten shan-yü].' The
consort was afraid of losing favor, so she said to the
shan-yü, 'The Han Son of Heaven also had his divinities
and spirits. It would be absolutely impossible to get
his territory.' Then the Hsiung-nu opened one corner,
through which he could escape." Yen Shih-ku adds, "Ying
Shao's explanation is based on Huan T'an's Hsin-lun.
Apparently Huan T'an came to this conclusion on his
own; the facts may well have been like that. This explanation is not found in the basic annals or in the
memoirs."

We see that Huan T'an's account agrees with
Ying Shao's in that it stresses the physical attractions
of the Chinese women, but they disagree on which method
was used to frighten the jealous wife of the barbarian
chieftain with their attractions. Huan T'an simply says
that the description was given verbally, while Ying Shao
suggests that portraits were used.

Through this we may see how history is transformed into fiction: 1) Shih chi 8, p. 73 ("The Basic
Annals of Emperor Kao") says only that the Hsiung-nu
besieged the Emperor for seven days before retiring.
(Chavannes, MH II, p. 390). 2) Shih chi 56, p. 14
("The Hereditary House of Chancellor Ch'en") adds that
"the exact plan used was secret, so no one today knows
just what happened." (Watson, Records I, p. 161).
3) Shih chi 110, pp. 26-27 ("Memoir on the Hsiung-nu")
gives a detailed account of the P'ing-ch'eng siege but
says that the Emperor was saved because he sent a messenger bearing generous gifts to the consort. (Watson,
Records II, pp. 165-66). Therefore, the tale of Ch'en
P'ing's ruse can be found only in his own biography,
which is hardly surprising. The ruse aroused interest
among the literati, including Liu Hsin and Huan T'an.
Huan tried, as was his wont, to reduce the inexplicable
element, suggesting a deliberate misrepresentation made
to the shan-yü's consort. However, because of Ying
Shao's account, which has erroneously been associated
with Huan T'an, it came to be believed that the first
Chinese portrait was painted about this time, in 201
B.C. This theory has been refuted by P. Pelliot, "Notes
sur quelques artistes des Six dynasties et des T'ang,"
pp. 213-18. Pelliot (on pp. 216-17) also analyzed the
short version of Huan T'an's text found at TPYL 381.3b
(159B). More recently, Max Loehr has discussed the
early development of portraiture in general in "The
Beginnings of Portrait Painting in China," pp. 210-14.

Chapter 15. <u>Mourning for Friends</u>

160

The <u>Chi-chieh</u> commentary to <u>Shih chi</u> 83, p. 21.

Yen 15.8a. Sun 10b.

In his well-known letter from prison, written
to King Hsiao of Liang,[1] which has also been included
in the <u>Wen hsüan</u> (33:3), Tsou Yang mentions a proverb:
"'Sometimes people who have lived together until their
hair is white regard each other as new acquaintances,
while those who meet on the road, halting their carriages, speak under inclined canopies[2] and regard each
other as old friends.' These words mean that it all
depends on whether there is a basis within for mutual
understanding. It does not matter whether the acquaint-
ance is new or old."

161

Li Hsien's commentary to <u>Hou Han shu</u> 1A, p. 5.

Yen 15.8a. Sun 12a.

Chuang Yu's[3] style name was Po-shih.

Previous translation and explanation: H. Bielenstein,
"The Restoration of the Han Dynasty," p. 112, note 1.

162

<u>TPYL</u> 614.4a. <u>PTSC</u> 101.1a.[4]   Yen 15.8a. Sun 15b.

Kao Chün-meng[5] had a broad knowledge of the
laws and regulations. He often bent over his desk
writing texts. The Office of Gentlemen in Charge of
Writings took pity on his advanced age and wished to do
this for him. But he refused, saying, "By writing it
myself I shall pay for the pain of having to proofread
it ten times over."

163

A   Li Hsien's commentary to <u>Hou Han shu</u> 59, pp. 2057-

58.[6] Hu San-hsing's commentary to <u>Tzu-chih t'ung-</u>

<u>chien</u> 38, Han 30, pp. 1216-17.

Yen 15.8a-b. Sun 12a.

Yang Hsiung[7] wrote the <u>Classic on Mystery</u>, believing that Heaven as well as the Way, were the Mystery. He said that the laws established by the sages
and worthies, and the affairs which they administered,
all take Heaven and the Way as their true clue and,
accordingly, embrace under them all species, kingly
government, human affairs, and laws and systems. Therefore, Fu Hsi calls it 'Change,'[8] Lao Tzu calls it 'the
Way,' Confucius calls it 'Origin,'[9] and Yang Hsiung
calls it 'Mystery." The <u>Classic on Mystery</u> consists of
three chapters which record the Way of Heaven, of Earth
and of Man. Three Substances are established--upper,
middle and lower--similar to the Three Classes presented in "The Tribute of Yü."[10]

Three times three makes nine, and nine times
nine makes eighty-one. Therefore, [the <u>Classic</u>] has
eighty-one diagrams. It uses [the number] four to count
[the lines of the diagrams],[11] beginning with one and
going up to four. [The diagrams] are repeated, connected, changed and alternated. In the end, when there
are eighty-one, a new round follows. Nothing may be
subtracted or added. For sorting out, thirty-five[12]
divining stalks of milfoil are used. The <u>Classic on</u>
<u>Mystery</u> consists of more than five thousand words of
text and twelve[13] chapters of commentary.

Previous translation: Pokora, "The Life," II, pp. 545-
46.

B   Wang Ying-lin, <u>K'un-hsüeh chi-wen</u> 9.13a.

Yen 15.8a-b. Sun 12a
(commentary).

Lao Tzu calls it 'Mystery;' Yang Tzu calls it
'Great Mystery.'

164

A Han shu 87B, p. 5136.   Yen 15.8b.

At that time, the Grand Minister of Works,
Wang I and the Communicator Yen Yu[14] heard that Yang
Hsiung had died. They said to Huan T'an, "You have
always praised the writings of Yang Hsiung. Will they
be sent down to future generations?"

Huan T'an said, "They will surely be sent down,
but you and I shall not see it.[15] People despise what
is near and admire what is far.[16] They saw for themselves Yang Tzu-yün's salary, position and appearance,
none of which could move the people, so they scorned
his writings."

Previous translation: Forke, Geschichte der mittel-
alterlichen chinesischen Philosophie, pp. 81-82.

B TPYL 432.6b.   Yen 15.8b.

Someone[17] asked, "What kind of man was Yang
Tzu-yün?"

My answer was, "He was gifted, wise, and possessed an open and penetrating mind. He could attain
the Way of the sages. Since the founding of the Han
dynasty, there has been no one like him."

Previous translation: Pokora, "The Life," II, pp. 551-
52.

C TPYL 602.2a.   Yen 15.8b. Sun 21b.[18]

Yang Tzu-yün's brilliance, reputation and prom-
inence surpassed that of the multitude. Since the
founding of the Han dynasty there has been no one like
him.

The State Master Liu Tzu-chü said, "What do
you mean by these words?"

Huan T'an replied, "There are hundreds of people
who had all-encompassing talents and were authors of
works; only the Grand Historian [Ssu-ma Ch'ien] has

written a very great book. As for the rest, theirs are
but small and fragmentary disquisitions,[19] which cannot
be compared with the Model Sayings and the Great Mystery[20] created by Yang Tzu-yün. People admire what
they hear and despise what they see; therefore, they
underrate and slight these works. If the Great Mystery
should be met by an Emperor who would take an interest
in affairs, he would surely rank it next to the Five
Classics."

Previous translation: Pokora, "The Life," II, pp. 551-
52.

D Lun-heng 13:39, p. 608.   Yen 15.8b.

      Wang Kung-tzu[21] asked Huan Chün-shan about Yang
Tzu-yün. Chün-shan replied, "Since the founding of the
Han dynasty there has been no one like him."

Previous translations: Forke, Lun-heng II, pp. 297-98;
Pokora, "The Life," II, p. 551.

E Liu Chih-chi, Shih t'ung 10:36, p. 15a.[22]

                        Yen 15.8b.

      In the past, when Yang Hsiung's Classic on
Mystery was completed, Huan T'an believed that, even
though it was despised by Yang's contemporaries, nevertheless, "after several hundred years this book will
certainly be sent down [to later generations]."[23]

Previous translation: Byongik, "Zur Wertheorie in der
chinesischen Historiographie auf Grund des Shih-T'ung
des Liu Chih-Chi (661-721)," Oriens Extremus, Vol. 4
(1957), p. 132.

F Commentary to Wen hsüan 3.1b.   Yen 15.8b.   Sun 12b.

      Today everyone reveres the ancient past and
scorns present times, admires what he hears and despises
what he sees.

G Commentary to <u>Wen hsüan</u> 47.43a.

Yen 15.8b.[24] Sun 14b.

Lao Tzu's heart is mysterious and remote, but it is in harmony with the Way.

165

Shih Nung.[25]   Yen 15.8b.

166

Lin Pao, <u>Yüan-ho hsing tsuan</u>, p. 130. Shih Nung.[25]

Yen 15.8a. Sun,
preface 4a.

An intelligent man, acting in accordance with the rites proper to a son.[26]

167

A <u>TPYL</u> 619.6a.   Yen 15.9a. Sun 23b.

Liang Tzu-ch'u and Yang Tzu-lin, who held with me the office of a Gentleman, liked to study. They wrote some ten thousand scrolls until their heads turned white. They once sent me some hundred items which they could not understand.[27] When I looked at their problems, I could generally understand them.

B Wang Ying-lin, <u>K'un-hsüeh chi-wen</u> 8.36a-b.

Sun, preface 4b.

[In the distant past, before books were printed from wooden blocks, those who liked to study suffered from the lack of books. Huan T'an's <u>Hsin-lun</u> mentions] Liang Tzu-ch'u and Yang Tzu-lin, who wrote ten thousand scrolls before their heads turned white.[28]

176

168

PTSC 68.4a-b.   Yen 15.9a.   Sun 15a.[29]

Chou Hu, the grandson of Chou Chih of Mou-ling,
did not write rhyme-prose, odes or complimentary pieces.
When he became a Department Head in the Grand Ministry
Over the Masses, he was in charge of a multitude of affairs and responsible for establishing the meaning of
the texts.[30]

NOTES: CHAPTER 15

1.   See, for example, Y. Hervouet, Un poète de cour sous les Han, p. 33. The letter has been translated by E. von Zach, Die Chinesische Anthologie II, pp. 722-27.

2.   The term ch'ing-kai 傾蓋 ("inclined canopies") occurs in K'ung-tzu chia-yü II, 8b, which is translated by R. P. Kramers as follows: "When Confucius went to T'an, he met Master Ch'eng on the way. Under the inclined canopies [of their carriages], they conversed the whole day very affectionately" (cf. K'ung-tzu chia-yü, pp. 237 and 333, for an explanation). It is not clear whether Tso Yang was alluding to the tradition used by the K'ung-tzu chia-yü.

3.   Because Chuang was the taboo personal name of Emperor Ming, Wang Mang's general Chuang Yu is given as "Yen Yu" in Hou Han shu and other sources of that time. P. Pelliot studied the possible semantic relationship between the two words chuang and yen in a note in JA, Vol. 20(1912), p. 168.

4.   PTSC 101.1a has the same text as TPYL 614.4a, but it does not include the quote in the last sentence of the fragment.

5.   This man cannot be identified, but the style name Chün-meng was quite common during the Former Han period. Sun gives only Kao Chün. Apparently Kao Chün-meng was a frustrated official with literary ambitions.

6.   This is the biography of the famous astronomer Chang Heng. Li Hsien says that Chang Heng greatly admired Yang Hsiung's T'ai hsüan ching.

7.   This should read "Yang Tzu-yün."

8.   This statement reflects the theory that Fu-hsi was the author of the Book of Changes.

9.   This statement reflects the theory that Confucius was the author of the Ch'un-ch'iu. The first word of the Ch'un-ch'iu is yüan 元 , which could mean "origin" or "first" as in "first year" (yüan nien 元 年). There has been much speculation about its meaning; see J. Legge, The Ch'un Ts'ew, pp. 1 and 4. Tung Chung-shu, of course, did not ignore this problem;

see O. Franke, Studien zur Geschichte, p. 301, note 1.
Even Wang Ch'ung mentions the yüan principle of the
Ch'un-ch'iu, associating it with Yang Hsiung's T'ai-
hsüan; see Lun-heng 29:84, p. 1174 (with the detailed
explanation by Huang Hui), and Forke, I, p. 88. During
the Han period, the term yüan also played a certain role
in calendrical computations, denoting an epochal cycle
of 4617 years; see Sivin, "Cosmos and Computation in
Early Chinese Mathematical Astronomy," p. 15.

10.   These three classes of tribute were gold, silver,
and copper, according to the Book of Documents III:I:VII:
52; Legge, p. 115. For a detailed explanation, see
ibid., pp. 110-11, sub. 44.

11.   This may refer to the four categories of the
T'ai-hsüan ching, which consists of three fang, nine
chou, twenty-seven pu, and eighty-one chia, or, according to Huan T'an, it may refer to four multiplications
by 3, which total 81 (i.e., 1x3=3, 3x3=9, 9x3=27,
27x3=81). There are also 729 tsan in the T'ai-hsüan
ching ($729=3^6$).

12.   The commentator Liu Pin (1022-1088) is quoted
in the commentary to the Tzu-chih t'ung-chien 38 (5th
year t'ien feng, p. 1217) as saying that there should
be thirty-six stalks. The T'ai-hsüan ching itself sets
the number at thirty-six, which is a multiple of the
principal numbers three and four, ($4 \times 9=36$, or $2^2 \times 3^2=36$).

13.   Yen gives "thirteen chapters" instead of
"twelve."

14.   Yen Yu is really Chuang. See fragment 161,
note 3.

15.   Forke (Geschichte der mittelälterlichen chinesischen Philosophie, p. 81) believes that Huan T'an's
statement ends here and that the remaining sentences
express the ideas of the author of the Han Shu. But,
see note 16 below, which indicates why I believe that
the remaining sentences should also be attributed to
Huan T'an.

16.   Huan T'an's memorial to Emperor Kuang-wu ex-
presses similar sentiments: "It is the character
of all men to disregard the facts before their eyes
and to value strange things learned from rumor;" see
Hou Han shu 28A, p. 1015, and Pokora, "The Life," I,
p. 29. See also fragment 164C and F.

17.   Yen, apparently following 164D, adds the name
of Wang Kung-tzu or Wang I. See also note 21 below.

18.   Sun's quotation omits the introduction and begins with Liu Hsin's question.

19.   P. Pelliot has carefully explained the meaning
of ts'ui-ts'an 聚 殘 (here translated as "small
and fragmentary") in "Meou-tseu ou les doutes levés,"
p. 412, note 376.

20.   Both Yen and Sun add ching 經 ("classic"),
which would make the title of Yang's work the Classic
of Great Mystery.

21.   Wang Kung-tzu is Wang I, the Grand Minister of
Works; (see fragment 164A). Sun I-jang (quoted by Huang
Hui, and by Liu P'an-sui, Lun-heng chi-chieh, p. 282)
believes that Wang Kung (王 公) refers to Wang Mang
and that the character tzu (子) is superfluous. Sun
says, "Huan T'an served Wang Mang as an official.
Therefore, the Hsin-lun often calls Wang Mang by the
name Wang Weng (王 翁 "venerable old Wang"). This
Sir Wang (or Wang Kung 王 公) is the same man as the
'venerable old Wang.' When the TPYL [432.6b; fragment
164B] quotes the Hsin-lun, it does not say who [see
note 17 above] asked [about Yang Hsiung]. Thus, it is
possible to correct the omission." Neither of the two
modern editors of the Lun-heng, Huang Hui or Liu P'an-
sui, follow Sun I-jang's suggestion that it was Wang
Mang who had this discussion with Huan T'an.

22.   Chapter "Tzu-hsü" of the Shih t'ung is autobiographical. Liu Chih-chi says, "My talent is lower
[than that of Yang Hsiung], but my bearing is like that
of this earlier wise man. I recorded it in my heart
and thus consoled myself. But, I fear that there is
one point in which I differ from Yang Hsiung. Why?"

23.   Liu Chih-chi continues, "Later Chang Heng and
Lu Chi did indeed hold that it was incomparable, attaining [the level of the works of] the sages."

24.   Properly speaking, fragment 164F does not fit
the context of the other versions of the fragment. Yen
says that he included it in fragment 164 because Han shu
87B (p. 5136; fragment 164A) mentions Lao Tzu. Of
course, these are the words of Pan Ku; even Yen does
not attribute them to Huan T'an.

25.   The text has: "In Ch'i there was a worthy man, Shih Tzu, who wrote a book. See Mencius. Hsin-lun has Shih Nung." For Shih Tzu, see Mencius II:II:X:3-5; Legge, pp. 226-27. In view of the following fragment, the Hsin-lun which is referred to is Huan T'an's.

26.   This apparently refers to Shih Nung. The text quotes from Huan T'an's Hsin-lun. See also the fore-going fragment and note 25.

27.   Instead of ch'ang 嘗 ("once"), both Yen and Sun have ch'ang 常 ("often").

28.   This may mean that Liang and Yang spent a great deal of time copying out their own works.

29.   Sun has a shorter version: "Chou Chih of Mou-ling."

30.   Yen's word-order differs somewhat from that given in the text.

Chapter 16.   The Way of the Zither

There are two or three different translations
of the name of the musical instrument ch'in; it has been
called a lute, a harp and a zither. R. H. van Gulik
used the term "lute," as can be seen from the title of
his book devoted to the ch'in ideology, The Lore of the
Chinese Lute. Nakajima Chiaki (in the English resume
of his article, cited in note 6 to fragment 169A1)
translates ch'in as "harp," as does another eminent
Japanese musicologist, Kishibe Shigeo (see note 2 to
fragment 42A). But, L. E. R. Picken, who has recently
catalogued the Chinese musical instruments, translates
the term as "zither" (pp. 103-107), classifying it as
the first of the chordophones; see his "T'ang Music and
Musical Instruments."

169

Al   I lin 3.10b.   Yen 15.9a.   Sun 8b.

Shen Nung succeeded Fu Hsi as ruler of the Empire. He made a ch'in from the wood of the t'ung tree.
It was three ch'ih, six ts'un and six fen long, symbolizing the number [of days] in a full year.1 It was
one eight-[tenths] ts'un thick, symbolizing the multiple
of three and six. Above, it was circular and gathered
in, following the model of Heaven; below, it was square
and flat, following the model of earth. Above, it was
broad, while below, it was narrow, following the model
of the rituals2 between superiors and inferiors. Ch'in
means "to restrain."3 The sages and worthies of the
ancient past played the zither to cultivate their
hearts. In adversity, they would devote themselves to
perfecting their own persons and would not lose their
principles; therefore, a composition for [the zither]
was called a ts'ao ["principle"].4 In success, they
would devote themselves to perfecting the Empire, so
that there would be nothing that would not reach and
penetrate; therefore, a composition for the zither is
called a ch'ang ("penetration").5 The "Yao ch'ang" has
been lost6 and is no longer preserved. The "Shun ts'ao"
sounds clear and subtle. The "Viscount of Wei ts'ao"
sounds clear and pure. The "Chi-tzu ts'ao" sounds pure
and overflowing.7

182

A2   TPYL 596.6b.   Ch'u-hsüeh chi 16.4b.

Yen 15.9a.   Sun 3b.

Shen Nung succeeded Fu Hsi as ruler of the Empire. Above, he looked for a model in Heaven; below,
he took his model from the earth. From near, he took
[his model] from his own person; from far, he took it
from all beings. Then, for the first time, he made a
ch'in of wood cut from the t'ung tree. He tied silk to
create a string, thus attaining communion with Divine
Virtue, and concord with the harmony of Heaven and
earth.

Variations of this paragraph may be found in IWLC 44.2b-
3a; TPYL 814.3a; Chang Ch'iao's commentary to Fu I's
Ch'in fu in Ku-wen yüan 21, pp. 451-52; commentary to
Wen hsüan, 13.19a and 28.28a; TPYL 956.6a; and IWLC
88.35a.

B   Commentary to Wen hsüan 34.5a.   Yen 15.9a.   Sun 3a.

The decoration on the ch'in is forty-five fen
long;[8] its length before the decoration is eight fen.

C   TPYL 579.5b.   Ch'u-hsüeh chi 16.4b.

Yen 15.9b.   Sun 4b.

Shen Nung made a seven-stringed ch'in, which
was sufficient to bring him into communion with the ten
thousand beings, and [to allow him] to scrutinize and
order chaos.

D1   TPYL 579.5b.   Ch'u-hsüeh chi 16.4a.

Yen 15.9b.   Sun 3b.

Among the eight sounds,[9] that of silk[10] [i.e.,
strings] is the finest; and [among silk instruments]
the ch'in is supreme.

D2   Commentary to Wen hsüan, quoting Huan T'an's Hsin-

lun.   Yen 15.9b.   Sun 3a.

     The eight sounds are broad and extensive. The
virtue of the ch'in is most abundant.

E   Ku Yeh-wang, Yü p'ien 16, p. 60, 2.

                                     Yen 15.9b.   Sun 3a.

     [The ch'in] was created by Shen Nung. The
meaning of ch'in is "to restrain." The superior man
keeps to it in order to restrain himself.

F   Commentary to Wen hsüan 18.7b.   Yen 15.9b.   Sun 3a.

     On [the composition of] the "Shun ts'ao:"
Shun's saintly virtue was mysterious and remote.11
Then he rose to become the Son of Heaven. He sighed,
longing for his parents, [and thought that] the exalted
position of Lord on High was not worth keeping. He
drew forth his ch'in and composed the ts'ao.

G1   PTSC 109.5b.   Yen 15.9b.   Sun 3b.

     On [the composition of] the "Yü ts'ao:" In
the past, in the Hsia period, there was a flood which
surrounded the mountains and immersed the hills. Then
Yü drew forth his ch'in and made a ts'ao. Its sound
was clear and, at the same time, narrow,12 flowing like
a small stream that wished to become a deep river.

G2   Commentary to Wen hsüan 12.1b.   Sun 3b (commentary)

     In the time of Yü of the Hsia dynasty, the
waters of this flood were singing.

H1   TPYL 916.9b.   Commentary to Wen hsüan 18.6b.

                                     Yen 15.9b.   Sun 3a.

     On [the composition of] the "Viscount of Wei
ts'ao:" The Viscount of Wei mourned the imminent end

of the Yin dynasty, but nothing could be done. Seeing the wild swans flying on high, he drew forth his ch'in and composed a ts'ao. Its music was clear and pure.[13]

H2 Commentary to Wen hsüan 18.7a.   Yen 15.9b (commentary). Sun 3a.

His performance was like the cry of a wailing wild goose.[14]

I1 TPYL 84.5b.   Yen 15.9b-10a. Sun 4a-b.

On [the composition of] the "King Wen ts'ao:" In the time of King Wen, Chou Hsin was unprincipled. He melted metal and made a gridiron[15] and filled a pond with overflowing wine. The courtiers in the palace murdered one another until their bones and flesh became a mire. He had a jade room, as well as a jasper terrace.[16] Many clouds appeared, shading the wind. The sound of his bells[17] rose like thunder, shaking Heaven and earth.

King Wen himself abided by the laws and regulations, secretly practicing benevolence and righteousness.[18] He drew forth his ch'in and composed a ts'ao. Therefore, its sound was tumultuous and agitated, with fearsome chüeh notes and thunderous shang notes.

I2 PTSC 41.5b.   Yen 15.10a. Sun 4b
                                        (commentary).

Chou Hsin melted metal into a gridiron; he made a pond of overflowing wine. Bones and flesh became a mire.

J1 Commentary to Wen hsüan 11.5b-6a.

                            Yen 15.9b. Sun 2b.

Ch'in: There is the "ts'ao" ["principle of playing the ch'in"] of Po I. When he encountered an unusual situation, he devoted himself exclusively to perfecting his own person; therefore, [his playing of the ch'in] was called a ts'ao [or "principle"].

J2 Commentary to Wen hsüan 16.4b. (Sun 2b, commentary).

Ch'in: On the "Po I ts'ao:" In adversity, he
devoted himself to perfecting his own person and not
losing his principles; therefore, [his composition for
the ch'in] was called a ts'ao [or "principle"]. This
means "to elevate oneself and become encouraged."[19]

J3 Commentary to Wen hsüan 17.7a.   Yen 15.10a (commen-
                                              tary).
                                      Sun 2b (commentary).

Ch'in: There is the "Po I ts'ao."

J4 Commentary to Wen hsüan 18.2b.   Yen 15.10a (commen-
                                              tary).
                                      Sun 2b.

The "Po I ts'ao" is like the cry of a wild
goose.[20]

K Commentary to Tu Yu's T'ung-tien 144.7b.

                              Yen 15.9a-b. Sun 3b.

The five strings: the first string is called
the kung tone and thereafter follow the shang, chüeh,
chih, and yü [strings]. Kings Wen and Wu each added
one string to make the "smaller kung" and the "smaller
shang" [strings].[21]

L Commentary to Wen hsüan 18.3b.   Yen 15.9b. Sun 2b.

The lower chih:[22] The seven strings gather together this pivot [of all things].[23]

M Commentary to Wen hsüan 18.10b. Yen 15.9b. Sun 3a.

[When the zither is] loud, it is not noisy,
clamorous or reckless.[24] [When the zither is] soft,
it does not sink and become inaudible.[25]

170

Li Hsien's commentary to Hou Han shu 36, pp. 1306-
1307.[26]   Yen 15.10a. Sun 4a.

  Master K'uang of Chin was an expert in the study
of tones. Duke Ling of Wei was about to visit Chin.
At night he lodged on the shore of the river P'u, and
during the night he heard some new music. He summoned
Master Chüan and told him, "Listen to this and write it
down for me."

  [Master Chüan] replied, "I have it."

  Afterwards they went to Chin, where Duke P'ing
of Chin entertained them. When they became drunk with
wine, Duke Ling said, "I have some new music which I
would like to have performed before you." Then he ordered Master Chüan to play the ch'in. But before the
end [of the performance], Master K'uang halted it, saying, "This is the music of a destroyed country."[27]

171

A P'ei Sung-chih's commentary to San-kuo chih, Shu

 chih 12.17a-b.   Yen 15.10a-11a. Sun 1a-2b.

  Yung-men Chou, [summoned] because of his [skill
in playing] the ch'in, paid a visit to the Lord of Meng-
ch'ang,[28] who said, "Sir, you can play the ch'in. Can
you also make me sad?"[29]

  "[You ask me]," Chou replied, "whom I can make
sad. There are those who were at first exalted and
later humbled; who were once rich and now are poor; and
who, rejected and oppressed, dwell in poor alleys and
have no intercourse with their neighbors. These cannot
compare with those whose person and talents are noble
and beautiful, who carry substance in their heart and
embrace the truth, but who meet with slander and en-
counter calumny, and who are enmeshed by ill-feeling
and cannot win trust. These cannot compare with those
who love but, without a quarrel, are parted from their
loved ones during their life; and who must leave for
some distant and remote land, not knowing when they will
see their loved ones again. These cannot compare with

those who, when young have no father or mother, who,
full-grown, have no wife nor child, who, going out, are
neighbor to the wild marsh and, coming in, dwell in a
hole dug in the ground, and who are in want by day and
by night and cannot borrow. Men such as these need only
hear the cry of a flying bird or the sighing of the
autumn wind through the branches to become sorrowful.
As soon I draw forth my lute for them, they will heave
long sighs and, without exception, grieve and weep.

"But you, Sir, live at present in large mansions
and high halls, in inner rooms reached by doors leading
to doors. Curtains are dropped; fresh breezes enter.
Singers and performers stand before you. Flatterers
and sycophants serve at your side. Musicians strike
up dances from Ch'u. Concubines from Cheng sing songs
to beguile your ears, while their practiced charms se-
duce your eyes. Playing on the water, you sail in dragon boats with feather banners hoisted. You drum and
fish in fathomless pools.[30] Roving in the wilderness,
you climb above the plains[31] and race in vast parks.
Strong cross-bows bring down birds from on high. Val-
iant men roast[32] wild game. Wine is served and you amuse
yourself. You are drunk and forget to come home. At
such a time you value Heaven and earth less than your
finger.[33] Even someone who is skilled at playing the
zither could not move Your Highness."

The Lord of Meng-ch'ang replied, "It is indeed
so."[34]

Yung-men Chou said, "But I have observed, Sir,
that there is a reason why you are incessantly sad.
Sir, you are the man who fights for the position of Emperor and who has frustrated Ch'in. You are the one
who aligned the Five Kingdoms to attack Ch'u, so the
Empire is never at peace. There is [always] either a
vertical or a horizontal alliance. If the vertical alliance succeeds, Ch'u will become King; if the horizontal alliance succeeds, Ch'in will be Emperor. Should
the strength of Ch'in and Ch'u be used as a retribution
against your weak Hsieh, it would be like grinding a
billhook to attack the morning mushroom.[35] Among informed gentlemen, there are none who do not shiver on
Your Highness' account.

"Constant prosperity is not the Way of Heaven.
Cold and heat advance and retreat. One thousand autumns
and ten thousand years from now, the spirits in your

ancestral temple will no longer be offered sacrifices.
High towers will tumble down and curbed lakes fill up.
Wild thorns will grow on your grave,[36] and foxes and
wild cats will build their lairs there. Wandering children and herd-boys will shuffle their feet and sing on
your grave. Is not the honor and dignity of the Lord
of Meng-ch'ang also like this?"

Thereupon, the Lord of Meng-ch'ang heaved a long
sigh. Tears came to his eyes but he did not weep. Yung-
men Chou drew forth his ch'in and played it gently. He
plucked the kung and chih tones and struck the chüeh
and yü tones until a song was made. Sighing and sobbing,
the Lord of Meng-ch'ang listened and said, "Master, when
you play the ch'in, you instantly turn me into a man
whose country has been destroyed."

B Li Shan's commentary to Wen hsüan quotes thirteen
times from fragment 171A, with some unimportant textual
variants. Yen gives these textual variations in his
"complete" text, so I will merely list here those places
in the commentary where they can be found. They are,
in order of decreasing length: 46.1b, 23.22b, 41.1b,
39.32a, 37.3a, 21.25b, 18.32a, 30.28a, 43.24b, 60.29b,
35.26a, 42.13a, 31.4b, and 28.1b.

172

A TPYL 248.7b.   Yen 15.11a-b.

Under Emperor Hsüan, during the yüan-k'ang and
shen-chüeh periods,[37] the Lieutenant Chancellor reported
the names of those who could play court music on the
ch'in and se. Chao Ting from Po-hai and Lung Te from
the Kingdom of Liang were summoned to the Wen-shih Hall
and appointed Gentlemen-in-Attendance.

B PTSC 71.3a.   Yen 15.11a-b.

Under Emperor Hsüan, during the yüan-k'ang and
shen-chüeh periods, Chao Ting from Po-hai and Lung Te
from the Kingdom of Liang were summoned to the Wen-shih
Hall and appointed Gentlemen-in-Attendance. Both were
familiar with books on the ch'in.

173

Commentary to <u>Wen hsüan</u> 24.4b.   Yen 15.11b.   Sun 14a.

Among those instrumentalists[38] at the Yellow
Gates who were skilled at playing the <u>ch'in</u>, Jen Chen-
ch'ing and Yü Ch'ang-ch'ien could teach the number of
intervals. Their excellent songs were tunes handed
down from the ancient past.

174

<u>TPYL</u> 581.5a.   Yen 15.11b.   Sun 4b.

Ch'eng Shao-po, an instrumentalist, piped on
the <u>yü</u>.[39] When he saw Chang Tzu-hsia, the Marquis of
An-ch'ang,[40] playing the <u>ch'in</u>, he told him, "As far
as musical tones[41] are concerned, if you are not familiar
with over a thousand songs, you cannot be considered an
expert."

NOTES: CHAPTER 16

1.   One ch'ih consists of ten ts'un, or one hundred
fen; the ch'in was 366 fen long, and 366 is the number
of days in a leap year. A "Ch'in ts'ao" (composed, perhaps, by Ts'ai Yung), quoted in Ch'u-hsüeh chi 16.la,
asserts that it was Fu Hsi, rather than Shen Nung, who
invented the ch'in. Nevertheless, Hsü Chien's appended
commentary says that Shih pen, Shuo wen and Huan T'an's
Hsin-lun all agree in giving the credit to Shen Nung.

2.   Sun gives t'i 體 ("form"), instead of li 禮
("rituals").

3. 禁 The editors of I lin found the character chin
illegible, but it is clear in fragment 169E.

4.   Ts'ao 操 or "principle." The bibliographical
chapters of the T'ang dynastic histories call Huan T'an's
study on the ch'in, "Ch'in ts'ao," instead of the original "Ch'in tao;" see T'ang shu ching-chi i-wen ho chih,
p. 31. Ts'ai Yung's work on the same theme is called
Ch'in ts'ao. Semantically, there is no great difference
between the meanings of tao 道 ("way") and ts'ao.
Tung-ch'ang 通 暢 ("reach and penetrate") indicates
that everything will, unimpeded, attain self-fulfill-
ment.

5.   This sentence is quoted in the commentary to
Wen hsüan 18.6b.

6.   The commentary to Wen hsüan 18.6b has Yao ch'ang
i 堯 暢 逸 ("The 'Yao ch'ang' is lost"). But Sun
has yao ch'ang ching i 堯 暢 經 逸 ("the 'Yao ch'ang
classic' is lost"). The word ch'ang, which is a musical
term associated with the ch'in, has been analyzed by
E. Chavannes in MH II, pp. 160-61, note 3. Chavannes
shows that there are two different characters 暢 and
暢 ; the meaning of the first is "s'étendre, péné-
trer." Jao Tsung-i (in the study cited in note 29 to
fragment 171A also interprets the term ch'ang (t'ung
ch'ang 通 暢) to mean "all-penetrating." Another
important study on the use of the ch'in during the Han
dynasty is that by Nakajima Chiaki, "Gakin no ongaku
shisō ni tsuite."

7.   溢 ("overflowing"). Sun has chi 激 ("agitated").

8.   One <u>fen</u> is 0.231 cm.

9.   The "eight sounds" refers to the eight kinds of instruments, which are, respectively, made of silk, bamboo, metal, stone, wood, earthenware, leather, and gourd.

10.   The text of the <u>Ch'u-hsüeh chi</u> 16.4a is somewhat different: "that of string [is most?]..."

11.   <u>PTSC</u> 7.3a quotes this sentence from Huan-tzu.

12.   The text has <u>ai</u> 隘 ("a pass," "narrow"), Sun has <u>i</u> 益 ("growing"), and Yen has another <u>i</u> 溢 ("overflowing"). See note 7 above.

13.   This last statement can also be found near the end of fragment 169A1. It is not included in the version found in the commentary to <u>Wen hsüan</u> 18.6b.

14.   See fragment 169J4.

15.   The story of Chou Hsin is told in <u>Lü-shih ch'un-ch'iu</u> 23:4, p. 301; Wilhelm, p. 410. Apparently, accused men were forced to walk on the glowing gridiron and were burned by the coals when they fell, much to Chou Hsin's delight.

16.   These precious stones, among others, are mentioned in <u>Huai-nan-tzu</u> 8, p. 118. Kao Yu, who has commented on both the <u>Lü-shih ch'un-ch'iu</u> and the <u>Huai-nan-tzu</u>, believes that <u>hsüan</u> 璇 ("jade") and <u>yao</u> 瑤 ("jasper") should be read as <u>hsüan</u> 旋 ("revolving") and <u>yao</u> 搖 ("swaying"), which would be translated as a "revolving room" and a "swaying terrace." His theory is corroborated by <u>Lü-shih ch'un-ch'iu</u> (cf. note 15 above), which also mentions a leaning palace.

17.   See <u>Li chi</u>, "Yüeh chi," XVII:III:15; Legge II, p. 120.

18.   The fact that King Wen did this "himself" and "secretly" shows his integrity. His respect for law and his practice of benevolence were not a mere public display.

19.   Compare fragments 169J1 and 2 with 169A1.

20.   See 169H2.

21.   Sun adds, "These explanations are not consistent.
As for the original creator of the ch'in, some say it
was Fu Hsi, while others say Shen Nung. None of the
different authors' explanations can be verified." Sun
thought the statements in fragment 169K are exclusively
those of Huan T'an, but Yen correctly points out that
the last part was added by Tu Yu. See also note 1 above.

22.   The meaning of the phrase "the lower chih" is
obscure.

23.   Shu Yao ("pivot") is also the name of the North
Star or Polar Star, which was believed to be the pivot
of Heaven.

24.   The term liu-man 流漫 (or 慢) ("reckless")
associated with the new music, is found in Hsün Tzu's
treatise on music, 14:20:5, p. 253; Dubs, p. 251. See
also Shih chi 87, p. 32; Bodde, China's First Unifier,
pp. 41-42.

25.   This passage may explain fragment 169D1, which
asserts that the ch'in is supreme among stringed instruments.

26.   This commentary from the Hsin-lun is appended
to the Hou Han Shu's account of Fan Sheng's fervent refusal to acknowledge the Tso chuan as a Classic.

27.   This is a short version of a well-known story
related in Shih chi 24, pp. 72-74; Chavannes, MH III,
pp. 287-88. Gimm (Das Yüeh-fu, pp 96-101) discusses
it in great detail.

28.   The Lord of Meng-ch'ang was T'ien Wen. A more
elaborate version of this story can be found in Shuo
yüan 11.8a-11a.

29.   Jao Tsung-yi has made two studies which shed
light on this text: "The Relation between Principles
of Literary Criticisms in the Wei and Tsin Dynasties
and Music--Illustration of Literature through Music,"
and "Lu Chi Wen-fu li-lun yü yin-yüeh chih kuan-hsi."
The principle of sadness is mentioned by Lu Chi in §87
of his Wen fu; A. Fang, "Rhyme-prose on Literature,"
p. 541.

30.   Shuo yüan 11.10a has, "...you drum and pipe in
fathomless pools."

31.   This refers to hunting, as Shuo yüan, ibid., makes clear.

32.   The term ko 㧁 ("roast") is explained in Lü-shih ch'un-ch'iu 23:4, p. 301; Wilhelm, p. 410. A slightly different explanation is given by Yen Shih-ku in his commentary to Han shu 85, p. 5001. See fragment 169I1, note 15.

33.   This alludes to Mencius VI:I:XIV, 4-5, where Mencius explains that all the parts of the body must be properly nourished. In his translation, Legge (p. 417) says, "He who nourishes one of his fingers, neglecting his shoulders or his back, without knowing that he is doing so, is a man who resembles a hurried wolf. A man who only eats and drinks is counted mean by others--because he nourishes what is little to the neglect of what is great."

34.   In Shuo yüan 11.1a, T'ien Wen totally rejects Yung-men Chou's conclusion.

35.   This alludes to Chuang-tzu I:I:I:2; Legge, p. 166. Chao-chün 朝 菌 (here translated as "morning mushroom") is also the name of an insect which, like the morning mushroom, lives only for a very short time.

36.   For the thorns, ching and chi, see fragment 38, note 19.

37.   The yüan-k'ang period was from 65 B.C. to 62 B.C., and the shen-chüeh period, from 61 B.C. to 58 B.C.

38.   Kung 工 ("instrumentalists"). Gimm (Das Yüeh-fu, p. 120, sub 426) translates kung-jen 工人 as "Instrumentalisten." See also fragment 119, note 47.

39.   Gimm (Das Yüeh-fu, pp. 126-27, sub 2-3) translates this as "Mundorgel."

40.   Chang Tzu-hsia appears to be Chang Hung, who, according to Han shu 19B, p. 1329, was promoted to Colonel of the Elite Cavalry in 2 B.C., from the post of Grand Master of Ceremonies. His father, Chang Yü (died in 6 B.C.), was an expert on the Book of the Changes and was regarded as a connoisseur of music (Han shu 81, p. 4889).

41.   Yin 音 (here translated as "musical tone"); for a more complete definition, see Gimm, Das Yüeh-fu, p. 550, sub 13.

Table I

Comparative Tables of the Fragments with the Editions

by Yen K'o-chün and Sun P'ing-i

Fragment	Chapter	Yen	Sun
1	1	13.2a	14a
2		13.2a	26a, 23a
3	2	13.2b	11a, 4b-5a
4		13.2b	14b
5		13.2b	18a
6		13.2b-3a	20a, 5a
7	3	13.3a	5a
8		13.3a	20b
9		13.3a	
10		13.3a	21a
11		13.3a-b	20a
12		13.3b	5a
13		13.3b-4a	
14		13.4a	
15		13.4a	9a
16		13.4a	15a
17		13.4a	15a
18		13.4a	14a
19		13.4a	14a
20		13.4a	5a
21		13.4b	
22		13.4b	24a
23		13.4b	14b
24		13.4b-5a	17b
25		13.5a	17b
26		13.5a	5a-b
27		13.5a	14b
28		13.5a-6a	
29		13.6a	5b
30		13.6a	5b
31		13.6a	
32	4	13.6b-7a	
33		13.7a	15b
34		13.7a	15b
35		13.7b	
36		13.7b	18a-b
37		13.7b	
38		13.8a	
39		13.8a	
40		13.8a-b	22b

Fragment	Chapter	Yen	Sun
41	5	13.8a	
42		13.8b	6a
43		13.8b	22a
44		13.8b-9a	17a
45		13.9a	6a
46		13.9a	14a
47		13.9a	24a
48		13.9a-b	17a-b
49		13.9b	20b
50		13.9b	24a
51		13.9b	25a
52	6	14.1a-b	
53		14.1b-2b	
54		14.2b	9b
55		14.2b-3a	23b
56		14.3a	22b
57		14.3a	25b
58		14.3a	
59		14.3b	11a
60		14.3b	6b
61		14.3b	9b
62		14.3b	12b
63		14.3b	16a
64		14.4a	13a
65		14.4a-b	
66		14.4b-5a	25a
67	7	14.5a	6b
68		14.5a	6b
69		14.5a	6b-7a
70		14.5a	7a
71		14.5a	13b
72		14.5a	13b
73		14.5a	14b
74		14.5b	15a
75		14.5b	18a
76		14.5b	21a
77		14.5b	25a
78		14.5b	
79	8	14.5b-6a	25b-26a
80		14.6a	7a-b
81		14.6a	7b
82		14.6a-b	11b
83		14.6b	26a
84		14.6b-8a	

Fragment	Chapter	Yen	Sun
85		14.8a	26a
86		14.8a	26a
87	9	14.8b	13b
88		14.8b	11b
89		14.8b	7b
90		14.8b-9a	23a-b
91		14.9a	20b-21a
92		14.9a	
93		14.9a	18a
94		14.9b	12b
95		14.9b-10a	15a
96		14.10a	
97		14.10a	7b
98	10	14.10a	7b
99		14.10a	13b
100		14.10a-b	20a-b
101		14.10b	19b
102		14.10b-11a	16b-17a
103		14.11a	
104		14.11a	22b
105	11	15.1a	8a
106		15.1a	8a, 21a
107		15.1a	11b
108		15.1a-b	20a
109		15.1b	11b
110		15.1b	8a
111		15.1b-2a	11b
112		15.2a	18a
113		15.2a	16a
114		15.2a	19b
115		15.2a-b	
116		15.2b	
117		15.2b	18a
118		15.2b	
119		15.2b	13b
120		15.3a	15a
121		15.3a	14b
122		15.3a	23a
123		15.3a	15a
124		15.3a	4a
125		15.3a	20b
126		13.3a-b	9b, 13a
127		15.3b	
128		15.3b	25a
129		15.3b	9a

Fragment	Chapter	Yen	Sun
130		15.3b	
131		15.3b	9a
132		15.4a	16a
133		15.4a	19b
134		15.4a-b	18b
135		15.14b	21b
136		15.4b	19b
137		15.4b	11a
138		15.5a	24b
139	12	15.5a	15b
140		15.5a	8a
141		15.5a-b	14b
142		15.5b	[15b]
143	13	15.5b	8a
144		15.5b	8a
145		15.5b	Pref. 3b
146		15.5b	8a-b
147		15.5b	8b, 13b
148		15.6a	13a
149		15.6a	24b
150		15.6a	13b, 13a, 9b
151		15.6a-b	12a
152		15.6b	23b
153		15.6b	21b
154		15.6b	
155		15.6b-7a	21a
156		15.7a	17b
157		15.7a-b	24b
158		15.7b	25b
159	14	15.7b-8a	10a-b
160	15	15.8a	10b
161		15.8a	12a
162		15.8a	15b
163		15.8a-b	12a
164		15.8b	
165		15.8b	Pref. 4a
166		15.9a	Pref. 4a
167		15.9a	23b, Pref. 4b
168		15.9a	15a
169	16	15.9a	2b-4b, 8b
170		15.10a	4a
171		15.10a-11a	1a-2b
172		15.11a-b	
173		15.11b	14a
174		15.11b	4b

Table II

Comparative Tables of the Fragments with the

Editions by Yen K'o-chün and Sun P'ing-i

Sun	Yen	Fragment
1a-2b	15.10a-11a	171
2b	15.9b	169J1 and 3
2b	15.9b	169C
2b	15.10a	169J4
2b	15.9b	169L
3a	15.9b	169F
3a	15.9b	169H1
3a	15.9b	169F
3a	15.9b	169M
3a	15.9b	169E
3a	15.9b	[169D1]
3a	15.9a	169B
3b	15.9a	[169A2]
3b	15.9a	169K
3b	15.9b	169G1
4a	15.3a	124
4a	15.10a	170
4a-b	15.9b-10a	169I1
4b	15.9b	169C
4b	15.11b	174
4b-5a	13.2a-b	3B
5a	13.2b-3a	6B
5a	13.3a	7
5a	13.3b	12
5a	13.4a	20 [and 26]
5a-b	13.5a	26
5b	13.6a	29
5b	13.6a	30
5b-6a	13.7b	35B
6a	13.8a	38B
6a	13.8b	42
6a-b	13.9a	45
6b	14.3b	60
6b	14.5a	67
6b	14.5a	68
6b	14.5a	69
7a	14.5a	70
7a	14.5a	71
7a	14.5b-6a	79A and C

Sun	Yen	Fragment
7a-b	14.6a	80
7b	14.6a	81
7b	14.8b	89
7b	14.8b	90B
7b	14.9b	94C
7b	14.10a	97
7b	14.10a	98A
8a	15.1a	105
8a	15.1a	106
8a	15.1b	110
8a	15.5a	140
8a	15.5b	143
8a	15.5b	144
8a-b	15.5b	146A
8b	15.5b	147
8b	15.9a	169A
9a	15.3b	129
9a	14.9a-b	93
9a	15.3b	131
9a	13.4a	15
9b	13.4a	15
9b	14.2a	54
9b	15.3a-b	126
9b	14.3b	62
9b	15.6a	150
10a	15.7b-8a	159
10b	15.8a	160
10b-11a	13.7b	35A
11a	13.2a-b	3A
11a	15.4b	137A and B
11a	14.3b	59
11b	15.1a	107
11b	15.1a	108
11b	15.1b	109
11b	14.6a	82D
11b	14.9a	90B
11b	14.8b	88
11b	15.1b-2a	111A and B
12a	15.6a	151A
12a	15.8a	161
12a-b	15.8a-b	163A
12b	14.9b	94A, B and C
12b	14.8b	90E
12b	14.3b	62

Sun	Yen	Fragment
12b	15.8b	164A and C
12b	13.4b	24B
13a	14.4a	64
13a	14.6a	80E
13a	15.6a	148A
13a	15.3a	126B
13a	14.6a	80D
13b	15.2b	119
13b	14.5a	72
13b	14.8b	87
13b	15.5b	147
13b	15.6a	150A
13b	14.10a	99
14a	15.11b	173
14a	13.9a	46
14a	14.2b	55, concl. n.
14a	13.4a	19
14a	13.4a	18
14a	13.2a	1
14b	14.5b	79C
14b	15.5a-b	141
14b	14.5a	73
14b	13.4b	23
14b	15.8b	164F
14b	13.2b	4
14b	14.10a	100, n.12
14b	13.5a	27
15a	15.3a	123
15a	14.5b	74
15a	13.4a	16
15a	13.4a	17
15a	15.3a	120
15a	15.9a	168
15a	14.9b	95
15b	15.5a	139
15b	14.10a	98B
15b	15.8a	162
15b	14.8b	90C
15b	15.5b, or 12.7b	[142]
15b	13.7a	34
15b	13.7a	33
16a	15.5a	140C
16a	14.3b	63
16a	15.2a	113
16a	15.4a	132

Sun	Yen	Fragment
16b	15.4b	135B
16b-17a	14.10b-11a	102
17a	14.9a	93B
17a	13.8b	42B
17a	13.8b	44
17a-b	13.9a	48B
17b	15.7a	156
17b	13.4b	24A
17b	13.5a	25A
17b	15.2a	112B
18a	15.2a	112A
18a	13.2b	5
18a	14.9b	93A
18a	15.2b	117
18a	14.5b	75
18a-b	13.7b	36
18b	15.4a	134
18b-19a	15.2a-b	115B
19b	15.2a	114A
19b	15.4a	133
19b	15.4b	136A
20a	15.1a	108A
20a	13.2b-3a	6
20a	13.3a	11B
20a-b	14.10a-b	100
20b	13.9b	49
20b	13.3a	8
20b	15.3a	125
20b-21a	14.9a	91
21a	15.6b-7a	155
21a	15.1a	106
21a	14.5b	76
21a	13.3a	10
21b	15.8b	164B
21b	15.8b	164C
21b	15.4b	135A
21b	15.6b	153
21b-22a	14.3b	60B
22a	14.1a-b	52, n.4
22a	13.8b	43
22b	13.8a-b	40
22b	14.3a	56
22b	14.11a	104
23a	15.3a	122
23a	13.2a	2B

Sun	Yen	Fragment
23a	14.8b	90A
23b	15.9b	167A
23b	14.2b-3a	55
23b	15.6b	152A
24a	13.4b	22
24a	13.9a	47
24a	13.9b	50
24b	15.5b	146B
24b	15.5a	138
24b	15.6a	149
24b	15.7a	157B
25a	13.9b	51
25a	15.3b	128
25a	14.5b	77
25a	14.4b-5a	66
25b	14.7b	84B
25b	14.3a	57
25b	15.7b	158B
25b-26a	14.5b-6a	79B
26a	14.8a	85
26a	13.2a	2A
26a	14.8a	86A
26a	14.6b	83A

New Fragments from the Hsin-lun

Not Included by Yen K'o-chün and Sun P'ing-i

175

The Ming-t'ang ta-tao lu 明堂大道錄 includes three quotations from the Hsin-lun.

The authorship of this book has caused considerable debate, but I believe it is correctly attributed to Hui Tung (1697-1758 A.D.). This attribution is accepted, for instance, by Hummel's Eminent Chinese of the Ch'ing Period I, p. 358; and H. Maspero's study of the Hall of Light, "Le Ming-t'ang," p. 30, note 1. On p. 60, note 4, Maspero says that the work is by one Hui Tien. This appears to be a misprint; the work was published posthumously, and the references were not verified (p. 2, note 1).

W. E. Soothill, however, who based his book, The Hall of Light: A Study of Early Chinese Kingship, in large part on the Ming-t'ang ta-tao lu, believes that it "was composed by Hui Tung-hsia, who is identified somewhat imperfectly with the celebrated historical and astronomical writer, Hui Shih-ch'i of Kiangsu, A. D. 1670-1741."[1] Hui Shih-ch'i was the father of Hui Tung, but Hummel (p. 357) does not give the style name "Tung-hsia" for either him or his son.

The Ming-t'ang ta-tao lu, which had become quite scarce (Soothill, p. 14), was later included in the well-known collection of reprints, Ts'ung-shu chi-ch'eng. This collection includes two other works on the same subject, the Ming-t'ang wen 問 by Mao Ch'i-ling (1623-1716 A.D.), and the Ming-t'ang k'ao 考 by an unknown author, probably of the Ch'ing dynasty, judging by his style of textual criticism. The Ssu-po ts'ung-k'an edition of the Ming-t'ang kao was reprinted from an earlier edition in the Wen-ching t'ang ts'ung-shu, which was edited, with the help of the famous scholar Sun Hsing-yen, by Sun P'ing-i, who also compiled Huan-tzu Hsin-lun. In an omission unusual for the Wen-ching t'ang ts'ung-shu, neither the author nor the editor of the Ming-t'ang k'ao is named, but Hsiao I-shan believes that it was in fact Sun P'ing-i who edited the text.[2] It is hard to believe that Sun, who, as the editor of

<u>Ming-t'ang k'ao</u> would be familiar with the quotations
therein which are attributed to Huan T'an, would include
in the <u>Huan-tzu Hsin-lun</u> only those quotations which
could be verified in original sources.

Mao Ch'i-ling's <u>Ming-t'ang wen</u>, probably the
oldest of the three works, is primarily a polemic a-
gainst Cheng Hsüan and does not include any fragments
from Huan T'an. This may be partially explained by
Mao's failure to give much attention to the opinions
of previous scholars, a fault for which he was chided
by the reviewer of his book in <u>Ssu-ku chüan-shu tsung-</u>
<u>mu t'i-yao</u> I, p. 501. Mao even fails to refer to those
fragments which had been incorporated into the <u>Ming-</u>
<u>t'ang ta-tao lu</u> and <u>Ming-t'ang k'ao</u>. It should be
pointed out that the authors of all these books suspected the reliability of the texts attributed to Huan
T'an.3

In fact, the contemporary historian Ku Chieh-
kang sharply criticized the Confucian literati, including the eminent scholar Juan Yüan (1768-1849 A.D.), for
their uncritical and unhistorical acceptance of any information on the Ming-t'ang, which was not mentioned
earlier than the <u>Mencius</u>. According to Ku Chieh-kang,
traditional scholars tried to prove that many ancient
buildings used for government and cultural purposes
were in fact the famous Ming-t'ang, even if there was
no historical support for their arguments. See his
study, "Juan Yüan Ming-t'ang lun" (On Juan Yüan's
Treatise "Ming-t'ang lun"), <u>Kuo-li ti-i Chung-shan</u>
<u>ta-hsüeh yü-yen li-shih yen-chiu-so chou-k'an</u> (1930),
pp. 4735-36.

A <u>Ming-t'ang ta-tao lu</u> 2, p. 45.

Shen Nung sacrificed in the Hall of Light,   4
which had a roof but did not have the four directions.
The Yellow Emperor's [Hall of Light was called] the
"Joint Palace." Yao's was called the "Five <u>Fu</u> Store"
[i.e., "houses"]. "<u>Fu</u>" means "to collect," so it is
said that the spirits of the Five Emperors assembled
there. The Shang people called the Great Apartment
the "Two-storied House." The sons of the Shang,5 Yü,
and the Hsia eliminated some of the ornaments, but
they added two eaves and four pillars. Therefore, the
name ["Two-storied House"] was adopted.

B <u>Ming-t'ang k'ao</u>, p. 2.[6]

Shen Nung sacrificed in the Hall of Light which had a roof but did not have the four directions.

C <u>Ming-t'ang ta-tao lu</u> 2, p. 51, and <u>Ming-T'ang k'ao</u>, p. 5,[7] quote, essentially, sentences three and four of fragment 175A.

D <u>Ming-t'ang ta-tao lu</u> 2, pp. 55-56, and <u>Ming-t'ang k'ao</u>, p. 7,[8] quote, essentially, sentences five, six, and seven of fragment 175A.

E <u>Ming-t'ang k'ao</u>, p. 20.

Thus was created a hall with four sides, each of which followed its own color, imitating the model of the four directions.[9]

F <u>Ming-t'ang k'ao</u>, pp. 13 and 17, gives the two quotations on the nine chambers, thirty-six doors and seventy-two lattice windows which can be found in fragment 93D. The commentator of the <u>Ming-t'ang k'ao</u> points out that the <u>Po-hu t'ung</u> corroborates the information.

I have made no attempt to analyze the reliability of these quotations by comparing them with the large body of literature which discusses the Hall of Light. Such an analysis may be helpful for a history of the building, but it is not critical to a study of Huan T'an. Therefore, I will merely make a short summary of what has been said in the introduction and notes: Mao Ch'i-ling, apparently the first of the three authors, quotes nothing from Huan T'an. Hui Tung, who may have written the <u>Ming-t'ang ta-tao lu</u>, is puzzled by some of Huan T'an's information, while the unknown author of the <u>Ming-t'ang k'ao</u> is openly critical of it.

176-187

The following fragments 176-87 are taken from the <u>Ch'i-kuo k'ao</u> (Study of the Seven Kingdoms) by Tung

Yüeh (1620-1676 A.D.).[10] Fragment 176 has been discussed thoroughly in my study, "The Canon of Laws by Li K'uei."[11] I have not translated three quotations on pp. 72, 233, and 275 of the Ch'i-kuo k'ao. The first of these is a short version of fragment 82D, while the other two are versions of fragment 40; see also, "The Canon," pp. 111-12.

In the above study, as well as in another article,[12] I have demonstrated the unreliability of fragment 176. I also suspect the authenticity of fragments 177-87, because they, too, are not corroborated by any fragment of Huan T'an's writings.

176

Ch'i-kuo k'ao, pp. 366-67 (Chapter 12, "The Penal Law of Wei"). Source: Huan T'an, Hsin-shu.

Li K'uei, the tutor of Marquis Wen of Wei, wrote The Canon of Laws. As he felt that nothing was more urgent for a kingly government than [the problem of] robbers and bandits, his laws started with "Robbers" and "Bandits." Since robbers and bandits must be charged and arrested, he wrote two sections on "Imprisonment" and "Arrests."[13] He compiled [the regulations of such crimes] as "frivolity and craftiness," "crossing city walls," "gambling and wild games,"[14] "dishonesty in borrowing and lending," "falling from purity" and "vile luxury," into one section, "Mixed Statutes." Moreover, in the "Criminal Statutes" he set forth [the rules for] the increase and diminishment [of punishment]. Hence, his writings amounted to a mere six sections in all.

Wei Yang[15] took these with him when he became Chancellor of Ch'in.[16] Hence, the two states of Ch'in and Wei share the penetrating formulation and the great severity of their laws.

The Regular Statutes[17] say, roughly, "He who kills a man will be executed, and his horse and property will be confiscated; this punishment will also apply to the clan of his chief wife. If he kills two men, the forfeiture will also extend to the clan of his mother. Prominent robbers will be sent to the frontier to serve as sentries; repeaters will be executed. Spies in the palace will be punished by having their knee-cap cut

off, and those who pick up lost items will be punished
by having their ribs cut, for such activities are said
to indicate an intent to steal."

His Mixed Statutes say, roughly, "If a man has
a chief wife and two concubines, his punishment will be
the cutting of his flesh,[18] but the punishment for having two chief wives is execution. If a chief wife com-
mits adultery, she will be banished to secluded quarters.[19] This is called 'prohibiting lewdness.'

"He who steals a [tiger] tally will be executed
and his house and property confiscated. He who steals
the great [official] seal will be executed. He who criti-
cizes the laws and ordinances of the State will be executed; his house and his property will be confiscated
and this forfeiture will extend to the clan of his chief
wife. This is called 'prohibiting craftiness.' If a
man crosses the city walls, he will be executed, but
if more than ten men, do this, their villages and clans
will be exterminated.[20] This is called 'prohibiting
the crossing of the city walls.'

"Gambling and wild games bring a fine of three
pinches[21] of gold. If the Crown-Prince is guilty of
this, he will be beaten with bamboo. If he does not desist, he will be subjected to a special beating with
bamboo, and if he again refuses to desist, another will
be installed as Prince. This is called 'prohibiting
[wanton] amusements.'

"If the [ruler's] many assistants do no work for
a period of more than one day, they will be interrogated.
[If they continue to do] nothing through a third, fourth
or fifth day, they will be executed. This is called
'prohibiting idleness.' If the chancellor accepts a
bribe of gold, all his close subordinates will be put
to death.[22] If officials [of ranks] lower than that of
'rhinoceros head' (or "general")[23] accept bribes of
gold, they will be executed. However, if they have accepted less than one i,[24] they will merely be fined,
not executed. This is called 'prohibiting the taking
of gold.' If, in his houses, a high dignitary has more
than one object [which is appropriate only for one of
the rank] of marquis, he will be executed, along will all
his relatives."

His Statutes on the Diminishment [of Punishment]
say, roughly, "If the criminal is under fifteen years

of age, the high punishments shall be diminished by
three degrees and the lower punishments by one degree.
If he is over sixty years of age, the small punishments
will be diminished according to the circumstances and
the great ones according to the principles." Since [the
reign of]Marquis Wu, this was observed as law.

Previous translation: Pokora, "The Canon of Laws",
pp. 101-102.

177

Ch'i-kuo k'ao, p. 370 (Chapter 12, "The Penal Law of

Wei"). Source: Huan T'an, Hsin-lun.

An ordinance of Wei: "Those who are unfilial
or who do not show proper respect to their elder brothers will be banished to the Eastern Desert."

Previous translation: Pokora, "The Canon of Laws,"
p. 102.

178

Ch'i-kuo k'ao, p. 347 (Chapter 12, "The Penal Law of

Ch'in"). Source: Huan T'an.

When King Hui-wen of Ch'in cut open the stomach
of worthy men, [his system of]penal law began to col-
lapse.

179

Ch'i-kuo k'ao, p. 354 (Chapter 12, "The Penal Law of

Ch'in"). Source: Huan T'an.

The emphasis which the Ch'in dynasty placed on
the law was even greater than the emphasis which the
Three Dynasties placed on ritual and music.

180

Ch'i-kuo k'ao, p. 357 (Chapter 12, "The Penal Law of

Ch'i"). Source: Huan T'an, Hsin-Lun.

King Hsüan of Ch'i implemented the law of the
metal blade.[25]

181

Ch'i-kuo k'ao, p. 99 (Chapter 2, "The Economy of Wei").

Source: Huan-tze, Hsin-lun.

In Wei, during the sacrifices on the height in
the third month, the agricultural official reads a rule
which says, "If the edges[26] of the plough are incomplete,
the hoe will not mire the way. All the spring fields
are level, as if they were straight. The summer fields
are [as irregular]as wild ducks. The autumn fields
trouble [your heart], for the coming of thieves cannot be
foreseen. When the best fields give the lowest yield
the women are fined. When the worst field gives the
highest yield, the women are rewarded."

182

Ch'i-kuo k'ao, pp. 192-93 (Chapter 5, "Place Names of

Chao"). Source: Huan Tze, Hsin-lun.

When the King was crowned in Han-tan, [people
bearing]presents came with empty hands.

183

Ch'i-kuo k'ao, p. 192 (Chapter 5, "Place Names of Ch'u").

Source: Huan tze, Hsin-lun.

The King of Ying liked slender waists, and the
people in the palace went hungry.[27]

210

184

Ch'i-kuo k'ao, p. 246 (Chapter 8, "Implements of Ch'u").

Source: Huan T'an, Hsin-Lun.

    King Chuang had a carriage built with sharp
points above and steep[28] points below. It was called
"the carriage of Ch'u."

185

Ch'i-kuo k'ao, p. 181 (Chapter 4, "The Palaces of Wei").

Source: Huan T'an.

    The King of Wei built an azure fishpond.

186

Ch'i-kuo k'ao, p. 214 (Chapter 6, "Social Customs of

Chao"). Source: Huan T'an, Hsin-lun.

    Roaming through Ta-ling, Marquis Hsiao rode out
by the Deer Gate. Ta-wu Wu[29] held back his horse and
said, "Now is a critical time for the ploughing. If we
miss work for one day, we shall not eat for one hundred
days!" Marquis Hsiao got down from his carriage, con-
fessed his error[30] and awarded Ta-wu Wu one hundred i
of gold.[31]

187

Ch'i-kuo k'ao, p. 234 (Chapter 7, "Music of Ch'u").

Source: Huan T'an, Hsin-lun.

    In the music of the lands along the Hsiao and
Hsiang[Rivers], square musical stones are..."[32]

188

Introduction to the novel, Fei-yen wai-chuan (The Un-

official Biography of Chao Fei-yen), in Shuo fu 32.25a.

The Shuo fu collection, the printed editions of
which are not very reliable, has been studied by P.
Pelliot,[33] who shares the view of some scholars that
the Fei-yen wai-chuan, the earliest specimen of the
ch'uan-chi 傳奇 genre,[34] was written during the
sixth century. The novel itself has been studied and
translated by W. Eichhorn.[35]

Chao Fei-yen was made the consort of Emperor
Ch'eng (chao hou 趙 后) on July 12, 16 B.C. By
its title (wai-chuan, rather than pieh-chuan), the Fei-
yen wai-chuan purports to be about this historical personality, but it is obviously fiction. To support his
pretense of historical accuracy, the author uses a kind
of historicization which is quite common in post-Han
literature and which has been excellently documented by
Y. Hervouet.[36]

According to the introduction to Fei-yen wai-
chuan, the author, Ling Hsüan,[37] was a contemporary of
Yang Hsiung and would know the stories about Chao Fei-
yen from his wife, who was the niece of a court lady.
Both the novel and its reputed author are highly suspect: the name Ling Hsüan is unusual and cannot be
found in Han sources, and the style of the novel contains anachronisms which are not appropriate to the Han
period.[38]

One of the devices by which the author attempts
to establish the historical authenticity of the text is
a reference to oral (yün 云) testimony by Huan T'an.
This is quoted in the introduction as follows: "During
the reign of Wang Mang, Pien Li from Mou-ling, who held
no office at that time, taught people calendric time
according to the Hsia-hou Shang version of the Book of
Documents.[39] In the keng-shih years,[40] when the Red
Eyebrows marched through Mou-ling, Pien Li left his
library behind and hid it in the mountains. When Liu
Kung entered his hut, he found Ling Hsüan's book. In
the second year of chien-wu,[41] Chia Tzu-i showed me the
book and said, 'Pien Li was taught to play the zither
by Ling Hsüan'..."

Previous translation: W. Eichhorn, "Das Fei-yen wai-
chuan," p. 124.

189

Commentary to <u>Wen hsüan</u> 31.12a, quoting Huan-tzu <u>Hsin-lun</u>.

Now, the authors of the <u>hsiao-shuo</u> represent [those who make] only small and fragmentary[42] utterings. The authors make these short books[43] by clothing their messages in comparisons with things close at hand.[44] But they contain words[45] worth heeding on the subjects of self-control and the regulation[46] of one's family.[47]

190

Liu Chün (or Liu Hsiao-piao 462-521), "Kuang Chüeh-chiao lun" (Extension of the Treatise on the Breaking of Friendship), in <u>Wen hsüan</u> 55.12a-b.[48]

All the five meanings [of friendship] are like buying and selling.[49] Thus, Huan T'an compared it[50] to a "market gate,"[51] while Lin Hui[52] used the metaphor[53] of sweet must.[54]

Li Shan, whose commentary to the <u>Wen hsüan</u> was written between 656 and 660 A.D., notes that no simile to the market (<u>shih</u> 市) can be found in the <u>Hsin-lun</u>, or in Huan T'an's literary works (<u>T'an chi</u>). For the significance of the market's relationship to <u>chiao</u> 交 ("friendship"), Li Shan quotes the ancient text, <u>Chan-kuo ts'e</u> ("Ch'i ts'e" 4:4; the following translation is of Li Shan's short version): "T'an Shih-tzu said to T'ien Wen, Lord of Meng-ch'ang, 'Can I fail to blame the officials and dignitaries of Ch'i?' The Lord of Meng-ch'ang said, 'Yes!' T'an Shih-tzu said, 'If one is wealthy and noble, people draw near; if one is poor and lowly, people stay away. Allow me to use the metaphor of a market. The market is full in the morning and empty in the evening. This is not because people like it in the morning or dislike it in the evening. They are seeking something that is there, so they go. When that something is no longer there, they leave. You, Sir, should not blame anyone.'"

Li Shan adds his own opinion: "I wonder whether, in this metaphor comparing friendship to the market, the character shih [of the name, T'an Shih-tzu 譚 拾 子] was not compared with Huan 桓 ." In other words, Li Shan suggests that the characters reconstructed by Liu Chün from the Chan-kuo ts'e as "Huan T'.an" had previously read "T'an Huan-tzu" instead of "T'an Shih-tzu." This is not a particularly strong argument since the two characters T'an and Huan would have had to have been transposed and the third character, tzu, omitted. Nevertheless, Lü Hsiang's commentary (see note 54 below) also suggests that there is some mistake in Liu Chün's text since no appropriate simile can be found in Huan T'an's works.

The fact that Li Shan and Lü Hsiang found no such text in Huan T'an's writings is not conclusive, for there is no evidence that they had access to all of Huan T'an's original works. Chu Mu, who was born some seventy years after Huan T'an's death, may have had more accurate source material, but his treatise has been lost.

Moreover, there is some additional evidence to support Liu Chün's reference. In his "Treatise on Destiny" ("Pien-ming lun") in Wen hsüan (54.16a-b), Liu Chün compares his own unsuccessful career with Huan T'an's. In my study, "Once More the Dates of Huan T'an" (pp. 655-57), I demonstrate that Liu Chün was "both deeply learned and interested in the Han period in general, as well as in Huan T'an in particular" (p. 656), and that Liu Chün had access to many Han books collected by Emperor Wen of the Northern Wei dynasty. In short, we have no reason to doubt the reliability of Liu Chün's information. Moreover, it is true that Huan T'an was fond of similes; see for example, fragments 84A, 116, 189, and 199.

There is still another, rather conclusive argument. About one hundred years after Liu Chün, the well-known poet Wu Yün briefly mentioned that "Huan T'an did not sell his friendship" (see fragment 200 for details). Thus, in Wu Yün's poem, Huan T'an is again associated with the mingling of the idea of trade and the character chiao 交 . Wu Yün was a historian, as well as a poet, and he wrote a commentary on ninety chapters of Fan Yeh's Hou Han shu, which includes Huan T'an's biography.

191

Commentary to <u>Wen hsüan</u> 53.13b, quoting Huan-tzu's

<u>Hsin-lun</u>.

    If his principles were to be cut off, his fate would depend on Heaven.

192

<u>Cheng-i</u> commentary to <u>Shih chi</u> 96, p. 4165, quoting

Huan T'an's <u>Hsin-lun</u>.

    Introductory note: Emperor Kao had eight sons. The second, whose mother was Empress Lü, became Emperor Hui; the third was Liu Ju-i, son of Lady Ch'i. At one time Emperor Kao, because of his love for Lady Ch'i, wanted to remove the boy who was then heir apparent and make Ju-i the new heir apparent in his place. Of course, his intention created enmity between the mothers, Empress Lü and Lady Ch'i. Eventually Ju-i became King of Chao. To protect the boy-king, who was only ten years old, the Emperor appointed the reliable high court official Chou Ch'ang as Chancellor of Chao, but Ju-i was poisoned in 193 B.C. Knowing this, Huan T'an suggested, some two hundred years later, another method by which Ju-i could have been protected.

    Instead of appointing Chou Ch'ang Chancellor of Chao, it would have been better to marry some girl from Empress Lü's family to Ju-i and have Lady Ch'i serve the Empress Lü well. Then Ju-i would not have died a violent death.[55]

193

<u>TPYL</u> 54.6b, quoting Huan Tzu.

    Upon entering a valley, Duke Huan of Ch'i asked an elderly man, "What valley is this?"

    The answer was, "They say that your servant is foolish and calls it the Valley of the Foolish Old Man."[56]

194

Wen-hsin tiao-lung 3:13, p. 35.2.

[All of Ssu-ma Hsiang-ju's mourning[57] for Erh-shih[58] took the form of a rhyme-prose.[59] Huan T'an described it:] "Its words, full of compassion[60] and sadness,[61] move the reader to sighs of pity."[62]

Previous translation: V.Y.C. Shih, The Literary Mind, p. 71.

195

Wen-hsin tiao-lung 6:29, p. 77.

[Huan Chün-shan said,] "When I read the elegant works of the men with us,[63] they are beautiful, but I would not choose them. But, when I read the works of Liu and Yang,[64] I often profit from them."

Previous translation: Shih, The Literary Mind, p. 167. F. Tökei, Genre Theory in China in the 3rd-6th Centuries, Budapest, 1971, p. 147.

196

Wen-hsin tiao-lung 6:30, p. 78, quoting Huan T'an's statement.

Each man of letters has his own taste. Some like the superficial and flowery style, having no knowledge of substance and depth; some praise profusion, having no vision of the trenchant and sparer.

Previous translation: Shih, The Literary Mind, p. 172.

197

Commentary to Wen-hsin tiao-lung 5:22, p. 62.1, quoting Huan T'an's Hsin-lun.

Fragment 197 is quoted in the commentary to Chapter 22 of <u>Wen-hsin tiao-lung</u>, a chapter devoted to the explanation of two characters, <u>chang</u> 章 and <u>piao</u> 表 (Shih, p. 126, "Memorial, Part I: 'The <u>Chang</u> and the <u>Piao</u>'"). Liu Hsieh explains that in a literary context, <u>chang</u> means "to make clear or articulate" and that <u>piao</u> means "to express one's own feelings" (Shih's translation, p. 127; for <u>chang</u>, see note 65 below). Liu Hsieh also points out that another meaning of <u>piao</u> is "to point," used in connection with measurement of time by means of a pointer's shadow cast by the sun on a sundial. The instrument <u>piao</u> ("pointer"), and its relationship to the table of measurement, <u>kuei</u> 圭 , was described in detail by Kao P'ing-tzu, in "Kuei piao ts'e-ching lun," pp. 293-306, especially p. 293. The <u>kuei</u> was laid horizontally on the earth (see note 66 below), while the <u>piao</u> was a post or rod made of wood, or later, during the Han dynasty, of bronze. Although the texts by Huan T'an and Liu Hsieh both turn on these two words, their meaning is rather different. Huan T'an's short text of only two lines is somewhat enigmatic, playing, as does Liu Hsieh, on the double meaning of the two characters in the philosophical and material contexts. Apparently Huan T'an wished to suggest that even invisible forces can and should be measured by objective criteria. For the shadow, see fragment 113.

The greatness of the two powers [Heaven and earth, or <u>yin</u> and <u>yang</u>] can be estimated by calendrical [<u>chang</u>] computation [<u>ch'eng</u>].[65] The movement of the three bonds [between the ruler and his minister, the father and his son, and the husband and his wife] can be estimated by a table [<u>kuei</u>] measuring the shadow of a pointer [<u>piao</u>].[66]

198

K'ung P'ing-chung, <u>Heng-huang Hsin-lun</u> 3, p. 31, quoting Huan T'an's <u>Hsin-lun</u>.[67]

Yang Tzu-yün [or Yang Hsiung] was always poor and distressed when he lived in Ch'ang-an. Particularly during this year [his condition] was extreme. When he lost his two sons,[68] he sorrowed and mourned them excessively. Both sons were sent back to Shu to be buried, exhausting [Yang's] funds. When [Yang] Hsiung was a Palace Grandee Without Specific Appointment, he fell

ill and died. He was so poor that there were no re-
sources left to arrange for his funeral. Because of
his poverty he was buried at Ch'ang-an. His wife[69]
left his grave and returned to Shu in the West. [Yang]
Hsiung's wrong lay in his disregard for possessions.
This was the blindness of an intelligent man.[70]

Previous translation: Pokora, "The Life," II, pp. 556-
57 (see also notes 131-136).

199

P'ei-wen yün-fu, p. 479.2, quoting Hsin-lun.

Duke Ling of Wei, when sitting with his Lady,
heard the noise of a rumbling vehicle which stopped at
the palace gate. The noise reappeared after passing
through the gate. The Duke asked the Lady if she knew
who had descended from the vehicle. She replied, "Chü
Po-yü!"

We do not know whether this quotation belongs
to Huan T'an's Hsin-lun or to a Hsin-lun written by
some other author. The story is found almost word for
word in Lieh-nü chuan 3.4a, which attributes it, apparently correctly, to Liu Hsiang, whom Huan T'an frequently used for a source. Both Duke Ling and Chü Po-yü are
mentioned elsewhere in Huan T'an's Hsin-lun (fragments
170 and 89, respectively), but this does not necessarily
mean that the present quotation was also written by Huan
T'an.

200

Wu Yün, Ch'u chih shou ch'un tso 初至壽春作, Chang

P'u (1602-1640 A.D.), ed., Han Wei Liu-ch'ao i-pai san-

chia chi, Vol. 81: "Liang Wu Chao-ch'ing chi," p. 27b.

Huan T'an did not sell his friendship.

For the context, see fragment 190, especially the end
of the accompanying note.

201

Wang Pao, "Ling-t'an pei," Han Wei Liu-ch'ao i-pai san-chia chi, Vol. 95: Pei Chou, "Wang Ssu-k'ung chi" [On the inscriptions on gravestones], p. 14b.

In his memorial, Ku Yung[71] used the image of a floating wind[72] which would not strike. Huan T'an wrote a treatise in which he made clear that it is difficult to sail on weak water.[73]

202

Shuo-fu 59.4a and Ku-chin shuo-pu ts'ung-shu, Part I, Vol. 5.1b, quoting Huan T'an's Hsin-lun.

In the Latter Han, when Chu Yu[75] was first studying in Ch'ang-an, the future Emperor [Kuang-wu] left to confer upon him the title of Marquis.[75] Chu Yu improperly ascended the parlor before the Emperor himself. Later, the Emperor himself went to Chu's state apartment and laughed, "I wonder if my host will be able to reject my parlor?"[76] But Chu Yu continued to enjoy his favor as before and, on several occasions, received rewards and affection.

Ku-chin shuo-pu ts'ung-shu, the preface of which is dated 1910, adapted this fragment from Shuo-fu. It is the only fragment from Huan T'an's Hsin-lun in Shuo-fu 59--fragment 188 belongs to Shuo-fu 32--which is not paralleled by a fragment in Yen.

Chu Yu 朱佑 may be identified as Chu Yu 祐 (died 47 A.D.), a general and a Confucianist who belonged to a powerful clan in Wan (Bielenstein, Restoration I, p. 101) and was a chief follower of Kuang-wu (ibid., p. 26, No. 25). The graphical difference between the two names is slight, and Bielenstein (p. 27, note 1) demonstrates that the name of the general has been written in many different ways (on this point, see also the chiao-pu commentary to Hou Han shu, p. 833).

Chu Yu's biography, Hou Han shu 22, is short but gives a balanced account of his life. At the very

end it includes the anecdote translated above, the text
of which is practically identical to that of the <u>Hsin-
lun</u>. The only significant difference is in the Emper-
or's speech, he is quoted as saying, "I wonder if my
host will be able to put away my parlance." The <u>Hou
Han shu</u> version is better, since it preserves the pun
on "parlor" (<u>chiang-she</u> 講 舍) and "parlance" (<u>chiang</u>
講).

Still another version of this anecdote is preserved in <u>Tung-kuan Han chi</u>, quoted in the commentary
to <u>Wen hsüan</u> 38.7b:

When the future Emperor [Kuang-wu] was first
studying in Ch'ang-an, he visited Chu Yu, who
often restrained the Emperor with "You need a
parlor [I read <u>she</u> 舍 "parlor" for <u>ching</u> 覓],
only then will you be able to speak." After
the Emperor ascended the throne, he went by
himself to Chu Yu's state apartment and asked,
"I wonder if my host will do away with my parlance?" Chu Yu said, "I would not dare do
that!"

This last version clearly states that the two allusions
to the Emperor's speech ("parlance") belong to two different occasions, separated by ten years or more. For
the quotation from the <u>Wen hsüan</u> commentary, see also
the <u>chiao-pu</u> commentary, p. 833.

Li Hsien's commentary to Chu Yu's biography in
<u>Hou Han shu</u> quotes still a different anecdote, which is
somewhat out of place:

When the Emperor lived in Ch'ang-an, he and
Chu Yu bought honey and mixed drugs. When
the Emperor remembered this occasion, he gave
Chu Yu a gallon of white honey. The Emperor
asked if he remembered how they bought honey
together in Ch'ang-an. Their intimacy was
<u>that</u> sincere!

These various anecdotes about Kuang-wu and Chu
Yu raise some problems, such as, why the version attributed to Huan T'an is identical to that of the <u>Hou Han
shu</u> rather than to that of <u>Tung-kuan Han chi</u>, which is
much older and is the source of the <u>Hou Han shu</u> version;
also, why is Huan T'an acknowledged as a source only
by the late, 14th century <u>Shuo fu</u> and not by the earlier

texts? Moreover, although the <u>Hsin-lun</u> mentions some
events which happened after the fall of Wang Mang, in
no other extant fragment does Huan T'an refer to persons living at that time.

Although I cannot offer conclusive proof, I
believe that this fragment is as unreliable as fragment
188. The anecdote related in <u>Hou Han shu</u> was probably
attributed to Huan T'an in order to enhance its reliability. No doubt, Huan T'an could have authored such
an anecdote, since he must have known Chu Yu, his younger contemporary, who acquired great authority and wealth.
I feel, however, that it was precisely the fact that he
could have written such an anecdote which led someone
in the 5th century or later to attribute it to Huan T'an.

203

K'ung Ying-ta, <u>Ch'un-ch'iu cheng-i</u> 4.4b (<u>SPTK</u>), quoting

Huan T'an.

Both <u>Tso Chuan</u> (Wen, 1st year, 625 B.C.; Legge,
pp. 228-230) and <u>Lun-heng</u> (21:63, pp. 890-92; Forke, I,
pp. 207-208) report that King Ch'eng of Ch'u, after his
strangulation, would not close his eyes when he was given
the unrespectable posthumous name of Ling. He closed
them only after he was given a more honorable epithet,
Ch'eng. Wang Ch'ung says that this was explained as
the act of the dead king's soul, but he suggests another, more rational theory; that is, the king's eyes
remained open immediately after his death because his
"vital fluid" was still abundant and closed naturally
as the fluid gradually disappeared. Thus, Wang Ch'ung
argues that the posthumous epithet had no connection
with the closing of the King's eyes. Undoubtedly, Wang
Ch'ung based his opinion on Huan T'an's text:

> After he strangled and died, his eyes would
> not close. They closed [only] when the
> corpse became cold. This had nothing to do
> with the rule on conferring posthumous names--
> be they good or bad.

204

Tu Yü, Ch'un-ch'iu ching-chuan chi-chieh 16.4b, quoting

Huan T'an.[77] Given in the Kuo-hsieh chi-yao reprint

of the 1720 edition of Feng Li-hua (Ming dynasty), Tso

hsiu, p. 1160.

Once more, both Tso chuan (Hsiang, 19th year, 553 B.C.; Legge, pp. 480, 482) and Lun-heng (21:63, pp. 891-92; Forke, I, pp. 206-208) tell the story of Officer Hsün Yen of Chin. After his death, his eyes protruded and his lips were shut so tightly that the traditional rite of putting a gem into his mouth could not be performed. Both these strange phenomena disappeared only when the corpse was told that his mission against Ch'i would be carried on despite his death. Again, both Wang Ch'ung and Huan T'an attempt to give rational explanations. Huan T'an said:

Hsün Yen fell ill, and his eyes protruded. Immediately after he died, his eyes would not close, but they did close when the corpse became cold. This was not caused by his knowledge [of the continuation of his mission].[78]

Wang Ch'ung quotes and explains two similar stories from Tso chuan in his chapter, "False Reports about the Dead." Wang failed to attribute his analysis to Huan T'an, as was his habit, but elsewhere he has only unrestricted praise for Huan T'an. Huan T'an's opinion is cited by two commentators to the Tso chuan, Tu Yü of the third century A.D. and K'ung Ying-ta[79] of the seventh century. Huang Hui, the modern commentator to the Lun-heng, quotes both quotations (Lun-heng chiao-shih, pp. 891-92), and they are explained in an excellent, if short, article by Chung Chao-p'eng, "Huan T'an ho Wang Ch'ung," p. 41.

In his rhyme-prose, "Grief for the Provinces South of the Yang-tzu" ("Ai chiang-nan fu" 哀江南 賦),[80] the influential poet Yü Hsin compares Huan T'an and Tu Yü:

There was Huan Chün-shan, a man of moral integrity and Tu Yüan-k'ai, whose life was well regulated; they both wrote books[81] to which they were able to append postfaces.[82]

NOTES: NEW FRAGMENTS FROM THE HSIN-LUN

1.   W. E. Soothill, The Hall of Light: A Study of Early Chinese Kingship, eds. Lady Hosie and G. F. Hudson, (London: 1951), p. 14.

2.   Hsiao I-shan, Ch'ing-tai t'ung shih, Vol. 5, Sixth Appendix: Table of the Works of Ch'ing Scholars, (Taipei: 1963), p. 503.

3.   See notes 6, 7, and 8 below.

4.   Fang 方 ("directions") is added here, in accordance with fragment 175B. In his commentary, Hui Tung says that ssu 四 ("four") refers to the ssu-ta 四達 ("four extremities").

5.   The text has Shang yü 商于 , but instead of yü, the Ming-t'ang k'ao, p. 7, gives tzu 子 ("sons").

6.   The Yü-lan, i.e., the T'ai-p'ing yü-lan, is given as the source of this passage, but no more specific information is provided. The TPYL chapter devoted to the Hall of Light is number 533, which does include a different quotation from Huan T'an's Hsin-lun (8b); see fragment 93A. The commentator, apparently the unknown author of the Ming-t'ang k'ao, says that the term Ming-t'ang was used first by the Chou philosophers and that the Yellow Emperor of the mythical past named the building Ho Kung 合宮 ("Joint Palace").

7.   Again, (see note 6 above) Ming-t'ang k'ao attributes this fragment to the T'ai-p'ing yü-lan. The author comments, "The term 'Five Fu' was first used during the reign of T'ang (i.e., T'ang Yü, or Yao). One certainly could not imitate the model of the Five Forces in one's sacrifices to the Five Supreme Rulers if the sacrifices were made in a four-cornered building." Hui Tung comments, "Huan T'an did not read the ch'an prognostication texts, but he, too, says that Yao had Five Fu. This means that he venerated the words of the ancient documents above all others. The wei prognostication books from the reigns of the Emperors Ch'eng and Ai cannot compare with them." Hui Tung, referring to Huan T'an's assertion to Emperor Kuang-wu that he would not read the ch'an texts, apparently believes that such an eminent scholar must have had access to original documents, rather than obtaining his information from the proscribed wei prognostication texts.

8.   The commentator to the <u>Ming-t'ang k'ao</u> does not accept the story of the Two-storied House and says flatly that the information on the additions is wrong.

9.   The <u>Ming-t'ang k'ao</u> says that the source of this statement is the <u>Ch'u-hsüeh chi</u>, but again (see note 6 above) gives no specific reference. A passage by Huan T'an on the subject of the <u>Ming-t'ang</u> is indeed quoted by <u>Ch'u-hsüeh chi</u> 13.18b (93A), but it is not the present fragment. In fact, this fragment is, with some slight differences, part of the quotation from <u>IWLC</u> 38.24b. See fragment 93C.

10.   Tung Yüeh, <u>Ch'i-kuo k'ao</u> (Study of the Seven Kingdoms), (Peking: Chung-hua shu-chü, 1956).

11.   T. Pokora, "The Canon of Laws by Li K'uei--A Double Falsification?"

12.   T. Pokora, "Two Answers to Professor Moriya Mitsuo: Part II, <u>Fa ching</u> and <u>Hsin-lun</u>." See Bibliography IIB21.

13.   The first part of the text of the <u>Canon of Laws</u> is almost identical to the "Treatise on Law" (<u>hsing-fa chih</u>) in Chin shu 30.5a-b (see note 16 below). To some extent, I have followed Hulsewé's translation of this text in <u>Remnants</u> I, pp. 28-29, in order to demonstrate the variances. For instance, the <u>Chin shu</u> here uses the titles "Nets" and "Arrests."

14.   <u>Po-hsi</u> 博戲 (here translated as "gambling and wild games") became, in the Han period, the name of a kind of military play.

15.   Wei Yang, i.e., Kung-sun Yang of Wei, is generally known as Shang Yang or Yang, the Lord of Shang.

16.   The text has <u>ju</u> 入 which would read "when he entered the Chancellorship of Ch'in." I prefer the <u>Chin Shu</u>, which gives <u>i</u> 以 ("when he became Chancellor of Ch'in"). From this point on, the texts of <u>Chin shu</u> and <u>Tung Yüeh</u> differ.

17.   For the translation of <u>cheng-lü</u> 正律 as "Regular Statutes," see Hulsewé, <u>Remnants</u> I, p. 68, note 66.

18. On p. 368, Tung Yüeh says that the unknown character 膩 may be a mistake for kuo 膩 ("to cut off the ear").

19. For the translation of kung 宮 as "secluded quarters," see Hulsewé, Remnants I, p. 127. The women who live in the secluded quarters serve as slaves.

20. Tung Yüeh (p. 369) says that laws such as this did not exist in other kingdoms during this period and that the laws of Wei were, in fact, even more cruel than those of Ch'in.

21. Following Yang K'uan's suggestion, I read lo 寽 ("pinch") instead of shih 市 , which makes no sense.

22. Apparently the Chancellor does not share his subordinates' unfortunate fate, as Tung Yüeh (p. 367) points out.

23. The Wei office of "rhinocerous head" (hsi-shou 犀首) was like a Ministry of War, as Tung Yüeh (p. 69) explains in some detail. Ssu-ma Piao, the author of a Hou Han shu, says that the "rhinoceros head" was like "the present rank of Tiger's Teeth General" (hu-ya chiang-chün 虎牙將軍).

24. There is some disagreement on the weight of one i 鎰 (or 溢); see HFHD I, p. 111, note 3; and W. Bauer, "Der Fürst von Liu," pp. 180-81, note 4. The term chin 金 (here translated as ["bribes of] gold") does not refer to real gold used in financial transactions which was designated as huang chin 黃金 ("yellow gold"); see HFHD I, p. 175, note 2.

25. Tung Yüeh, quoting Kuo yü, Ch'i yü says that the law allowed a criminal to atone for his offense by offering a metal sword.

26. Yü 羽 ("feathers") is interchangeable with shih 矢 ("arrow"); I believe that this refers to the sharpness of a point and have translated it as "edges."

27. This well-known story about King Ling of Ch'u is found in many texts, including Hsün-tzu, Han Fei-tzu, and the Hou Han shu. A more elaborate version is given in the Hsin-lun by Liu Chou; see Liu-tzu Hsin-lun 3:13 3:13.3a (Han Wei ts'ung-shu edition).

28.   Instead of the tou 斗 of the text, I read tou
阧 ("steep").

29.   Wu 戍 may also be read ch'eng 成 , as Takigawa Kametarō suggests (see the following note). Ta-wu
Wu, or Ta-ch'eng Wu, was Chancellor of Chao.

30.   This story can be found in Shih chi 43 (p. 44;
Chavannes, MH V, p. 63, and also p. 57), although Tung
Yüeh does not give this source. Only the last seven
characters, corresponding to the heading of the paragraph, are added to the Shih chi version. The attribution of the story to Huan T'an is highly suspect, since
none of the many commentators to the Shih chi refer to
Huan as its source. It is odd that the well-read Tung
Yüeh did not refer to its inclusion in the Shih chi.

31.   For the measure i and for the explanation of
gold see fragment 176, note 24.

32.   A character is missing in the text. Both rivers are in Hunan; the Hsiao is a tributary of the Hsiang.

33.   P. Pelliot, "Quelques remarques sur le Chouo
Fou," TP, pp. 163-220.

34.   Ibid., p. 192.

35.   W. Eichhorn, "Das Fei-yen wai-chuan."

36.   Y. Hervouet, Un poète de cour sous les Han--
Sseu-ma Hsiang-jou.

37.   Ling Hsüan 伶玄 , or Ling Yüan 伶元 , whose
style name was Tzu-yü 子于 . His name, Ling, may also
be interpreted as ling, or "Actor," Hsüan; see chapter
126 of the Shih chi, which discusses the actors, or yu-
ling 優伶 , Meng 孟 and Chan 旃 .

38.   See Eichhorn, pp. 123-24.

39.   Hsia-hou Shang shu 夏侯尚書 ("the
Hsia-hou Shang version of the Book of Documents"); Eichhorn (p. 124) translates, "...mit Hilfe des von Hsia-
hou Sheng redigierten Shu-ching (das heisst des Kapitels
Hung-fan) für die Leute die Kalenderzeiten festlegte."

40.   23-24 A.D.

41.   26 A.D.

42.   For an explanation of ts'ung ts'an 叢殘 ("small and fragmentary"), see fragment 164C, note 19. Ts'an ("fragmentary") is a derogatory adjective.

43.   Tuan-shu 短書 (translated here as "short books") is also used in fragment 2B and by Wang Ch'ung (Lun-heng 12:36, p. 560; Forke, II, p. 78, translates it as "trivial books"). The Classics were written on large bamboo tablets, which were, according to Wang Ch'ung, two feet and four inches long. Other, less important books were written on much smaller tablets. See Forke, Lun-heng II, p. 77, note 6, and, especially Tsien Tsuen-hsuin, Written on Bamboo and Silk, pp. 104-107. This traditional difference in size was later reflected in the derogatory evaluation of the ideas presented in "short" books; thus, in this sense tuan-shu might be translated as "deficient books." See Hou Wai-lu et al. (see note 47 below) who read tuan p'ien 篇.

44.   The whole text of this fragment with three textual variations, is quoted in the introduction to Hsü Chen-ngo, Han Wei Liu-ch'ao hsiao-shuo hsüan. The first variation: instead of the p'i-lun 譬論 ("comparisons") of the text, Hsü gives p'i-yü 喻.

45.   Hsü's second variation: instead of the tz'u 辭 ("words") of the text, Hsü has ts'e 策 ("strategy").

46.   Hsü's third variation: instead of the chih 治 ("regulation") of the text, Hsü has li 理 (also "regulation").

47.   Hou Wai-lu et al. (Chung-kuo ssu-hsiang t'ung-shih, Vol. 2, p. 204) quote this fragment in their analysis of the famous catalogue by Liu Hsiang and Liu Hsin.

48.   Liu Chün (462-521 A.D.) is a well-known author, as well as the commentator to the Shih-shuo hsin-yü by Liu I-ch'ing (403-444 A.D.). His essay extends to an earlier essay written by Chu Mu (100-163 A.D.), i.e., Chüeh-chiao lun, which is mentioned in Chu's biography in Hou Han shu 43, p. 1575, and in TPYL 410.6b. Liu Chün's text was translated by E. von Zach in Die Chinesische Anthologie: Übersetzungen aus dem Wen hsüan II, p. 962.

49.   The character chiao 交 means both "to barter, to bargain" and "intimacy, friendship."

50.   The term p'i 譬 ("compare") is also used in fragment 189. See note 44.

51.   Instead of shih 市 ("market"), Liu Chün uses Huan k'uei 闤闠 , referring only to the gate.

52.   Lin Hui is mentioned in Chuang-tzu II:20. His story about must, a substance so sweet that it only pleases the senses for a short period of time, is given there in more detail.

53.   Yü 諭 should be read as yü 喻 ("metaphor") as in fragment 189, note 44, or in PWYF, p. 1445:2, which quotes the present fragment.

54.   Lü Hsiang (ca. 720 A.D.), who wrote a commentary on Wen hsüan, says that must is sweet and therefore quickly spoils. See also note 52 above.

55.   Watson, Records I, pp. 260-61. After being murdered by Empress Lü in a most barbarous way, Lady Ch'i became an object of popular pity and a figure of fiction. See, for example, Hsi ching tsa chi 3.4a.

56.   The reliability of the quotation is supported by the fact that it is based on the account in Shuo yüan 7.3a which was one of Huan T'an's favorite sources. The Shuo yüan version is more elaborate: "Duke Huan of Ch'i, when out hunting, chased a deer into a mountain valley. He asked an old gentleman whom he saw there, 'What kind of valley is this?'"

        The gentleman answered, 'It is the valley of a stupid gentleman.'"

        Duke Huan inquired further and was told, 'It has my name.'"

57.   The thirteenth chapter of Wen-hsin tiao-lung is devoted to two terms, ai 哀 ("lament") and tiao 弔 ("mourning" or "condolence").

58.   Erh-shih is Hu-hai, the second emperor of the Ch'in dynasty.

59.　　The text of "Tiao Er-shih" is given in Ssu-ma Hsiang-ju's biography in Shih chi 117; Watson, Records II, pp. 331-32.

60.　　For the word ts'e 惻 (here translated as "compassion"), see fragment 84A, note 28.

61.　　For the word ts'ang 愴 ("sadness"), see fragment 134, note 84.

62.　　The power of music to arouse sadness has also been described by Huan T'an in fragment 171 (see note 29). This was exactly the point which interested Liu Hsieh, the author of Wen-hsin tiao-lung. Huan T'an and Yang Hsiung were greatly interested in Ssu-ma Hsiang-ju's fu, as may be seen from Yang Hsiung's letter translated in note 12 to fragment 80C.

63.　　For hsin chin 新進 ("new writers," "novices"), see fragment 80C, note 6.

64.　　"Yang" clearly refers to Yang Hsiung; "Liu" might be Liu Hsin, but more probably refers to Liu Hsiang, whose Shuo yüan was one of Huan T'an's favorite sources (see note 56 to fragment 193). It is, however, odd that these two men are not designated by their style names, i.e., Tzu-yün for Yang Hsiung and Tzu-chün for Liu Hsin. This may indicate either that "Liu" refers to both Liu Hsiang and Liu Hsin, or, more improbably, that the original text was modified by Liu Hsieh.

65.　　Chang ch'eng 章程 (translated here as "calendrical computation") is a stock phrase, the exact meaning of which has never been clear. In HFHD, I, p. 146, H. H. Dubs translates it as "the calendar and the measures." In his note 5 Dubs adds, "Ju Shun interprets this phrase as referring to the calendar and to weights and measures; Yen Shih-ku says the second part of this phrase refers to the standard models [for weights and measures]." See fragments 112B, note 22, and 163A, note 9.

66.　　Couvreur (Dictionnaire classique, p. 165), following Cheng Hsüan's commentary to the Chou li, translates [t'u] Kuei 土圭 as "tablette des mesures." Couvreur continues, "...elle avait quinze ts'uen 才 [ts'un-T.P.] de long, se plaçait horizontalement dans la direction du nord au sud, et reçevoit à midi l'ombre de gnomon 表 de huit tch'ĕu 尺 [ch'ih-T.P.] dressé à

son extremité au sud...Au moyen de la tablette des
mesures, on mesure l'étendue de la terre, détermine la
longuer de l'ombre au soleil, et cherche ainsi le milieu
de la surface de la terre."

67.   K'ung P'ing-chung was a poet who lived ca. 1040-
1105 A.D. This reference could establish that the Hsin-
lun was still extant in his time, after the fall of the
T'ang; however, most of this information may be also
found in fragment 104 (TPYL) which undoubtedly was written before the T'ang dynasty.

68.   Nan 男 ("sons"). His sons were probably fully
grown adults at the time of their deaths.

69.   The text has tzu 子 ("son"); however, the
original appears to have had ch'i-tzu 妻子, since Pi
Yüan quotes this term in his commentary to Ch'ang-an
chih 13.11b. Unfortunately, the term ch'i tzu may mean
either "wife" or "son"; for an explanation, see Ku Yen-
wu, Jih chih lu chi shih, p. 44. Since, according to
this fragment, Yang Hsiung's sons had already died, the
translation "wife" is more consistent.

70.   K'ung P'ing-chung adds, "This was Huan T'an's
opinion."

71.   Ku Yung (died 8 or 7 B.C.) was an eminent officer, as well as a scholar who specialized in portents.
He belonged to the group around the Tu family (Tu Ch'in
and Tu Yeh; see fragment 84A, note 24), and his memorials, written in an exquisite style, were very influential.

72.   Liu-feng 流風 ("floating wind"), is a pun
upon Mencius' use of the term in the sense of "auspicious emanating influence;" see Mencius (I I:I:8; Legge,
p. 182).

73.   Jo-shui 沏水 ("weak water"), may be the
name of the River Jo, mentioned in the Book of Documents (III:1:X:72, i.e., Yü kung; see Legge, pp. 123
and 124). The River Jo was situated in west Kansu and
was, apparently, not easily navigated.

       In Han times, the River Jo became an object of
a legend; in the 4th century, Kuo P'o stated that "its
water cannot support goose-down." See Shan-hai ching,
Chapter 16, translated and explained by H. H. Dubs in

"An Ancient Chinese Mystery Cult," p. 226, and notes 11 and 13. The connection of this legend with Han mythology is established by the text's reference to the goddess Hsi-wang-mu, whose cult was formed in 3 B.C.

74. This time designation must have been added later and cannot belong to Huan T'an's text, nor to the other versions.

75. According to his biography in Hou Han shu 22 (pp. 809-11), Chu Yu received his first marquisate ca. 24 A.D., his second in 26 A.D., and a third in 37 A.D.

76. See the analysis above for an explanation of this jibe.

77. Given in the Kuo-hsieh chi-yao reprint (T'aipei: 1968) of the 1720 edition of Feng Li-hua (Ming dynasty), Tso hsiu, p. 1160.

78. Tu Yü (or Huan T'an?) adds, "The Tso chuan follows his strange appearance and notes it."

79. K'ung Ying-ta's book is entitled either Ch'un-ch'iu cheng-i or Ch'un-ch'iu Tso-shih-chuan cheng-i.

80. See Yü Hsin, Yü Tzu-shan chi, I (Shanghai: 1945), p. 65.

81. Tu Yü was a very prolific writer, more than twenty of his works have now been identified.

82. With the exception of "Wang hsien fu" (fragment 205), no postface (hsü 序) to Huan T'an's works is known.

III. Other Writings by Huan T'an

It is not always easy to determine what was
written by Huan T'an and what was written by some other
author (see, for example, note 1 to fragment 8). Similarly, we cannot always say what was part of the Hsin-
lun and what comes from Huan T'an's other writings (see,
for example, note 13 to fragment 205). In what follows
I present each fragment from his other works separately,
just as Yen K'o-chün has done. At the same time, I relate the fragments to each other through the notes.
The problem of authorship is treated separately.

205

Rhyme-prose on Looking for Immortals (Wang hsien[1] fu).

I-wen lei-chü 78.16b. Pei-t'ang shu-ch'ao 102.4a.

Yen 12.7b. Preface:[2]

Being a Gentleman,[3] in my youth I accompanied
Emperor Hsiao-ch'eng to his sacrifices[4] at Kan-ch'üan
Palace and Ho-tung commandery.[5] First, the sacrifices[6]
were arranged in the Palace of Assembled Spirits at
Hua-yin.[7] This palace, situated under Mount Hua, was
built by Emperor Wu.[8] In the palace the Emperor wished
to reflect upon and gather together immortals,[9] such as
Wang Ch'iao and Ch'ih Sung Tzu;[10] therefore, the hall
was called the "Hall of Immortals." The upright gate
which faces the mountain from the south was called
"Looking-for-Immortals Gates." There I lived.[11] I
dared to take delight in lofty and beautiful[12] thoughts,
so I wrote a small fu on the wall:[13]

Behold Wang Ch'iao and Ch'ih Sung!
    Exhaling, they expel old [breath]; contracting,
they bring in fresh [breath].[14]
They bend and stretch, guiding their breath[15] through
their arteries; they collect the breath and conserve
the original.[16]
Their spirit circulates and nourishes their body,
flowing through every hindrance;
They ascend, rising through Emptiness and Nothingness[17] to reach an understanding of darkness and

light.[18]
Everything is visible to them. The Jade Woman[19]
is at their side.
Now that they have attained the Way of Immortality,
they are welcomed by spiritual and divine beings.
Then they mount a car drawn by blue dragons and red
horses.[20]
    Coming over the high and sharp black stone,[21]
they soar like the female phoenix and her male,
    Flying and coming together in the region of
purest air[22] at the terrace of T'ai-shan.
They breath in the juice of jade[23] and eat the
splendid iris.[24]
They rinse their mouths with jade liquid[25] and drink
the wine of gold.
Leaving the universe behind, they float with the
clouds.
Sprinkling a light vapor, they cross sloping cliffs.
Looking on vast[26] streams, they rise to the Gate of
Heaven.[27]
Riding a white deer, they keep company with unicorns.
In all directions they inspect the eight[28] extremi-
ties and return to the altar of Yen-hua.[29]
Oh, like vast waters, how overflowing![30] With
Heaven they revolve,
    Enjoying their non-striving.
Their longevity approaches that of Heaven and earth.

Previous translation: Pokora, "Huan T'an's Fu," pp.
363-65.

206

Discussion with Fu Yen.

Hou Han shu 18A, pp. 1011-12.

    Huan T'an is said to have conversed with Fu
Yen, the Marquis of K'ung-hsiang in 3 B.C. Huan T'an
advised him on how to handle the difficult situation
which arose when Emperor Ai began to show more interest
in the sister of Tung Hsien[31] than in his own Empress,
Fu Yen's daughter. Although Huan T'an's advice is presented in the form of a discussion between the two men,
there is no doubt that the historian Fan Yeh based his
account on a written source. It is also probable that

the source was Huan T'an himself because, among other
things, both the Empresses née Ch'en and Wei Tzu-fu are
mentioned in the present text, as well as in fragment
102 (see also fragment 62). Since the original text
was probably written by Huan T'an, I include it here.

[Huan T'an came forward and advised Fu Yen:]

"In the past, when Emperor Wu wished to make Wei
Tzu-fu his Empress, he secretly inquired into errors
committed by the Empress née Ch'en.[32] In the end, the
Empress née Ch'en was finally dismissed,[33] and Wei Tzu-
fu was eventually established in her place.[34] Now, Tung
Hsien enjoys the highest affection, and his younger sister is even more favored. Another Wei Tzu-fu incident
seems imminent.[35] How can one fail to be disturbed?"

Fu Yen, greatly frightened, said, "But what can
we do about it?"

Huan T'an replied, "An innocent person cannot
be punished; wickedness cannot prevail over an upright
man. A gentleman courts his ruler with his talent and
his knowledge; a woman woos her lord with her beguiling
ways. The Empress is young and has rarely experienced
trouble. Perhaps she will send frantically for doctors
and sorcerers,[36] or summon magicians and wizards from
outside the court.[37] You must be prepared for such
things.

"Moreover, Lord Marquis, as father of the Empress, you are high and mighty and associate with many
retainers.[38] Surely you will use them to strengthen
your position,[39] thereby inviting criticism and gossip.
It would be better to dismiss your followers courteously.
You must make every effort to be humble and earnest.
This is the way to cultivate oneself, to set right one's
family, and to avoid calamity."

Previous translation: Pokora, "The Life," I, pp. 18-20.

207

Huan T'an's Letter to Tung Hsien.

Hou Han shu 18A, p. 1012.

234

[When Tung Hsien[40] became Commander-in-Chief,
he heard of Huan T'an's fame and wished to become
friends[41] with him. But first Huan T'an sent a letter
to Tung Hsien in which he advised him on:]

The art of assisting in the governing of the
state and of preserving oneself.

Previous translation: Pokora, "The Life," I, p. 20.

208

Proposal on Regulation Projects

Han shu 29, p. 3085.

The last part of the Han shu chapter on drains
and ditches (Han shu 29) is probably based on Huan T'an's
account in the Hsin-lun. The main argument for this
suggestion is that Chapter 29 mentions many personalities which also appear in the Hsin-lun. Moreover, the
principal commentary to the Han shu, by the T'ang scholar Yen Shih-ku, frequently quotes from the Hsin-lun
(see, e.g., fragments 107, 108, and 109), elaborating
on the information provided by Pan Ku, the chief author
of the Han shu. H. Bielenstein convincingly demonstrates that the Yellow River changed its course sometime between 2 and 5 A.D., although this is not express-
ly mentioned in the Han shu.[42] On this occasion many
different proposals were submitted on how to deal with
the situation.[43] Although Emperor P'ing was still
nominally on the throne, all important matters of the
state were directed by Wang Mang.

The Han shu says, "When Huan T'an, from the
P'ei commandery, became Division Head of the Grand
Ministry of Works, he was put in charge of the propos-
als and said to Chen Feng:[44]

"'These many proposals certainly contain some
valid points. We should study them in detail. Everything may be prepared in advance and fixed according
to plan; then we can launch our action. The expenditure will not exceed several milliards.[45] We should
employ the labor of people who live from hand to mouth
and have neither occupation nor property. Whether they

are idle or employed, they must be clothed and fed all the same. If they are clothed and fed by the Imperial government,[46] and at the same time are employed by it, two birds will be killed with one stone. Thus, above we can continue the achievement of Yü, while below the people's distress can be removed.'

"In the time of Wang Mang, there was mere veneration of empty words, but no one put them into action."[47]

Previous translation: Pokora, "The Life," I, p. 51.

209

Statement on the Duties of Contemporary Government

Hou Han shu 28A, pp. 1013-15.   Yen 12.8a-9a.

Your servant has heard that the fall and rise of a country depend upon its political affairs.[48] Success or failure in political affairs depends upon one's counsellors.[49] If one's counsellors are wise and clear-sighted, then talented men will fill the court, and their principles will meet the demands of contemporary problems. If the counsellors are not clear-sighted, then the problems which they discuss will not correspond to contemporary needs and the actions which they take will be full of error.

All rulers who possess kingdoms wish to promote culture and establish the good.[50] But if they have not yet put their ways of governing into order, then what they call wise is strange.

Once King Chuang of Ch'u[51] said to Sun Shu-ao,[52] "I do not know any method by which to put my country into proper order."

Sun Shu-ao said, "If the country is hated by everyone, even when it is in 'proper order,' I am a-fraid, my King, that you will not be able to manage it."

The King asked, "Does this unmanageability depend only on the ruler or does it also depend on the minister?"

Sun Shu-ao replied, "When a lord treats his ministers with arrogance,[53] saying, 'Without me, there is no way for my minister to become rich and noble,' and a minister treats his lord with arrogance, saying, 'Without me, there is no way for my lord to be safe and secure,' then the lord of men may even lose his country without realizing why, and the minister may even become hungry and cold, not advancing in his career. If there is no harmony between ruler and minister, the affairs of the country cannot be settled."

King Chuang said, "I approve. I would like you, Chancellor, to work with the Grandees to settle the affairs of the country."[54]

One who is well-versed in government observes the ways of the people and spreads moral instruction accordingly, examines mistakes and sets up preventive measures accordingly. Might and virtue alternately hold sway, civil and military methods are each employed in turn. Only then will government be in tune with the times and impetuous men[55] be stilled.

In the past Tung Chung-shu said, "The ordering of a country is like a ch'in (zither) or a se (zither). When these are out of tune, they must be unstrung and strung anew."[56] It is difficult to carry out this re-stringing, and whoever thwarts the multitude will perish. This is why Chia I was expelled for his talent,[57] and Ch'ao Ts'o was made to die for his wisdom.[58] Even if men of outstanding ability are present, in the end no one will dare to speak out because everyone will be intimidated by examples from the past.

Moreover, with respect to establishing laws and prohibitions, one cannot completely stop up the evil in the world, but it is enough if the laws and prohibitions meet the wishes of the multitude and, in general, a policy is adopted which is most convenient to the country and profitable to government affairs.

Offices are established and civil servants nominated in order to manage the people.[59] Rewards are offered[60] and fines instituted in order to differentiate between the good and the bad. When evil men are punished and hurt, good men are blessed with happiness.

But now, the people kill and hurt one another. Even if their quarrels are settled by the law,[61] they form private grudges and feuds,[62] and their sons and grandsons take revenge on one another. In this way, the later hatred becomes deeper than the earlier hatred and can even result in the extermination of families and the destruction of careers. Yet the people commonly call this heroism! So, even if people are timid and weak, they force themselves to act in this way. This amounts to allowing people[63] to take matters into their own hands, so laws and prohibitions no longer exist.

Now, we should repeatedly explain[64] the old ordinances.[65] If official punishment has been meted out after a quarrel, but later, injury or death is brought about through private revenge, then, even if the offender should escape, his entire family should be banished to the border. The normal punishment of the one who has caused injury should be increased by two degrees, and he should not be allowed to hire anyone to redeem his punishment for him.[66] In this way, hatred and anger[67] will disappear of themselves, and robbery and thievery will be curbed.

The way to put a country into order is to promote the basic occupation and to suppress extraneous profits.[68] Therefore, the emperors of earlier times prohibited one person from practicing two professions and forbade traders and merchants from serving as officials.[69] By these methods, they prevented the accumulation and acquisition of the fields of the poor by the rich and powerful[70] and promoted a sense of modesty and shame.[71]

Now, rich traders and great merchants accumulate land and goods.[72] The young people of families of the intermediate rank serve as guarantors[73] for them and scurry on their behalf with the diligence of servants and slaves.[74] Meanwhile, the ground tax[75] [levied by merchants] yields an income comparable to that of the enfeoffed rulers.[76] As a result, the masses follow their example,[77] try to eat without ploughing and often gain access to luxuries[78] with which they indulge their ears and eyes.

Therefore, all traders and merchants should be ordered to watch and report on one another. If something could have been gained through their own effort [but was gained in some other way], their illicit profit should be given to the informer.[79] In this way,

they will concentrate on serving their own needs and
will not dare to give goods to others [in trade]. When
their affairs have diminished and their power weakened,
then their efforts will certainly revert to the fields.
Once the fields are cultivated, the harvest of grain
will be large, and the potential of the land will be
fully exploited.[80]

Furthermore, I have seen that when laws and
ordinances are invoked to decide matters, they are not
uniform in their lightness or severity; that is, for
one matter there are varying laws, and for the same
crime, different judgments. Consequently, villainous
officials can avail themselves of this[81] to do business--
they produce arguments to allow those whom they want to
save to live, while they apply judicial precedents[82]
[to condemn to death] those whom they want to damn.
This means that the law opens two gates.[83]

Now, an order should be issued that persons who
thoroughly understand the principles of justice and are
well versed in the laws and statutes should revise and
fix the rulings and judicial precedents[84] so as to uni-
fy the legal rules, to circulate them to the commanderies and kingdoms below, and to abolish antiquated stipu-
lations.[85] In this way, the Empire will know the proper
direction,[86] and in lawsuits there will produce neither
grievances nor abuse."

Previous translation: Pokora, "The Life," I, pp. 23-29.

210

On Repressing the Ch'an Texts and Increasing Rewards.

Hou Han shu 28A, pp. 1015-17.   Yen 12.9a-b.

Huan T'an's biography says that his second
memorial (translated above in fragment 209) was reported
to the Emperor but was not examined. Fan Yeh continues, "At this particular time the Emperor believed in
prognostications, which he often used to decide and
settle doubtful matters.[87] Also, rewards granted by
the Emperor were small and miserly, and the Empire was
not pacified by the expected time. Huan T'an submitted
another memorial which said:"

"Earlier your servant presented his humble
opinions, but he has not yet been blessed by being summoned to report. Overcome with bitterness and anguish,
I risk death to make another plea.[88] When the stupid
man makes plans, the only ones that are of benefit to
government policy are those that are in harmony with
the mind of the people and have a grasp of the real
state of affairs. It is the character of all men[89] to
disregard the facts before their eyes and to value
strange things learned from rumor.[90] From the records
of the early kings, we see that they all took humanity,
righteousness and the correct Way as their base and had
no room for strange, empty and boastful things. As for
the Way of Heaven, nature, and human fate, even the
sages found it difficult to speak of it. From Tzu-kung
on down they are not heard from on these matters.[91] How
much less can these matters be understood by shallow
scholars of later ages?

"Today all the artful and foxy, magicians of
small talent, as well as the soothsayers[92] disseminate
and reproduce diagrams and documents,[93] falsely praising
the records of prognostication. By deception and mis-
information,[94] by greed and dishonesty, they lead the
ruler astray.[95] How can we fail to suppress and banish
such things?[96]

"Your subject, T'an, ventures to say that he has
heard that Your Majesty deeply despises[97] the practices
of magicians who try to make gold and silver. This is
very wise indeed! But how mistaken you are when you
want to believe in and listen to the apocryphal records!
Even if their predictions were to occasionally correspond with the facts, their practices are of the same
class as divination by oracle bones[98] and numerology
with odd and even numbers.[99]

"It befits Your Majesty to deign to judge with
clear vision,[100] to manifest your sagely will, to reject
the distorted theories of the many mean men, to hand
down the correct meaning of the Five Classics, to put
vulgar, hearsay[101] opinions into order,[102] and to examine carefully the correct proposals of the learned
men.[103]

"Moreover, your servant has heard that masters
of magical practices are esteemed during periods of
security and peace, but that, during times of crisis,
armored and helmeted subjects are honored.[104] If,

although your sacred court has now begun to restore the
ancestral line of succession[105] and you have become the
ruler of men, the robbers and thieves in the four directions have not yet completely surrendered, it is because
you do not have the right schemes and plans.

"Your servant, T'an, humbly observes that, since
those who were forced to surrender during Your Majesty's
military operations received no great rewards to entice
them by favors and were even captured as enemies[106] and
robbed of their property, the commanders of the regular
troops and the chieftains of the rebels have become suspicious of each other.[107] Cliques and groups[108] form
and do not dissolve for years and months. The people
of the ancient past used to say, 'Everyone in the Empire
knows that one takes in order to get, but no one knows
that one gives in order to get.'[109] If Your Majesty
is really able to lighten the ranks,[110] increase the
rewards, and share dignities, then there will be none
who will not come at your bidding and none whom you
cannot persuade. There will be no direction which will
not open to you and no military expedition which will
not be victorious. In this way, you can make the narrow
wide, speed the slow, revive the extinct, and regain the
lost."

Huan T'an's biography goes on to discuss this
memorial:

Upon examining the memorial, the Emperor
[Kuang-wu] was even more displeased. Later,
he summoned a council to deliberate upon a
site for the Spiritual Tower.[111] The Emperor
said to Huan T'an, "I want to decide this[112]
according to prognostication.[113] What do
you think?"

T'an remained silent for a long time,
finally replying, "Your servant does not read
prognostications."[114]

The Emperor asked for an explanation.
Once more T'an[115] strongly condemned prognostications as being contradictory to the canonical books.[116] The Emperor, infuriated, said,
"Huan T'an opposes the teachings of the sages
and disowns the law.[117] Take him below and
behead him!"

Huan T'an kotowed for such a long time
that blood flowed from his head. He was
pardoned only much later.[118] Sent from the
capital to be an Assistant Administrator in
the commandery of Liu-an,[119] he was full of
sorrow.[120] On the way he fell ill and died.
He was over seventy[121] years old.[122]

Previous translation: Pokora, "The Life," I, pp. 29-33.

211

Commentary to <u>Wen hsüan</u> 3.41a, quoting Huan T'an, "Shang
pien-i" 上便宜 (Memorial on What is Advanta-
geous). Yen 12.9b.

Kuan Chung was Duke Huan's guide.

212

Commentary to <u>Wen hsüan</u> 30.20a and 56.30a, quoting Huan
T'an, "Ch'en pien-i" 陳便宜 (Statement on What
is Advantageous). Yen 12.9b.

By "the achievement of the hegemons" we mean a
state in which the law is clear and straight, in which
the bureaucracy is disciplined and ordered, and in which
the stern authority of ordinances prevails.

213

<u>Ch'i-shih</u> 啓事 (Notice). Quoted by Yen without
attribution.

All officials with an income of two thousand
piculs, who wear plain jackets and sheep garments, and
use ordinary wooden cups for eating and drinking are

242

deceiving, false and cunning. They merely want to gain
a reputation and seek after fame.

214

Commentaries to Wen hsüan (45.24b, 43.30b, 56, 34b),

quoting Huan T'an, "Ta Yang Hsiung shu" 桓譚答揚雄書

("A Letter in Reply to Yang Hsiung").   Yen 12.10a.

Tzu-yün, (you) have diligently tasted the choice
meat of the Way.[123]

Previous translation: Pokora, "The Life," II, p. 533.

215

TPYL 763.7a, quoting Huan T'an, "Shang shih" 上事

(Esteeming Affairs).

Confucius asked a butcher about to slaughter a
cow if there was a particular method[124] used in slaugh-
tering? The answer was, "A cut must be exactly in the
middle in order to open up (the cow) and butcher it.
An examination of the sinews[125] must be arranged in the
middle. Only then is the final conclusion taken before
the cow is struck."[126]

216

The So-yin commentary to Shih chi 47, p. 25.

Lun-yü XVII:5 tells the story of Kung-shan Fu-
jao (known in the Shih chi as Kung-shan Pu-niu), who,
in 502 or 501 B.C., rebelled in Lu, seized the forti-
fied city of Pi, and invited Confucius to come to him.
The story is repeated in Shih chi 47, p. 25 ("The Hereditary House of Confucius"). Confucius himself was
inclined to accept the invitation, but Tzu-lu tried to
disuade him. At this point in the anecdote, Ssu-ma

Ch'ien puts seventeen characters into the mouth of Confucius which cannot be found in any other source, including the vast compendium of Confucian lore, the K'ung-tzu chia-yü: "Wen and Wu of the Chou rose from Feng and Hao, respectively, to become kings. Although Pi is now but a small place, might it not play the same role?"

Such a statement was, at least for the later orthodoxy, definitely sacrilegious, since it implied that Kung-shan Fu-jao, a military upstart of somewhat dubious character, might seize the throne of the Chou. Moreover, it indicated that Confucius would be willing to rise with the rebel, or even become the king himself, thus breaking his loyalty to the rulers of Lu and Chou. Perhaps, since the source of Ssu-ma Ch'ien's addition is unknown, we may conclude that the Han historian was attempting to criticize Confucius in a bitter and scandalizing way, besmirching his impeccable reputation. H. G. Creel's negative opinion of Chapter 47 of the Shih chi in his Confucius and the Chinese Way (pp. 244-48) might conform to this suggestion, but B. Watson takes the opposite approach in Ssu-ma Ch'ien: Grand Historian of China (pp. 167-74). For details of the affair itself, see Creel (pp. 35-36, and note 13 on p. 299) which discusses the attempts of modern scholars to prove that the incident did not happen at all. A T'ang scholar not mentioned by Creel, Ssu-ma Cheng (8th century A.D.), comments:

"If we examine the [K'ung-tzu] chia-yü and the writings of Confucius, these words are nowhere to be found. Therefore, Huan T'an, too, believed that this was a false accusation."

Of course, because of Ssu-ma Cheng's Confucian bias, it is to be expected that he would try to disprove "the false accusation" and affirm Confucius' loyalty; however, this does not in itself invalidate his commentary. However, it is clear from fragment 137 that Ssu-ma Cheng was not a reliable historian; he clearly misinterpreted Huan T'an's statement on Tung-fang Shuo. It is possible that, in this particular case, he was misusing the authority of Huan T'an, an eminent Han scholar, to prove that Confucius could have not been impeached.

NOTES: OTHER WRITINGS BY HUAN T'AN

1.   PTSC 102.4a, IWLC 78.16b and Yen 12.7b give the
name as "Hsien fu," while PTSC 12.4a quotes "Hsien wang
[fu]," which is probably a mistake for "Wang hsien [fu]"
望 仙 賦 . K'ung Kuang t'ao's edition of PTSC,
published in 1888, uses the latter, preferable form.
It corresponds to the name "Looking-for-Immortals Gate"
and to Huan T'an's feelings as described in the last
sentence of his preface. Furthermore, names composed
of two characters were commonly used as titles for
rhyme-prose (fu).

2.   PTSC 102.4a only quotes the preface (hsü 序 ,
which may also be translated as "postface," since it is
frequently placed at the end of a work) which is not
mentioned by any other source.

3.   IWLC 78.16b has chung-lang 中 郎 ("Gentleman
of the Household"). PTSC 102.4a has two different quotations. The first, which is attributed to Huan T'an's
Hsin-lun (fragment 142), has feng-ch'e lang 奉 車 郎
("Gentleman of the Imperial Carriages"), while the second, from "Hsien fu" has only lang 郎 ("Gentleman").
Although the title chung-lang existed in Huan T'an's
time, Huan T'an himself did not use it. The title feng-
ch'e lang is also given to Huan T'an by TPYL 215.9a
(see fragment 125, note 60); Huan T'an attained this
rank when he was only seventeen years old (sixteen by
European computation; see fragment 125, note 59). The
short form, lang ("Gentleman"), which I adopt, may be
an abbreviation of one of those titles; it is given in
Huan T'an's biography in Hou Han shu 28A, p. 1011.

4.   IWLC 78.16b has chiao 郊 ("sacrifice"), while
PTSC 102.4a has pu 部 ("subordinate"). Yen hesitated
between the two. In the modern edition of PTSC (see
note 1 above) he originally used chiao, but Ku Ch'ien-
li changed it to pu, and Yen later accepted this modification. The IWLC cannot be lightly dismissed, since
it is in accord with the account in Han shu 10 (see
HFHD II, p. 407). See also note 6 below.

5.   Ho-tung commandery was in western Shansi near
the Yellow River.

6.   Following the reading pu (see note 4 above),

another acceptable translation may be; "The subordinate [officials] first..."

7.　　The town of Hua-yin can still be found between the Wei River and Mount Hua-shan in eastern Shensi on the railroad from Lo-yang to Sian. However, Hua-yin is also an old name for Mount Hua-shan itself; M. Kaltenmark, Le Lie-sien tchouan, p. 160, note 1.

8.　　Han shu 28A (p. 2489) confirms this but gives no date for the building of the palace. Its construction is not mentioned in the "Annals of Emperor Wu."

9.　　PTSC 102.4a has a fuller version, chi-ling-kung huai hsien-cho 集 靈 宮 懷 仙 者 which is more intelligible and thus preferable: "In the Palace of Assembled Spirits the Emperor wished to reflect on immortals such as..."

10.　　Wang Ch'iao and Ch'ih Sung Tzu are well-known Taoist Immortals, usually associated with each other. Ch'ih Sung Tzu 赤 松 子 was said to be the Master of Rain in the time of the legendary Shen Nung. Wang Ch'iao (or Wang-tzu Ch'iao 王 子 喬) was the heir apparent of King Ling of Chou (571-545 B.C.). Some of the earliest of the many legends which have surrounded them are recorded in Chan-kuo ts'e 2:3:17 and, later, in Yüan yu ("The Far-Off Journey"). See D. Hawkes, Ch'u Tz'u: The Songs of the South, p. 82, for Ch'ih Sung, and p. 83, for Wang Ch'iao. More material is collected in Lieh-hsien chuan, Chapters 1 and 28; see especially the abundant notes to Kaltenmark's translation, Le Lie-sien tchouan, pp. 35-42 and 109-14. P. Pelliot refers to a rich literature on Wang Ch'iao in his article, "Meou-tseu ou les doutes levés," p. 406, note 364, and to literature on Ch'ih Sung Tzu in note 365 on p. 407.

　　　　Both immortals are discussed by Pan Piao in his "Lan-hai fu" (Yen, Ch'üan Hou Han wen 23.4b), and by the poet Hsi K'ang (see Holzman, La vie et la pensée de Hi K'ang, pp. 20 and 139, 23 and 140). Hsi K'ang also refers to Huan T'an directly (Holzman, pp. 114, 172) and indirectly, when speaking of Mister Tou (fragment 82D, note 21; Holzman, pp. 106, 169). The first of the above quotations from Hsi K'ang is important for an understanding of Huan T'an's reaction to the Taoist practices. See note 16 below for the Taoist practices.

11.　The text has hu 戶 , but I follow Yen in reading chü 居 ("to live"). The four characters of this
last short sentence are not found in IWLC 78.16b.

12.　Instead of the miao 妙 ("beautiful") of the
text, Yen reads another miao 眇 ("subtle").

13.　This is the last character of the quotation
from "Hsien fu hsü" 仙 賦 序 in PTSC 102.4a. Another, similar quotation on the same page comes from
the Hsin-lun, not from this rhyme-prose. It seems hardly possible that "Rhyme-prose on Looking for Immortals"
was part of the Hsin-lun; more likely, it was part of
Huan's literary works (chi 集 ; see the commentary to
fragment 190).

　　The quotation from Hsin-lun was shortened by
Huan T'an or some later editor. Yen included it in
his reconstructed 12th chapter, "Tao fu" (see fragment
142). Sun 15b (fragment 142, note 11) attributes his
quote to the same source; his text, however, is sub-
stantially different and cannot be found in PTSC. It
reads as follows: "In my youth, when I was a Gentleman of the Imperial Carriages, Emperor Hsiao-ch'eng
favored Kan-ch'üan Palace. I wished to write on the
wall; therefore, I wrote a fu to eulogize and praise
the behavior of the two Immortals. I received a command to write a "Rhyme-prose on the Immortals" (Hsien
fu) on the wall of Kan-ch'üan Palace."

　　Yen includes three characters, i sung-mei 以頌
美 ("To eulogize and praise"), which cannot be found
in the PTSC 102.4a version of the "Hsien fu hsü" (preface) but are included in Sun's version of the Hsin-lun
quote, translated above. In fact, Yen's version makes
little sense since he did not also add the four characters "the behaviour of the Immortals."

14.　This verse bears a strong resemblance to Chuang-
tzu 4:15, p. 87, which describes Taoist breathing exercises: "...inhaling and exhaling of the old breath and
taking in new..." (t'u-ku na-hsin 吐 故 納 新 ;
Legge, I, p. 364).

15.　The character yin 引 ("to guide") is here
connected with the compound tao-yin 導 引 ("gymnastics").

16. __Yüan ch'i__ 元氣 ("the original breath") is
translated by Maspero in "Les procédés de 'nourrir le
principe vital' dans la réligion taoïste ancienne,"
p. 206, as "Souffle Originel." A theory on this "original" or "primal" breath was not fully developed until
the T'ang dynasty, which considered it to be a kind of
"personal" breath. Taoist breath exercises were closely
connected with gymnastics (__tao-yin__). Ch'ih Sung Tzu and
Wang Ch'iao were each identified with a system of gymnastics. A description of these two systems, which is
crucial to understanding this rhyme-prose, is given by
Maspero, pp. 415-17, 422-23.

17. For the expression __hsü wu__ 虛無 ("Emptiness
and Nothingness"), see P. Pelliot, "Meou-tseu ou les
doutes levés," __TP__, No. 19 (1920), pp. 397-98, note 324.

18. __Yu ming__ 幽明 (translated as "darkness and
light") could mean "death and life."

19. A character referred to as early as the __Book of
Songs__, __yü-nü__ 玉女 ("Jade Woman") became one of the
Taoist goddesses (Yen Shih-ku, commentary to __Han shu__
87A, p. 5078). According to __Shen-i ching la__ (attributed
rather arbitrarily to Tung-fang Shuo), she lived in a
mountain in the Eastern desert (for __Tung-huang__ 東荒
or "Eastern Desert," see fragment 177). __Lieh-hsien
chuan__ 44 refers to the "sanctuary of the Jade Woman"
(Kaltenmark, p. 178; see also __Han shu__ 25B, p. 2145),
and Yang Hsiung, in his "Kan-ch'üan fu" (Wen hsüan 7.4a;
__Han shu__ 87A, p. 5078; von Zach, __Die Chinesische Anthol-
ogie__, I, p. 97), associates her with the other Taoist
deities Hsi-wang-mu and Fu-fei. Chang Heng, in his
"Ssu-hsüan fu" (__Wen hsüan__ 15.5b; von Zach, I, p. 224),
makes the same association and also says that the Jade
Woman comes from Mount T'ai-hua (or Hua-shan), also
called Hua-yin (see note 7 above). See also Y. Hervouet,
__Sseu-ma Siang-jou__, pp. 299-300, 315, and E. H. Schafer,
__TP__, Vol. 50 (1963), p. 261, note 1.

     In his commentary to __Wen hsüan__ 15.5b, Li Shan
identifies the Jade Woman with the Hairy Woman (Mao-nü
毛女) from __Lieh-hsien chuan__ 54. Pao-p'u-tzu (11.13a;
__Monumenta Serica__, Vol. II, 1946, pp. 24-25; and Kaltenmark, __Le Lie-sien tchouan__, p. 160, note 4) says that,
during the reign of Emperor Ch'eng, this Hairy Woman
was found by hunters in the Chung-nan Mountain. Her
style name was Jade Lady (__Yü-chiang__ 玉姜). Li Shan's

identification, if correct, would explain why the Jade
Woman is unknown in earlier Taoism, since she would re-
present a feature peculiar to Hsien-Taoism. Neither
Maspero ("Les procédés," p. 377, note 1) nor W. Eichhorn
("Eine Erzählung aus dem Wen-chien hou-lu", p. 173, note
24) recognized this possibility.

 Thus, the Jade Woman is a Taoist goddess associated with Hua-shan. She bears a certain resemblance to
the Mysterious Woman (Hsüan nü 玄女). Although of
Taoist origin, she was later identified with Kundalini
of the Yoga system; see J. Filliozat, "Taoïsme et Yoga,"
Dan Viêt-Nam, Vol. 3 (1949), p. 119.

20. K'ang-hsi tzu-tien quotes a commentary to the
"Yüeh ling" chapter of the Li chi, which says that t'eng
騰 designates draft animals (Legge I, p. 266). The
term ch'ing-lung 青龍 ("blue dragon") can also be
found there (Legge, I, p. 251) in connection with the
Emperor's carriage. Pan Piao uses similar terms in his
"Lan-hai fu" (Yen, Ch'üan Hou Han wen 23.4b). For "blue
dragon," see also E. H. Schafer, TP, Vol. 50 (1963),
p. 261, note 1.

21. The reference to the black stone calls to mind
the "Tzu-hsü fu" by Ssu-ma Hsiang-ju (Wen hsüan 7.7b).

22. Yang Hsiung frequently mentions "the region of
purest air" in e.g., his "Kan-ch'üan fu" (Wen hsüan
7.1b, Han shu 87A, p. 5068). The two characters chiao
膠 and ko 葛 may also be interpreted as referring
to the Chiao Mountain, in Shantung, and Mount Ko-hsien,
in Chekiang; the latter is famous as a home of immortals.

23. Maspero translates Yü-i 玉液 ("the juice of
jade") as "la liquer du Jade" ("Le Taoïsme," in Mélanges
posthumes, II, p. 107). He describes the substance in
detail in a paragraph on the absorption of the saliva
("Les procédés," p. 362): "L'absorption de la salive
...accompagne ordinairement les pratiques du Souffle;
on profite de ce que la bouche est fermée pour recueillir
la Liquer du Jade, c'est-à-dire la salive en abondance
sous la langue, en remplir la bouche et, en penchant la
tête, l'avaler pour qu'elle aille en haut réparer le
cerveaux et en bas baigner les cinq viscères." See also
Kaltenmark, Le Lie-sien tchuan, p. 37, and P. Pelliot,
in "Meou-tseu ou les doutes levés," p. 381, note 266.

24.   Hua-chih 華芝 ("splendid iris") is also mentioned in "Kan-ch'üan fu" (Wen hsüan 7.1b; Han shu 87A,
p. 5069; von Zach, I, p. 94). Fu Ch'ien's commentary
says it is a hua-kai 蓋 , an umbrella with the emblem
of a splendid iris which is used on the Emperor's carriages.

25.   Yü-chiang 玉漿 ("jade liquid") is translated
by Maspero as "le Bouillon de Jade" ("Le Taoïsme," p.
113); the term also means "saliva." The saliva is not
to be absorbed, as note 23 shows, but plays an important
role in the absorption of breath. The first step of the
Taoist procedure was to hold the breath for a long period of time. In the following difficult step one must
"close up the breath" (pi ch'i 閉氣 and avoid passing
it out through the mouth, nose, or any other orifice.
The "jade liquid" must fill the mouth to prevent the
breath from leaking out.

26.   In accordance with Yen, I read ts'ang 滄
("vast") for the ts'ang 倉 ("hurried, flurried") of
the text.

27.   This probably refers to the Gate of Heaven on
T'ai-shan.

28.   In accordance with Yen, I read pa 八 ("eight"),
instead of the graphically similar character, ju 入
("to reach"). Pa is also used in Pan Piao's "Lan-hai
fu" (see note 20 above).

29.   "The altar of Yen-hua" may refer to Yen-tzu, a
mountain near T'ien-shui in Kansu. The sun is said to
sink into a cave on Mount Yen-tzu every night.

30.   The second hu 乎 is not given by IWLC and was
correctly added by Yen. The term comes from Mencius
(III:I:IV:7; Legge, p. 250).

31.   See fragment 207, note 40.

32.   Li Hsien's commentary presents a brief survey
of these events, which are described in detail in Han
shu 97A, pp. 5568-71. For more than ten years the Empress née Ch'en had been the legal wife of Emperor Wu,
but she had not borne a son by him. The Emperor fell
in love with Wei Tzu-fu, whose career has been vividly
described by M. Wilbur, Slavery in China during the
Former Han Dynasty, pp. 298-99. Her younger brother
was the famous general, Wei Ch'ing.

33.   According to <u>HFHD</u>, II, p. 41, the Empress née Ch'en was dismissed on August 20, 131 B.C.

34.   According to <u>HFHD</u>, II, p. 49, the Empress née Wei was established on April 30, 128 B.C., only after she gave birth to a son, Liu Chü. She had previously borne three daughters. See also note 32 above.

35.   The <u>Ssu-pu pei-yao</u> edition of <u>Hou Han shu</u> has the wrong character <u>fu</u> 夫 ("man") instead of the <u>pien</u> 變 ("transformation") of Wang Hsien-ch'ien's edition.

36.   The Empress née Ch'en attempted to regain the love of her husband, Emperor Wu, by means of a love potion produced by black magic. Unfortunately, the result was the reverse of what she had hoped; the Empress was executed, together with over three hundred people who were accused of taking part in these magical practices. See <u>HFHD</u>, II, pp. 17-19, and other literature quoted in note 25 to fragment 102. Huan T'an had every reason to believe that the neglected Empress née Fu, also estranged from her husband, would resort to the same remedy in her despair, thereby courting a fate like that of the Empress née Ch'en.

37.   The Empress was indeed interested in magicians and in their art of "yellow and white," the production of gold.

38.   <u>Pin-k'o</u> 賓客 ("retainers"). At this time numerous memorials were presented to the Emperor criticizing the ownership of large numbers of slaves, and proposals were made to limit their acquisition. These criticisms were apparently directed against retainers as well. In some cases the position of the retainers may have been very similar to that of the slaves.

39.   In accordance with <u>Tz'u hai</u>, I prefer <u>shih</u> 勢 ("position") to the <u>i</u> 執 ("skill") of the text.

40.   Tung Hsien was a young and powerful protégé of Emperor Ai. He became Commander-in-Chief in July of the year 1 B.C. and was deposed a few weeks later, on August 16, when Emperor Ai died.

41.   For an explanation of <u>chiao</u> 交 ("friends"), see the commentary to fragment 190.

42.   Bielenstein, The Restoration, I, pp. 145-51 and 153; see also The Life, I, p. 53.

43.   The proposals are translated in The Life, I, pp. 48-51.

44.   Chen Feng was a high dignitary who gained his first post in 8 B.C. (Han shu 19B, p. 1311) and became a close collaborator of Wang Mang. In 2 A.D., he became the Grand Minister of Works (ibid., p. 1330), a post which he filled until January 15, 9 A.D. (HFHD, III, p. 263). In December of the year 10 A.D. or in January of 11 A.D., Chen Feng committed suicide, in part because of the intrigues of his own son (HFHD, III, pp. 308-10). Chen Feng's successor in the office of the Grand Minister of Works was Wang I, who is also mentioned in the Hsin-lun (see fragment 164A, note 17 to fragment 164B, and note 21 to fragment 164D).

45.   "Milliard" is a provisional translation of the term i-wan 億萬 . Wan is, of course, "ten thousand," but i may mean any one of several different numbers: 100,000; 1,000,000; 10,000,000; or even 100,000,000. I-wan is, simply, an immense number (see Dai Kanwa jiten, I, pp. 944-45, and No. 1178.30). However, since Huan T'an speaks of "several i-wan," he is clearly referring to a specific number. A similar large number, ch'ien-wan 千萬 (possibly 10,000,000), was examined by M. Wilbur in Slavery, p. 281, note 6: "This might be read 'several thousand up to a myriad [cash],' wan being the terminal figure. Certainly, the term ch'ien-wan at times means thousand times myriad (see Couvreur, Dictionaire classique, p. 106), and it must mean that here, for several thousand or a myriad is not a large figure for money in Han times." In a letter of October 22, 1965, Professor L. S. Yang writes, "I suggest that i-wan as a real number was the same as wan-wan or i (100,000,000) in Han times. Hou Han shu 64.13a-b [i.e., 24, p. 1246--T.P.] refers to the wealth of Shih-sun Fen, which amounted to i-i ch'i-ch'ien wan 一億七千萬 , or 170,000,000. Hou Han shu 81.5a [i.e., 41, p. 1823--T.P.] states that the government owed people debts amounting to several tens of i-wan, which must have been a real number too." This means that Huan T'an's estimate of several i-wan represented approximately one-tenth of what would be the government debt one hundred years later (in 110 A.D.) and thus could have been quite realistic.

Incidentally, it is significant that the immensely rich Shih-sun Fen does not have a biography in Hou Han shu. Moreover, he is mentioned only once in the large dynastic history and even then in relation to an affair which actually happened some twenty years later, under the Emperor Shun.

46.　　The meaning of the term hsien-kuan 縣官 (here translated as "Imperial government") is also ambiguous. H. H. Dubs (HFHD, I, p. 311, note 3.5, and II, p. 64) translates it as "government" or "imperial government." N. L. Swann (Food and Money in Ancient China, p. 167, note 192) suggests that the "reference may be to the county official himself," while A. F. P. Hulsewé, (Remnants, I, p. 381, note 176) treats the problem exhaustively, saying that "it is not always easy to make a decision" and that hsien-kuan in the term hsien tao kuan ("offices of the prefectures and marches") 'definitely does not indicate the central government, but the prefecture and nothing else." B. Watson reflects this ambiguity; in his translation from Shih chi 122, pp. 17-18, he translates the term twice as "district officials" and once as "the government" (Records, II, p. 430). Perhaps we should accept the opinion of L. S. Yang (see note 45 above): "I wonder whether it is always necessary to make a distinction between central government and local government, because, after all, the prefects and magistrates were all agents of the imperial government."

47.　　The last sentence appears to belong to Huan T'an, because Pan Ku's evaluation (or eulogy) is found in the following sentence. Moreover, since Huan T'an's conclusion clearly is not part of his dialogue with Chen Feng, I believe that the entire text was copied by Pan Ku from the Hsin-lun.

48.　　In translating cheng-shih 政事 as "political affairs," I follow H. H. Dubs, The Works of Hsüntze, p. 36. Legge, in Confucian Analects (XI:II:2; pp. 237-38), has "administrative talents;" in the Works of Mencius (VII:II:XII:3; p. 483), Legge has "[the great principles] of government and their various business."

49.　　"The Counsellors" (Fu-tso 輔佐) is the title of Chapter 5 of Chia I's Hsin-shu.

50.　　A similar sentence is found in a memorial by Huan T'an's contemporary, Ts'ai Mao, which is quoted in Hou Han shu 28, p. 960.

51.   King Chuang of Ch'u reigned from 613 to 591 B.C. and is traditionally regarded as one of the Five Hegemons.

52.   Sun Shu-ao was a Chancellor of Ch'u. His biography is found in <u>Shih chi</u> 119, pp. 2-4. He is frequently mentioned in early literature, as, for example, in <u>Tso chuan</u> (Legge, p. 318) and in <u>Mencius</u> (Legge, p. 446.

53.   For an example of such an arrogant lord, see Su Ch'in's biography in <u>Shih chi</u> 69, p. 47. The term <u>chiao chün</u> 驕 君 ("arrogant lord") also occurs in the short fifth chapter of Lu Chia's <u>Hsin-yü</u>. The title of the chapter, "Pien-huo" 辨 惑 ("Discerning Error") is the same as that of the thirteenth chapter of Huan T'an's <u>Hsin-lun</u>.

54.   The story of King Chuang and Sun Shu-ao may be found in the collection of anecdotes, <u>Hsin hsü</u> (2, p. 12), generally attributed to Liu Hsiang. Huan T'an did not quote this story verbatim but adapted and shortened it. Liu Hsiang's version shows that Sun Shu-ao was extremely critical of his ruler. Another story about Sun Shu-ao, the second of the three included by Ssu-ma Ch'ien in Chapter 126 of the <u>Shih chi</u>, shows a "Sun Shu-ao redivivus." After Sun Shu-ao's death, an ironical critic (<u>ku-chi</u>), Meng, imitates his behavior so convincingly that the same King Chuang is forced to promise to give more care to Sun Shu-ao's wife and children, who had become destitute after the death of the eminent and selfless chancellor.

55.   The term <u>tsao jen</u> 躁 人 ("impetuous men") alludes to the <u>I Ching</u>, "Hsi-tz'u chuan." R. Wilhelm (<u>I Ging: Das Buch der Wandlungen</u>, p. 272) translates it as "Aufgeregte Menschen machen viele Worte," while Couvreur (<u>Dictionnaire classique</u>, p. 901) has "un homme d'un caractère ardent (multiplie les paroles)." Hui Tung, in his commentary quoted by Wang Hsien-ch'ien, says that the term means "people who privately deliberate on the government of the country." In the last, autobiographical chapter of his <u>Lun-heng</u>, Wang Ch'ung alludes to this line in the <u>I Ching</u>, saying that some people call him a man of many words because of the great size of his book (30:85, p. 1193; Forke, I, p. 77).

56.   This is a quote from Tung Chung-shu's first memorial to Emperor Wu, given in Han shu 56, p. 4001, with some variations. The text has been translated by W. Seufert, "Urkunden zur staatlichen Neuordnung unter der Han-Dynastie," MSOS, Vols. 23-25 (1922), p. 26. A similar text is found in the "Treatise on the Rules for Ceremonious Behaviour and on Music," in Han shu 22, p. 1911, translated by Hulsewé (Remnants, I, p. 435): "I [would beg] to liken it to a lute or a zithern. When these are very much out of tune, they have to be unstrung, and strung anew; then they can be strummed. When, in carrying out an administrative [policy], this is not enacted to a serious extent, it must be changed and transformed anew; then there can be order." The text of Pan Ku's Han shu is based upon Huan T'an; a similar adaptation is noted by Hulsewé, Remnants, I, p. 312. Of course, both texts were originally derived by Huan T'an from Tung Chung-shu, but his reasoning is significantly different from that of Tung Chung-shu. Tung Chung-shu stresses the necessity of administrative reforms, while Huan T'an uses the same anecdotes as examples of persons who suffered greatly because they were not understood by their contemporaries. This is, in a slightly different form, Wang Ch'ung's constantly recurring theme of the frustration of ministers and officials.

57.   Chia I lived ca. 201-169 B.C. At the age of twenty, he was appointed a Scholar of Erudite Learning (po-shih) by Emperor Wen, and only a year later he became a Grand Palace Grandee. However, before long Chia I was banished to Ch'ang-sha because of the slanders of envious courtiers who feared his wisdom and growing power.

58.   Ch'ao Ts'o was an eminent politician and scholar during the reigns of Emperors Wen and Ching. He correctly recognized the danger which the existence of large fiefs not administered by the Emperor's officials created for the stability of the dynasty. Therefore, in 154 B.C., he proposed to liquidate these fiefs according to the system practiced by the Ch'in dynasty. This proposal, of course, was strongly opposed by the holders of these fiefs. It led directly to the rebellion of the Seven Kingdoms in the same year; to save the situation, the Emperor sacrificed Ch'ao Ts'o. Apparently Huan T'an compared the conflicts in his own official career with Ch'ao Tso's death, a "reward" for his meritorious work on behalf of the Han dynasty. The stories of Chia I and Ch'ao Ts'o may be found in Han shu 48, pp. 3687-3740, and 49, pp. 3751-78, respectively.

59.　　Dai Kan Wa Jiten 9812.238 quotes both this line and a similar, less realistic statement from the Po-hu t'ung 7.31a:　"Therefore, the division of the land into principalities is not for the sake of the Feudal Lords; neither is the institution of administrative offices and bureaus for the sake of the Ministers and great officers.　It is all for the benefit of the people." (Translation by Tjan Tjoe Som, II, p. 416.)

60.　　Dai Kan Wa Jiten 27784.57 quotes this, preferring hsüan-shang 懸賞 ("rewards are offered") to hsien-shang 縣賞.

61.　　The term fu-fa 伏法 (here translated as "settled by the law") is translated by B. Watson as "to fall before the law" (in his translation of Han shu 62, p. 4266; Ssu-ma Ch'ien, Grand Historian of China, p. 63) and by A. Forke as "[to suffer death] according to the law" (Lun-heng, I, p. 157; Lun-heng 6.20, p. 255).

62.　　See note 67 below.

63.　　Perhaps jen 任 ("to allow") should be read for jen 人 ("people"), as in the biography of Hsieh Hsüan, the well-known jurist and elder contemporary of Huan T'an (Han shu 83, p. 4928).　If we accept jen 任, it would be synonymous with t'ing 聽 ("to allow, to permit") and would not change the translation in any way. Dai Kan Wa Jiten 29211.100 translates t'ing-jen 聽任 as "makaseru" ("to leave anything to another's care," "to leave a person do anything").

64.　　Shen 申 means "repeatedly."　Shen ming 申明 ("repeatedly explain") is a legal term.　See, for example, Shih-chi 25, p. 5; Chavannes, MH III, p. 295: "[Ces royaumes] développèrent et éclaircirent les lois de la guerre; les récompenses et les châtiments furent d'une absolue certitude..." Shih chi 64, p. 4:　"[Ssu-ma Jang-chü] repeatedly explained the discipline (shen-ming yüeh-shu 申明約束)."　Shen by itself means "evident, clear" in the legal context, as in Hou Han shu 16, p. 631:　"The crime is not evident and there are no proofs" (tsui wu shen cheng 罪無申證).　Li Hsien's commentary to this line says that shen means ming-pai 明白 ("to understand, evident, clear").

65.　　Hui Tung quotes from commentaries to several ancient texts by Wang Pao and Cheng Chung in order to prove that such an ordinance really did exist in the

Han period. No such ordinance is listed in Hulsewé,
Remnants, I, pp. 42-47, where Hulsewé discusses all the
ordinances of which we now have knowledge. However,
J. L. Kroll does convincingly demonstrate that at least
one ordinance not listed by Hulsewé did exist; see his
"Notes on Han Law." Huan T'an's text on revenge (or
vendetta) was quoted and translated by Masabuchi Tatsuo
in "The Yu Hsia [游 俠] and the Social Order in
the Han Period," 3, p. 94. There is a more thorough
treatment of the vendetta in Han times in Makino Tatsumi,
Shina Kazoku kenkyū, p. 417-87. Explaining blood revenge in Chinese law, Ch'ü T'ung-tsu also translated
Huan T'an's passage, emphasizing its importance, since
"we do not know exactly when the taking of revenge became illegal and punishable by the law." Huan T'an's
memorial "seems to imply that revenge was prohibited,
at least at the end of the Former Han Dynasty, and that
Huan T'an was merely asking Emperor Kuang-wu to imple-
ment a law already in existence" (Law and Society in
Traditional China, p. 80).

66.   Ku-shan 雇山 (here translated "to redeem his
punishment for him") literally means "a hired mountain."
Li Hsien's commentary to Hou Han shu 1A, p. 34, explains
the term as a redemption which can be made by hiring
people to fell trees in the mountains. See also the
detailed explanation in Dubs, HFHD, III, pp. 69-70,
note 4.5.

67.   Ch'ou-yüan 仇 怨 ("hatred and anger") is
identical with yüan-ch'ou 怨 仇 . Ch'ou-yüan
occurs, among other places, in Shih-chi 55, p. 19; W.
Bauer ("Der Fürst von Liu," p. 169) translates, "[Leute
welche Sie zeitlebens] aufs bitterste gehasst haben,"
but the same text paraphrased in Liu Hsiang's Hsin-hsü
10.9b (chapter Shan, mou B) gives yüan-ch'ou. Yüan-
ch'ou is identified by Dai Kan Wa Jiten 10479.13 with
yüan-ch'ou 怨 讎 , which is also used in this memorial; see the text to note 62 above.

68.   The "root" or "basic" occupation is, of course,
agriculture, while extraneous profits are those acquired
by trade.

69.   Li Hsien's commentary mentions the laws of the
first Han Emperor Kao which prohibited the sons and the
grandsons of merchants from becoming officials. This
ordinance is also mentioned by Hulsewé (Remnants, I,
p. 151, note 159), who says that his source is Huan

T'an's memorial, written about 30 A.D. Hulsewé is probably referring to Huan T'an's memorial as quoted in the Tung-kuan Han chi; see note 79 below and the order by Emperor Kao which Dubs translates in HFHD, I, p. 120. See also the following note 70 and Ying-shih Yü, Trade, p. 18, note 32.

70. The term ping-chien 幷兼 ("the accumulation and acquisition of the fields of the poor by the rich and powerful") is found in Chung-ch'ang T'ung's Ch'ang-yen, in Chapter Sun-i (quoted in Hou Han shu 49, p. 1780) and in Chapter Li-luan (ibid., p. 1776), where it is used to characterize the ruling methods of the Ch'in. The same term is used again, in the same context, in Hou Han shu 80A, p. 2855, by Fan Yeh. Li Hsien (Chapter 19, p. 729; see also 26, p. 966) comments, "Ping-chien means that the powerful and rich, by means of their wealth and influence, unite and secure (ping-ch'ü 幷取) the fields of the poor and take and possess (chien-yu 兼有) them" (translation by H. H. Dubs, in HFHD, II, p. 68, note 17.2).

In order to understand properly these two characters, it is also necessary to analyze the reversed binom, chien-ping. The new dictionary, Chung-wen ta-tz'u-tien (Vol. II, 9379.24) says that ping-chien is the same as chien-ping and quotes several sources, such as Kuan-tzu, Shih chi 6, Han shu 24, Mo-tzu, Hsin-shu, and the "Wang-tao" Chapter of Tung Chung-shu's Ch'un ch'iu fan lu in support of its suggestion. Wen Ying, whose commentary is quoted in Han shu 5, sixth year yüan-shou, and translated by Dubs, says, "Those who 'had taken concurrently (chien-ping)' were the families who enjoyed official salaries; They were not permitted to rule their estates and concurrently (chien) to take the advantages (given to) unimportant common people. Although the merchants might be rich, they were not, again concurrently (chien) to hold fields and residences, to have guest-(retainers), or to plow and farm" (HFHD II, p. 68, note 17.2).

H. H. Dubs resumes, "Wen Ying seems to imply that there were three classes: (1) officials and nobility, who might possess fields and residences and entertain guest retainers, (2) farmers, and (3) merchants. Farmers were granted many privileges by the Ch'in and Han dynasties; Emperor Wu tried to keep the officials and merchants from claiming the advantages granted to farmers by prohibiting merchants from owning farm land."

The term chien-ping is also used in the treatise
on economy in Han shu 24, which is translated by N. L.
Swann: "That is why tradespeople absorb (rights of)
farmers, and farmers therefore are drifting from place
to place." The author comments further (note 187):
"...Here...occurs the term translated 'absorb,' or 'to
take possession of' [i.e., chien ping--T.P.]. It is
used only once in the treatise, whereas the two parts
reversed, ping-chien, is a term with a different meaning, that is 'to monopolize,' 'to tyrannize.'" See
N. L. Swann, Food and Money in Ancient China, p. 156
and note 187.

Still another interpretation is offered by
A. F. P. Hulsewé in Remnants, I, p. 90: "...'harsh
officials' turned against members of their own 'gentry'
class...the locally prominent...are accused again and
again of 'encroaching,' i.e., of extending their power
at the expense of the lesser folk, especially by dispos-
sessing them of their land."

71.   A "sense of modesty and shame" is one of the
basic Confucian virtues.

72.   The text has fang t'ien huo 放田貨 (here
translated as "accumulate land and goods") which may
mean "sell land and goods" (see Dai Kan Wa Jiten,
13133.62, under fang-huo). Nevertheless, Huan T'an apparently had the merchants who bought the land of poor
peasants in mind. Wang Hsien-ch'ien points out that
the Palace edition reads ch'ien-huo 錢貨 ("money
and goods"), while our text of the Hou Han shu is corroborated by the Tung-kuan Han chi. Wang is correct,
but the significant variation is in the Tung-kuan Han
chi, which has shou t'ien-huo 收田貨, rather than
fang t'ien-huo (Chapter 4, p. 20b, in the edition by
Yao Chih-yin, Hou Han shu pu-i, or in the edition Ssu-
pu pei-yao of the Tung-kuan Han chi 19, p. 69b). The
two characters fang and shou are graphically similar;
I prefer shou.

73.   This section is quoted by the Dai Kan Wa Jiten,
1, p. 789, and in Chung-wen ta tz'u-tien 694.74. Ho
Ch'ang-chün studied the position of the "middle" families (chung-chia 中家) of the Former Han in his
Lun Liang-Han t'u-ti chan-yu hsing-t'ai ti fa-chan, pp.
14-22.

74.   Ch'en-p'u 臣僕 (here translated as "servants and slaves"). Perhaps these terms were used by

speakers to refer to themselves as a polite form of
modesty when speaking to persons of higher rank. The
use of the term in the Han period may have been archaic.
This suggestion is reinforced by its use in Han shu (73,
p. 4647), which discusses ancient times. However,
neither of these suggestions adequately explains its use
in this text.

75.　　　"Ground tax" is the translation of the term shui
税 given by N. L. Swann, Food and Money, p. 371.
For a systematic study of the term, see R. C. Blue, "The
Argumentation of the 'Shih-huo chih' Chapters of the Han,
Wei, and Sui Dynastic Histories," pp. 108-10. On page
110, the author translates a commentary by Yen Shih-ku:
"Shui means collecting the income from their arable
fields..." Chavannes (MH, III, p. 542, note 6) says
that the term shui "désigne le redevance du quinzième
prélevé sur toutes les productions du sol et de l'in-
dustrie." Huan T'an was probably referring to the land-
rent, but Li Hsien's commentary explains the term shou-
shui 收 税 as describing the levying of interest
from loans. The Tung-kuan Han chi, quoted by Li Hsien,
says, "The sons of families of intermediate rank serve
as guarantors, receive the accounts, and report to the
throne. They scurry, bow and prostrate themselves like
servants and slaves. [The merchants] just sit and di-
vide the profit." Huan T'an's criticism goes even further. For "families of intermediate rank," see note 73
above; for rich merchants, see the following note 76.

76.　　　Several of Huan T'an's observations are similar
to those made by Ssu-ma Ch'ien in his chapter on the
money-makers, Shih chi 129.

77.　　　I prefer mu 慕 ("to follow," "an example") for
the original mu 慕 ("to desire," "to long for"), a
preference shared by Dubs, HFHD, II, p. 409, and by
Wilbur, Slavery, p. 422. When commenting on Dubs's
translation of the term mu-i 慕 義 , C. S. Goodrich
explains the word mu: "The word is used not so much of
actions as of feelings, and here probably indicates an
alleged desire or yearning on the part of the barbarians
to conform with the Chinese principles. 'To yearn for'
...or even 'to desire to imitate'...comes, I think,
closer to representing the specific meaning of the Chinese expression;" see Goodrich's "Professor Dubs's
Translation of the Biography of Wang Mang," p. 115, and
also note 65.

260

78.   See Dubs and Wilbur, quoted in the note above.

79.   For the translation of tsang 臧   as "illicit profit," see Hulsewé, Remnants, I, pp. 178-79. The
more detailed account of the Tung-kuan Han chi is quoted
by Li Hsien: "The merchants frequently have access to
extravagant and lavish things, like white gauze, open-
work variegated and embroidered silk, colors and toys,
thus indulging people's ears and eyes and utterly exhausting their wealth. This plants extravagance in the
lower classes and establishes the root of poverty. Then,
how is it possible to make people thrifty and austere,
wealthy and content? Customs are difficult to change
abruptly, and people cannot be reformed quickly. It is
necessary to suppress the channels [by which they grow
extravagant] and let bad customs gradually wither of
themselves." The style of Huan T'an's memorial, as
quoted in the Tung-kuan Han chi, differs radically from
the version in Hou Han shu. Tung-kuan Han chi appears
to be quoting from an imperial edict; there are certain
similarities with the edict by Emperor Ch'eng, published
in 13 B.C. and translated in HFHD, II, pp. 408-09.

     Huan T'an's proposal that the informer be re-
warded with the money gained through illegal withdrawal
of taxes or other machinations which he reported was
not an original idea. For example, the treatise on
economy in Han shu 24B says, "If anyone fails to make
his estimate [and pay his tax or] makes an incomplete
report, he should be sent out to serve on a frontier
post for one year, and his strings of cash [that is,
his fortune] should be confiscated. He who could be
able to accuse in law another [of breaking these regu-
lations], to him would be given one half [of the cul-
prit's fortune]." (Translation by Swann, Food and Money, p. 282.) It is quite probable that, as in the case
of his suggestion on revenge (see the text to note 66
above), Huan T'an was merely proposing that the new
Emperor revive the old regulation.

80.   Chin ti-li 盡地力 (here translated "fully
exploited") was translated by J. J. L. Duyvendak (The
Book of the Lord Shang, p. 51) as the name of the agricultural school of "intensive culture."

81.   The term yin-yüan 因緣 ("to avail oneself") is defined in Li Hsien's commentary to the Hou
Han shu 46, p. 1662, as i-fu i sheng ch'ing-chung 依
附以生輕重, which is, in turn, explained by the

Tz'u hai (under yin-yüan) as "profiting from the law
by the misuse of official documents."

82.   Pi 比 , may also be translated as "comparison;" see Hulsewé, Remnants, I, pp. 51 or 60.

83.   The greater part of this passage has been translated by Hulsewé, Remnants, I, p. 338, p. 389 (note 199)
and p. 421 (note 343). My translation differs in only
a few respects. As Hulsewé correctly points out, there
are interesting similarities between Huan T'an's memorial and Pan Ku's treatise on law in Han shu 23, p. 1997.
The Han shu text is translated by Hulsewé in Remnants,
I, p. 349; "...the law will no [longer] have two appli-
cations; the lightness or severity [of the punishments]
will correspond to the [gravity of the] crimes and the
lives of the people will remain intact."

84.   The four characters ming-hsi lü-ling 明習律令
are used in Han shu 23, p. 1987; see Hulsewé, Remnants,
I, p. 340. The term chiao-ting 校定 ("revise and
settle") is quoted by Dai Kan Wa Jiten 14713.72 and by
Chung-wen ta-tz'u-tien 15043.21 as having been first
used by Huan T'an. Both dictionaries identify it with
a later binome, chiao-ting 校訂 . Liu Hsiang collated (chiao 校) the books in the private library
of the Palace, but he did not settle (ting 定) them.
(Han shu 10, p. 316; HFHD II, p. 386 and note 6.1. See
also Han shu 36, p. 3401). Ting 定 means to "fix"
or "settle" something, such as a literary text or an
obligatory norm.

85.   Most of this sentence has been translated by
Hulsewé in Remnants, I, pp. 59-60, note 40.

86.   The text has fang-chih 方知 ("direction");
Li Hsien's commentary prefers fa 法 ("law") for fang.
Wang Hsien-ch'ien and Ch'ien Ta-chao, quoted in the
chiao-pu commentary, point out that the Palace edition
has chih-fang (p. 1035). The term is from Lun yü XI:
25:4 (Legge, p. 247). See also Hulsewé, Remnants, I,
p. 358, note 49.

87.   For an early use of the term hsien-i 嫌疑
("doubtful matters"), see, for example, Hsün-tzu 15:21,
p. 267, translated by Dubs, p. 271. See also Shih chi
130, p. 22, translated in Watson, Ssu-ma Ch'ien, p. 51.
Dai Kan Wa Jiten 6618.8 points out that hsien-i is also
a legal term referring to the investigation of the facts
of a crime.

88.   The method of addressing the Emperor is studied
by Dubs in HFHD, I, pp. 99-100, note 2. Similar terms,
such as, "stupid opinion...deserving ten thousand
deaths," can be found in a memorial by Ku Yung (Han shu
85, p. 5005; see fragment 201, note 71), who was famous
for his sharp remonstrances with Emperor Ch'eng.

89.   A summary of this last part of Huan T'an's biography is given in L. Wieger, Rudiments: Textes historiques, Vol. 2 (1904), pp. 800-01.

90.   For similar statements by Huan T'an, see fragment 164C.

91.   Lun-yü V:12, translated by Legge, pp. 177-78:
"Tsze-kung said, 'The Master's personal display of his
principles and ordinary descriptions of them may be
heard. His discourses about man's nature, and the way
of Heaven, cannot be heard.'"

92.   I translate shu 數 as "soothsayers," in accordance with Duyvendak's translation "statistical methods,"
referring to numerical speculations in The Book of the
Lord Shang, pp. 96 and 205. See also E. M. Gale, Discourses on Salt and Iron, p. 18, note 4. A detailed
explanation of the term shu, based on a study by Ch'en
P'an, is given by Hulsewé in Remnants, I, p. 360, note
71. Ch'en Chung-fan, in the commentary to this text
found in his Han-Wei Liu-ch'ao san-wen hsüan (Shanghai:
1956), p. 154, explains the term shu-shu as "the officials of the Ming t'ang, Hsi and Ho, of astrology and
divinity."

93.   T'u 圖 ("diagrams") and shu 書 ("documents")
are tools of prognostication (ch'an 讖), as has been
shown by Ch'en P'an (see note 92 above), who published
several studies on them. See also note 113 below and,
for a more detailed bibliography, The Life, II, p. 526,
note 22. The two terms t'u and shu appear to be short
forms of Ho-t'u ("the Chart of the Yellow River") and
Lo-shu ("the Writing of the River Lo"). A thorough
condemnation of prognostications, falsely attributed to
Confucius, can be found in Huan T'an's fragment 68.
About half a millenium later, the famous literary critic
Liu Hsieh also strongly denounced prognostications, to
which he devoted a chapter of his Wen-hsin tiao-lung
(1.4, "Cheng wei;" Shih, The Literary Mind, pp. 21-25).
Liu Hsieh believes that the apocrypha appeared during
the reigns of Emperor Ai and P'ing. He mentions Emperor

Kuang-wu's great infatuation with them, as well as Huan T'an's opposition (Shih, p. 24). For Ch'en P'an, see also fragment 68, note 3.

94. The term ch'i-huo 欺 惑 ("deception and mis-information" occurs earlier in Hsün-tzu 3.6, p. 57; Dubs, p. 78.

95. The heroism displayed in this passage has been pointed out by, among others, Hang Shih-chün (1696-1773 A.D.), in his Chu-shih jang-i, p. 2. For Liu Hsieh's comment, see note 93 above. See also note 114 below. In his commentary to Hou Han shu (1B, p. 46), Li Hsien says that, according to the Shuo-wen, the meaning of the character kua 註 ("to deceive, mislead") is iden-tical with that of wu 誤 ("to impede, mistake").

96. Again, similar terms on "suppressing and banish-ing arrogant and envious favorites" may be found in Han shu 85, p. 5010 (see note 88 above).

97. According to Dai Kan Wa Jiten 25593.160, the term ch'iung-che 窮 折 ("deeply despises") occurs only in Huan T'an's biography.

98. In the chiao-pu 校 補 commentary (p. 1035), Wang Hsien-ch'ien calls attention to the fact that, ac-cording to Ch'ien Ta-chao, most editions have the char-acter pu 卜 ("to foretell"), but that the edition of Mao Chin has shih 十 ("ten"), while the Fu-chien edi-tion has hsiao 小 ("small"). The translation follow-ing these variations, would be: "...like divining from ten (or, "from a small group of") even and odd numbers."

99. Li Hsien's commentary explains the text as "to hit the mark by chance" (ou-chung 偶 中), but Hui Tung refutes his explanation. A version of this passage in modern Chinese is given in Ku Chieh-kang, Han-tai hsüeh-shu shih-lüeh (Shanghai: 1948), p. 204.

100. The last three characters, ch'ui ming t'ing 垂 明 聽 ("to condescend to judge with clear sight") are also used in Han shu 23, p. 1986, and trans-lated by Hulsewé in Remnants, I, p. 339.

101. The expression lei-t'ung 蠱 同 ("hearsay") originates in Li chi I:I:III:3:11. Legge (I, p. 75) translates, "Let him not appropriate [to himself] the words [of others], nor [repeat them] as [the echo does the] thunder." See fragment 28, note 31.

102.   I prefer the character lüeh 略 ("to put into order"), given by the Ssu-pu pei-yao (or Palace) edition, for Wang Hsien-ch'ien's chao 昭 ("to display").

103.   T'ung-jen 通人 ("learned men"). Wang Ch'ung, displaying his typical ironical attitude towards the literati, defines t'ung-jen, as well as other categories of scholars: "Whoever is able to explain one Classic is a scholar (ju-sheng 儒生). Those well-versed in ancient and modern literature are learned (t'ung-jen); those who collect books and records and present memorials to the throne are men of letters (wen-jen 文人); and those never in need of ingenious thoughts to compose themselves, joining paragraphs and chapters, are eminent scholars (hung-ju 鴻儒)." (Lun-heng 13:39, p. 607; Forke, II, p. 296.) Huan T'an may not have shared Wang Ch'ung's taste for ironical distinctions and probably was referring to intelligent men in general.

104.   Huan T'an may be alluding to a similar sentence in the biography of Han Fei-tzu, in Shih chi 63, p. 15: "When there is urgent need, soldiers with armor and helmets are used." In fact, Chang Shou-chieh's commentary to this Shih chi text and Li Hsien's commentary to the Hou Han shu are identical.

105.   Emperor Kuang-wu is praised in similar terms in a memorial of 39 A.D.: "The virtue of Your Majesty unites Heaven and earth. You have restored the unity of our ancestors" (Hou Han shu 1B, p. 62). Huan T'an's text has tsu 祖 for "ancestor," while the Hou Han shu has tsung 宗 .

106.   The term lu 虜 ("captured as enemies") is discussed in great detail in Wilbur, Slavery in China, pp. 99-100, note 2.

107.   For the explanation of the term hu-i 狐疑 (literally, "suspicious as a fox"), see HFHD, I, p. 238, note 4, or Chavannes, MH, II, p. 458, note 2.

108.   The term tang-pei 黨輩 ("cliques and groups") is also used in the fifth chapter of Lu Chia's Hsin-yü (see fragment 209, note 53).

109.   This alludes to Tao te ching 36.

110.   "To lighten the ranks" is the meaning of ch'ing-ch'üeh 輕爵 according to Li chi 30 (Legge, II, pp.

356-57). We should also take note of a very similar
sentence in Hsün-tzu (8:12, p. 159), which reads kuei-
ch'üeh ch'ung-shang 貴爵重賞 ("to raise honor and
increase rewards").

111. In my article, "Once More the Dates of Huan
T'an" (pp. 654-55), I have demonstrated that this council was held in 28 A.D. at the Cloud-Terrace (Yün-t'ai)
and that the main subject of discussion was the recognition of the Tso chuan and Fei Chih's Book of Changes.
The imprecise information given by this Hou Han shu
text has caused much misunderstanding among later scholars, as shown in my article, "The Dates of Huan T'an."

112. The chiao-pu commentary (p. 1035) notes that
the Fu-chien edition, as well as several other texts,
adds the character i 以 : wu yü i ch'an chüeh chih 吾
欲 以 讖 決之 , an addition which has no significant
effect on the meaning of the line.

113. For the term ch'an 讖 I have adopted the
translation "prognostication," suggested by D. Bodde
in his translation of Fung Yu-lan, A History, II, p.
89ff.

114. Tung-kuan Han chi (16, p. 69b) puts more emphasis on Huan T'an's refusal: "Never in my life have
I studied prognostications." Of course, Huan T'an's
answer was only a polite refusal to give his opinion.
Certainly he was familiar with prognostications, as was
everyone of that time. Moreover, we have evidence of
his knowledge from the Hsin-lun and other sources (see
for example, note 93 above). Huan T'an's reply to
Kuang-wu became a symbol of heroism and has been frequently quoted as such. For instance, the well-known
T'ang writer, Han Yü, mentions it in his Lien-chü, Han
Ch'ang-li ch'üan chi 104a. Han Yü also had a good opinion of Wang Ch'ung whom he ranked, together with Wang
Fu and Chung-ch'ang T'ung, as one of the three worthy
men of the Latter Han. See Hou Han san-hsien tsan san-
shou, in his Han Ch'ang-li wen-chi (chia-chu), 1. p. 33;
ed. Chung-kuo hsüeh-shu ming-chu, Wen-hsüeh ming-chu 3,
1, Taipei, 1960. Chang Ping-lin and Liang Ch'i-ch'ao
even considered Huan T'an's Hou Han shu biography important enough to include in their collection of important literary texts, Chung-kuo hsüeh-shu lun-chu chi-
yao (1930), pp. 137-40. See also note 95 above.

115. The word "once more" probably refers to Huan
T'an's third and last memorial.

116.   At this point Wang Hsien-ch'ien adds his own
opinion: "The prognostications did in fact contradict
the classical books. But Kuang-wu had gained the throne
by means of prognostications, as everyone in the Empire
knew. Even if this [argument by Huan T'an] could not
compare with the other affair [i.e., Kuang-wu's gaining
the throne], it would, nevertheless, have been advis-
able to conceal [his opinion] somewhat." Kuang-wu became furious because he regarded Huan T'an's opposition
to the prognostications as tantamount to disloyalty to
his restored dynasty.

117.   The Emperor is not referring to the "law" in a
judicial sense but to the "law" ruling the upper strata
of Han society. Hui Tung quotes a similar passage from
Hsiao ching XI: "...when the authority of the Sage is
disallowed, that is the disowning of (all) law." (Legge,
The Hsiao King, p. 481). Of course, the concepts of law
and morality were closely related, as may be seen from
the term for one of the most heinous crimes, pu-tao 不道
("impious"). Later, the term fei-sheng wu-fa 非聖無法
("to oppose the teachings of the sages and disown the
law") became very common; see, for example, J. R. Levenson, Liang Ch'i-ch'ao and the Mind of Modern China
(1959), p. 37, note 7.

118.   Tung-kuan Han chi (p. 69b) says, "Because of
this, Huan T'an lost the Emperor's confidence. He was
never called back and never restored [to his previous
place]."

119.   Liu-an is now in west Anhwei province. On the
changes in the administrative status of Liu-an, see
Pokora, "The Dates of Huan T'an," pp. 672-74, as well
as the articles by Chiang Liang-fu, pp. 47-49, and
Moriya Mitsuo, pp. 677-83, quoted, respectively, in
Ar. Or., No. 33 (1965), p. 79, and No. 34 (1966), p.
494. See also the bibliography below (II:12:13). The
post of Assistant Administrator was not a low position,
although it was a serious demotion.

120.   The term hu-hu 忽忽 (here translated as "full
of sorrow") has many meanings. For example, B. Watson,
in his translation of Ssu-ma Ch'ien's letter to Jen An
(Han shu 62, p. 4271), translates it literally as "be-
fuddled" (Ssu-ma Ch'ien, p. 66).

121.   A. Forke (<u>Geschichte der mittelälterlichen
chinesischen Philosophie</u>, p. 102) says that Huan T'an
died at the age of 69.   Apparently, Forke overlooked
the term <u>yü</u> 餘 ("more") and subtracted one year from
the seventy, according to the Chinese system of calcu-
lating age.   Hsieh Ch'eng, <u>Hou Han shu</u> 4a (Yao Chih-yin,
ed., <u>Hou Han shu pu-i</u>) and <u>Pei-t'ang shu-ch'ao</u> 102.3b
give Huan T'an's age as seventy years.

122.   The last two paragraphs are also found in the
<u>Tung-kuan Han chi</u> 16, p. 69b, in a shorter form, but,
with the exception of the first sentence, in essentially
the same wording.

123.   A letter sent by Yang Hsiung to Huan T'an is
quoted in note 12 to fragment 80C.   The commentary to
<u>Wen hsüan</u> 46.35b quotes another fragment from this or
another letter: "Looking towards the wind (i.e., the
virtuous influence of the king or sage), the shadows
(of the people) follow, and instruction is accomplished
of itself (i.e., without the king or sage uttering in-
structions)."

124.   <u>Tao</u> 道 ("a way" or "the Way").

125.   Instead of the <u>chu</u> 筯 ("chopsticks") of the
text I read <u>chin</u> 筋 ("sinews").

126.   I could find no source for this fragment.
<u>TPYL</u> 828.1a-3a quotes many texts on slaughtering, but
none of them casts any light on the present text.

ADDENDA

p. 33, to the note 1: It is probable that Huan T'an
followed Chia I who in his memorial Ch'en cheng
shih ("Statement on Government Affairs") used
this term; cf. Han shu 48, p. 3716.

p. 38, commentary to fragment 45: Sung Chung-weng is
evidently identical with Sung Hung (died ca.
35 A.D.) whose courtesy name was Chung-tzu,
"the second son;" Chung-weng, "the second venerable old man" might have been a polite form
used by Huan T'an. (For Wang Weng = Wang Mang
see fragment 11, note 7).

p. 70, add to the note 16: Both instruments are mentioned in the chapter on music in the Li chi
XVII, 14 as exhortating to practice the virtue.
Cf. also Hsün-tzu 14, 20, 11, p. 255 (Köster,
p. 267) and Tjan Tjoe Som, Po Hu T'ung, p. 405,
note 122 (different character for the instruments).

p. 102, add to the note 38: The term "wonderful
treatises" (ch'i-lun 奇 論) may also be
found in the Lun-heng 11, 56, p. 811; it is
translated by A. Forke (I, p. 477) as "modern
writings."

p. 212, Commentary to fragment 189: Previous super-
ficial translation by Yang Hsien-i and Gladys
Yang in Lu Hsün, A Brief History of Chinese
Fiction, Peking, 1959, p. 1.

p. 360, add before the item Kung-sun Lung: Kung-sun
Fu-jao or Kung-sun Pu-niu 公 山 弗 擾 ,
弗 扭 , politician (6th-5th cent. B.C.), 216
(comm.).

Bibliographies

I. Editions of Hsin-lun

There are only two complete, published recon-
structions of the Hsin-lun. A third reconstruction has
been compiled but has never been published.

The earliest editor was Sun P'ing-i (Sun Feng-
i?), whose style name was either Feng-pu 鳳 埔 (according to Ssu-pu pei-yao shu-mu ts'ung-shu, tzu-pu
子 部 33b and DKJ 6987.428) or Feng-ch'ing 鳳 卿 (according to Huang I-chou 6a and Takeuchi, p. 371; cf.
below 11A 3 and 4). We have no information on the dates
of his life other than the fact that he edited the large
collection, Wen-ching-t'ang ts'ung-shu, which was published between 1797 and 1802 A.D. (Hummel, ECCP II, p.
737). In the colophon to his Huan-tzu Hsin-lun (see I 1
below), Sun says he is from Shen-yang 瀋 陽 . The SPPY
shu-mu ts'ung-shu, instead gives Ch'eng-te 承 德 , while
Hsiao I-shan (Ch'ing tai t'ung-shih, Vol. 5, p. 503)
places him in Cho-chou in Chihli province. All of these
places are in Northern China (or Manchuria). Sun compiled twenty texts in his Wen-ching t'ang ts'ung-shu,
including the Huan-tzu Hsin-lun and Ming-t'ang k'ao.

The most well-known compiler of the Hsin-lun
is Yen K'o-chün (1762-1843 A.D.), to whom Tu Lien-che
devoted (in Hummel, ECCP II, pp. 910-12) three large
pages. Frustrated by being refused admission to the
staffs of the official compilation projects, Yen compiled one large work including quotations from 3,495
authors. This undertaking took twenty-seven years
(1808-1836 A.D.). According to Tu Lien-che, the first
part of this collection, which is called Ch'üan shang-
ku San-tai Ch'in Han San-kuo Liu-ch'ao wen, contained
prosaic texts from Han through Sui and was to be printed
in 1815. Unfortunately, the project did not materialize
(see, however, the information below I 2) and it was
only during 1887-93 that Yen's work was finally printed.
This does not, of course, mean that the unpublished
collection was unknown before this time.

Huang I-chou 黃 以 周 (1828-1899 A.D.), a less
well-known scholar, also took an interest in Huan T'an.
We know from his own account (see below IIA 3) that at
first he only had access to the edition by Sun P'ing-i.

Only later did he gain access to Yen K'o-chün's edition, although he was acquainted with the short description of the reconstructed Hsin-lun found in Yen's T'ien-ch'iao man-kao (see below IIA 2). Huang I-chou relied on Sun's edition, adding new fragments from Ch'ün-shu chih-yao and re-ordering it according to the substantive relationships between fragments. Sun P'ing-i had merely reproduced the fragments as found in different books. Consequently, different versions of the same fragment are given in several places of his reconstruction without any cross-reference. Unlike Sun, both Huang and Yen tried to reconstruct the lost original system of the Hsin-lun. Huang's reconstruction was not published during his lifetime, nor was it later published by Hsü Tseng 許增 (1842-1903 A.D.) to whom Huang had bequeathed his manuscript. It first appeared in 1912 in the published edition by Takeuchi (see below IIA 4).

Other editions include:

1. Sun P'ing-i 孫馮翼 , Huan-tzu Hsin-lun 桓子新論. In the collection Wen-ching-t'ang ts'ung-shu 問經堂叢書 , Chia-ch'ing 7 (1802 A.D.). Peking National Library No. 635 324 13. Reprinted in the Ssu-pu pei-yao collection. The University Library in Cambridge, No. FB 55.16.2, has a slightly different edition with a preface by Chang Chiung 張炯 , published in Chin-ling (Nanking), Chia-ch'ing 6 (1801 A.D.). The collection Lung-hsi ching-she ts'ung-shu 龍谿精舍 , published by a Mr. Cheng 鄭氏 from Ch'ao-yang 潮陽 , includes Huan-tzu Hsin-lun. Peking University Library 9100. 0298 65-70; University Library in Cambridge FB 59. 48. 11.
   For Sun P'ing-i, see also IIA 1.

2. Yen K'o-chün 嚴可均 , Huan-tzu Hsin-lun. In Ch'üan Hou Han wen, Chapter 12.7a-10a and Chapters 13-15 of the collection Ch'üan shang-ku San-tai ch'in Han San-kuo Liu-ch'ao wen 全上古三代秦

漢三國六朝文, published in <u>Chia-ch'ing</u> 25 (1815
A.D.). The entire collection has been republished
many times. Yen's reconstruction is much larger
than Sun's because it includes the important fragment 84A from <u>Hung-ming chi</u> (see also I 6 and IIA 8
and 10 below) and fifteen fragments from Wei
Cheng's <u>Ch'ün-shu chih-yao</u> (see below IIIA 11),
which were rediscovered in Japan; detailed information is given in P. Pelliot, "Notes de Bibliographie Chinoise I., Le <u>Kou Yi Ts'ong Chou</u>," BEFEO,
No. 2 (1902), pp. 315-40. For Yen K'o-ch'ün, see
also IIA 2.

The collection <u>Chih-hai</u> 指海 , published in 1843
by Ch'ien Hsi-tso (ca. 1801-1844 A.D.), the famous
owner of the <u>Shou-shan ko</u> library, also includes
in part 13, <u>Huan-tzu Hsin-lun</u>. It includes quotations from the <u>Ch'ün-shu chih-yao</u>, but it is difficult to say what its relation to the edition by Yen
K'o-chün was. In any case, the edition in <u>Chih-hai</u>
is better than Sun's but inferior to Yen's. University Library in Cambridge FB 55. 88. 13.

Other, less complete editions:

3. Ching-shan tzu 荊 山 子 , <u>Ch'in feng</u> 琴 諷 ,
    <u>Hsin-lun</u>, in the collection <u>Chu-tzu hui-han</u>
    諸 子 彙 函   21.1a-2b. Includes only
    fragment 171A; title refers to remonstration by
    means of the zither. The commentary explains that
    Huan T'an was called "Ching-shan-tzu" because he
    stood aloof from the people and frequently hid under
    Ching Mountain.

4. The Ming print of the <u>Shuo-fu</u> 説郛 , chapter
   59 entitled "Tan" 弓 , 1a-3b, includes twelve
   quotations from <u>Hsin-lun</u>; another edition, <u>Ch'ung-
   chiao Shuo fu</u> 重校 , includes ten other quotations. A recent reprint (Taipei, 1963) excludes
   the chapter containing these quotations. All the
   fragments quoted in <u>Shuo-fu</u>, with the exception of
   fragment 202, may be found in other editions. See
   the commentary to fragment 202; see also fragment
   188, for another, suspect fragment from the <u>Shuo-fu</u>.

5. The collection <u>Ku-chin shuo-pu ts'ung-shu</u> 古今説
   部叢書 I:5:1a-b, published in 1910 A.D. by Wang
   Wen-ju 王文濡 , includes the same twelve fragments as the Ming edition of <u>Shuo-fu</u> referred to
   above. See also fragment 202.

6. <u>Hsin-lun</u>, <u>Hsing-shen</u> 新論, 形神 . Reprint
   of fragment 84A from <u>Hung ming chi</u> (see IIIA 21)
   5.4b-5b (pp. 208-210), with annotation (pp. 210-11)
   and translation into modern Chinese (pp. 211-14),
   in <u>Chung-kuo che-hsüeh-shih tzu-liao hsüan-chi:
   Liang-Han chih pu</u> 中國哲學史資料選輯兩漢之部
   (Peking, 1960).

7. Huan T'an, selection of fragments with commentary
   in <u>Chung-kuo che-hsüeh-shih chiao-hsüeh tzu-liao
   hui-pien; Liang-Han pu-fen</u> 中國哲學史教學資料彙
   編,兩漢部份, Vol. 2 (Peking, 1964) (third edition),
   pp. 339-54. In the translation <u>Liang-Han pu-fen</u>.

II. Studies on Huan T'an and the <u>Hsin-lun</u>.

A. In Chinese and Japanese, chronologically:

1. Sun P'ing-i, <u>Huan-tzu Hsin-lun hsü</u> 序 , <u>K'ao-cheng</u> 考 證 , p.1a-3a and 3a-b in the <u>Ssu-pu pei-yao</u> edition of his <u>Huan-tzu Hsin-lun</u>. See I 1.

2. Yen K'o-chün, <u>Huan-tzu Hsin-lun hsü</u> 敍 in <u>T'ieh-ch'iao man kao</u> 鐵橋漫稿 , 5.24a-25a. Reprint (Taipei, 1964), in the collection <u>Chung-kuo wen-hsüeh ming-chu ti-liu-chi</u> 中國文學名著第六集 . See I 2.

3. Huang I-chou, <u>Huan-tzu Hsin-lun hsü</u> 敍 in <u>Ching-chi Tsa-chu</u> 儆季襍著之四, 4, Tzu hsü 子序 5b-6a. See introduction to I above.

4. Takeuchi Yoshio 武内義雄 , "Kantan Shinron ni tsuite" 桓譚新論二就行 , <u>Shinagaku</u> 支那學 , No. 2 (4) (1921), pp. 244-58. Translation into Chinese by Chiang Hsia-an 江俠菴 , "Huan T'an Hsin-lun k'ao" 考 , Appendix (<u>Fu-lu</u> 附錄) to <u>Hsien Ch'in ching-chi k'ao</u> 先秦經籍考 , Vol. 2 (Shanghai, Commercial Press, 1933), pp. 365-76.

5. Jung Chao-tsu 容肇祖 , "Huan T'an ti ssu-hsiang" 桓譚的思想 , in "Tung Han chi-ke cheng-chih-chia ti ssu-hsiang" 東漢幾個政治家的思想 (The Thought of Some Politicians of Eastern Han), <u>Kuo-li ti-i Chung-shan ta-hsüeh yü-yen li-shih-hsüeh yen-chiu-so chou-k'an</u> 國立中山大學語言歷史學研究所周刊, No. 2 (January 8, 1927), pp. 33-41.

6. Narita Hirao 成田衡夫 , "Kantan no tetsugaku"

桓譚の哲學 , <u>Kangakkai zasshi</u> 漢學會雜誌,
No. 5 (3) (1937), pp. 1-12.

7. Hsiao Kung-ch'üan 蕭公權 , "Huan T'an chih
    Chung-ch'ang T'ung" 桓譚至仲長統 , in <u>Chung-</u>
    <u>kuo cheng-chih ssu-hsiang</u> 中國政治思想 ,
    Part 2 (Taipei, 1961), (original edition, Shanghai,
    1947), pp. 308-09.

8. Kuan Feng 关鋒 , "Hsin-lun Hsing-shen tso-che
    ts'un-i: Fu-chi" 新論形神作者存疑 , in
    <u>Wang Ch'ung che-hsüeh ssu-hsiang yen-chiu</u> 王充哲學
    思想研究 (Shanghai, 1957), pp. 139-42, 142-44.
    See I 6 and IIA 10.

9. Hou Wai-lu 侯外廬 , Chao Chi-pin 趙紀彬 , Tu
    Kuo-hsiang 杜國庠 , and Ch'iu Han-sheng 邱漢生 ,
    "Wang Ch'ung ti shih-tai i-chi 'cheng-tsung' yü
    'i-tuan,' wei-hsin-chu-i yü wei-wu-chu-i tou-cheng
    ti yen-chin" 王充的時代以反"正宗"與"異端,"唯心主義與,
    唯物主義斗爭的演進 in <u>Chung-kuo ssu-hsiang t'ung-</u>
    <u>shih</u> 中國思想通史 ,Vol. 2 (Peking, 1957), pp. 257-61.

10. Chung Chao-p'eng 鍾肇鵬 , "Hsin-lun Hsing-
    shen ti tso-che ying tuan-kuei Huan T'an" 新論形神
    的作者应断归桓譚 , <u>Renwen Zazhi</u> (Jen-wen tsa-chih)
    人文雜誌 , No. 2 (1959), pp. 34-36. See <u>RBS</u>
    5, No. 746.

11. ____ , "Huan T'an ho Wang Ch'ung" 桓譚和王充 ,
    <u>Chiang-hai hsüeh-k'an</u> 江海學刊 , No. 5 (1963),
    pp. 40-43.

12. Feng Yu-lan 馮有瀾 , "Huan T'an tui hsing,
    shen kuan-hsi ti wei-wu-chu-i-ti chien-chieh chi-
    ch'i fan tui shen-mi-chu-i-ti tou-cheng" 桓譚对形神
    关系的唯物主义的見解及其反对神秘主义的斗争
    in <u>Chung-kuo che-hsüeh-shih hsin-pien</u>

中國哲學史新編 , Vol. 2 (Peking, 1964), pp. 242-44.

13. Chiang Liang-fu 姜亮夫 and T'ao Ch'iu-ying 陶秋英 , "Huan T'an i-nien ti t'ao-lun" 桓譚疑年的討論 , Hangchow ta-hsüeh hsüeh-pao 杭州大學學報 , No. 1 (1963), pp. 45-56. Partial translation of and reply to 3 below; for rejoinder, see 5 below.

14. Moriya Mitsuo 守屋美都雄 , "Kantan no sei sotsu nendai" 桓譚の生卒年代 , Suzuki Shun kyōju kan-reki kinen Tōyōshi ronsō 鈴木俊教授還歷記念東洋史論叢 (Tokyo, 1964), pp. 669-84. Reprinted in the posthumous edition of a partial edition of Moriya's studies: Chūgoku kodai no kazoku to kokka 中國古代の家族と國家 , Tōyōshi kenkyū sōkan 東洋史研究叢刊 , No. 19 (Kyoto, 1966), pp. 585-99. Reply to 3 below and 13 above; for rejoinder, see 6 below.

15. _____ , "Ri Kai no Hō-kei ni kansuru ichi mondai" 李悝の法經に關する一問題 , Chūgoku kodai-shi kenkyū 中國古代史研究 , Vol. 2 (1965), pp. 311-50. Reprinted in Chūgoku kodai no kazoku to kokka (see 14 above), pp. 548-84. Reply to 7 below; for rejoinder, see 6 below.

15a. Kanō Naoki 狩野直喜 , Kan Tan no Shinron 桓譚の新論 , Ryo-Kan gakujutsu kō 兩漢學術考 (Tokyo, 1954), pp. 171-7. Originally lectures held in 1924-1925.

B. In Western Languages:

1. Alfred Forke, "Huan T'an," in Geschichte der mittelälterlichen chinesischen Philosophie (Hamburg, 1934), pp. 100-10.

2. Timoteus Pokora, "La vie du philosophe materialiste Houan T'an," _Mélanges de sinologie offerts a Monsieur Paul Démieville I, Bibliotheque de l'Institut des Hautes Études Chinoises_, Vol. XX (Paris, 1966), pp. 191-208.

3. _____, "The Dates of Huan T'an," _Archiv Orientální_, No. 27 (1959), pp. 670-77. See 13 and 14 above.

4. _____, "Once more the Dates of Huan T'an," _ArOr_, No. 29 (1961), pp. 652-57.

5. _____, "Last Note on the Dates of Huan T'an: Answer to Professor Chiang Liang-fu and T'ao Ch'iu-ying," _ArOr_, No. 33 (1965), pp. 79-82. See 13 above.

6. _____, "Two Answers to Professor Moriya Mitsuo," _ArOr_, No. 34 (1966), pp. 494-504. See 14 and 15 above, 7 below.

7. _____, "The Canon of Laws by Li K'uei: A Double Falsification?" _ArOr_, No. 27 (1959), pp. 96-121. See 15 above.

8. _____, "Huan T'an's 'Fu on Looking for the Immortals' (Wang-hsien fu)," _ArOr_, No. 28 (1960), pp. 353-67. See fragment 205.

9. _____, "The Necessity of a More Thorough Study of Philosopher Wang Ch'ung and of His Predecessors," _ArOr_, No. 30 (1962), pp. 231-57.

10. _____, "The Life of Huan T'an," _ArOr_, No. 31 (1963), pp. 1-79, 521-76. Includes (pp. 16-38) a full translation of Huan T'an's biography from _Hou Han shu_ 28A and from Yüan Hung's _Hou Han chi_.

III. Sources

  A. Sources of the Fragments

1. Ch'ang-tuan ching 長短經 . By Chao Jui 趙蕤 (8th cent. A.D.). Tu-hua-chai ts'ung-shu 讀畫齋 叢書 . 21.

2. <u>Cheng-i commentary</u>, see <u>Shih-chi</u>.

3. <u>Chi-chieh commentary</u>, see <u>Shih-chi</u>.

4. <u>Ch'i-kuo k'ao</u> 七國考 . By Tung Yüeh 董説 (1620-1686 A.D.). (Peking, 1956). 40, 176-87.

5. <u>Chin-shu</u> 晉書 . <u>Po-na</u>. 115A.

6. <u>Ching-tien shih-wen</u> 經典釋文 . By Lu Te-ming 陸德明 (556-627 A.D.). In <u>Pao-ching-t'ang ts'ung-shu</u> 拘經堂叢書 . 90E, 94B.

7. <u>Ch'u-hsüeh chi</u> 初學記 . By Hsü Chien 徐堅 (659-729 A.D.). In <u>Chiou-chou shu-wu</u> 九州書屋 (reprint: Peking, 1962). 5, 36, 75, 79C, 83B, 93A, 112A-B, 113A, 117, 151B, 159A2, 169C, 169D1.

8. <u>Ch'un-ch'iu</u> 春秋 . Translation: J. Legge, "The <u>Ch'un Ts'ew</u> with the <u>Tso Chuen</u>," <u>The Chinese Classics</u>, Vol. V, Hong Kong, 1872.

9. _____. Commentary by K'ung Ying-ta 孔穎達 (574-648 A.D.). See 203.

10. _____. Commentary by Tu Yü 杜預 (222-284 A.D.). See 204.

11. <u>Ch'ün-shu chih-yao</u> 羣書治要 . By Wei Cheng 魏徵 (581-643 A.D.). In <u>SPTK</u>. 11A, 13, 28, 32, 37, 38A, 39, 41, 48A, 52, 53, 58, 65.

12. <u>Fa yen</u> 法言 . By Yang Hsiung 揚雄 . In <u>Chu-tzu chi-ch'eng</u>.

13. <u>Fa-yüan chu-lin</u> 法苑珠林 . By Tao-shih 道士 (fl. 650-664 A.D.), In <u>SPTK</u>. 134A, 152D.

14. <u>Han shu</u> 漢書 . By Pan Ku 班固 (32-92 A.D.). In Wang Hsien-ch'ien 王先謙 , <u>Han shu pu-chu</u> 漢書補注 , <u>WYWK</u>. For translation, see <u>HFHD</u>. 164A, 208.

15. _____. Commentary by Li Ch'i 李奇 (fl. 200 A.D.). 12.

16. _____. Commentary by Yen Shih-ku 顏師古 (579-645 A.D.). 82D, 88, 90B, 103, 107, 108B, 109.

17. Heng-huang Hsin-lun 珩璜新論 . By K'ung
    P'ing-chung 孔平仲 (ca. 1040-1105 A.D.). In
    SPTK. 198.

18. Hou Han shu 後漢書 . By Fan Yeh 范曄
    (398-446 A.D.). In Wang Hsien-ch'ien 王先謙 ,
    Hou Han shu chi-chieh 後漢書集解 , WYWK, 206,
    207, 209, 210.

19. ____ . Commentary by Liu Chao 劉昭 (fl. 502-
    519 A.D.). 15, 54, 93D, 126A, 131A.

20. ____ . Commentary by Li Hsien 李賢 (651-684
    A.D.). 62, 126B, 161, 163A, 170.

21. Hung-ming chi 弘明集 . By Seng-yu 僧祐
    (445-518 A.D.). In SPTK. 84A.

22. I lin 意林 . By Ma Tsung 馬總 (8th-9th
    cent. A.D.). In SPPY. 3B, 6B, 7, 9 (Jen-tzu),
    12, 20, 26, 29, 30, 35B, 38B, 42A, 45, 60A, 67,
    68, 70, 71, 79A, 80A, 81, 89, 94C, 97, 98A, 105,
    106B, 110, 136A, 140A, 143, 144, 146A, 147, 169A1.

23. I-wen lei-chü 藝文類書 . By Ou-yang Hsün 歐
    陽詢 (557-641 A.D.). Ed. 1879 (reprint: Peking,
    1959). 24A, 25A, 42B, 44, 48B, 79C, 80C, 93C,
    102, 111B, 132, 140B, 151A, 159D, 205.

24. Ku-chin shuo-pu ts'ung-shu 古今説部叢書 . See
    Bibliography I 5. 202.

25. Ku-wen yüan 古文苑 (T'ang). Commentary by Chang
    Ch'iao 章樵 (fl. 1228-1233 A.D.). In
    SPTK. 96.

26. K'un-hsüeh chi-wen 困學紀聞 . By Wang
    Ying-lin 王應麟 (1223-1296 A.D.). In SPTK.
    55, 90D, 163B, 167B.

27. K'ung Ying-ta, see Ch'un-ch'iu.

28. <u>Li chi</u> 禮記 . Translation: J. Legge, <u>The Li Ki: The Sacred Books of China</u> XXVII-XXVIII; <u>The Texts of Confucianism</u> I-II, Oxford, 1885. See also IIIB 21.

29. _____. Subcommentary, see 25B.

Li Hsien, see <u>Hou Han Shu</u>.

30. <u>Liang-shu</u> 梁書 . Po-na. 118.

31. Liu Chao, see <u>Hou Han shu</u>.

32. Liu Chün 劉峻 (462-521 A.D.), see 190.

33. <u>Lun-heng</u> 論衡 . By Wang Ch'ung 王充 (27-ca. 97 A.D.). In Huang Hui 黃暉 , <u>Lun-heng chiao-shih</u> 論衡校釋 (reprint: Taipei, 1964). Translation: A. Forke, Lun-heng I-II, Leipzig, 1907, 1911 (reprint: New York, 1962). 31, 79C, 130, 154D.

34. <u>Ming-t'ang-k'ao</u> 明堂考 . Probably by Sun P'ing-i 孫馮翼 (18th-19th cent. A.D.). In <u>SPTK</u>. 175B and E.

35. <u>Ming-t'ang ta-tao lu</u> 明堂大道錄 . By Hui Tung 惠棟 (1697-1758 A.D.). In <u>TSCC</u>. 175A, C and D.

36. <u>Pao-p'u tzu</u> 抱朴子 . By Ko Hung 葛洪 (284-363 A.D.). In <u>Chu-tzu chi-ch'eng</u>. Translation: J. R. Ware, <u>Alchemy, Medicine, and Religion in the China of A.D. 320</u>, Cambridge, Mass., 1966. 151C, 154, 157A.

37. <u>Pei-t'ang shu-ch'ao</u> 北堂書鈔 . By Yü Shih-nan 虞世南 (558-638 A.D.). Edition by K'ung Kuang-t'ao 孔廣陶 , 1888 (reprint: Taipei, 1962). 14, 17, 22, 33, 34, 44, 63, 79C, 80B and E, 90, 95, 98B, 101, 114B, 120, 126B, 127, 132, 136B, 139, 142, 150B, 151A, 162, 168, 169G1, 169I2, 172B, 205.

38. P'ei-wen yün-fu 佩文韻府 . Compiled in
    1711. In WYWK. 52, 199.

39. Po K'ung liu-t'ieh 白孔六帖 . By Po Chü-i
    白居易 (772-846 A.D.) and K'ung Chuan 孔傳
    (Sung). Undated edition in the Library of Peking
    University. 79C, 80E, 135B, 159C.

40. Po-wu chih 博物志 . By Chang Hua 張華
    (232-300 A.D.). In Han Wei ts'ung-shu 漢魏叢書.
    145, 151C, 152E.

41. San-fu huang-t'u 三輔黃圖 , 6th century.
    In SPPY. 151A.

42. San-kuo chih 三國志 . Commentary by P'ei
    Sung-chih 裴松之 (372-451 A.D.). In
    SPPY. 171A.

43. Shen-hsien chuan 神仙傳 . By Ko Hung 葛洪.
    In Han Wei ts'ung-shu. 151C.

44. Shih-chi 史記 . By Ssu-ma Ch'ien 司馬遷 .
    In Takigawa Kametaro 瀧川龜太郎 , Shiki kaichū
    kōshō 史記會注考證 (Peking, 1954). For trans-
    lation, see MH.

45. ____. Cheng-i commentary 正義 . By Chang
    Shou-chieh 張守節 (8th cent. A.D.). 3A, 192.

46. ____. Chi-chieh commentary 集解 . By
    P'ei Yin 裴駰 (fl. 465-472 A.D.). 35A, 150D,
    159A, 160.

47. ____. So-yin commentary 索隱 . By
    Ssu-ma Chen 司馬貞 (fl. 713-742 A.D.). 59,
    137A-B.

48. Shih-chieh chi 世界記 . By Seng-yu 僧祐
    (455-518 A.D.). See 116.

49. Shih-lei fu 事類賦 . By Wu Shu 吳淑 (947-
    1002 A.D.). (Chien-kuang-ko ts'ang pan 劍光閣藏板,
    1865). 108A, 115.

50. <u>Shih-t'ung</u> 史通 . By Liu Chih-chi 劉知幾
(661-721 A.D.). In <u>WYWK</u>. 94C, 118, 164E.

51. <u>Shu-i chi</u> 述異記 . By Jen Fang 任昉 (460-
508 A.D.) or Tsu Ch'ung-chih 祖沖之 (429-500
A.D.). Probably compiled after mid-T'ang. Un-
dated edition in the Peking University Library.
61.

52. <u>Shui-ching chu</u> 水經注 . By Li Tao-yüan 酈道元
(467-527 A.D.). <u>Kuo-hsüeh chi-pen ts'ung-shu</u>
<u>chien-pien</u> (Shanghai, 1936). 111A, 151A.

53. <u>Shuo fu,</u> T'ao Tsung-i (ca. 1320-1368 A.D.), see
Bibliography I 4. 43, 44, 63, 80E, 90B, 188, 202.

54. <u>So-yin commentary.</u> See <u>Shih chi.</u>

55. <u>Sui-hua chi-li</u> 歲華紀麗 . By Han Ao 韓鄂.
(T'ang). In <u>TSCC</u>. 112A, 151C.

56. <u>Sui-shu</u> 隋書 . <u>Po-na.</u> 134B.

57. <u>T'ai-p'ing huan-yü chi</u> 太平寰宇記 . By Yüeh
Shih 樂史 (930-1007 A.D.). (Nanking, 1882).
83A.

58. <u>T'ai-p'ing yü-lan</u> 太平御覽 . By Li Fang 李昉
(925-996 A.D.), compiled in 982. In <u>SPTK</u>. 2A-B,
3A, 6A, 8, 10, 11B, 22, 24A, 40, 43, 44, 47, 49-51,
55-57, 60B, 63, 66, 70, 76-78, 79B-C, 80C and E,
82A-B, 84B, 85, 86A, 90A, 91, 93A-B, 94A, 98B, 100,
102, 104, 106A, 132-133, 135A, 136A and C, 138,
141, 146B, 149, 150C, 151A, 152A-C, 153, 155, 156A,
157B, 158A-B, 159B, 162, 164B-C, 167A, 169A2, 169C,
169D1, 169H1-2, 169I1, 172A, 174, 193.

59. "Pien tao lun" 辨道論 . By Ts'ao Chih
曹植 (192-232 A.D.). In <u>Kuang-Hung-ming chi</u> 廣
弘明集 , compiled in 664. In <u>SPPY</u>. 82C, 152F,
156B.

60. Tu Yü, see Ch'un ch'iu.

61. T'ung-tien 通典 . By Tu Yu 杜佑 (735-812 A.D.). Commentary. Shanghai, 1902, 169K.

62. Tzu-chih t'ung-chien 資治通鑑 . By Ssu-ma Kuang 司馬光 . Peking, 1956.

63. _____. Commentary by Hu San-hsing 胡三省 (1230-1302 A.D.). 163A.

64. Wang Pao 王襃 , see 201.

65. Wen-hsin tiao-lung 文心雕龍 . By Liu Hsieh 劉勰 (ca. 465-522 A.D.). In SPPY. Translation: V. Y. C. Shih, New York, 1959. 194-97.

66. Wen hsüan 文選 . By Hsiao T'ung 蕭統 (501-531 A.D.). Ed. Liu-ch'en chu, SPTK. Translation: E. von Zach, Die Chinesische Anthologie: Übersetzungen aus dem Wen Hsüan, Cambridge, 1958. 189-91.

67. _____. Commentary. 1, 4, 16, 18-19, 23, 24B, 27, 46, 55, 62, 64, 72-74, 79C, 80D-E, 87, 99, 119, 121, 123, 126B, 147, 148A-B, 150A, 164F-G, 169B, 169D2, 169F, 169G2, 169H1, 169J1-3, 169L-M, 171B, 173, 189, 193, 211, 212, 214.

68. Wu-hsing ta-i 五行大義 . By Hsiao Chi 蕭吉 (fl. 605 A.D.). Shanghai, 1926. 92.

69. Wu-li hsiao-chih 物理小識 . By Fang I-chih 方以智 (1611-1671 A.D.). In WYWK. 86B.

70. Wu Yün 吳筠 , see 200.

71. Yü Hsin 庾信 , see 204.

72. Yü-p'ien 玉篇 . By Ku Yeh-wang 顧野王 (519-581 A.D.). In Ta kuang-i Yü-p'ien 大廣益, SPTK. 169E.

73. Yüan-ho hsing tsuan 元和姓纂 . By Lin Pao 林寶 (fl. 812 A.D.), Shanghai, 1968. 165, 166.

B. Other Sources

1. Analects. Legge, J., Confucian Analects in The Chinese Classics, Vol. I (reprint: Hong Kong, 1960).

2. Book of Changes. Legge, J., I Ching: Book of Changes in Sacred Books of the East, Vol. XVI, Texts of Confucianism, Part II. Oxford, 1882 (re-edition: New York, 1964).

3. Book of Documents, see Shu-ching.

4. Chan-kuo ts'e 戰國策. Shanghai, 1926. Translation: Crump, J. I., Jr., Chan-Kuo Ts'e, Oxford, 1970; Crump, J. I., Jr., Intrigues: Studies of the Chan-kuo ts'e, Ann Arbor, 1964.

5. Chiang-yün-lou shu-mu 絳雲樓書目. In TSCC. See Wang Chung-min below V 77.

6. Chin-lou-tzu 金樓子. By Emperor Yüan of Liang 梁元帝. In Chih-pu-tsou-chai ts'ung-shu 知不足齋叢書.

7. Ch'in ts'ao 琴操. Attributed to Ts'ai Yung 蔡邕 or to K'ung Yen 孔衍. In TSCC.

8. Chuang-tzu 莊子. In Wang Hsien-ch'ien 王先謙. Chuang-tzu chi-chieh 莊子集解, Shanghai, 1956. Translation: Legge, J., The Writings of Kwang-zze in The Sacred Books of China, Vol. XXIX-XXX; The Texts of Taoism, Vol. I-II, Oxford, 1891. See also Pozdneeva, L. D., Ateisty, materialisty, dialektiki drevnego Kitaja: Jan Čžu, Leczy, Čžuanczy (Atheists, Materialists, and Dialecticians of Ancient China: Yang Chu, Lieh Tzu, Chuang Tzu), Moscow, 1967.

9. Han Yü 韓愈, "T'ung-su lien-chü" 同宿聯句, in Han Ch'ang-li ch'üan chi 韓昌黎全集. In SPPY.

284

10. ____, "Hou Han san hsien tsan [san shou]" 後漢
三賢贊三首, in Han Ch'ang-li wen-chi chiao-
chu 韓昌黎文集校注. Chung-kuo hsüeh-shu ming-
chu 中國學術名著, Wen-hsüeh ming chu 文學名著.
3:1. Taipei, 1960.

11. Hsi-ching tsa-chi 西京雜記. Author unknown. In SPTK.

12. Hsi K'ang chi 嵇康集. By Hsi K'ang (223-
262 A.D.). Reprinted in Holzman, D., La vie et la
pensée de Hi K'ang, Leiden, 1957.

13. Hsiao-ching 孝經. Translation: Legge, J.,
The Shu King, The Religious Portions of the Shih
King, The Hsiao King in The Sacred Books of the
East, Vol. III, Part I, Oxford, 1889.

14. Hsin-hsü 新序. Attributed to Liu Hsiang.
In Han-Wei ts'ung-shu. See also IV 5 below.

15. Hsün-tzu 荀子. In Chu-tzu chi-ch'eng.
Translation: Dubs, H. H., The Works of Hsüntze,
London, 1928; Köster, H., Hsün-tzu: Die Schriften
des Philosophen Hsün, Kaldenkirchen, 1967.

16. Huai-nan-tzu 淮南子. In Chu-tzu chi-ch'eng.

17. I-ching 易經, see Book of Changes.

18. Kory∅-sa 高麗史. By Ch'∅ng In-ji 鄭麟趾.
P'yongyang, 1957.

19. K'ung-ts'ung-tzu 孔叢子. In SPTK.

20. Lao-tzu 老子. In Chu Ch'ien-chih 朱謙之,
Lao-tzu chiao-shih 老子校釋, Shanghai, 1958.

21. Li chi 禮記. Translation: Couvreur, F. S.,
'Li Ki,' ou Mémoires sur les Bienséances et les
Cérémonies, Vol. I-II, Hokienfou, 1913; Legge, J.,
The Li Ki in The Sacred Books of China, Vol. XXVII-
XXVIII, The Texts of Confucianism, Vol. I-II, Ox-
ford, 1885.

22. Lieh-hsien chuan 列仙傳 , see Kaltenmark, M., below V 64.

23. Lieh-tzǔ 列子 . In Chu-tzu chi-ch'eng. Translation: Graham, A. C., The Book of Lieh-tzu: A New Translation, London, 1960.

24. Lun-yü 論語 , see Analects, IIB 1 above.

25. Lü-shih ch'un ch'iu 呂氏春秋 . In Chu-tzu chi-ch'eng. Translation: Wilhelm, R., Frühling und Herbst des Lü Bu We, Jena, 1928.

26. Ming-shih 明史 . Shanghai, 1923.

27. Nihonkoku genzaisho mokuroku 日本國見書目錄 . By Fujiwara no Sukeyo 藤原佐世 . In Obase Keikichi 小長谷惠吉 , Nihonkoku genzaisho mokoroku kaisetsukō 日本國見書目錄解説稿 . Tokyo, 1956.

28. Ma Kuo-han 馬國翰 , Yü-han shan-fang chi i shu 玉函山房輯佚書 . 1884.

29. Mencius 孟子 . Translation: Legge, J., The Works of Mencius in The Chinese Classics, Vol. II, (reprint: Hong Kong, 1960).

30. Shang-shan-t'ang Sung Yüan pan ching-ch'ao chiuch'ao shu-mu 上善堂宋元板精鈔舊鈔書目 [or Shang-shan-t'ang shu-mu]. By Sun Ts'ung-t'ien 孫從漆 and Ch'en Chun 陳準 . Originally in Ch'iuliu-chai ts'ung-shu 湫漻爾叢書 (reprint: Shanghai, 1929).

31. Shen-i ching 神異經 . Attributed to Tung-fang Shuo 東方朔 . In Han Wei ts'ung-shu. See also V 40 below.

32. Shih-chi 史記 . Bibliography IIIA 44. Translations: see MH, Bodde, D., and Watson, B.

33. Shu-ching 書經 . Translation: Legge, J., The Shoo King in The Chinese Classics, Vol. III

(reprint: Hong Kong, 1960).

34. Shuo-yüan 説苑 . Attributed to Liu Hsiang 劉向 . In Han Wei ts'ung-shu.

35. Sui shu ching-chi chih 隋書經籍志 . Shang-hai, 1955.

36. T'ang shu ching-chi i-wen ho chih 唐書經籍藝文合志 . Shanghai, 1956.

37. Tso-chuan 左傳 . See Ch'un-ch'iu in Biblio-graphy IIIA 8.

38. Tung-kuan Han chi 東觀漢記 . By various authors (1st-2nd cent. A.D.). In SPPY.

39. Wang Shih-chen 王世貞 , [Tseng-chi] Ch'ih tu ch'ing ts'ai 增集尺牘清裁 . 1571.

40. Wu-li lun 物理論 . By Yang Ch'üan 楊泉 . Reconstruction: Sun Hsin-yen, P'ing-chin-kuan ts'ung-shu 1:3, Peking, 1885.

41. Yang Shen 楊慎 . Ch'ih-tu ch'ing-ts'ai 赤牘清裁 . See Wang Shih-chen above 39.

42. Yao Chih-yin 姚之駰 , Hou Han shu pu-i 後漢書補逸 . 1773.

43. Yen-tzu ch'un-ch'iu 晏子春秋 . Attributed to Yen Ying 晏嬰 or Liu Hsiang 劉向 . In Chu-tzu chi-ch'eng.

44. Yü-hai 玉海 . By Wang Ying-lin 王應麟 . Taipei, 1964.

IV. Literature in Chinese and Japanese

1. Ch'ang Pi-te 昌彼得 , "Hsi Han ti ma cheng" 西漢的馬政 (The Horse Policy during the Western Han), in Ch'in Han shih chi chung-ku shih ch'ien-ch'i yen-chiu lun-chi: Ta-lu tsa-chih shih-hsüeh

ts'ung-shu 秦漢史及中古史前期研究論集：大陸雜
誌史學叢書 (Collection of Studies on the History
of the Ch'in and the Han, and on the Early Medieval
History: Collection of History of the Continent
Magazine) 1:4. Taipei, 1960. Pp. 58-62.

2. Chang Shun-hui 張舜徽 , Chung-kuo li-shih yao-
chi chieh-shao 中國歷史要籍介紹 (Introduction
to Chinese Historical Writing), Wuhan, 1957.

3. Chang Tsung-yüan 章宗源 , Sui-shu ching-chi chih
k'ao cheng 隋書經籍志考證 . In Pu-pien,
Vol. 4, pp. 4943-5037.

4. Chang Yen 張嚴 , "Yen K'o-chün Ch'üan shang-
ku San-tai Ch'in Han San-kuo Liu-ch'ao wen pien-
tz'u te-shih p'ing-i" 嚴可均宅上古三代秦漢三國六朝文
編次得失平議 (Evaluation of Success and Failure
in the Composition of Yen K'o-chün's Ch'üan shang-
ku San tai Ch'in Han San kuo Liu ch'ao wen), Ta-lu
tsa-chih 大陸雜誌, Vol. 21 (1960), pp. 8-11.

5. Chao Chung-i 趙仲邑 , "Hsin hsü shih lun"新序試論
[On the Hsin-hsü], Chung-shan ta-hsüeh hsüeh-pao
中山大學學報 , No. 3 (1957), pp. 170-83.

6. Chao I 趙翼 , "Kuang-wu hsin ch'an shu" 光武信
讖書 (Kuang-wu Trusted the Prognostication Texts),
in Nien-erh shih cha-chi 廿二史劄記 (Notes
on Twenty-two Histories). Peking, 1963.

7. Ch'en Ching-ho 陳荊和 , "Chiao-chih ming-ch'eng
k'ao" 交趾名稱考 (On the Nomenclature of
"Kiao-tche:" Its Origin and Application), Wen-shih-
che hsüeh-pao, Vol. 4 (1952), pp. 79-130.

8. Ch'en Chung-fan 陳中凡, Han Wei Liu-ch'ao san-
wen hsüan 漢魏六朝散文選 (Selection of the Prose
of the Han, Wei and Six Dynasties). Shanghai,
1956.

9.   Ch'en I-chen 陳以震 , "Lun Liu Hsiu" 論劉秀
     (On Liu Hsiu), <u>Szechwan ta-hsüeh hsüeh-pao</u>, No. 3
     (1957), pp. 83-91.

10. Ch'en P'an 陳槃 , "Ch'an-wei ming-ming chi ch'i
     hsiang-kuan chih chu wen-ti" 讖諱命名及其相關之
     諸問題 (On the Nomenclature of <u>Ch'an-Wei</u> and Other
     Relevant Problems), in <u>Li-shih yü-yen yen-chiu-so</u>
     <u>chi-k'an</u>   歷史語言研究所集刊   , Vol.
     21 (1949), pp. 19-42; and <u>Yu-shih hsüeh-pao</u> 幼獅
     學報 (The Youth Journal), Vol. 1, No. 1 (1958),
     pp. 1-35.

11. _____. "'Chin pu-te tz'u ming-hsing ch'u hsi-fang'
     chih chu wen-t'i" 「禁不得祠明皇出西方」之諸問
     題 (The Problems of the Phrase "It was Prohibited
     to Worship the Bright Star which Rose in the West"),
     <u>Ch'ing chu Chu Chia-hua hsien-sheng ch'i-shih sui</u>
     <u>lun-wen chi</u> 慶祝朱家華先生七十歲論文集
     <u>Ta-lu tsa-chih t'e-k'an</u> 大陸雜誌特刊 , Vol. 2.
     Taipei, 1962, pp. 369-75.

12. Ch'en Te-yün 陳德芸 , <u>Ku-chin jen-wu pieh-ming</u>
     <u>so-yin</u> 古今人物別名索引 (Index of Other Names
     of Antiquity and Present). Shanghai, 1937 (re-
     print: 1965).

13. Chiang Shih-jung 江世榮 , "Yu kuan Chuang-tzu
     ti i-hsieh li-shih tzu-liao" 有關莊子的一些歷史資料
     (Some Historical Materials on Chuang Tzu), <u>Wen-shih</u>
     (Literature and History), Vol. 1 (1962), pp. 221-24.

14. Chiang Tsu-i 蔣祖怡 , <u>Wang Ch'ung ti wen-hsüeh</u>
     <u>li-lun</u> 王充的文學理論 (Wang Ch'ung's Literary
     Theory). Shanghai, 1962.

15. Ch'ien Mu 錢穆 , "Liu Hsiang Hsin fu-tzu nien-
     p'u" 劉向歆父子年譜 (Chronological Biography
     of Father and Son, Liu Hsiang and Liu Hsin), <u>Ku-shih</u>
     <u>pien</u> 古史辨 , Vol. 5 (1935), pp. 101-249.

16. ____, Hsien-Ch'in chu-tzu hsi-nien 先秦諸子繫年 (Chronological Studies of the Pre-Ch'in Philosophers). Shanghai, 1936; second edition: Hong Kong, 1956.

17. ____, Liang-Han ching-hsüeh chin-ku-wen p'ing-i 兩漢經學今古文平議 (On the Schools of New and Ancient Exegesis of the Classics during the Two Han Dynasties), Kowloon, 1958.

18. Ch'ien Pao-ts'ung 錢寶琮 , "Kai-t'ien shuo yüan-liu k'ao" 蓋天說源流考 (The Origin of the Kai-t'ien Theory), K'o-hsüeh-shih chi-k'an 科學史季刊 (History of Science Quarterly), No. 1 (1958), pp. 29-46.

19. Chou Shou-ch'ang 周壽昌 , Han shu chu chiao-pu 漢書注校補 (Revised Commentary to Han shu). Shanghai, 1937.

20. Chou Yü-t'ung 周予同 , Ching chin-ku-wen hsüeh 經今古文學 (Study of the New and Old Schools of Exegesis of the Classics). Peking, 1955.

21. ____ and T'ang Chih-chün 湯志鈞 , "Wang Mang kai-chih yü ching-hsüeh-chung ti chin-ku-wen hsüeh wen-t'i" 王莽改制與經學中的今古文學問題 (The Reforms of Wang Mang and the Problem of the Study of the New and Old Schools of Exegesis of the Classics), Kuang-ming jih-pao 光明日報 (May 15, 1961), p. 2.

22. Ch'üan Tsu-wang 全祖國 , Chi-ch'i t'ing chi wai-pien 鮚埼亭外編 . In SPTK.

23. Chu I-tsun 朱彝尊 , Ching i k'ao 經義考 . In SPPY.

24. Chung-wen ta tz'u-tien 中文大辭典 , Vol. 1-40. Taipei, 1962-68.

25. Erh-shih-wu shih pu-pien 二十五史補編 (Addenda to the Twenty-five Histories). Vol. 2-4. Shanghai, 1937 (reprint: Peking, 1956).

26. Fan Wen-lan 范文瀾 , Wen-hsin tiao-lung chu 文心雕龍注 . Peking, 1959.

27. Feng Yu-lan, see Bibliography II 11.

28. Han Ch'üeh 寒爵 , "T'an so-wei 'ku-chi chia' Tung-fang Shuo" 談所謂「滑稽家」東方朔 (On the So-called "Ironical Critic" Tung-fang Shuo), Fan-kung yüeh-k'an 反攻月刊 , No. 256 (July 1963), pp. 21-24.

29. Hang Shih-chün 杭世駿 , Chu-shih jan-i 諸史然疑 Peking, Harvard-Yenching Institute, Supplement No. 2, 1932.

30. Ho Ch'ang-ch'ün 賀昌羣 , Lun Liang-Han t'u-ti chan-yu hsing-t'ai ti fa-chan 論兩漢土地佔有形態的發展 (On the Development of the Forms of Land Possession during the Two Han Dynasties). Peking, 1956.

31. Ho Liang-chün 何良俊 , Ssu-yu-chai ts'ung shuo 四有齋叢説 . 1567 (republication: Shanghai, 1959).

32. Hou K'ang 侯康 , Pu Hou Han shu i-wen chih 補後漢書藝文志 . In Pu-pien, Vol. 2, pp. 2105-30.

33. Hou Wai-lu 侯外廬 , "Chung-kuo che-hsüeh-shih chung-ti wei-wu-chu-i chuan-t'ung" 中國哲學史中的唯物主義傳統 (The Materialist Tradition in the History of Chinese Philosophy), Hsin chien-she 新建設 No. 4 (1963), pp. 1-11.

34. ____, "Fang I-chih: Chung-kuo ti pai-k'o-ch'üan-shu-p'ai ta che-hsüeh chia" 方以知一中國的百科全書

派大哲學家 (Fang I-chih: China's Great Ency-
clopaedist-Philosopher), Li-shih yen-chiu 歷史
研究 (1957), Vol. 6, pp. 1-21, and Vol. 7, pp.
1-25. See also Bibliography II 8.

35. Hsiao I-shan 蕭一山 , Ch'ing tai t'ung-shih
清代通史 (General History of the Ch'ing
Period). Vol. 1-5. Taipei, 1963.

36. Hsiao Kung-ch'üan, see Bibliography IIA 7.

37. Hsieh Kuo-chen 謝國楨 , "Han-tai hua-
hsiang k'ao" 漢代畫像考 (Study of Han
Period Portraiture), in Chou Shu-t'ao hsien-sheng
liu-shih sheng-jih chi-nien lun-wen chi 周叔弢先生
六十生日紀念論文集 (Collected Articles on
the Occasion of the 60th Birthday of Chou Shu-
t'ao). Peking, 1951 (reprint: Hong Kong, 1967),
pp. 354-94.

38. Hsü Chen-ngo 徐震堮 , Han Wei Liu-ch'ao
hsiao-shuo hsüan 漢魏六朝小說選
(Selection of Fiction from the Han, Wei and Six
Dynasties Period). Shanghai, 1956.

39. Huang Shih 黃奭 , Han-hsüeh-t'ang ts'ung-shu
漢學堂叢書. Preface: 1925.

40. Jan Chao-te 冉昭德 , "Kuan-yü Han-tai sheng-
ch'an nu-li yü sheng-ch'an-li shui-p'ing wen-
t'i" 關於漢代生產奴隸與生產水平問題
(On the Problem of Slaves in Production and the
Level of Productive Forces in Han Period), Li-
shih yen-chiu, No. 8 (1958), pp. 51-58.

41. ____, "Han-tai ti ta-chia, chung-chia ho hsiao-
chia" 漢代的大家中家和小家 (The Great, Middle
and Small Families of the Han), Kuang-ming jih-
pao 光明日報 , Supplement Shih-hsüeh 史
學 (January 15, 1964).

292

42. Jao Tsung-i 饒宗頤 , "Hsi Han chieh-i chuan" 西漢節義傳 (Biographies of Chaste and Loyal Men of the Western Han), <u>Hsin Ya hsüeh-pao</u>, Vol. 1, No. 1 (1955), pp. 157-208.

43. ____, "Hsin shu hsü mu" 新書序目 (Introduction and Table of Contents of the Hsin History), <u>Tse-shan pan-yüeh-k'an</u> 責善半月刊 , Vol. 1, No. 3 (1940), pp. 48-50.

44. ____, "Lu Chi Wen-fu li-lun yü yin-yüeh chih kuan-hsi" 陸機文賦理論與音樂之關係 (The Theory of Lu Chi's Rhyme-prose on Literature in its Relation with Music), <u>Chūgoku bungaku hō</u> 中國文學報 , Vol. 14 (1961), pp. 22-37.

45. Juan Yüan 阮元 , <u>Ssu-k'u wei-shou shu-mu t'i-yao</u> 四庫未收書目提要. Shanghai, 1955.

46. Jung Chao-tsu, <u>Wei Chin ti tzu-jang-chu-i</u> 魏晉的自然主義 (Naturalism during the Wei and Chin Dynasties). Shanghai, 1935.

47. K'ang Yu-wei 康有為 , <u>Hsin Hsüeh wei ching k'ao</u> 新學偽經考 (Study of the Classics Falsified by the Scholarship of the Hsin Dynasty). Peking, 1931.

48. Kao P'ing-tzu 高平子 , <u>Hsüeh li san lun</u> 學曆散論 (Studies on Chinese Calendar Science and Astronomy). Nankang, 1969.

49. ____, "Kuei piao ts'e ching lun" 圭表測景論 (On the Measurement of the Shadow on the Sundial by the Instruments <u>kuei</u> and <u>piao</u>), <u>Ch'ing-chu Chu Chia-hua hsien-sheng ch'ih-shih sui lun-wen chi</u>, <u>Ta-lu tsa-chih t'e-k'an</u>, Vol. 2, Taipei, 1962, pp. 293-306.

50. Kishibe Shigeo 岸邊成雄 , "Kugo no engen" 箜篌の淵源 (The Origin of the Chinese Harp), in

Kōhogaku zasshi 考古學雜誌 , Vol. 39, No. 2 (1953), pp. 77-96; and Vol. 39, No. 3-4 (1954), pp. 169-84.

51.　Ku Chieh-kang 顧頡剛 , "Chan-kuo Ch'in Han chien jen-ti tsa-wei yü pien-wei" 戰國秦漢間人的造偽與辨偽 (Forgeries and Their Refutation by Chinese Scholars from 403 B.C. to 220 A.D.), Shih-hsüeh nien-pao 史學年報 , Vol. 2, No. 2 (1935), pp. 209-48.

52.　_____, "Juan Yüan Ming-t'ang-lun" 阮元明堂論 (Juan Yüan's Ming-t'ang-lun), Kuo-li ti-i Chung-shan ta-hsüeh yü-yen li-shih hsüeh yen-chiu-suo chou-k'an, No. 121 (March 5, 1930), pp. 4735-36.

53.　_____, Han-tai hsüeh-shu shih-lüeh 漢代學術史略 (Outline History of the Han Period Civilization). Shanghai, 1935, 1948. Reprinted under the title Ch'in Han fang-shih yü ju-sheng 秦漢方士與儒生 (Magicians and Confucian Literati in the Ch'in and Han Periods), Shanghai, 1955.

54.　Ku Huai-san 顧懷三 , Pu Hou-Han-shu i-wen chih 補後漢書藝文志 . In Pu-pien, Vol. 2, pp. 2131-2304.

55.　Ku Yen-wu 顧炎武 , Jih chih lu [chi shih] 日知錄集釋 . Shanghai, 1933.

56.　Kuan Feng, see Bibliography IIA 8.

57.　Lao Kan 勞榦 , "Lun Han tai ti yu-hsia" 論漢代的游俠 (On the Knights Errant of the Han Dynasty), Wen-shih-che hsüeh-pao 文史哲學報 , Vol. 1 (1950), pp. 237-52.

58.　_____, Ch'in Han shih 秦漢史 (History of the Ch'in and Han Dynasties). Taipei, 1955.

59.　_____, "Han-tai ti 'shih-shu' yü 'ch'ih-tu'" 漢代的「史書與「尺牘」(The "Letters" and "Foot-tablets" of the Han Dynasty), Ta-lu tsa-chih 大陸雜誌 , Vol. 21, No. 1 (1960), pp. 69-72.

294

60. _____, "Lun Hsi-ching tsa-chi chih tso-cho chi
ch'eng-shu shih-tai" 論西京雜記之作者及成書時代
(On the Authorship and Date of the Hsin-ching tsa-chi),
Li-shih yü-yen yen-chiu so chi-k'an, Vol. 33 (1962),
pp. 19-34.

61. Liang Jung-jo 梁容若 , "Chung-kuo wen-hsüeh-
shih shang ti wei-tso i-tso yü ch'i ying-hsiang" 中國文學
史上的偽作擬作與其影響 (The Influence of Falsely-attribu-
ted Works and Imitations on Chinese Literature), Tung-
hai hsüeh-pao 東海學報 (Tunghai Journal), Vol. 6,
No. 1 (1964), pp. 41-53.

62. Liu P'an-sui 劉盼遂 , "Yen T'ieh-ch'iao
Ch'üan shang-ku San-tai Ch'in Han wen pu" 嚴鐵橋全上
古三代秦漢文補 (Supplement to Yen K'o-chün's
Ch'üan shang-ku San-tai Ch'in Han wen), Pei-p'ing t'u-
shu-kuan kuan-k'an 北平圖書館館刊
Vol. 5, No. 1 (1931).

63. Liu Shih-p'ei 劉師培 , "Ch'in ts'ao pu shih"
琴操補釋 , in Liu Shen-shu hsien-sheng i-shu
劉申叔先生遺書 , Vol. 36 (1908).

64. Lo Ken-tse 羅根澤 , Chu-tzu k'ao-so 諸子
考索 (Examination and Inquiry into the Philosophers). Peking, 1958.

65. Ma Hsien-hsing 馬先醒 "Han shih lun-chu
lei-mu" 漢史論著類目 (A Classified Catalogue of
Articles and Books on the History of the Han Dynasty).
Chinese Culture, Vol. 10, No. 3 (1969), pp. 103-70;
No. 4, pp. 105-57; Vol. 11, No. 1 (1970), pp. 124-78;
No. 2, pp. 69-187.

66. Makino Tatsumi 牧野巽 , Shina kazoku
kenkyū 支那家族研究 (Study of the Chinese
Family). Tokyo, 1944.

67.　　Nakajima Chiaki 中島千秋 , "Gakin no ongaku shisō ni tsuite" 雅琴の音樂思想りにて (The Ideology of Court Music), Shinagaku kenkyū, Vol. 13 (1955), pp. 54-71.

68.　　Pan Piao 班彪 , "Lan-hai fu" 覽海賦 In Yen, Ch'üan Hou Han wen 23.4a-5b, adapted from IWLC, 27.

69.　　Ssu-k'u ch'üan-shu tsung-mu t'i-yao 四庫全書總目提要 . By Chi Yün and others. Vol. 1-4. In WYWK, Shanghai, 1933.

70.　　T'ai Ching-nung 臺靜農 , "Liang Han yüeh-wu k'ao" 兩漢樂舞考 (Ritual and Social Songs and Dances During the Han Dynasty), Wen-shih-che hsüeh-pao, No. 1 (1950), pp. 253-308.

71.　　Tai Chün-jen 戴君仁 , "Ho-t'u Lo-shu ti pen-chih chi ch'i yüan-lai ti kung-yung" 河圖洛書的本質及其原來的功用 (The Essence and Original Function of the Ho-t'u Lo-shu), Wen-shih-che hsüeh-pao, No. 15 (1966), pp. 163-180.

72.　　T'an Chieh-fu 譚戒甫 , Kung-sun Lung-tzu hsing-ming fa-wei 公孫龍子形名發微 . Peking, 1957 (reprint: 1963).

73.　　T'ang Chün-i 唐君毅 , "Ch'in Han i-hou t'ien-ming ssu-hsiang chih fa-chan" 秦漢以後天命思想之發展 (The Development of Ideas on the Will of Heaven Since the Ch'in and Han Periods), Hsin Ya hsüeh-pao, Vol. 6, No. 2 (1964), pp. 1-61.

74.　　T'ien Ch'ang-wu 田昌五 , Wang Ch'ung chi ch'i Lun-heng 王充及其論衡 (Wang Ch'ung and his Lun-heng). Peking, 1958.

75.　　Tseng P'u 曾樸 , Pu Hou Han shu i-wen chih p'ing k'ao 補後漢書藝文志抨考 . In Pu-pien, Vol. 2, pp. 2447-2566.

76. Uchiyama Toshihiko 內山俊彥, "Yō Sen no shisō" 楊泉の思想 (The Idea of Yang Ch'üan: A Milestone of the Rationalistic View of Nature), Shirin 史林, Vol. 50, No. 1 (1967), pp. 69-87.

77. Wang Chung-min 王重民, "Chiang-yün-lou shu-mu pa" 絳雲樓書目跋 (Postface to the Catalogue of Chiang Yun Lou), Kuo-li Pei-p'ing t'u-shu-kuan yüeh-k'an 國立北平圖書館月刊, Vol. 3, No. 5 (1929), pp. 577-79.

78. Wang I-t'ung 王伊同, "Tz'u-hai k'an wu" 辭海列誤, Tsing Hua Journal of Chinese Studies 清華學報, Vol. 2 (1960), pp. 131-42.

79. Wang Kuo-wei 王國維, "Ming-t'ang-miao t'ung-k'ao" 明堂廟通考, Kuan-t'ang chi-lin 觀堂集林, Vol. 1, No. 3, pp. 123-53. Reprint: Peking, 1959. See Heffer, J., for translation.

80. Wang Li 王力, Han-yü shih kao 漢語史稿 (History of Chinese), Vol. 1-3. Peking, 1957-1958.

81. Wang Shih-chen 王世貞, I-yüan chih-yen 藝苑卮言. Shanghai, 1925.

82. Wang Shu-min 王叔岷, Liu-tzu chi-cheng 劉子集證. Taipei, 1961.

83. _____, "Lun chien ku-chu lei-shu yü chiao-ting ku-shu chih kuan-hsi" 論檢古注類書與斠定古書之關係 (A Study of the Relationship between the Old Annotated Encyclopedias and the Textual Criticism of Ancient Books), Wen-shih-che hsüeh-pao, Vol. 10 (1961), pp. 15-37.

84. Wen I-to 聞一多, Ku-tien hsin-i 古典新義 (New Meaning of Old Records). Shanghai, 1948. Vol. II of Wen I-to ch'üan chi 聞一多全集.

85. Wen T'ing-shih 文廷式, Pu Chin shu i-wen chih 補晉書藝文志. Pu-pien 3, pp. 3703-95.

86. Yamada Taku 山田琢, "Shunjū hōhen setsu ni tsuite" 春秋褒貶説について(A Study of the Phrase Pao-pien found in the Ch'un-ch'iu), Tōhōgaku 東方學, Vol. 37 (1969), pp. 1-15.

87. Yang Hsiang-k'uei 楊向奎, Chung-kuo ku-tai she-hui yü ku-tai ssu-hsiang yen-chiu 中國古代社會與古代思想研究 (A Study of Ancient Chinese Society and Ancient Thought). Vol. 1, Peking, 1962.

88. Yang Shen 楊愼, Sheng-an ch'üan chi 升菴全集 (Collected Writings of Yang Shen). In WYWK.

89. ____, Tan ch'ien tsa-lu 丹鉛雜錄. In TSCC.

90. Yao Chen-tsung 姚振宗, Hou-Han-shu i-wen chih 後漢書藝文志. In Pu-pien, Vol. 2, pp. 2305-2445.

91. Yasui Kōzan 安居香山, "Zushin no keisei to sono enyō ni tsuite no kōsatsu.-Kōbu kakumei zenho o chūshin to shite" 圖讖の形成をその延用についての考察光武革命前後を中心てして(A Study of the Formation of Tu-ch'en, Fortune-Telling Documents, and Amplification of Them--Mainly Centering Around the Period Before and After the Kuang-wu Revolution), Tōhōgaku 東方學, Vol. 27 (1964), pp. 48-63.

92. Yü Chia-hsi 余嘉錫 (or Yü Chi-yü 余季豫), Ssu-k'u t'i-yao pien-cheng 四庫提要辦證. Peking, 1958.

93. Yü Ching-jang 于景讓, "Shih ching chi" 釋荊棘 (The Ching and Chi Plants Elucidated). Ta-lu tsa-chih 大陸雜誌, Vol. 14, No. 12 (1957), pp. 1-8.

94. Yü Ying-shih 余英時, "Han Chin chih chi shih chih hsin tzu-chüeh yü hsin ssu-ch'ao" 漢晉之際士之新自覺與新思潮 (The New Self-Consciousness

298

of the Literati Between the Han and Chin Dynasties and the New Trends of Thought), Hsin Ya hsüeh-pao 新亞學報, Vol. 4, No. 1 (1959), pp. 25-144.

95.   ____, "Tung-Han cheng-ch'üan chih chien-li yü shih-tsu ta-hsing chih kuan-hsi: Lüeh-lun Liang Han chih chi cheng-chih pien-ch'ien-ti she-hui pei-ching" 東漢政權之建立與士族大姓之關係：略論兩漢之際政治變遷的社會背景 (The Establishment of the Political Power of the Later Han Dynasty and Its Relation with the Distinguished Clans and Noble Families: A Summary of the Social Background of Political Change in the Two Han Dynasties), Hsin Ya hsüeh-pao, Vol. 1, No. 2 (1956), pp. 209-80.

V. Literature in Other Languages

1.   Balazs, E., Chinese Civilization and Bureaucracy: Variations on a Theme. New Haven, 1964.

2.   Bauer, W. "Der Fürst von Liu," ZDMG, Vol. 106, No. 1 (1956), pp. 166-205.

3.   ____, "Das P'ai-hang-System in der chinesischen Namengebung," ZDMG, Vol. 107 (1957), pp. 595-634.

4.   ____, "Der chinesische Personenname: Die Bildungsgesetze und hauptsächlichsten Bedeutungsinhalte von Ming, Tzu und Hsiao-Ming. Wiesbaden, 1959.

5.   Bielenstein, H., "The Restoration of the Han Dynasty with Prolegomena on the Historiography of the

6.   ____, "The Civil War," BMFEA, Vol. 31 (1959), pp. 1-287.

7.   ____, "An Interpretation of the Portents in the Ts'ien Han-shu," BMFEA, Vol. 22 (1950), pp. 127-43.

8.   ____, "The People," BMFEA, Vol. 39 (1967), pp. 1-202.

Hou Han shu," BMFEA, Vol. 26 (1954), pp. 1-81, 82-209.
9.   Blue, R. C., "The Argumentation of the 'Shih-huo
chih' Chapters of the Han, Wei, and Sui Dynastic Histories," HJAS, Vol. 11 (1948), pp. 1-118.
10.   Bodde, D., China's First Unifier: A Study of the
Ch'in Dynasty as Seen in the Life of Li Ssu, 280-208
B.C. Leiden, 1938 (reprint: Hong Kong, 1967).
11.   ____, Statesman, Patriot, and General in Ancient
China: Three Shih Chi Biographies of the Ch'in Dynasty
(255-206 B.C.). New Haven, 1940.
12.   ____ and Morris, C., Law in Imperial China:
Exemplified by 190 Ch'ing Dynasty Cases. Cambridge,
Mass., 1967.
13.   Bridgman, R. F., "La médecine dans la Chine antique," Mélanges chinois et bouddhiques, Vol. 10 (1955),
pp. 1-213.
14.   Camman, S., "Types of Symbols in Chinese Art,"
in A. F. Wright (editor), Studies in Chinese Thought,
Chicago, 1953, pp. 195-231.
15.   ____, "The Magic Square of Three in Old Chinese
Philosophy," History of Religions, Vol. 1 (1961), pp.
37-80.
16.   Chan Wing-tsit, Chinese Philosophy 1949-1963:
An Annotated Bibliography of Mainland China Publications.
Honolulu, 1967.
17.   Chatley, M., "The Heavenly Cover: A Study in
Ancient Chinese Astronomy," Observatory, Vol. 61 (1938),
pp. 10-21.
18.   Ch'en Ch'i-yün, "A Confucian Magnate's Idea of
Political Violence: Hsün Shuang's (128-190 A.D.) Interpretation of the Book of Changes," TP, Vol. 54, No. 1-3,
(1968), pp. 73-115.

300

19. _____, "Hsün Yüeh and his Shen-chien: A Confucian Minister's Reflections on the Downfall of His Dynasty," unpublished dissertation, Harvard University, 1966.

20. _____, "Textual Problems of Hsün Yüeh's (148-209 A.D.) Writings: The Han chi and the Shen-chien," Monumenta Serica, Vol. 27 (1968), pp. 208-32.

21. Ch'ü T'ung-tsu, Law and Society in Traditional China. Paris, 1961 (second edition, 1965).

22. Couvreur, S., Dictionnaire Classique de la Langue Chinoise. Reprint: Peiping, 1947.

23. Crawford, R. B., "The Social and Political Philosophy of the Shih-chi," JAS, Vol. 22, No. 4 (1963), pp. 401-16.

24. Creel, H. G., "What is Taoism?" JAOS, Vol. 76 (1956), pp. 139-52.

25. Diény, J.-P., Aux Origines de La Poésie Classique en Chine: Étude sur La Poésie Lyrique à L'époque des Han. Leiden, 1968.

26. Dill, J., "Untersuchungen zum Charakter und Struktur der gegen die 'Öffentliche Ordnung' verstossenden Bewegung des Zeitraums 1-33 in China," unpublished dissertation, Berlin, 1965.

27. Dobson, W. A. C. H., Late Han Chinese: A Study of the Archaic - Han Shift. Toronto, 1964.

28. Dubs, H. H., "An Ancient Chinese Mystery Cult," Harvard Theological Review, Vol. 35 (1942), pp. 221-40.

29. _____, "The Beginnings of Alchemy," Isis, Vol. 38 (1947), pp. 62-86.

30. _____, "The Origins of Alchemy," Ambix, Vol. 9 (1961), pp. 23-36.

31. _____, "Theism and Naturalism in Ancient Chinese Philosophy," Philosophy East and West, Vol. 9, No. 3-4 (1960), pp. 163-72. See also HFHD and Bibliography IIIB 15.

32.   Dull, Jack L., "A Historical Introduction to the Apocryphal [Ch'an-Wei] Texts of the Han Dynasty," unpublished dissertation, Seattle, 1966.

33.   Duyvendak, J. J. L., The Book of the Lord Shang: A Classic of the Chinese School of Law. London, 1928.

34.   Eichhorn, W., "Das Fei-yen wai-chuan," Wissenschaftliche Zeitschrift der Karl-Marx-Universität Leipzig: Gesellschafts- und Sprachwissenschaftliche Reihe, Vol. 10, No. 1 (1961), pp. 123-32.

35.   ____, "Eine Erzählung aus dem Wen-chien hou-lu," Oriens Extremus, Vol. 2 (1955), pp. 167-74.

36.   Fang, A., "Rhyme-prose on Literature: The Wen-fu of Lu Chi (261-303 A.D.)," HJAS, Vol. 14 (1951), pp. 527-66.

37.   Feng, H. Y., and Shryock, J. K., "The Black Magic in China known as Ku," JAOS, Vol. 55 (1935), pp. 1-30.

38.   Filliozat, J., "Taoïsme et Yoga," Dan Viêt-Nam, Vol. 3 (1949), pp. 113-19.

39.   Forke, A., see Bibliography IIB 16 and IIIA 33.

40.   Franke, H., "Zur Textkritik des Shen-i ching," Oriens Extremus, Vol. 8 (1961), pp. 131-35

41.   Franke, O., Geschichte des chinesischen Reiches. Vol. 1-5   Berlin, 1930-1953.

42.   ____, Studien zur Geschichte des konfuzianischen Dogmas und der chinesischen Staatsreligion: Das Problem des Tsch'un-ts'iu und Tung Tschung-schu's Tsch'un-ts'iu fan-lu. Hamburg, 1920.

43.   Fung Yu-lan (trans D. Bodde), A History of Chinese Philosophy. Vol. 1-2. Princeton, 1952-1953.

44.   Gabain, von, A., "Ein Fürstenspiegel: Das Sin-yü des Lu Kia," MSOS, Vol. 33 (1930), pp. 1-82.

45.   Gimm, M., "Das Yüeh-fu tsa-lu des Tuan An-chieh: Studien zur Geschichte von Musik, Schauspiel und Tanz in

der T'ang Dynastie," Asiatische Forschungen, Band 19, Wiesbaden, 1966.

46.   Goodrich, C. S., "Professor Dubs's Translation of the Biography of Wang Mang, " JAOS, Vol. 79 (1959), pp. 104-23.

47.   Graham, A. C., "The Composition of Gongsuen Long tzyy," Asia Major, Vol. 5, No. 2 (1956), pp. 147-83.

48.   _____, "The Date and Composition of Liehtzyy," Asia Major, Vol. 8, No. 2 (1961), pp. 139-98. See also Bibliography IIIB 23.

49.   _____, "Two Dialogues in the Kung-sun Lung-tzu: 'White Horse' and 'Left and Right'," Asia Major, Vol. 11 (1965), pp. 128-52.

50.   Gulik, van, R. H., The Lore of the Chinese Lute: An Essay in Ch'in Ideology. Tokyo, 1941.

51.   Haeger, J. H., "The Significance of Confusion: The Origins of the T'ai-p'ing yü-lan," JAOS, Vol. 88, No. 3 (1968), pp. 401-10.

52.   Haenisch , E., Lehrgang der klassischen chinesischen Schriftsprache, Vol. 4. Leipzig, 1957.

53.   Hawkes, D., Ch'u Tz'u: The Songs of the South. Oxford, 1959.

54.   Heffer, J., "Ming-t'ang miao ch'in-tung-k'ao: Ausschluss über die Halle der lichten Kraft, ming-t'ang, über den Ahnentempel miao, sowie über die Wohnpaläste (Wohngebäude), ch'in," Ostasiatische Zeitschrift (1931), pp. 17-35, 70-86.

55.   Hervouet, Y., Un poète de cour sous les Han: Sseu-ma Siang-jou. Paris, 1964.

56.   Hirth, F., "Bausteine zu einer Geschichte der chinesischen Literatur," TP, Vol. 6 (1895), pp. 314-32, 416-46; Vol. 7 (1896), pp. 295-322, 481-507.

57.   Ho Peng Yoke, The Astronomical Chapters of the Chin Shu. Paris, 1966.

58.   Holzman, D., "The Conversational Tradition in Chinese Philosophy," Philosophy East and West, Vol. 6, No. 2 (1956), pp. 223-30. See also Hsi K'ang.

59.   Hu Shih, "The Concept of Immortality in Chinese Thought," Harvard Divinity School Bulletin (1945-46), pp. 23-46.

60.   Hughes, E. P., Two Chinese Poets: Vignettes of Han Life and Thought. Princeton, 1960.

61.   Hulsewé, A. F. P., "Notes on Historiography of the Han Period," in W. E. Beasley and E. G. Pulleyblank (eds.), Historians of China and Japan (London, 1961), pp. 31-43.

62   _____, Remnants of Han Law: Introductory Studies and Annotated Translation of Chapters 22 and 23 of the History of the Former Han Dynasty, Vol. 1.   Leiden, 1955.

63.   Jao Tsung-yi, "The Relation between Principles of Literary Criticism in the Wei and Tsin Dynasties and Music--Illustration of Literature Through Music," unpublished paper, presented at the Eleventh Conference of Young Sinologues, Padua, 1958.

64.   Kaltenmark, M., Le Lie-sien tchouan: Biographies légendaires des Immortels taoistes de l'antiquité. Peking, 1953.

65.   _____, "Les Tch'an-wei," Han-hiue, Vol. 2, No. 4 (1949), pp. 363-73.

66.   Kierman, F. A., Jr., Ssu-ma Ch'ien's Historiographical Attitude as Reflected in Four Late Warring States Biographies. Wiesbaden, 1962

67.   Kishibe Shigeo, "The Origin of the K'oung-Hou," Tōyō ongaku kenkyū, Vol. 14 (1957), pp. 1-51.

68.   Knechtges, D. R., "Yang Shyong, the Fuh and Han
Rhetoric," unpublished dissertation, Seattle, 1968.

69.   Koh Byongik, "Zur Werttheorie in der chinesischen
Historiographie auf Grund des Shih-T'ung des Liu Chih-
Chi (661-721)," Oriens Extremus, Vol. 4, No. 1 (1957),
pp. 5-51; No. 2, pp. 125-81.

70.   Kopetsky, E. E., "A Study of Some Han Fu of
Praise, The Fu on Hunts, Sacrifices, and Capitals,"
unpublished dissertation, New Haven, 1969.

71.   Kraft, B., "Wang Shih-chen (1526-1590): Abriss
seines Lebens," Oriens Extremus, Vol. 3 (1958), pp. 169-
201.

72.   Kramers, R. P., K'ung Tzu Chia Yü: The School
Sayings of Confucius. Leiden, 1960.

73.   Kroll, J. L., "Notes on Han Law," TP, Vol. 51,
No. 2-3 (1964), pp. 125-39.

74.   ____, Syma Cjan' -istorik (Ssu-ma Ch'ien: Historian). Moscow, 1970.

75.   Künstler, J. M., "Deux biographies de Tcheng
Hiuan," Rocznik orientalistyczny, Vol. 26 (1962), pp.
23-64.

76.   Lanciotti, L., Considerazioni sull'estetica
letteraria nella Cina antica: Wang Ch'ung ed il sorgere
dell'autonomia delle lettere. Rome, 1965.

77.   Levenson, J. R., Liang Ch'i-ch'ao and the Mind
of Modern China. Cambridge, Mass., 1953 (reprint: 1959).

78.   ____ and Schurman, F., China: An Interpretative
History, From the Beginnings to the Fall of Han. Berkeley, 1969.

79.   Lévy, A., "Études sur trois récueils anciens de
contes chinois," TP, Vol. 52 (1965), pp. 97-148.

80.   Liebenthal, W., "The Immortality of Soul in
Chinese Thought," Monumenta Nipponica, Vol. 8 (1952),
pp. 327-97.

81.   Lo Hsiang-lin, "The Southward Expansion of Chinese Expansion of Chinese Civilization and the Advance-
ment of Learning in Kwangtung Province," in W. Eberhard,
(ed.), Symposium on Historical, Archaeological and
Linguistic Studies on Southern China, South-East Asia
and the Hong Kong Region (Hong Kong, 1967), pp. 139-49.
82.   Lo Jung-pang, "China's Paddle-wheel Boats:
Mechanized Craft Used in the Opium War and Their Historical Background," Tsing Hua Journal of Chinese Studies, N.S. II (1960), pp. 189-215.
83.   Loehr, M., "The Beginnings of Portrait Painting
in China," Trudy Dvadcat' pjatogo meždunarodnogo kon-
gressa vostokovedov, Vol. 5 (Moscow, 1963), pp. 210-14.
84.   Loewe, M., Records of Han Administration, Vol.
1-2. Cambridge, 1967.
85.   Masabuchi Tatsuo, "The Yu-hsia and the Social
Order of the Han Period," Annals of the Hitotsubashi
Academy, Vol. 3, No. 1 (1952), pp. 84-101.
86.   Maspero, H., "Le Ming-t'ang et la crise religieuse avant les Han," Mélanges chinois et bouddhiques,
Vol. 9 (1951), pp. 1-71.
87.   _____, "Les procédés de 'nourrir le principe
vital' dans la réligion taoïste ancienne," JA, Vol. 229
(1937), pp. 177-252, 353-430.
88.   _____, "Le Taoïsme," Mélanges posthumes dur les
réligions et l'histoire de la Chine, Vol. 2. Paris,
1950.
89.   Mather, R. B., "The Controversy over Conformity
and Naturalness during the Six Dynasties," History of
Religions, Vol. 9, No. 2-3 (1969-1970), pp. 160-80.
90.   Miyazaki Ichisada, "Les villes en Chine à l'époque des Han," TP, Vol. 43 (1960), pp. 376-92.

306

91.   Mondolfo, R., "La filosofia como problematica y
su continuidad historica," Revista de Filosofia de la
Universidad de Costa Rica, Vol. 1, No. 1 (1957), pp.
9-17.
92.   Needham, J., Science and Civilization in China,
Vol. 1: Introductory Orientations, Cambridge, 1954.
Vol. 2: History of Scientific Thought, Cambridge, 1956.
Vol. 3: Mathematics and the Sciences of Heavens and the
Earth, Cambridge, 1959. Vol. 4: Physics and Physical
Technology: I, "Physics," Cambridge, 1962; II, "Mech-
anical Engineering," Cambridge, 1965; and III, "Nautical
Engineering," Cambridge, 1970.
93.   _____, Wang Ling and de Solla Price, D. J.,
Heavenly Clockwork: The Great Astronomical Clocks of
Medieval China--A Missing Link in Horological History.
Cambridge, 1960.
94.   O'Connor, J. (ed.), Modern Materialism: Readings
on Mind-Body Identity. New York, 1969.
95.   Pelliot, P., "La gravure sur pièrre des classi-
ques en caractères anciens sous les Wei," TP, Vol. 23
(1924), pp. 1-4.
96.   _____, "Notes de bibliographie Chinoise I: Le
Kou Yi Ts'ong Chou," BEFEO, Vol. 2 (1902), pp. 315-40.
97.   _____, "Notes sur quelques artistes des Six
dynasties et des T'ang," TP, Vol. 22 (1923), pp. 215-91.
98.   _____, "Meou-tseu ou les doutes levés," TP,
Vol. 19 (1920), pp. 255-433.
99.   _____, "Quelques remarques sur le Chouo Fou,"
TP, Vol. 23 (1924), pp. 163-220.
100.   Perelomov, L. S., "O roli ideologii v stanolenii
despotičeskogo gosudarstva v drevnem Kitae" (On the Role
of the Ideology during the Establishment of the Despotic
State in Ancient China), Narody Azii i Afriki, No. 3
(1967), pp. 62-73.

101.   Petrov, A. A., Van Čun: Drevnekitajskij materialist i prosvetitel (Wang Ch'ung: Materialist and Enlight-
ener in Ancient China). Moscow, 1954.
102.   Picken, L. E. R., "T'ang Music and Musical Instruments," TP, Vol. 55 (1969), pp. 74-122.
103.   Pokora, T., "The Canon of Laws by Li K'uei--A
Double Falsification?" ArOr, Vol. 27 (1959), pp. 96-121.
104.   _____, The First Interpolation in the Shih-chi,"
ArOr, Vol. 29 (1961), pp. 311-15.
105.   _____, "How Many Works Were Written by Wang
Ch'ung (27-97 A.D.)?" ArOr, Vol. 25 (1957), pp. 658-59.
106.   _____, "Huan T'an and Yang Hsiung on Ssu-ma
Hsiang-ju: Some Desultory Remarks on History and Tradition," JAOS, Vol. 91 (1971), pp. 431-38.
107.   _____, "An Important Crossroad of the Chinese
Thought," ArOr, Vol. 29 (1961), pp. 64-79.
108.   _____, "The Need for a More Thorough Study of
the Philosopher Wang Ch'ung and of his Predecessors,"
ArOr, Vol. 30 (1962), pp. 238-39.
109.   _____, "Notes on New Studies on Tung Chung-shu,"
ArOr, Vol. 33 (1965), pp. 256-71.
110.   _____, "On the Origin of the Notions T'ai-p'ing
and Ta-t'ung in Chinese Philosophy," ArOr, Vol. 29
(1961), pp. 448-54.
111.   _____, Review of Bodde, D., China's First Unifier, ArOr, Vol. 37 (1969), p. 131-32.
112.   _____, Review of Needham et al., Heavenly Clockwork, ArOr, Vol. 29 (1961), pp. 490-94.
113.   _____, "Two Answers to Professor Moriya Mitsuo:
Part II, Fa ching and Hsia-lun," ArOr, Vol. 34 (1966),
pp. 496-503.
114.   _____, "Two Recent Commented Editions of the
Lun-heng," ArOr, Vol. 34 (1966), pp. 593-601.

115. ____, "The Works of Wang Ch'ung," ArOr, Vol. 36 (1968), pp. 122-34.

116. Quistorp, M., "Männergesellschaft und Alters-klassen im alten China," MSOS, Vol. 18 (1915), pp. 1-60.

117. Reinhard, K., Chinesische Musik. Eisenach, 1956.

118. Rickett, W. A., Kuan-tzu: A Repository of Early Chinese Thought. Hong Kong, 1965.

119. Rogers, M. C., "Sung-Koryø Relations: Some In-hibiting Factors," Oriens Extremus, Vol. 11, No. 1-2 (1958), pp. 194-202.

120. Sargent, G. E., "The Intellectual Atmosphere in Lingnan at the Time of the Introduction of Buddhism," in W. Eberhard (ed.), Symposium on Historical, Archaeo-logical and Linguistic Studies on Southern China, South-East Asia and the Hong Kong Region (Hong Kong, 1967), pp. 161-71.

121. Seufert, W., "Urkunden zur staatlichen Neuordnung unter der Han-Dynastie," MSOS, Vol. 23-25 (1922), pp. 1-50.

122. Shigezawa Toshio, "The Significance of Contra-dictions as Seen in the Ideology of Wang Fu," Acta Asiatica, No. 2 (1961), pp. 30-39.

123. Sivin, S., "Cosmos and Computation in Early Chinese Mathematical Astronomy," TP, Vol. 55 (1969), pp. 1-73.

124. Smith, H., "Transcendence in Traditional China," Religious Studies, Vol. 2, No. 2 (1967), pp. 185-96.

125. Soothill, W. E., The Hall of Light: A Study of Early Chinese Kingship. London, 1951.

126. Soper, A. C., "The 'Dome of Heaven' in Asia," The Art Bulletin, Vol. 29 (1947), pp. 225-48.

127. Soymié, M., "L'éntrevue de Confucius et de Hsiang T'o," JA, Vol. 242 (1954), pp. 311-91.

128.   Sprenkel, van der, O. B., Pan Piao, Pan Ku, and the Han History. Canberra, 1964.

129.   Swann, N. L., Food and Money in Ancient China: The Earliest Economic History of China to 25 A.D. Princeton, 1950.

130.   T'ang Yung-t'ung (trans. W. Liebenthal), "Wang Pi's New Interpretation of the I ching and the Lun-yü," HJAS, Vol. 10 (1947), pp. 124-61.

131.   Tjan Tjoe Som, Po Hu T'ung: The Comprehensive Discussion in the White Tiger Hall: A Contribution to the History of Classical Studies in the Han Period. Vol. 1-2. Leiden, 1949, 1952.

132.   Tsien Tsuen-hsuin, Written on Bamboo and Silk: The Beginnings of Chinese Books and Inscriptions. Chicago, 1963.

133.   Wagner, R. C., "Die Auflösung des legalistischen Staatsmodells gegen Ende der Han," ArOr, Vol. 35 (1967), pp. 244-61.

134.   Waley, A., "Notes to Johnson's A Study of Chinese Alchemy," BSOAS, Vol. 6 (1930-1932), pp. 1-24.

135.   _____, Ballads and Stories from Tun-huang. London, 1960.

136.   Ware, J. R., The Sayings of Chuang Chou. New York, 1963.

137.   Watson, B. (trans.), Records of the Grand Historian of China. Vol. 1-2, New York and London, 1961.

138.   _____ (trans.), Records of the Historian: Chapters from the Shih chi of Ssu-ma Ch'ien. New York, 1959.

139.   _____, Ssu-ma Ch'ien: Grand Historian of China. New York, 1958.

140.   Welch, H., The Parting of the Way: Lao Tzu and the Taoist Movement. Boston, 1957 (reprint: 1966).

141. Whitaker, K. P. K., "Tsaur Jyr and the Introduction of Fannbay into China," BSOAS, Vol. 20 (1958),
pp. 585-97.

142. Wilbur, M., Slavery in China during the Former
Han Dynasty. Chicago, 1943.

143. Wilhelm, H., "The Scholar's Frustration: Notes
on a Type of 'Fu'," in J. K. Fairbank (ed.), Chinese
Thought and Institutions (Chicago, 1957), pp. 310-19,
398-403.

144. Wilhelm, R., I Ging: Das Buch der Wandlungen.
Vol. 1-2, Jena, 1924.

145. Yang Lien-sheng, "Great Families of Eastern
Han," in E-tu Zen Sun and J. deFrancis, Chinese Social
History: Translations of Selected Studies (Washington,
1956), pp. 103-34.

146. Yü Ying-shih, "Life and Immortality in the Mind
of Han China," HJAS, Vol. 25 (1964-1965), pp. 80-122.

147. _____, Trade and Expansion in Han China: A
Study in the Structure of Sino-Barbarian Economic Relations. Berkeley, 1967.

148. Zach, von, E., "Yang Hsiung's Fa Yen (Worte
strenger Ermahnung): Ein Philosophischer Traktat aus
dem Beginn der Zeitrechnung," Sinologische Beiträge,
Vol. IV. Batavia, 1939.

149. _____, "Zur Verteidigung des chinesischen
Philosophen Yang Hsiung," Monumenta Serica, Vol. 1
(1935-1936), pp. 186-91.

INDEX OF PROPER NAMES, SUBJECTS, AND TERMS

Note: The numbers in the Index below refer to fragment numbers and notes to fragments, not to page numbers. "Comm." refers to the commentary that precedes the text of the fragment.

Ch'in　泰　: kingdom of, 1, 10, 11, 171A, 176, 178,
　　179; dynasty of, 52, 209 (nn. 58, 70).

Ch'in　琴 (zither), Chapter 16 passim, 82A-D, 169A1-
　　G1, H1, I1 and J1-3 (and comm., nn. 1, 4), 170,
　　171A, 172A-B, 173, 174, 188, 209.

Ch'in Chin-chün　泰近君　, see Ch'in Kung.

Ch'in Chün-yen　泰君延 , see Ch'in Kung.

Ch'in Kung　泰恭　, prolific commentator (older
　　contemporary of Huan T'an), 88 (and nn. 1-2).

Ch'in Shih Huang-ti　泰始皇帝　(First Sovereign
　　Emperor of the Ch'in), 11B, 52, 53.

Ch'in-tao　琴道 (The Way of the Zither), by
　　Huan T'an, 169A1 (n. 4).

Ch'in-ts'ao　琴操 ("The Principle of the
　　Zither), by Ts'ai Yung or Huan T'an, 132B
　　(n. 79), 169A1 (nn. 1, 4).

Ch'in Yen-chün　泰延君　, see Ch'in Kung.

China (Chung-kuo　中國), 53.

Ching　荆 (type of plant), 38A (n. 19), 171A (n. 36).

Ching: Duke of Ch'i　齊景公　(547-490 B.C.), 74
　　(and n. 13), 84A (and n. 29); Duke of Sung 宋景公
　　(516-456 B.C.), 58 (and n. 33); Emperor of Han
　　景帝 (156-140 B.C.), 19 (n. 15), 28 (and n. 38),
　　34 (n. 10), 42, 53, 209 (n. 58).

Ching Chün-ming　京君明 , see Ching Fang.

Ching Fang　京房 , musician (77-36 B.C.), 32A (n. 1).

Ching Province　荆州 , in Kiangsu, 152D.

Ching Tzu-ch'un　景子春 , foreteller (probably Huan
　　T'an's contemporary), 50.

Ch'ing-lung　青龍 (blue dragon), 205 (n. 66).

Ch'ing-ming festival　清明 , 132A (n. 77).

Ch'ing Province　青州 , in Shantung, 32E.

Gentleman (lang 郎), 113A, 125 (n. 60), 126A
(n. 63), 154, 155, 162, 167A, 205 (n. 3); at
the Palace, 100 (n. 11), 125 (n. 60), 205
(n. 3); at the Yellow Gate, 126A, 157A; Attendant at the Gate, 157B; in Attendance, 172A-B;
of Imperial Carriages, 125 (and n. 60), 142,
205 (nn. 3, 13); of the Household, 125 (n. 60),
205 (n. 3).
Ghosts (shen 神), 40.
Gimm, M., 119 (n. 47), 170 (n. 27), 173 (n. 38), 174
(nn. 39, 41).
God (shen 神), 41, 80 (n. 12), 140A; of the soil
and grain, 22.
Goepper, R., 93A (n. 25).
Gold (chin 金), 28 (and n. 40), 56, 83A, 126, 148A
(n. 7), 149, 154, 157A (n. 36), 163A (n. 10),
176 (and n. 14), 186 (and n. 31), 206 (n. 37);
as a medicine, 154; production of, 210; wine,
205; yellow, 176 (n. 24); ribbons, 188.

Goodrich, C. S., 209 (n. 77).
Government, 11A, 22, 26, 32C-D, 55 (n. 21), 105, 171
(comm.), 208 (n. 46), 209 (nn. 48, 55, 76);
central, 208 (n. 46); debt, 208 (n. 45); imperial, 208 (and n. 46); kingly, 163A, 176;
local, 208 (n. 46); policy, 210; servant, 65.
Governor, 84A (n. 24), 128A (n. 68).
Graham, A. C., 134 (nn. 78, 79), 135A (n. 87), 135B
(n. 89).
Grand Augur (t'ai-pu 太卜), 90C.

Heart (<u>hsin</u> 心), a constellation, 58.

Heaven, 37, 41, 53, 67, 86A, 91, 93A-D, 112A-B, 115B, 134, 152F (n. 28), 163A, 169A1-2, 169I1, 171A, 193, 205, 210 (n. 105); Yao corresponding with, 97; authority of, 58; center of, 115B; cover of, 115B; movement of, 115A-B; neglect and esteem of, 133A; opposition to, 58; pivot of, 115B; production of drugs, 86A; purposeful activities of, 86A; response of, 91; substance of, 92; Way of, 163A, 210 (and n. 91); will of, 99; <u>yang</u>, 134A.

Heffer, J., 93A (n. 25).

Hegemon (<u>pa</u> or <u>po</u> 霸), 3A, 6A, 9, 10, 212.

Hereditary Houses (<u>shih-chia</u> 世家), 118 (n. 46), 159A (n. 3).

Hervouet, Y., 117 (n. 13), 160 (n. 1), 188 (comm.), 205 (n. 19).

Hirth, F. (1845-1927 A.D.), 89 (comm.).

Ho 和 , see Pien Ho.

Ho Ch'ang-ch'ün 賀昌羣 , contemporary historian, 209 (n. 73).

Ho Ch'ü-p'ing 霍去病 , Han general (ca. 141-117 B. C.), 59 (n. 35).

<u>Ho-kung</u> 合宮 (Joint Palace), 175B (n. 6).

Ho-nan 河南 , commandery in Honan, 66 (n. 65).

Ho Shan 霍嬗 , Han official (d. 110 B.C.), 59 (n. 35).

<u>Ho-t'u</u> 河圖 (River Chart), 68 (n. 66), 210 (n. 93).

Ho-tung 河東 , commandery in western Shansi, 142, 205 (and n. 5).

Ho Tzu-hou 霍子侯 , see Ho Shan.

Holzman, D., 148 (n. 8), 151C (comm.), 205 (n. 10).

Honor, 53, 77, 143, 164F, 169A1, 171A, 206, 210 (and n. 104); empty, 52.

Huai-nan-tzu 淮南子 , attributed to Liu An, 2B, 29
    (n. 44), 48 (comm.), 52 (n. 1), 61 (n. 40),
    82 (n. 18), 89 (n. 6), 169I1 (n. 16).

Huan 齊桓公 , Duke of Ch'i (685-643 B.C.), 53 (and
    n. 6), 65, 83A-B, 96 (n. 41), 192 (and n. 55),
    211.

Huan Chieh 桓階 , high official (d. after 220 A.D.),
    8 (n. 1).

Huan Chieh pieh-chuan 桓階別傳 , 8 (n. 1).

Huan Chieh-tzu 桓階子 , 8 (n. 1).

Huan Chün-shan 桓君山 , see Huan T'an.

Huan Fan 桓範 , Wei minister (fl. 249 A.D.), 8
    (n. 1).

Huan Mao 桓茅 , 35A (comm.), 90C.

Huan T'an 桓譚 , (ca. 43 B.C.-28 A.D.), 2B (and
    n. 4), 3 (comm.), 8 (n. 1), 11A (n. 6), 14
    (n. 12), 22 (comm.), 24 (n. 21), 25B (n. 27),
    28 (nn. 31, 37, 38, 41), 31 (and n. 49), 32A
    (n. 2), 34 (n. 10), 36 (nn. 16, 17), 37 (n. 18),
    38A (n. 19), 42A (and n. 2), 44 (n. 6), 47
    (n. 10), 52 (n. 1), 53 (nn. 7, 18), 55 (n. 21),
    58 (n. 31), 59 (n. 35), 61 (n. 37), 68 (n. 3),
    72 (n. 8), 74 (n. 13), 78, 80D (nn. 12-13),
    81 (n. 14), 82B-D (nn. 20-21), 84A (nn. 24, 26,
    27), 84B (comm.), 85 (n. 32), 86A (nn. 34-35),
    87 (n. 34), 88 (n. 2), 89 (n. 6), 93D (comm.,
    n. 31), 94 (nn. 34, 35), 95 (n. 37), 96 (nn.
    39-40), 100 (n. 16), 102 (n. 20), 103 (comm.,
    n. 27), 104 (nn. 28, 31), 107 (comm.), 108B
    (nn. 10, 12), 110 (n. 13), 113 (n. 24), 114
    (nn. 28-29), 115A (and nn. 30, 35, 38), 116
    (and n. 40), 117 (n. 43), 118 (n. 46), 125

Iron, 130 (n. 72).

Irony: critics, see ku chi; in Wang Ch'ung, 210 (n. 103).

Irrigation, 108A-B (and n. 12).

Jade, 20; strung, 91, 112B; juice, 205 (and n. 23); letter, 138; liquors, 205 (and nn. 23, 25); piece of, 93B; room, 169I1; utensil, 138; Dam (pi-yung 辟雍), 93A-B; Lady (Yü-chiang 玉姜), style name of Hairy Woman, 205 (n. 19); Woman (Yü-nü 玉女), 205 (and n. 19).

Jan Chao-te 冉昭德 , contemporary historian, 128A (n. 69).

Jao Tsung-yi 饒宗頤 , contemporary historian, 169A (n. 6), 171A (n. 29).

Jen An 任安 , official (contemporary of Ssu-ma Ch'ien), 209 (n. 61), 210 (n. 120).

Jen Chen-ch'ing 任真卿 , musician (probably a contemporary of Huan T'an), 173.

Jen I 任弈 , author of Jen-tzu (end of Han), 9 (n. 2).

Jen Ku 任嘏 , author of Jen-tzu tao-lun (2nd-3rd cent. A.D.), 9 (n. 2).

Jen Shuang 任爽 , perhaps identical with Jen I, 9 (n. 2).

Jen-tzu 任子 by Jen I, 9 (comm.).

Jen-tzu tao-lun 任子道論 , by Jen Ku, 9 (n. 2).

Joint Palace, see Ho kung.

Ju-i, see Liu Ju-i.

Ju-sheng 儒生 , scholar, 210 (n. 103).

Ju Shun 如淳 , commentator (189-265 A.D.), 197 (n. 65).

Juan Yüan 阮元 , scholar (1768-1849 A.D.), 175 (comm.).

Judge, 210.

359

Ku Yung 谷永 , high official and scholar (d. 8
   or 7 B.C.), 200 (comm., n. 71), 210 (n. 5);
   顧雍, chancellor of Wu (168-243 A.D.), 78.
Kua-wu 詿誤 (deceive), 210 (n. 95).
Kuan Chung 管仲 , chancellor of Ch'i (d. 645 B.C.),
   28, 53, 65 (and n. 50), 103 (n. 26), 117 (n.
   43), 211.
Kuan Lung-feng 關龍逄 , virtuous minister
   (18th cent. B.C.), 28 (and n. 38).
Kuan Ping 關並 , colonel (contemporary of Huan
   T'an), 107 (and n. 2), 134A (n. 80).
Kuan-tung 關東 , region east of Han-ku pass, 79A
   (n. 3).
Kuan-tzu 管子 , eclectic book, 117 (n. 43), 209
   (n. 70).
Kuan Tzu-yang 關子揚, see Kuang Ping.
Kuang-wu 光武 , Han Emperor (25-58 A.D.), 93 (comm),
   94 (n. 34), 164A (n. 16), 175 (n. 7), 202
   (comm.), 209 (n. 65), 210 (nn. 93, 105, 114,
   116).
K'uang 師曠 , music teacher (6th cent. B.C.),
   170.
Kuei 圭 (table of measurement), 197 (and comm.,
   (n. 66).
Kuei-lin 桂林 , region in southwest China,
   61 (n. 37).
K'un-ming 昆明池 , lake in Shang-lin park in Ch'ang-
   an, 151A.
Kundalini, 205 (n. 19).
kung 宮 : (secluded quarter), 176 (n. 19); (musical
   tone), 124, 169K, 171A; smaller (shao kung
   少宮), 169K.
Kung-jen 工人 (instrumentalist), 173 (n. 38).

Kung-kung 共工 , minister to Yao (24th-23th cent.), 2B.

Kung Sheng 龔勝 , scholar (Huan T'an's contemporary), 51 (n. 18).

Kung-sun Lung 公孫龍, (4th-3rd cent. B.C.), 32A, 135A-B (and nn. 87, 89).

Kung-sun Shu 公孫述 , rival of Kuang-wu (d. 36 A.D.), 158A (n. 46).

Kung-sun Yang 公孫鞅 , see Shang Yang.

Kung-tu 公都 , disciple of Mencius, 32A (n. 1).

Kung-yang chuan 公羊傳, 94A (n 34).

Kung-yang Kao 公羊高, author of the Kung-yang chuan (3rd-2nd cent. B.C.), 94A-B.

K'ung 控 or 椌 (musical instrument), 75 (and n. 15).

K'ung Ch'iu 孔丘 , see Confucius.

K'ung-hou 箜篌 (musical instrument), 42A-B (and n. 2).

K'ung-hsiang, Marquis of 孔鄉侯 , see Fu Yen.

K'ung Kuang-t'ao 孔廣陶 , editor (fl. 1861-1889 A.D.), 205 (n. 1).

K'ung P'ing-chung 孔平仲, poet (ca. 1040-1105 A.D.), 198 (nn. 69-70).

K'ung-ts'ung-tzu 孔叢子 , by K'ung Fu, 25B (n. 27).

K'ung-tzu chia-yü 孔子家語 , by Wang Su, 160 (n. 2), 216 (comm.).

K'ung Ying-ta 孔穎達 , scholar (574-648 A.D.), 204 (comm., n. 79).

K'ung-yü 空語 (fiction), 2B (n. 4).

Kuo, Mr., 郭氏 , (7th cent. B.C.), 53.

Kuo-chiao 郭椒 (name of an ox), 25A (and n. 25).

Liu Heng 劉恒 , or Emperor Wen, 100 (nn. 9, 11).

Liu Hsiang 劉向 , scholar (79-8 B.C.), 2B (and
n. 4), 53 (n. 6), 86 (n. 34), 98A-B (and n. 1),
136C (n. 96), 157A (n. 37), 188 (comm.), 189
(n. 47), 195 (n. 64), 199 (comm.), 209 (nn.
54, 67, 84).

Liu Hsieh 劉勰 , author of Wen-hsin tiao-
lung (ca. 465-522 A.D.), 80 (n. 13); 194 (n.
62), 195 (n. 64), 197 (comm.), 210 (nn. 93, 95).

Liu Hsin 劉歆 , scholar (ca. 50 B.C.-23 A.D.),
82C (and nn. 19-20), 86A (n. 34), 87 (n. 1),
98A-B (n. 1), 129 (and n. 70), 130 (and n. 71),
135A (n. 87), 156A, 156B (nn. 33, 34), 159A
(and n. 3), 164C (and n. 19), 188 (comm.), 189
(n. 47), 195 (n. 64).

Liu I-ch'ing 劉義慶 , author (403-444 A.D.),
190 (n. 48).

Liu Ju-i 劉如意 , son of Emperor Kao (d. 193
B.C.), 191 (comm.).

Liu Jung 劉榮 , eldest son of Emperor Ching
and Lady Li (d. 146 B.C.), 28 (n. 36).

Liu Keng-sheng 劉更生 , see Liu Hsiang.

Liu Kung 劉恭 , official (1st cent. B.C.-1st cent.
A.D.), 188.

Liu P'an-sui 劉盼遂 , contemporary commentator,
164B (n. 21).

Liu Pang 劉邦 , 11A (n. 4), 36, Emperor Kao, 11A
(n. 4), 36 (n. 17).

Liu Pin 劉攽 , commentator (1022-1088 A.D.), 163
(n. 12).

Liu Po-sheng 劉伯生 , nephew of Liu Hsin (1st
cent. B.C.-1st cent. A.D.), 86A (n. 34).

Liu Po-shih 劉伯師 , nephew of Liu Hsin (1st
cent. B.C.-1st cent. A.D.), 84A-B, 86A (n. 34).

Mars, planet (<u>Huo-hsing</u> 火 星), 58.

Masabuchi Tatsuo 增 淵 龍 夫 , contemporary historian, 209 (n. 65).

Maspero, H. (1883-1945 A.D.), 93A (n. 25, comm.), 116 (n. 40), 175 (comm.), 205 (nn. 16, 19, 23, 25).

Master, see Confucius, 210 (n. 91); of Rain, 205 (n. 10); in Charge of Robbers (<u>chu-shou-tao</u> 主 守 盜), 66; Yang, see Yang Hsiung.

Māyā (<u>huan</u> 幻), 152D (n. 34).

Medicine, 102 (n. 25), 116 (n. 40), 157A-B; for prolonging life, 154.

Mencius 孟 子 , philosopher (ca. 390-305 B.C.), 6 (n. 6), 32A (nn. 1-2), 84A (n. 25), 131B (n. 73), 165 (n. 25), 171A (n. 33), 175 (comm.), 201 (n. 72), 205 (n. 30), 209 (nn. 48, 52).

Meng (優) 孟 , half-legendary personality of the Warring Kingdoms period, 137B (n. 97), 188 (comm.).

Meng-ch'ang, Lord of 孟嘗君 , see T'ien Wen.

Meng Ford 孟 津 , in Honan, 91.

Meng Sun 孟 孫 , officer (Huan T'an's contemporary), 45.

Merchant, 209 (and nn. 69, 79); rich, 209 (nn. 70, 75-76).

Metal, 92, 169D1 (n. 9), 169I1-2 (and n. 15).

Middle Gate (<u>chung-men</u> 中 門), 43.

Middle way (<u>chung-tao</u> 中 道), 94C (n. 35).

Mien-shang 綿上 , mountain in Shansi, 132 (n. 77).

Military: expedition, 55 (n. 20), 102, 210; forces, 96 (n. 41); methods, 209; operations, 3A-B, 52, 100, 210; play, 176 (n. 14).

Min Tzu-ch'ien 閔 子 騫 , disciple of Confucius (5th cent. B.C.), 28 (n. 35).

Office of the Masters of Writing (<u>shang-shu kuan</u> 尚
書官), 15.
Officer, 32E, 52, 102, 204; fighting, 48A; great, 209
(n. 59).
Officer of the Commander-in-Chief, 108B (nn. 11-12).
Official, 41, 66, 85, 154, 164D (n. 21), 190 (comm.),
209 (and nn. 69-70); agricultural, 181; at the
frontier, 135B; county, 208 (n. 46); documents
209 (n. 81); frustrated, 209 (n. 56); harsh,
209 (n. 70); high, 19 (n. 15), 66 (n. 65);
hundred, 212; lower, 209; musical, 119 (n. 47);
robes, 100; salary, 209 (n. 70); upright, 19
(n. 15), 65; villainous, 209.
Old Duke Tan-fu, or Ku-kung Tan-fu, see T'ai-wang.
Old Text school of the exegesis of the Classics, 88
(n. 2), 103 (n. 27); praise of, 90A.
Omen, 43, 58-59, 68; auspicious, 91 (n. 15).
Oppression, 38A-B, 171A; of the Hsiung-nu, 53.
Order, 93C-D, 170, 209 (and n. 56), 210 (and n. 102),
212.
Ordinance (<u>ling</u> 令), 32D, 93B, 176-177, 209 (and
n. 65).
Origin (<u>yüan</u> 元), 163A.
Otter, 86A-B.
Ou Yeh, producer of swords (Spring and Autumn period),
13.
<u>Ourouparia rhynchophylla</u> (<u>kou-teng</u> 歐治), 86A.
Owl, 60A-B.
Ox: of the Duke Hsüan of Ch'i, 38A; power of, 128A
and C; famous, 25A.
Oyster, 2B.
<u>Pa-shu</u> 巴菽 , (Szechwan tree), 86A (n. 37).

Shu 蜀 , commandery in Szechwan, 51, 104, 198.

Shu-ching 書經 , see Book of Documents.

Shui 稅 (groundtax), 209 (n. 75).

Shui-ching chu 水經注 , by Li Tao-yüan, 108A (n. 9), 110 (n. 16).

Shui-ch'ung 水舂 (water-pestles), 128A (n. 68).

Shui-p'ai 水排 (water bellows), 128A (n. 68).

Shui-tui 水碓 (water-pestles), 128A (n. 68).

Shun: 舜 , Emperor (2255-2206 B.C.), 15, 35A (n. 11), 52, 65, 97, 132 (n. 77), 169F; 順 , Late Han Emperor (126-144 A.D.), 208 (n. 45).

Shun-yü K'un 淳于髡 , politician and humorist (4th cent. B.C.), 13 (n. 11), 48A-C (and n. 12).

Shuo-fu 說郛 , collection by T'ao Tsung-i, 98 (n. 2), 188 (comm.), 202 (comm.).

Shuo-wen 說文 , dictionary by Hsü Shen, 169A1 (n. 1), 210 (n. 95).

Shuo-yüan 說苑 , by Liu Hsiang, 74 (n. 13), 171A (nn. 28, 30, 31, 34), 192 (comm., n. 55), 195 (n. 64), 199 (comm.).

Siege, 159A-B (and n. 3).

Sight, 82A-D, 92, 155, 156A, 164A, C and F.

Silk, 51, 154 (n. 31), 157B, 169A2, D1 (n. 9); of different kinds, 209 (n. 79).

Silkworm, 86B.

Silver, 56, 149, 157A (n. 36), 163A (n. 10); production of, 210; "liquid," 157A (n. 38).

Sincerity (hsin 心), 3A, 171A.

Singer (ch'ang 倡), 119, 171A.

Sivin, N., 112 (n. 22), 163A (n. 9).

Six arts (liu-i 六藝), 102.

Six Kingdoms (liu kuo 六國), 82D (n. 21), 135A.

Skin, 84A (and n. 26), 152F (n. 28); of fox, 151A.

135A; in <u>Chin-shu</u> 30, 176 (n. 13); <u>on the Rules</u>
<u>for Ceremonious Behavior and Music</u> (<u>Li-yüeh</u>
<u>chih</u>　禮 樂 志), in <u>Han shu</u> 22, 209 (n.
56); <u>on the Feng and Shan Sacrifices</u>, by Ssu-
ma Hsiang-ju, 117 (n. 43).
Tree, 43, 84A, 92, 156A-B, 209 (n. 66); bent, a sign
of calamity, 58; Szechwan, 86A (n. 37).
Trial, 43, 49, 50, 65.
"Tribute of Yü," see <u>Yü kung</u>.
<u>Tsa-lun</u>　雜 論 , probably <u>Hsin-lun</u>, 108B (n. 10).
Ts'ai Mao　蔡 茂 , official (24 B.C.-47 A.D.),
209 (n. 50).
Ts'ai Yung　蔡 邕 , scholar (133-192 A.D.), 145
Comm.), 169A1 (nn. 1, 4).
<u>Tsan</u>　贊 ; unit in the <u>T'ai-hsüan ching</u>, 163 (n. 11).
<u>Tsang</u>:　藏 (viscera), 116 (n. 40);　臧 (illicit
profit), 209 (n. 79).
Ts'ang-wu　蒼 梧 , commandery in Kwangtung, 75
(and n. 15).
<u>Tsao-jen</u>　躁 人 (impetuous men), 209 (n. 65).
Ts'ao Chih　曹 植 , poet (192-232 A.D.), 82C
(n. 20), 84A (n. 26), 152F (n. 28), 156B (nn.
37-38).
Ts'ao Kuei　曹 劌 , see Ts'ao Mo.
Ts'ao Mo　曹 沫 , general (7th cent. B.C.), 96
(and n. 41).
Ts'ao P'i　曹 丕 , Emperor Wen of Wei (187-226
A.D.), 79 (n. 5), 103 (n. 27).
Ts'ao Shen　曹 參 , first Han chancellor (d. 190
B.C.), 32D (and n. 4), 36.
Ts'ao Tsang　曹 臧 , see Ts'ao Mo.
Tseng Shen　曾 參 , Confucius' disciple (504-
436 B.C.), 28 (n. 35).

Tung Chung 董忠 , rebel (d. 23 A.D.), 38A (n. 19).

Tung Chung-chün 董仲君 , magician (fl. 6 B.C.-
6 A.D.), 152A-F (and nn. 39-40).

Tung Chung-shu 董仲舒 , philosopher (ca. 179-
104 B.C.), 2A (and n. 3), 6 (n. 7), 102 (n. 20),
117 (n. 43), 209 (and nn. 56, 70).

Tung-fang Shuo 東方朔 , eccentric hermit (154-
93 B.C.), 32A, 42A, 137A-B (and n. 97), 205
(n. 19), 216 (comm.).

Tung Hsien 董賢 , catamite of Emperor Ai (d.1
B. C.), 62 (and n. 42), 206, 207 (comm., n. 40);
sister of, 206 (and n. 31).

Tung-huang 東荒 , see Eastern Desert.

Tung-kuan Han chi 東觀漢紀 , historical source,
94C (n. 35), 202 (comm.), 209 (nn. 69, 72, 79,
84).

Tung Yüeh 董説 , writer and scholar (1620-1686
A.D.), 40 (comm.), 82 (comm.), 176 (and nn.
15, 18, 20, 22-23), 180 (n. 25), 186 (n. 30).

T'ung 桐 (tree), see Wu-t'ung.

T'ung-jen 通人 (intelligent man), 210 (n. 103).

Tutor (shih 師), 176.

Tzu-ch'ang 子場 , mistake for Tzu-yang, 107 (n. 3).

Tzu-cheng 子政 , see Liu Hsiang.

Tzu-chih t'ung-chien 資治通鑑 , by Ssu-ma
Kuang, 163A (n. 12).

Tzu-chün 子駿 , see Liu Hsin.

Tzu-fu 子夫 , see Wei Tzu-fu.

Tzu-hou 子侯 , or Ho Tzu-hou, see Ho Shan.

Tzu-hsü 子胥 , or Wu Tzu-hsü, see Wu Yüan.

"Tzu-hsü fu" 子虛賦 (Rhyme-prose on Sir Fantasy),
by Ssu-ma Hsiang-ju, 205 (n. 21).

Yen K'o-chün 嚴可均 , editor (1762-1843 A.D.),
1 (n. 1-2), 3 (n. 2-3), 8 (n. 1), 10 (n. 3),
14 (n. 13), 20 (n. 18), 24B (comm.), 28 (nn.
34, 42), 32B (comm.), 35B (n. 13), 40 (n. 25),
41 (comm.), 44 (n. 6), 48A (n. 13), 60C, 61
(n. 39), 66 (nn. 66, 71), 74 (n. 12), 77 (n.
18), 80C (n. 12), 84A (n. 27), 86A (n. 38),
90A (n. 7), 90E (n. 10), 93D (n. 31, comm.),
95 (n. 38), 96 (n. 40), 99, 100 (nn. 12, 15),
104 (nn. 29-30), 105 (n. 1), 108A (n. 5), 110
(n. 17), 111B (n. 20), 112 (n. 22), 114A (n. 27),
118 (n. 46), 120 (n. 48), 122 (n. 54), 124
(n. 58), 125 (n. 60), 134 (nn. 81, 84), 136C
(n. 96), 138 (n. 98), 139 (n. 1), 142 (n. 11),
148A (n. 8), 149 (n. 11), 150B (n. 14), 151A
(n. 20), 158B (nn. 45, 49-50), 159A (n. 2),
163A (n. 12), 164A (nn. 17, 20, 24), 167 (n.
27), 168 (n. 30), 169G1 (n. 12), 171B, 202
(comm.), intr. to Part III, 205 (nn. 3, 11-13,
20, 25, 28-29), 215 (n. 126).

Yen-ling 延陵 , in Kiangsu, 96 (n. 39).

Yen-shih, see Yen-chih.

Yen Shih-ku 顏師古 , historian (579-645 A.D.),
55 (n. 20), 82C (n. 21), 103 (comm.), 108B
(nn. 7, 10), 110 (n. 13), 157A (n. 37), 159A
(n. 3), 169I1 (n. 15), 197 (n. 65), 205 (n.
19), 208 (comm.), 209 (n. 75).

Yen-tzu 崦子 , see Yen.

Yen-tzu 晏子,嬰 , or Yen Ying, Minister in Ch'i
(ca. 580-500 B.C.), 84A (and n. 29).

Yen-tzu ch'un-ch'iu 晏子春秋 , attributed to
Yen Ying, 84A (n. 29).

414

MICHIGAN PAPERS IN CHINESE STUDIES

No. 1.   The Chinese Economy, 1912-1949, by Albert
Feuerwerker.

No. 2.   The Cultural Revolution: 1967 in Review, four
essays by Michel Oksenberg, Carl Riskin, Robert Scala-
pino, and Ezra Vogel.

No. 3.   Two Studies in Chinese Literature: "One Aspect
of Form in the Arias of Yüan Opera" by Dale Johnson; and
"Hsü K'o's Huang Shan Travel Diaries" translated by Li
Chi, with an introduction, commentary, notes, and bibliography by Chun-shu Chang.

No. 4.   Early Communist China: Two Studies: "The Fu-
t'ien Incident" by Ronald Suleski; and "Agrarian Reform
in Kwangtung, 1950-1953" by Daniel Bays.

No. 5.   The Chinese Economy, ca. 1870-1911, by Albert
Feuerwerker.

No. 6.   Chinese Paintings in Chinese Publications, 1956-
1968: An Annotated Bibliography and An Index to the
Paintings, by E. J. Laing.

No. 7.   The Treaty Ports and China's Modernization:
What Went Wrong? by Rhoads Murphey.

No. 8.   Two Twelfth Century Texts on Chinese Painting,
"Shan-shui ch'un-ch'üan chi" by Han Cho, and chapters
nine and ten of "Hua-chi" by Teng Ch'un, translated by
Robert J. Maeda.

No. 9.   The Economy of Communist China, 1949-1969, by
Chu-yuan Cheng.

No. 10. Educated Youth and the Cultural Revolution in
China by Martin Singer.

No. 11. Premodern China: A Bibliographical Introduction, by Chun-shu Chang.

No. 12. Two Studies on Ming History, by Charles O.
Hucker.

No. 13. Nineteenth Century China: Five Imperialist
Perspectives, selected by Dilip Basu, edited with an
introduction by Rhoads Murphey.

No. 14. Modern China, 1840-1972: An Introduction to Sources and Research Aids, by Andrew J. Nathan.

No. 15. Women in China: Studies in Social Change and Feminism, edited with an introduction by Marilyn B. Young.

No. 16. An Annotated Bibliography of Chinese Painting Catalogues and Related Texts, by Hin-cheung Lovell.

No. 17. China's Allocation of Fixed Capital Investment, 1952-57, by Chu-yuan Cheng.

No. 18. Health, Conflict, and the Chinese Political System, by David M. Lampton.

No. 19. Chinese and Japanese Music-Dramas, edited by J. I. Crump and William P. Malm.

No. 20. Hsin-lun (New Treatise) and Other Writings by Huan T'an (43 B.C. - 28 A.D.), translated by Timoteus Pokora.

Price: $3.00 (US) each

except $4.00 for special issues #6, #15, and #19

and $5.00 for #20

Prepaid Orders Only

NON SERIES PUBLICATION

Index to the "Chan-Kuo Ts'e," by Sharon Fidler and J. I. Crump. A companion volume to the Chan-Kuo Ts'e translated by J. I. Crump. (Oxford: Clarendon Press, 1970). $3.00

MICHIGAN ABSTRACTS OF CHINESE AND
JAPANESE WORKS ON CHINESE HISTORY

No. 1. The Ming Tribute Grain System by Hoshi Ayao,
translated by Mark Elvin.

No. 2. Commerce and Society in Sung China by Shiba
Yoshinobu, translated by Mark Elvin.

No. 3. Transport in Transition: The Evolution of
Traditional Shipping in China, translations by Andrew
Watson.

No. 4. Japanese Perspectives on China's Early Modernization: The Self-Strengthening Movement, 1860-1895
by K. H. Kim.

Price: $4.00 (US) each

Prepaid Orders Only

Michigan Papers and Abstracts available from:
Center for Chinese Studies
University of Michigan
Lane Hall
Ann Arbor, Michigan 48104
USA

Printed and bound by CPI Group (UK) Ltd, Croydon, CR0 4YY

13/04/2025

14656536-0004